Racial Formation in the Twenty-First Century

Racial Formation in
the Twenty-First Century

EDITED BY

Daniel Martinez HoSang
Oneka LaBennett
Laura Pulido

UNIVERSITY OF CALIFORNIA PRESS

BERKELEY LOS ANGELES LONDON

Portions of chapter 2 were previously published in James Kyung-Jin
Lee, "The Transitivity of Race and the Challenge of the Imagination,"
PMLA, vol. 123, no. 5, (October 2008): 1550–1556. Portions of chapter
9 were previously published in Devon W. Carbado and Cheryl Harris,
"The New Radical Preferences," 96 *California Law Review* 1139 (2008).
Portions of chapter 11 were previously published in Nicholas De Genova,
"Antiterrorism, Race, and the New Frontier: American Exceptionalism,
Imperial Multiculturalism, and the Global Security State," *Identities,* vol. 17,
no. 6 (2010).

University of California Press, one of the most distinguished university
presses in the United States, enriches lives around the world by advancing
scholarship in the humanities, social sciences, and natural sciences. Its
activities are supported by the UC Press Foundation and by philanthropic
contributions from individuals and institutions. For more information, visit
www.ucpress.edu.

University of California Press
Berkeley and Los Angeles, California

University of California Press, Ltd.
London, England

Library of Congress Cataloging-in-Publication Data

   Racial formation in the twenty-first century/edited by
Daniel Martinez HoSang, Oneka LaBennett, Laura Pulido.
    p. cm.
   Includes bibliographical references and index.
   ISBN 978-0-520-27343-6 (cloth : alk. paper)
   ISBN 978-0-520-27344-3 (pbk. : alk. paper)
   1. Omi, Michael. Racial formation in the United States.   2. United
States—Race relations.   3. Racism—United States.   4. Race.
5. Racism.   6. Sexism.   I. HoSang, Daniel.   II. LaBennett, Oneka.
III. Pulido, Laura.
   E184.A1O4637   2012
   305.800973—dc23

                                            2012010842

Manufactured in the United States of America

20   19   18   17   16   15   14   13   12
10   9   8   7   6   5   4   3   2   1

In keeping with a commitment to support environmentally responsible and
sustainable printing practices, UC Press has printed this book on Rolland
Enviro100, a 100 percent postconsumer fiber paper that is FSC certified,
deinked, processed chlorine-free, and manufactured with renewable biogas
energy. It is acid-free and EcoLogo certified.

Dedicated to the memory of Peggy Pascoe (1954–2010) and Clyde Woods (1957–2011)

CONTENTS

List of Illustrations   ix

Introduction   1
Daniel Martinez HoSang and Oneka LaBennett

PART ONE
RACIAL FORMATION THEORY REVISITED   19

1 · Gendering Racial Formation   23
Priya Kandaswamy

2 · On the Specificities of Racial Formation: Gender and Sexuality
in Historiographies of Race   44
Roderick A. Ferguson

3 · The Transitivity of Race and the Challenge
of the Imagination   57
James Kyung-Jin Lee

4 · Indigeneity, Settler Colonialism, White Supremacy   66
Andrea Smith

PART TWO
RACIAL PROJECTS AND HISTORIES OF RACIALIZATION   91

5 · The Importance of Being Asian: Growers, the United Farm
Workers, and the Rise of Colorblindness   95
Matthew Garcia

6 · The Unbearable Lightness of Being (Black): Legal and Cultural
Constructions of Race and Nation in
Colonial Latin America   116
Michelle A. McKinley

7 · Race, Racialization, and Latino Populations
in the United States   143
Tomás Almaguer

8 · Kill the Messengers: Can We Achieve Racial Justice without
Mentioning Race?   162
Gary Delgado

9 · The New Racial Preferences: Rethinking
Racial Projects   183
Devon W. Carbado and Cheryl I. Harris

PART THREE
WAR AND THE RACIAL STATE   213

10 · "We didn't kill 'em, we didn't cut their head off":
Abu Ghraib Revisited   217
Sherene H. Razack

11 · The "War on Terror" as Racial Crisis: Homeland Security,
Obama, and Racial (Trans)Formations   246
Nicholas De Genova

12 · Racial Formation in an Age of
Permanent War   276
Nikhil Singh

Conclusion · Racial Formation Rules: Continuity, Instability,
and Change   302
Michael Omi and Howard Winant

Bibliography   333
List of Contributors   361
Acknowledgements   365
Index   367

ILLUSTRATIONS

FIGURES

4.1. Traditional Model for People-of-Color Organizing or Ethnic Studies *67*

4.2. Three Pillars of White Supremacy *68*

TABLES

8.1. Myths, Racial Beliefs, and Frames *169*

8.2. Contesting Racial Ideologies *170*

8.3. Dos and Don'ts of Framing Public Discourse about Social Problems *172*

Introduction

Daniel Martinez HoSang and Oneka LaBennett

In the preface to the first edition of *Racial Formation in the United States,* Michael Omi and Howard Winant wrote: "To study race in the United States is to enter a world of paradox, irony, and danger. In this world, arbitrarily chosen human attributes shape politics and policy, love and hate, life and death. All the powers of the intellect—artistic, religious, scientific, political—are pressed into service to explain racial distinctions, and to suggest how they may be maintained, changed, or abolished" (1986, xiii).

This edited volume, arriving twenty-five years after the first publication of *Racial Formation in the United States,* brings together thirteen essays from scholars in a wide range of fields to again "enter a world of paradox, irony, and danger." The contributors explore far-reaching concerns: slavery and land ownership; labor and social movements; torture and war; sexuality and gender formation; indigeneity and colonialism; genetics and the body. From the ecclesiastical courts of seventeenth century Lima to the cell blocks of Abu Ghraib, the essays draw from Omi and Winant's influential theory of racial formation, which they defined as "the sociohistorical process by which racial categories are created, inhabited, transformed, and destroyed" (1994, 55). The contributors share many of Omi and Winant's theoretical convictions about the centrality of race to all social and political structures in the United States, the "unstable and 'decentered' complex of social meanings" that constitute race, the dynamic relationship between social movements and the state, the interaction between micro- and macro-level dimensions of race, and a refusal to reduce race to other categories of analysis, such as class, ethnicity, or nation (Omi and Winant 1994, 55).

At the same time, the contributors ask an array of questions not fully elaborated in Omi and Winant's original work: How is the gendered and sexual basis of racial formation most productively theorized? How do theories about the biological basis of race continue to shape assumptions about the social and political construction of race? How might racial formation theory effectively engage issues of indigeneity, war making, and settler colonialism? *Racial Formation in the Twenty-First Century* explores these and other questions, building on twenty-five years of scholarship since Omi and Winant's generative insights first came to light.

THE GENEALOGY OF *RACIAL FORMATION* IN THE UNITED STATES

In a 1982 speech delivered to the Colorado Bar Convention, Ronald Reagan's solicitor general, Rex E. Lee, offered a provocative defense of the administration's stance on civil rights. Since his election two years earlier, Reagan had come under criticism by major civil rights groups on a number of important issues. In a recent case before the U.S. Supreme Court, for example, Lee had written a brief in support of a California effort to end mandatory desegregation programs in public schools; the subsequent ruling marked the first time that students attending desegregated schools were reassigned to segregated ones as a result of a court order. The administration had also refused to take a stance against a Texas law banning undocumented students from public schools, and reversed the position of two previous Republican presidents by withdrawing legal support for the Internal Revenue Service's denial of tax exemptions to private schools that practice racial discrimination.[1]

Lee insisted, however, that it would be erroneous to assume that the Reagan administration did not wholly support civil rights. "What is it that qualifies a legal position as 'pro–civil rights' or 'anti–civil rights?'" he asked. "Certainly not the fact that the position is advanced, or opposed, by any certain group." Defining civil rights as rooted in the "pursuit of individual rights and individual interests," he contended, "it would be a profound disservice" to the American public "to assume that all positions espoused by certain groups automatically deserve the label 'pro–civil rights'"[2]

Two decades earlier, at the height of the desegregation struggle centered in the U.S. South, there was little disagreement about the policy positions that determined whether someone could be identified as "pro–civil rights" or "anti–civil rights"; the terms appeared self-defining. Lee's insistence by the early 1980s that the Reagan administration could dismantle deseg-regation policies in the name of protecting civil rights marked a power-ful transformation within U.S. racial politics. Reagan could make potent appeals to white political identity while claiming to operate within the ethical norms of liberal anti-racism. He could denounce "welfare queens" and champion "states' rights" in the heart of Dixie while steadfastly insist-ing on his own racial innocence. And he could draw in the supporters of unapologetic segregationists like George Wallace while still declaring his resolute support for civil rights (Edsall and Edsall 1992).

As Lee delivered his 1982 address, two recent PhD's from the University of California, Santa Cruz, were at work on a lengthy essay attempting to make sense of the landscape that produced this contradictory political discourse. Michael Omi and Howard Winant's article "By the Rivers of Babylon: Race in the United States" appeared the following year in the *Socialist Review*; both scholars served as members of the journal's San Francisco Bay Area editorial collective.[3] Their project, as they would later explain, aspired "to comprehend the recent tumultuous decades and to assess their meanings for a broader understanding of race in the U.S." (Omi and Winant 1994, 2). The seventy-five-page essay, published across two issues, began by taking inventory of the explicit racial dimensions of the conservative resurgence in the early 1980s: the Reagan administration's dismantling of school desegregation and affirmative action programs, the rise of hate crimes against people of color, a surge in attacks against immi-grants, and the resurrection of a white revanchist "politics of resentment" committed to reversing the gains of the civil rights era.

But the article also noted the formation of a "new racism," an ideologi-cal reconstitution of racial subordination that relied on implicit references to race woven "throughout the social fabric." In response to the "great transformation" brought about during the 1960s by the Civil Rights Movement, and the new forms of racial subjectivity, collectivity, and meaning secured by ascendant social movements, new articulations of racial meaning and power were emerging. The great transformation did not expel racism from cultural, political, or social life in the United States, or even lessen its impact. Instead, according to this periodization, a new "reconstitution of racial oppression" was unfolding fueled by "society-wide political struggle" (Omi and Winant 1983, 34). The new racism, they contended, encompassed a wide range of issues, including crime, unemployment, welfare, housing, gun control, tax cuts, militarism, and even nuclear power.

Omi and Winant made clear that the motive forces of this new racism were rooted in the U.S. right. The main thrust of the article, however, addressed the anemic response of the U.S. left, which they described as "unable to gauge the depth and appeal of a new 'racial discourse' that doesn't need to make explicit references to race." They argued that the "left often misreads contemporary currents; it's encumbered with dogmatic understandings of what race and racism are, and it lacks the necessary vision to mount effective anti-racist campaigns. Racism is, in fact, endemic to much of the left itself" (1983, 35). Omi and Winant contended that this political myopia was often predicated on a reductionism that treated race as derivative of economically determined contradictions rather than as a central axis of social relations.[4] Figures on the left and right increasingly shared the view that after the passage of landmark civil rights and anti-discrimination legislation in the 1960s and 1970s, race had become an anachronistic category of political analysis, masking more fundamental conflicts rooted primarily in culture, geography, and the economy.

The framework developed in Omi and Winant's *Socialist Review* essay, which introduced many of the central concepts published three years later in the first edition of *Racial Formation in the United States,* offered an alternative account, conceptualizing race as both central to all social relations and politically and ideologically transient. They held that "race establishes the identity of human subjects, it structures social conflict and social cohesion, and it is deeply woven into other aspects of existence" (1983, 56). The state in particular loomed large in this analysis. "Every state institution," they argued, "is a racial institution," linked in a network by "history, mandate, internal composition, and constituency" to the prevailing racial order. They focused particular attention on "the pattern of conflict and accommodation which takes place over time between racially based social movements and the policies and programs of the state" (1983, 78).

At the same time, Omi and Winant insisted that the meaning of race and the logics of a racial order could never be fully fixed; race was an "unstable and 'decentered' complex of social meanings constantly being transformed by political struggle" (1994, 55–56). Drawing from the Italian theorist Antonio Gramsci, Omi and Winant called attention to the changing sociohistorical and ideological basis of racial meaning, identity, and power. Race was, in this view, always a subjectivity in formation, or as

James Kyung-Jin Lee suggests in his contribution to this volume, "race is better described as a verb than a noun, as production rather than destiny."[5]

To be sure, Omi and Winant were not the first scholars to conceptualize race in this manner. The *Socialist Review* essay drew from a number of historians in particular, including Alexander Saxton and Selig Perlman, who attended to the constellation of ideological struggle and meaning that gave rise to particular alignments of racial power and hierarchy. *Racial Formation* also emerged at a time when other scholars and activists were exploring the basis of political subject formation and social identity in more fluid and less deterministic ways. Stuart Hall, Gloria Anzaldua, Cherrie Moraga, and others similarly conceptualized race in nonreductionist, contradictory, and explicitly political ways that also challenged the perceived orthodoxies of established leftist politics.[6]

What *Racial Formation* would provide to other scholars and activists was a kind of political vocabulary and shared framework through which to analyze and locate the role of race in structuring broader social formations; it became a tool to use as much as a theory to dissect. Indeed, Omi and Winant devoted extensive attention within both editions of the book to an extended application of racial formation theory to the political terrain of the 1980s (and later the early 1990s). The analysis explored the construction of an emerging racial order in both Reagan's and Clinton's America that incorporated many of the signifiers and referents of the civil rights era even as it disavowed the continued impact of racial inequities by celebrating the tropes of colorblindness and post-racial triumph. Ultimately, it would be in these applications of racial formation theory that Omi and Winant's work would have the greatest impact. That is, while the portion of their book outlining the basis of racial formation theory has now been excerpted in dozens of introductory textbooks and readers in sociology, ethnic studies, and other disciplines, its broader influence has been in facilitating a large body of scholarship that implicitly or explicitly applies racial formation theory to a wide range of questions and empirical topics.

RACIAL FORMATION THEORY: DEBATES AND
CONVERGENCES

In the late 1990s both conservative and liberal scholars and public commentators increasingly embraced the argument that race was not a biological "fact," arguing instead that "race is an ideological construct, understood in the sense of an 'illusion' that explains other 'material' relationships in distorted fashion" (Winant 1994, 14). Howard Winant rejected this "race as illusion" approach, insisting that the effects of race cannot simply be "abolished by acts of will" for the very reasons he and Omi emphasized in *Racial Formation*; race is a salient, pervasive component of American society that has held ideological and material currency for more than half a millennium. "U.S. society," Winant contended, "is so thoroughly racialized that to be without racial identity is to be in danger of having no identity" (Winant, 1994, 14, 16).

Omi and Winant insisted that the prevailing paradigms about race within the social sciences—which alternatively conceptualized race as a marker of class, ethnicity, or nation—contributed to this myopic view. While they acknowledged that the class, ethnicity, and nation paradigms retained some analytic utility, each also "missed the manner in which race has been a *fundamental* axis of social organization in the U.S." (Winant 1994, 12; emphasis in original). This position has been polemical. Multiple scholars, including historians such as Barbara Jeanne Fields and sociologists such as Mara Loveman, Robert Miles, Rudy Torres, and Leonard Gordon, have questioned the utility and centrality of this conceptualization of race.[7] To put Omi and Winant's work into a richer context, it is worth considering these critiques, along with converging theorizations from other sociologists, historians, and anthropologists.

Echoing broader critiques of racial formation theory, sociologist Mara Loveman takes Omi and Winant to task for relying on examples specific to the United States alone in making generalizations about the utility of race-based versus ethnicity-based theories. Loveman contends that such an approach undermines an understanding of race and racism in other periods and locations, and that it fails to account for the racialization of Irish and Italian immigrants in particular (Loveman 2009). Along similar lines, but with an emphasis on class, cultural studies scholar E. San Juan Jr. (2009) suggests that Omi and Winant overemphasize the independent significance of race while too quickly dismissing class as a key analytic concept. For San Juan, to fully understand and rectify structural racism and its constitutive concepts (such as "colorblindness") we must take into account "global capitalism's endemic crisis, imperialist military interventions by the U.S. state, sharply intense inequality of nation-states and peoples, classes within national polities, regional conflicts, etc." (San Juan Jr. 2009). He therefore advocates a "historical-materialist critical framework," concluding that racism is "an instrumentality of class rule." Ultimately, San Juan rejects Omi and Winant's "racial state" for a "capitalist state."

Anthropologists have, like Omi and Winant, acknowledged the shortcomings of the ethnicity paradigm. Ethnicity can be understood as a "process by which individuals and groups [come] to understand, or understand themselves as separate or different from others," based on social practices such as "language, religion, rituals, and other patterns of behavior" (Yu 2007, 103). A key conjunction between *Racial Formation* and contemporaneous anthropological approaches to race rests in Omi and Winant's clear delineation of the ways in which the ethnicity approach has been co-opted by conservative political projects to undo civil rights–era programs and policies in the name of creating a "colorblind" society. In addressing this conflicted legacy, anthropologist Faye Harrison notes two critical shortcomings that followed Franz Boas's early strides in dismantling the biological validity of race. "A myopic view of the kinds of questions cultural anthropology could attempt to answer," Harrison argues, "inhibited Boasian anthropology from producing the kind of ethnographic research on African Americans that could explicate the workings of racism" (Harrison 1998, 612). Moreover, Harrison laments that the early work invalidating race as a biological fact was rarely followed up by sustained attention to the "processes that engender the *social construction* of race" (Harrison 1998, 611; emphasis in original). Harrison acknowledges that although ethnicity has been a useful concept for addressing processes of "cultural identification," "as it has been conceptualized and approached in much of anthropological analysis, [ethnicity] has not adequately accounted for the processes of racial formation" (Harrison 1998, 613 [quoting, in part, Harrison 1995, 48]). Omi and Winant similarly delineated the limitations of the ethnicity paradigm, arguing that it ignored the specific circumstances of U.S. racial minorities (Omi and Winant 1994, 22).

RACE THEORY SINCE *RACIAL FORMATION*

As broader debates reveal, and as the essays in this volume emphasize, convergent and competing theories have contributed to our understanding of race since the publication of *Racial Formation*. Omi and Winant's work can be placed in dialogue with developments in critical race theory and theories of intersectionality from the 1970s through the 1990s (Crenshaw et al. 1995; Crenshaw 1991b; Bell 1973). The insistence on the socially constructed nature of race for which Omi and Winant continue to be most widely cited, combined with their focus on social justice concerns, links the two authors with a range of contemporary critical race theorists (Delgado and Stefancic 2000; Valdes, Culp, and Harris 2002), with researchers who utilize intersectionality (McCall 2005; Bedolla 2007; Hancock 2004), and with scholars in geography, cultural studies, American studies, and other interdisciplinary fields. As Patricia Price notes, early critical race theory "emphasized the racialized aspects of advantage which were more often than not enshrined and upheld by the law" (Price 2009, 148). Indeed, this "dialectical engagement with liberal race discourse and with critical legal studies" (Crenshaw 2002, 9), framed around "an insistence on progressive race consciousness, on systemic analysis of the structures of subordination, and on multi-intersectional or multidimensional critiques of power relations," came to define critical race theory (Valdes, Culp, and Harris 2002, 2). Critical race theorists placed particular emphasis on the experiences of African Americans, problematized the results of civil rights–era legislation, and prioritized activism in an effort "not merely to understand the vexed bond between law and racial power but to *change* it" (quoted in Price 2009, 151; emphasis in original). Critical race theory, like racial formation theory, employed a U.S.-centered approach and drew criticism from feminist scholars. These criticisms receive new, constructive ruminations within this volume.

Beyond critical race theory and intersectionality, Omi and Winant can be placed in conversation with a host of racial theorists. For example, their marking of race as a powerful social construct is also central to the work of Stuart Hall and Paul Gilroy, two scholars who propelled shifts in cultural studies, American studies, and racial theory more generally, and for whom cultural production has always been a primary site of analysis. Even though these scholars' approaches have divergent attributes, Omi and Winant are often cited in the company of Hall and Gilroy as seminal contributors to racial theory.[8] One can find shared elements among Hall's, Gilroy's, and Omi and Winant's conceptualizations of black expressive culture, for example, as predicated on a resistance that destabilizes hegemony. In discussing slave music, Omi and Winant write, "with its figuring of suffering, resistance, perseverance, and transcendence, . . . the slaves incorporated elements of racial rule into their thought and practice, turning them against their original bearers" (1994, 67). Hall's theorizations, based on the hybrid character of black diasporic identity, are also taken up by Paul Gilroy, whose articulation of black Atlantic culture emphasizes the common routes that link black expressive culture. Foregrounding common experiences of oppression rather than defining blackness in relation to Africa as an "actual or mythical" homeland, Gilroy conceptualized black Atlantic communities as constructed in defiance of racial essentialism and as connected through popular cultural productions (Gilroy 1993; Thomas and Clarke 2006, 13). Gilroy cautions that just as reifying racial identities creates hierarchies, so too can the focus on hybridity, "arguing that both positions are, in a sense, essentializing."[9] Touching on the dangers of the ethnicity paradigm that Omi and Winant identified, Stuart Hall has endeavored to rescue ethnicity from being "deployed . . . in the discourse of racism" (Hall 1993, quoted in Koshy 2008, 1554). Hall's concept of "new ethnicities" falls in line with how literary studies has theorized the concepts of race and ethnicity. This field highlighted transnational literary influences, multilingual traditions that traversed national boundaries, and multinational public spheres produced by the translation and circulation · of texts, ideas, and people. By focusing on the circuits of ethnicity formation in conjunction with racial formation and exploring these relations in and across nations, such studies diverge from sociological models of racial formation in which the state plays a central role (Koshy 2008, 1554).

RACIAL FORMATION BEYOND THE UNITED STATES

Several contributors to this volume also take the study of race beyond the borders of the United States. Coterminous with Hall's reworking of ethnicity and Gilroy's concept of the black Atlantic, researchers interested in immigration, ethnicity, diasporic identities, and social networks have explored these processes through transnational and global lenses. Pioneered by Linda Basch, transnationalism centers around the study of deterritorialized social practices, defined as "the processes by which migrants forge and sustain simultaneous multi-stranded social relations that link together their societies of origin and settlement (Basch 2001, 118). Occurring along both macro and micro lines, these transnational social relations inform racial, ethnic, gender, class, and sexual identities (Basch 2001, 118). Transnationalism has been applied to explicating the connections between local and global constructions of race and ethnicity in settings and contexts too numerous to summarize here.[10]

While the research done within the framework of transnationalism has proven to be invaluable in illustrating the processes by which social networks operate across national boundaries, the transnational rubric has also been criticized for "obscur[ing] the role of racial categorizations and racisms in contemporary social fields" (Thomas and Clarke 2006, 2). Following the increasing attention to late-twentieth-century conditions of transnational production and consumption, a host of theorists have attempted to theorize race within the processes of globalization (Bhattacharyya, Gabriel, and Small 2002; Marable 2004; Winant 2001; da Silva 2007). The late Manning Marable, for example, revised DuBois's famous quote to offer: "The problem of the twenty-first century is the problem of global apartheid" (Marable 2004). Marable identified a new "New Racial Domain"—distinct from "earlier racial formations"—forged and empowered by transnational capitalism and neoliberal state policies (Marable 2004). Still, theorizing race and racism globally, Deborah Thomas and Kamari Clarke argue, has been a challenging endeavor marked by scholarly trepidation stemming from the anti-essentialist shift (Thomas and Clarke 2006, 2).

Although anti-essentialism critiqued biological constructions of race, it "has also mitigated against generalized formulations of racial processes across time and space" (Thomas and Clarke 2006, 2). Thus, theorizing race at the global scale can be problematic because it conjures questions of whether there is "an absolute truth of racial difference everywhere" (Thomas and Clarke 2006, 2). For their part, Thomas and Clarke attempt to overcome these pitfalls by offering a historically grounded exploration of the ways in which race shapes and is shaped by global transformations. They do this, in part, by utilizing terms like *racial formation* to interrogate processes in distinct national contexts—processes that have similar effects on people's lives, but that are practiced in complex and dissimilar ways (Thomas and Clarke 2006, 3–4).

RACIAL FORMATION IN THE TWENTY-FIRST CENTURY

Profound political, social, economic, and cultural transformations have continued to mark the United States since the second edition of *Racial*

Formation was published in 1994. Omi and Winant proved quite prescient in anticipating the continuous disavowal of civil rights and racial justice issues on the part of the centrist New Democrats in the 1990s. Across multiple issues, including assaults on affirmative action, immigration, bilingual education, and welfare; the dramatic rise of the prison complex; and restrictions on reproductive justice and women's rights, Democrats and their liberal allies continually proved unwilling or unable to protect many of the modest redistributive programs secured during the long Civil Rights Movement. The enormous U.S. military power in Iraq and Afghanistan unleashed in the wake of September 11 has demonstrated the co-constitutive relationship of race-making and war-making. Indeed, the contradictions of race in Obama's ascent to the White House—at once incorporating and disavowing the long legacy of racial subordination in the United States—demonstrates the continued relevance of racial formation theory.

SCOPE OF THE VOLUME

The contributors to this volume utilize racial formation theory as a point of departure and a shared framework to engage and explore new questions. The essays demonstrate that twenty-five years after its first publication, *Racial Formation* continues to provide generative insights into a broad range of scholarly and political issues and debates. The essays put Omi and Winant in dialogue with multiple scholarly developments in critical race theory and address gaps in their profoundly influential framework, particularly in relation to gender, sexuality, and global racializations.

Although there are many intersecting themes across the essays, the volume has been organized into three sections: "Racial Formation Theory Revisited"; "Racial Projects and Histories of Racialization"; and "War and the Racial State." Each part contains a brief introduction of the essays therein, discussing their particular resonance with *Racial Formation,* while also briefly addressing the convergences and divergences among the contributors. Readers will see that although the essays in each section reflect thematic imbrications, the boundaries created between parts are in fact porous.

The essays in part I, "Racial Formation Theory Revisited," explicitly engage with the theoretical commitments and assumptions within *Racial*

Formation, extending these concepts in new directions. In "Gendering Racial Formation," gender studies scholar Priya Kandaswamy puts racial formation theory "into conversation with intersectional analysis by highlighting the ways that attention to gender and sexuality might alter the key terms of Omi and Winant's theory and the ways that their understanding of processes of racialization might enrich approaches to intersectionality." Comparing the U.S. welfare state in the mid-1990s to the Freedmen's Bureau in the Reconstruction South, Kandaswamy analyzes two aspects of Omi and Winant's theory—racial projects and the relationship between the state and social movements—as important avenues toward a more complex understanding of intersectionality.

In an incisive essay titled "On the Specificities of Racial Formation: Gender and Sexuality in Historiographies of Race," American studies scholar Roderick A. Ferguson interrogates the particular historiographical assumptions animating Omi and Winant's work, and the ways the historical periodization they deploy marginalizes particular gendered and sexual racial subjects. As Ferguson explains, much of Omi and Winant's work rests on a "declension hypothesis," in which the bold and transformative anti-racist movements of the 1950s and 1960s became fractured and destabilized in the face of an insurgent New Right in the 1970s and 1980s. This periodization, Ferguson makes clear, "occludes anti-racist movements that were no less significant than the social formations around civil rights and national liberation . . . [movements that were] initiated by women of color and queers of color within the United States."

James Lee's essay, "The Transitivity of Race and the Challenge of the Imagination," offers a close reading of several passages in the first and second editions of *Racial Formation* to explore the impact the book had on scholars in the humanities. Lee explains: "We [humanists] picked up *Racial Formation* in 1994 because it provided a language for what seemed either too deterministic or too inchoate, because it taught us that knowing the world of race as it is might, against prevailing evidence, help us in the humanities disrupt the assumption that race's remainder was only negativity and loss."

In "Indigeneity, Settler Colonialism, White Supremacy," Andrea Smith interrogates the ways that the dominant theoretical frameworks used within both Native studies and ethnic studies, including racial formation theory, prevent a full engagement with the historical and contemporary realities of white settler colonialism. She argues that white supremacy operates through multiple and intersecting logics, rendering subjects who are simultaneously oppressed and complicit in the oppression of others. Smith's provocative essay insists that unless Native studies and critical race scholarship can "center [on] the analytics of settler colonialism, both intellectual projects [will] fall back on the presumptiveness of the white supremacist, settler state." Such political projects, she warns, "can do no more than imagine a kinder, gentler settler state founded on genocide and slavery."

The essays in part II, "Racial Projects and Histories of Racialization," apply and reconceptualize Omi and Winant's theorization of racial projects and racialization across a range of time and places. Historian Matthew Garcia's "The Importance of Being Asian: Growers, the United Farm Workers, and the Rise of Colorblindness" explores processes of racial formation among rural California grape growers. The essay compares the ways both Armenian and Japanese immigrants "challenged the boundaries of citizenship and whiteness," resulting in historically distinct paths of racialization. In particular he shows the extent to which people of color may be complicit in supporting white supremacy as seen in the life of a Japanese American grower.

In "The Unbearable Lightness of Being (Black): Legal and Cultural Constructions of Race and Nation in Colonial Latin America," legal scholar Michelle McKinley examines the fascinating archival records of seventeenth-century ecclesiastical courts in Lima, Peru, to "explore the way that ideas of blood purity were worked out (retained, shaped, transformed) in a slaveholding, colonial milieu in which extensive race mixing occurred." McKinley demonstrates the surprising continuities between early modern discourses of universal humanism and contemporary debates over multiculturalism.

For Tomás Almaguer, the history of colonial racializations continues to shape the ways in which Latino ethnic groups racialize one another. In "Race, Racialization, and Latino Populations in the United States," Almaguer investigates the changing meaning of race and racial categories for Latinos in general and for Mexicans and Puerto Ricans in particular, arguing that Latinos occupy a unique position betwixt and between "race" and "ethnicity." Noting the marked increase in the U.S. Latino population, which currently surpasses African Americans as the largest racial-ethnic group, Almaguer explores Latinos' practice of shunning U.S. census racial categories in favor of their own self-definitions, which are often reminiscent of Spanish colonial racializations.

In "Kill the Messengers: Can We Achieve Racial Justice without Mentioning Race?" scholar activist Gary Delgado argues that some racial justice advocates have lost sight of one of the central interventions of *Racial Formation*—that "race in U.S. political culture is always predominant and always evolving." He explores the apprehension, evinced by liberal political campaign consultants and media strategists during public debates over affirmative action and immigration, about explicitly mentioning race and racism or challenging the belief among many white voters that a colorblind meritocracy now prevails in the United States. Racial justice, he insists, cannot be secured through racial silence, but instead requires developing "new frameworks for understanding and communicating the reality of race in the twenty-first century."

In "The New Racial Preferences: Rethinking Racial Projects," legal scholars Devon Carbado and Cheryl Harris use Omi and Winant's conceptualization of racial projects to examine the ways that the principles of "race neutrality" and "race preferences" operate in debates over affirmative action. Using the example of hypothetical personal statements written by Barack Obama and Clarence Thomas in their law school applications, they contend that bans on references to race in these statements constitute a "new racial preference [that] gives a priority or advantage to applicants who choose to suppress (or are perceived as suppressing) their racial identity over those who do not so choose (or are so perceived)." Carbado and Harris also raise important questions about the ways in which "good" (anti-racist) and "bad" (racist) racial projects become distinguished.

Part III, "War and the Racial State," includes three powerful essays that bring Omi and Winant's theorizations on the relationship between racial formation and state violence to bear on the post-9/11 era. Popular cultural narratives about Abu Ghraib form the analytical center for Sherene H. Razack's essay, "'We didn't kill 'em, we didn't cut their head off': Abu Ghraib Revisited." Razack notes how critical responses to Abu Ghraib targeted the torture policies of the Bush administration, while "rank-and-file torturers" were largely unexamined. Razack's polemical questions—"How do contemporary narratives about the wrongness of torture at Abu Ghraib mediate terror? How do we write effectively against torture?"—force us to confront the "systematic dehumanization of the other" that torture represents.

In "The 'War on Terror' as Racial Crisis: Homeland Security, Obama, and Racial (Trans)Formations," anthropologist Nicholas De Genova frames the election of Barack Obama within a historical moment of racial crisis and an expansion of state violence. De Genova examines the "global war on terror" to explore how Obama's construction as a "post-racial" subject is intricately intertwined with long-standing notions of American exceptionalism. De Genova describes this moment as the ascension of "'the emerging hegemony of the racial project of neoliberalism,' which evades any frank acknowledgment of racial themes" in order to pronounce the end of racism.

Nikhil Singh's essay, "Racial Formation in an Age of Permanent War," traces the political backdrop against which *Racial Formation* was written not only to highlight its contribution to understanding race in the U.S. context but also to interrogate how contemporary global theorizations of race are inextricably connected to sovereign violence. For Singh, it is neither political struggle nor scientific codification, but rather sovereign violence that "'overdetermines' the field of racial meanings and effects." This field of racial meanings, Singh argues, is increasingly complex and sharply bifurcated, is rendered invisible under "colorblind jurisprudence," yet gradually reattached to state augmentation that violently excludes categories of persons deemed security threats.

Michael Omi and Howard Winant conclude the volume with their essay, "Racial Formation Rules: Continuity, Instability, and Change." They discuss the genesis of racial formation theory, review the political context from which it emerged, and describe the key theoretical currents that influenced their work. Initially, they explain, their book was all but ignored by the social scientists and anti-racist activists they sought to address. It was scholars in other disciplines, such as history, literary studies, and law, who first embraced *Racial Formation* before it circulated widely among their initial target audience. Their essay then considers various "post-racial scenarios" that the United States might confront in the near future, each animated by different assumptions about particular fault lines of racial conflict and solidarity. The essay concludes with an extended consideration of the tensions and possibilities authorized by the crisis of colorblindness. They call for an anti-racist practice that both exploits the numerous contradictions inherent within colorblind politics and discourse while still asking readers to confront two vexing questions: "What do you want *your* race consciousness to be?" and "What would a racial justice–oriented social policy look like *to you?*" They insist: "Our actions and ideas—both individual and collective—should be seen as political projects that have the potential to undo racial injustice and generate broader racial equality, indeed greater freedom in every way."

All of the contributors to this volume embrace Omi and Winant's conclusion that no racial regime is permanent because race is always in formation. Race, they argued in 1994, is "always politically contested." What has been done can be undone. What has been made can be unmade. All crises contain the seeds of change. They urge us, even when confronting the most violent and dehumanizing practices of racial domination, not to take refuge in a despondent fatalism. For even if "race will *always* be at the center of the American experience," new chapters about this experience remain to be written (Omi and Winant 1994, 5).

NOTES

1. "Administration Asks Court to Back Prop 1," *Los Angeles Times,* Feb. 2, 1982, p. A10. On the California ballot case, see HoSang 2010, chapter 4. On the administration's relationship with the conservative legal movement, see Teles 2008.

2. "Justice Official Defends Reagan on Rights," *Los Angeles Times,* Oct. 3, 1982, p. A5.

3. The *Socialist Review* had editorial collectives in Boston, New York, and the Bay Area. The Bay Area collective included organizer Gary Delgado (a contributor to this volume) as well as scholars David Plotke, Dana Takagi, and Michael Kazin, among others.

4. For one notable example, see W. J. Wilson 1980.

5. See Lee's "The Transitivity of Race and the Challenge of the Imagination" in this volume.

6. According to scholar-activist Bob Wing (2007), the term "racial formation" was previously introduced in a series of essays written by Harry Chang, a Korean immigrant and educator active in Marxist study circles in the Bay Area in the 1970s.

7. Loveman 1999; Fields 1990; Miles and Torres 2007. The thrust of Gordon's evaluation is that *Racial Formation* overstates the authors' own theoretical applicability while understating those of others: "The *problem* in their critique is the neglect of the *theoretical evolvement* of what the authors reasonably classify as ethnicity-based, class-based, and nation-based theories. . . . The theoretical problem is that Omi and Winant far overstate the negation of race and racisms

among ethnicity-based theoreticians. The desire to sink ethnicity-based theory simply discards, by extension, some of the most widely cited critical theory modifications" (Gordon 1989, 133; emphasis in original). For Gordon these modifications include work by Etzioni (1949); Merton (1949); Westie (1964); Albrecht, De Fleur, and Warner (1972); and Smith (1981).

8. See, for example, Miles and Torres (2007, 70), who compare Omi and Winant to Gilroy; and Nguyen (2008), who puts Omi and Winant in dialogue with Hall and Gilroy. See also Koshy (2008), who engages Omi and Winant with Hall.

9. Maira 2002, 191.

10. Some examples include Ong 1999; Appadurai 1991; Glick Schiller, Basch, and Szanton-Blanc 1992; Matory 2005; and Sen and Samad 2007.

---- ·

PART ONE

Racial Formation Theory Revisited

The essays in this section underscore racial formation theory's enduring intellectual force. The contributors revisit Omi and Winant, demonstrating how the roots of racial formation continue to develop as scholars addressing topics from gender and sexuality to indigeneity and settler colonialism, and spanning disciplines from literary studies and American studies to sociology, adapt the racial formation framework to portray a complex, evolving picture of racialized, gendered, classed, and sexualized subjects.

The charge that racial formation theory, like critical race theory, subsumes gender to privilege race as "the primary axis of disadvantage in the U.S." (Price 2009, 151), finds new, analytical currency in an essay by Priya Kandaswamy that utilizes legal scholar Kimberlé Crenshaw's concept of intersectionality alongside racial formation theory. Intersectionality initially sought to explain how the experiences of women of color are simultaneously "the product of intersecting patterns of racism and sexism, and how these experiences tend not to be represented within the discourses of either feminism or antiracism" (Crenshaw 1991b: 1243–1244). Like Omi and Winant, Crenshaw was critical of the intellectual movement to reject race as an analytical category. She maintained, however, that "recognizing that identity politics takes place at the site where categories intersect thus seems more fruitful than challenging the possibility of talking about categories at all" (Crenshaw et al. 1995: 299). Following Crenshaw, Kandaswamy addresses the unexplored opportunities in *Racial Formation* to theorize gender and race as mutually constitutive. Her essay juxtaposes the profound effect *Racial Formation* has had on the field of ethnic studies with its relatively obscure place within women's and gender studies, using this conundrum to investigate why theories that analyze the historical production of race and gender have not adequately engaged with one another. The chapter interrogates the alleged gender deviance of black women on welfare, comparing this to similar discourses surrounding black women's citizenship during Reconstruction to advance an intersectional reading of Omi and Winant's work. Kandaswamy explains "both how racial formation is a gendered and sexualized process and how the theoretical framework of intersectionality might better account for the dynamic processes through which racial categories are constructed."

Rather than seeing race, gender, class, and sexuality as discrete axes that cross each other, Kandaswamy rejects the imagined singularity of these structures, describing them as intrinsically conjoined. These "intertwined issues of race, gender, sexuality, and class" also form the basis for Roderick Ferguson's fresh periodization of anti-racist mobilizations in "The Gender and Sexual Historiography of Racial Formation." For Ferguson, Omi and Winant's attention to the rise of the new right in the 1980s obscures the proliferation of feminist and queer organizing that took place during this time that made strident anti-racist claims. Moreover, this organizing challenged many of the core assumptions of a unified politics of racial identity by demonstrating the complex "reality of dissension, conflict, and heterogeneity within anti-racist formations." Ferguson's erudite critique of *Racial Formation* positions the text "not as a canonical object whose theorizations and pronouncements we must obey, but as a field of investigation that is alive and beating."

This understanding of *Racial Formation's* legacy as "alive and beating" is applied in James Kyung-Lee's excursion into the literary archive in "The Transitivity of Race and the Challenge of the Imagination." While Ferguson uses Omi and Winant's notion of the "great transformation" to delineate the emergence of women- and queer-of-color activism, Kyung-Lee takes up Omi and Winant's representation of the transformed political landscape of the 1960s and 1970s as a springboard for reflecting on the authors' "settled understanding" of the racial present by the publication of *Racial Formation's* second addition. Omi and Winant's understanding of the Reagan era's racial topography resonated with the thinking of Kyung-Lee and his colleagues in the humanities, who turned to *Racial Formation* in the years between the publication of the first edition in 1986 and the second edition in 1994. Here, Kyung-Lee offers a close reading of "tense and transitivity" in the two editions and argues that in spite of the melancholic inheritance of the "post-racial" era that Omi and Winant describe, their work is still premised on the notion "that the racial imagination, like power, is not something that is seized, but an act, many acts in fact, of creativity." It is because of this "startling capacity" of race to "helps us imagine anew" that Lee retains optimism for envisioning "a racial future worth securing."

A reengagement with Omi and Winant's concept of the racial state figures prominently in Andrea Smith's "Indigeneity, Settler Colonialism, White Supremacy." For Smith, insufficient exchange between ethnic studies and Native studies prevents us from imagining an alternative to the racial state. Smith unpacks Omi and Winant's notion of the state as inherently racial to question how it might be possible to eradicate white supremacy while presuming the permanency of the U.S. state. She argues that racial theorists and scholars in Natives studies can work toward "transcendent change" by accounting for how settler colonialism intersects with white supremacy. Comparing the strategies used by a range of Native scholars and activists in the United States, including the collaboration between indigenous and immigrant groups to fight the 2010 Arizona bill allowing police to arrest "suspected" undocumented immigrants, with the development of indigenous struggles in Latin America, Smith boldly calls for "theoretical and political projects that address the intersections of settler colonialism and white supremacy simultaneously," in order to build "a politics of liberation that engages us all."

ONE

Gendering Racial Formation

Priya Kandaswamy

Michael Omi and Howard Winant's *Racial Formation in the United States* has had a profound effect on the development of the field of ethnic studies. The most important insights of the book—that race is not reducible to ethnicity, class, or nation; that racial categorization shifts and changes over time; and that the state is a preeminent site of racial struggle—have become well-established truths amongst critical race theorists. In staking out the significance and meaning of terms like *race, racism, the racial project,* and *racial formation* itself, Omi and Winant developed a vocabulary that enabled discussion of how race comes to be as it is and how race and the meanings associated with it change over time. In addition to delineating the racial formation framework, Omi and Winant's work identified why the study of race and processes of racialization matters. Demonstrating that race was neither an essential fact nor an illusion, they argued that it was best understood as the sedimentation of a vast array of racial projects, as a category produced and reproduced every day at scales ranging from quotidian interactions to macro-level social and political processes. By shifting the question from What is race? to How does race come to be? they emphasized that racial politics happens in the very constitution of race, not just as political struggle between already existing racial groups.

Its influence on ethnic studies notwithstanding, Omi and Winant's work has, however, received far less attention within women's and gender studies. Despite the fact that within the last two decades the field has increasingly recognized the social construction of race as an important component of understanding both women's experiences and gendered structures of power, *Racial Formation* as a text has still not found a place within women's and gender studies curriculum and scholarship.[1] This is no doubt partly because the neglect of gender and naturalization of sexual difference is a significant shortcoming of the book. However, it may also indicate that, despite the increasing recognition of the importance of thinking about race and gender together, theoretical frameworks that examine the processes by which race and gender are historically produced have not sufficiently engaged each other (Glenn 1999). The critique of the lack of attention to gender in Omi and Winant's work has been part of a more generalized acknowledgement of the tendency of ethnic studies as a field to center men of color in its analysis and of women's studies to center white women. Both of these fields have struggled to sufficiently account for the experiences of women of color and the articulations of race, gender, and other forms of difference. In recent years, "intersectionality" has emerged as a concept that both names this absence and signifies the development of a growing arena of scholarship that theorizes the relationship between race and gender as simultaneous and interacting structures of power.

This essay seeks to put Omi and Winant's theoretical framework of racial formation into conversation with intersectional analysis by highlighting the ways that attention to gender and sexuality might alter the key terms of Omi and Winant's theory, and the ways that Omi and Winant's understanding of processes of racialization might enrich approaches to intersectionality. I suggest that racial formation is fundamentally a gendered and sexualized process and argue that viewing race as unstable, historically produced, and changing in the ways that Omi and Winant demonstrate complicates the meaning of intersectionality. Specifically, I focus on two different aspects of Omi and Winant's theory—the racial project itself (what Omi and Winant term the building block of racial formation) and the trajectory of racial politics (what Omi and Winant call the relationship between the state and social movements). I argue that these two concepts provide important openings through which to elaborate the historical embeddedness of race, gender, sexuality, and class in each other. To illustrate these points, I first place Omi and Winant's work within the context of the development of scholarship on intersectionality and then turn to the specific example of the historical development of the U.S. welfare state, a site where the contradictions of the racialized and gendered state are particularly apparent.

Omi and Winant define race as "a concept which signifies and sym-bolizes social conflicts and interests by referring to different types of human bodies" (Omi and Winant 1994, 55). In Omi and Winant's formulation, race is a category grounded not in biological difference but rather in what perceived bodily differences come to mean in the context of particular social struggles. To emphasize this point, Omi and Winant make a telling comparison to gender. In one of the few men-tions of gender in the book, they argue, "In contrast to the other major distinction of this type, that of gender, there is no biological basis for distinguishing among human groups along the lines of race" (Omi and Winant 1994, 55). This statement is elaborated in the footnotes with the explanation that gender is a social construct that is grounded in a natural biological division between the sexes. In contrast to race, which has no legitimate biological basis, Omi and Winant write, "the biological divi-sion of humans into sexes—two at least, and possibly intermediate ones as well—is not in dispute" (Omi and Winant 1994, 18n4). While Omi and Winant's analysis politicizes the very construction of bodily differ-ence as the basis for racial categories, it relegates gender politics to the struggle over the social meaning of categories firmly anchored in natural sexual difference.

Often cited as evidence of the text's failure to adequately engage feminism, this brief discussion of gender reveals fundamental problems with how Omi and Winant theorize gender and its relationship to race. Although inaccurate, Omi and Winant's understanding of sex and gender in fact mirrors the dominant strand of second wave feminist thinking at the time the book was written. Second wave feminists employed the term *gender* to challenge biological determinism, not by calling into question the naturalness of sex categories per se, but by shifting the debate to the terrain of the cultural meaning of those categories. In doing so, these feminists took for granted that there was a natural category of women who were the subjects of feminism, an assumption that has since been thoroughly chal-lenged. A number of theorists have pointed out that this approach failed to recognize the ways that biological categorization of people into sexes is a cultural and political practice inseparable from social relations of gender. Rather than seeing sex as the real foundation for a socially constructed gender, these theorists argue that beliefs about gender play a fundamental role in constituting how the naturalized sexed body materializes (Butler 1993; Fausto-Sterling 2000).

Recourse to a natural category of sex has also grounded the category of women in an essential sameness that has enabled the claim that women share a set of common experiences and a common oppression. Feminists of color have critiqued the ways that this idea of "universal sisterhood" has been used to center the concerns of white, economically privileged women and to justify imperialism and racism within feminist movements.[2] They have argued that the category of women is in fact marked by internal differences rather than by any fundamental sameness amongst women. At the time *Racial Formation* was written, these critiques had not necessarily gained the attention they deserved within predominantly white women's studies programs, but they had already been substantially made. Ironically, in uncritically employing second wave white feminists' theorization of gender, Omi and Winant actually reproduced the marginalization of women of color within both women's studies and ethnic studies.

The deeper problem reflected in Omi and Winant's discussion of gender lies in the framing of the question itself. In the above-quoted statement, Omi and Winant focus on how race is like or not like gender. This positioning of race and gender as potentially analogous represents them as distinct categories to be compared rather than as imbricated categories that are constructed simultaneously and that gain their meaning in and through each other. This is not a problem unique to Omi and Winant's work, but rather one that can be seen within efforts to theorize race within women's and gender studies, as well. As Evelyn Nakano Glenn notes, the fact that much of the scholarship on race and gender developed on independent trajectories has meant not just the exclusion of the experiences of women of color but also a failure to seriously consider the co-constitutive nature of categories such as race, gender, class, and sexuality (Glenn 1999). In relation to Omi and Winant's theory of racial formation, this oversight suggests a difficulty more fundamental than that of simply examining how a socially constructed category of race intersects with an equally socially constructed category of gender. Rather, thinking about race and gender as constituted in and through each other challenges Omi and Winant's assertion that race is an independent and distinct category of analysis that can be thought about in isolation from other kinds of difference. While Omi and Winant's insistence that race is not reducible to anything else is still useful (particularly in revealing the limits of ethnicity theory, economic reductionism, and nation-based ideas of race), in the contemporary moment it seems necessary to recontextualize race in relation to other axes of power and difference. In other words, the irreducibility of race should not be taken to mean that race develops in isolation from other categories of difference. Rather, race must both be seen as an important entity in its own right but also as fundamentally inseparable from the gendered, sexualized, and classed contexts in which ideas of race and racial categories develop.

In recent years, the rubric of intersectionality has emerged as the most prominent sign under which work that attempts to theorize race and gender together happens within ethnic studies and women's and gender studies. The language of intersectionality has its origins in women of color feminism. While this feminist tradition has a long history, texts such as the Combahee River Collective's groundbreaking statement of black feminist politics (Combahee River Collective 1983); Gloria Hull, Patricia Bell Scott, and Barbara Smith's edited collection *All the Women Are White, All the Blacks Are Men, but Some of Us Are Brave* (Hull, Scott, and Smith 1993); and Cherríe Moraga and Gloria Anzaldúa's edited collection *This Bridge Called My Back* (Moraga and Anzaldúa 1981) articulated a women of color feminist politics out of which the concept of intersectionality in its contemporary incarnation emerged. These texts emphasized the inseparability of race, class, gender, and sexuality, powerfully arguing that social movements that grappled with only one of these forms of inequality effectively negated the existence of women of color. Within academic feminism, critical race theorist Kimberlé Crenshaw coined the term *intersectionality* just a few years after the first publication of *Racial Formation* in order to elucidate the very specific ways that women of color were rendered invisible in activist and legal frameworks that centered either on race or gender. In her work on discrimination law, for example, Crenshaw made visible the unrecognizability of black women within a legal structure that required them to frame their claims as individuals who were either black or female (Crenshaw 1991a; see also Crenshaw 1991b).

Despite the profound impact that intersectionality has had upon ethnic studies and women's and gender studies, a number of tensions and difficulties surround the current usage of the term. Within women's and gender studies, the language of intersectionality is often appropriated to mean putting together already existing theoretical frameworks, or including the experiences of those "left out" of white feminist projects, in a way that evades theoretical consideration of race altogether. Thus, grappling with intersectionality is often mistakenly reduced to a call to include the experiences of women of color. Sidestepping the challenge to feminism inherent in the theoretical and political project of intersectionality, this framework of inclusion fails to confront racism for a number of reasons. First, to include women of color into women's and gender studies leaves the core concepts of the field intact and suggests that the lives of women of color are just another area of study that can be analyzed in the same way that white women's experiences have been. Rather than take seriously the theories of race and gender and the feminist politics that emerge when the experiences of women of color are centered, inclusion simply invites women of color into a project that has already been defined in relation to the experiences of white women (Alarcón 1991; A. Smith 2004). Instead of taking intersectionality as a call to fundamentally transform (or abandon) frameworks that cannot grapple with racial difference, inclusion frequently preserves those frameworks as they are by simply adding to them. Second, inclusion often fails to take into account the relationality of different women's experiences and instead repositions white women's experiences as the norm from which experiences of women of color differ. As Elsa Barkley Brown notes, the point is not just that women of color and white women have different experiences but rather that racism is a structure of power in which "white women live the lives they do in large part because women of color live the ones they do" (E. Brown 1992, 298). Finally, including the experiences of women of color does not require the development of theoretical approaches that demonstrate how race is gendered and gender is raced beyond the scale of individual experiences. What emerges from inclusion is a focus on accounting for different identities rather than on critically interrogating the mechanisms of power by which particular identities are produced as such.

While the metaphor of intersectionality has been a critical first step that has enabled a wealth of scholarship that both brings together theories of race and gender and draws attention to the experiences of women of color, it is also limited by the fact that it implies discrete axes of oppression that intersect in particular locations. This limitation of the intersection metaphor perhaps contributes to the misreading of the term noted above. The tendency has often been to see the intersections of race, gender, sexuality, and class as static locations (usually embodied in women of color) where the otherwise independent trajectories of racism, patriarchy, heterosexism, and capitalism converge rather than seeing these intersections as cuts that completely fracture the imagined singularity of these structures. In her reading of the work of women of color feminists of the late 1970s and early 1980s, Grace Kyungwon Hong defines intersectional analysis as "an analytic mode that does not privilege one site of identification over another, but insists on the importance of race, class, gender, and sexuality as interlocking and mutually constitutive" (Hong 2006, ix–x). In Hong's formulation, intersectionality is not an area of study but rather a methodological approach or "a reading practice, a 'way of making sense of' that reveals the contradictions of the racialized and gendered state" (Hong 2006, x). Such an intersectional reading of Omi and Winant's work potentially elaborates both how racial formation is a gendered and sexualized process and how the theoretical framework of intersectionality might better account for the dynamic processes through which racial categories are constructed. Two particularly useful concepts emerge from Omi and Winant's framework as openings for this kind of reading: the racial project and the trajectory of racial politics.

First, as the "building block" of racial formation, a racial project "is simultaneously an interpretation, representation, or explanation of racial dynamics, and an effort to reorganize and redistribute resources along particular racial lines" (Omi and Winant 1994, 56). A key element of Omi and Winant's theory of racial formation, racial projects link what race means in particular contexts to how social life is racially organized in relation to those meanings. This approach to theorizing the social construction of race moves away from both a purely discursive analysis of racial meanings and a strictly structural analysis that takes already established racial categories as simply the basis of hierarchical social organization. Instead, Omi and Winant's framework stresses that the shape and meaning of racial categories evolve in conjunction with struggles to organize resources through those very categories. As such, racial categories can neither be taken for granted as stable constructions nor divorced from the social contexts in which they develop. Racial formation is the accumulation of both macro-level and everyday racial projects through which race itself is constantly produced and reproduced. Omi and Winant's formulation suggests a different way of thinking about racial politics, not as a struggle between already existing racial categories but rather as a struggle over the very meaning of race and the forms of social organization those meanings enable.

However, despite these invaluable insights, Omi and Winant's framework presumes that race and racial politics evolve in isolation from other axes of power and difference. The absence of consideration of gender and sexuality is particularly striking given how centrally the regulation of the reproduction of racialized populations has figured in the making of race. In addition, examination of the ways that ideas of gender have developed in relation to practices of colonialism, slavery, racialized labor exploitation, and defining national identity suggests that the process of constructing and regulating gender often works as (though perhaps not exclusively as) a racial project. Omi and Winant trace the origins of modern ideas of race to European colonization of the Americas, arguing that the processes of conquest and enslavement consolidated Western concepts of racial difference (Omi and Winant 1994, 61–62). However, conquest was also a process through which modern ideas of gender and heterosexuality were consolidated and imposed on colonized peoples as a technique of domination (Lugones 2007). Not only did colonists frequently employ sexual violence to secure their domination, but patriarchal hierarchies of gender were used as a reference point through which racial hierarchy could be naturalized (A. Smith 2005). The making of race and the making of gender were thus inseparable rather than isolated processes, suggesting the importance of analyzing the gendered and sexualized dynamics of racial formation more broadly. This insight is particularly valuable because it moves away from the idea that these axes of differentiation develop independently and then intersect in particular bodies or locations. Instead, it locates gender and sexual politics firmly within the terrain of racial politics.

A second concept that provides a useful starting point for elaborating the relationship between racial formation theory and theories of intersectionality is what Omi and Winant call the "trajectory of racial politics," or the relationship between the racial state and social movements. Omi and Winant argued that the state is structured by race, that the state doesn't intervene in racial conflict but rather is a site of racial conflict (Omi and Winant 1994, 82). They identified the trajectory of racial politics as shaped by both the racial state and by social movements that engage the state in efforts to rearticulate the terms of racial discourse. Particularly in the post–civil rights era racial hegemony, the racial state secures its legitimacy not simply through repression but also through the incorporation and containment of social movements' demands. Not only does the state absorb dissent, it insulates itself from challenges to the racial organization by limiting the terms in which political claims can be made (86–87). In thinking about how hegemony is constituted in relation to multiple constructions of difference, Omi and Winant suggest that "race, class, and gender (as well as sexual orientation) constitute 'regions' of hegemony, areas in which certain political projects can take shape." They note that "it is crucial to emphasize that such 'regions' are by no means autonomous. They overlap, intersect, and fuse with each other in countless ways" (68).

Omi and Winant's theorization of the state and social movements provides a crucial opening for elaborating intersectional analysis. In thinking about the racial state, it is vital to recognize that Marxist and feminist theorists have made similar observations about the state as structured by capitalism and patriarchy. However, theorizations of the racial state, the patriarchal state, and the capitalist state have not sufficiently engaged each other. For example, within scholarship on the U.S. welfare state, Marxists have explored how the welfare state emerges as a means of regulating the working class, while antiracist scholars point to the ways that welfare policy was structured to maintain racial segregation, thereby ensuring the continued exploitation of African American labor. At the same time, feminist scholars have argued that the U.S. welfare state is organized around gendered ideas of citizenship that define women primarily in terms of their roles as mothers and relegate them to programs within a two-tiered welfare state that are seen as charity rather than entitlements.[3] These three different theories of the welfare state have developed largely in isolation from each other despite the fact that they are in effect seeking to describe the same sets of state practices and interrelated dimensions of the meaning of citizenship.[4]

What Omi and Winant call absorption and insulation have been important areas of inquiry within intersectional analysis as well. One of the most valuable contributions of intersectionality has been to highlight how the separation of race, gender, and sexuality within social movements has frequently provided the ground for state absorption and insulation against more radical claims. For example, Cathy Cohen persuasively argues that the black community has gained certain forms of recognition and inclusion in U.S. political structures by marginalizing gays and lesbians. This "secondary marginalization" constitutes a kind of absorption and insulation in that black leaders gain access to certain forms of power on the condition that they adhere to dominant norms of respectability and police their own communities' demands. As a result, the fact that only some concerns can legitimately count as black issues insulates the state from a more multidimensional critique (Cohen 1999). Similarly, the mainstream feminist movement has adopted an approach to violence against women that emphasizes criminalization. Because it effectively employed the terms of the state, this approach has enabled the movement to gain national recognition to the extent that major legislation has been passed and an Office on Violence Against Women has been created within the Department of Justice. However, feminists of color have shown that this strategy stemmed from a failure to center the experiences of women who by virtue of their race, class, sexuality, and/or immigration status might experience the state not as a protector of women but rather as a perpetrator of violence (Crenshaw 1991b; Richie 2005; Incite!: Women of Color Against Violence 2006). On the one hand, absorption into the state prevents a deeper critique of structural violence against women. On the other hand, the fact that the state recognizes only political claims made in its own terms such as through the rubric of criminalization means that social movements that seek recognition from the state are encouraged to frame their demands in ways that benefit only the most privileged members within a category.

RACIAL FORMATION, INTERSECTIONALITY, AND
THE U.S. WELFARE STATE

To illustrate the value of developing an intersectional understanding of racial formation, I now look specifically at the restructuring of the U.S. welfare state in the mid-1990s and the practices of the Freedmen's Bureau in the Reconstruction South. When read in relation to this historical case, more contemporary debates about "welfare reform" present some interesting problems for thinking about racial formation and the racial state. First, race, in particular, operated as a kind of absent presence in the discourse about "welfare reform." While the welfare legislation adopted in 1996 was the culmination of decades of highly racialized debate and had clearly racialized impacts, race as such is never explicitly mentioned in the law and is difficult to pin down in the discourse surrounding the law. Instead, representations of gender deviance (for example, "sexual promiscuity" or what were deemed "bad mothering practices") were often what marked a subject as racialized in a context in which political discourse strove to remain formally colorblind. This suggests that representations of gender work to signify and constitute racial categories, or, in Omi and Winant's words, that gender itself operates as a racial project. Second, to remedy the threat that women on welfare supposedly posed to the nation's foundational "family values," the law forced welfare recipients to work outside of the home while measuring their value as citizens by their ability to conform to dominant ideals of the heteronormative family. This contradiction reveals the ways that the state's patriarchal interests in regulating women as wives and mothers within the family and its interests in regulating women as a racialized workforce do not necessarily neatly align. This example forces us to consider both how the same bodies can be simultaneously subject to different regulatory impulses and how the contradictory investments of the state are displaced or sutured over so that state power might appear unified when it is not. Finally, the political popularity of a policy that had severe consequences for women, working-class populations, people of color, immigrants, and particularly those who occupy more than one of those categories begs the question, Why did oppositional social movements largely fail to substantially challenge the law? Putting racial formation theory in dialogue with a more intersectional approach provides some insight into how consent for the dismantling of the welfare state was secured and how a state built around and through multiple forms of inequality maintains itself.

The objectives of the Personal Responsibility and Work Opportunity Reconciliation Act (PRWORA) of 1996 were rooted in the belief that welfare enabled a cultural degeneracy amongst recipients that under-mined two of the defining institutions of American citizenship—work and marriage. Replacing a federal entitlement with the state-run Temporary Assistance to Needy Families (TANF) program, PRWORA established a five-year lifetime limit on welfare assistance, mandatory work require-ments including workfare programs, stricter paternity identification and child support enforcement practices, and narrower eligibility criteria that denied or limited assistance to legal immigrants, unwed teenage mothers, and individuals convicted of felony drug crimes. Notably, the text of the law opens with the proclamation that "marriage is the foundation of a successful society," and within public discourse the law was largely pack-aged as an effort to restore the "family values" that had supposedly been undermined by a welfare system thought to promote single motherhood. However, while the law cast marriage promotion as a policy goal, it pri-marily focused on forcing women on welfare into the low-wage labor market either through mandatory work programs as a condition of aid or by denying them welfare assistance altogether. The desire to shore up the heteropatriarchal family was in effect employed to force low-income mothers to work outside the home.

To understand this contradiction, it is necessary to examine how race, gender, sexuality, and class have structured anti-welfare discourse in the post–civil rights era. The "welfare queen," a figure central to this discourse, illuminates the way that racial projects often gain their meaning through gender and sexuality. Popularized in the 1980s by Ronald Reagan and taken up by proponents of welfare reform, the mythic welfare queen is most frequently imagined as a black woman who both lives in a state of hyperdependency on government assistance and, in doing so, aggressively threatens to undermine national well-being. Seen as lazy and sexually irresponsible, she is often depicted as having children in order to increase her welfare check and as eschewing labor discipline, preferring to live off of hardworking taxpayers instead. Transmitting her corrupt values intergenerationally, she is held responsible for the perpetuation of a degenerate culture that keeps her and her children trapped in poverty.[5] In the mid-1990s, this representation was further elaborated to include Latina immigrants who were portrayed as coming to the United States in search of welfare benefits and bringing with them a culture of poverty that undermined American family values such as hard work and sexual restraint (Chang 2000). The antithesis of both the good mother and the good worker, the "welfare queen" embodies excesses of sexuality, entitlement, immorality, dependency, and irresponsibility that justified state austerity in particularly racialized and gendered ways. These representations defined the problem to be solved as undeserving black women whose dependency on welfare threatened national morality, and thus displaced the question of economic, racial, and gender inequality almost entirely.

Scholars have responded to these overwhelming and omnipresent narratives about women on welfare through a wide range of sociological research that disproves common myths about welfare recipients. For example, Kathryn Edin and Laura Lein have painstakingly documented the ways that most single mothers on welfare were forced to supplement their welfare checks with various forms of paid labor in order to survive even prior to the institution of mandatory work requirements in 1996 (Edin and Lein 1997). Similarly, Kristin Luker has demonstrated that the moral panic over teenage pregnancy in the 1980s and 1990s was overblown and that teenage pregnancy by no means causes poverty (Luker 1996). Dorothy Roberts demonstrates how popular myths about welfare recipients are flawed, such as the idea that welfare encourages women to have children and causes dependency and the notion that marriage can solve the problem of single mothers' poverty (Roberts 1997). Amidst the endless debates about immigrants' use of social services, many scholars have argued that welfare benefits are not a significant factor in shaping migration patterns (Sassen 1998), and a number of studies have documented how immigrants use relatively few social services and as a group contribute more in taxes than they use in services.[6] The above-mentioned critiques of common myths about welfare receipt are hardly obscure. They have all surfaced within public debates about the welfare system at some point, but despite the fact that these are rational, well-supported, and even somewhat obvious social scientific arguments, they have failed to stick within public discourse about welfare.

Omi and Winant's concept of the racial project suggests the importance of assessing representations such as the "welfare queen" not just in terms of their veracity but also in terms of the work they do to reiterate and rearticulate racialized social structures. This theoretical approach moves beyond simply thinking of racial stereotypes as flawed representations and instead asks where these representations come from, why the public believes them, and how these representations come to appear as truths difficult to dislodge within a particular constellation of power relationships. Politically, this shift suggests a way of moving the terrain of political struggle away from questions about the truthfulness of representations, where it often gets mired (i.e., struggles over whether welfare recipients are deserving or not, whether immigrants are useful members of society or not, or whether criminalized people are innocent or not), to a more critical interrogation of the ways that the language of deservingness, usefulness, and innocence is always already connected to racialized structures of power.

A look at history reveals that the "welfare queen" is not so much a recent invention as it is a rearticulation in a particular historical context of a set of paradoxes that have defined black women's formal inclusion in the institutions of citizenship. These paradoxes derive from black women's unique location in relation to regimes of labor discipline, sexual regulation, and racial exclusion. The articulation of these regimes of power in historical moments of crisis often presents ideological and material contradictions for the state. As discussed below, these contradictions are frequently displaced onto black women's bodies by exacting an impossible set of obligations as the defining feature of their formal inclusion in citizenship. In juxtaposing the contemporary racial project of the welfare queen against an older historical example, I suggest that these contradictions are central to processes of racial formation and that the articulations of race, gender, and sexuality that inhere in the development of the very terms of citizenship continue to shape contemporary racial politics.

The practices and discourses that evolved in relation to black women's citizenship during Reconstruction resonate strongly with contemporary debates about welfare and reveal how gender functions in the production of racialized exclusion from citizenship rights. As one of the first institutions of the U.S. welfare state, the Freedmen's Bureau was charged with the task of incorporating newly emancipated populations in the institutions of U.S. citizenship. Many contradictions emerged in efforts to include black women in institutions of citizenship that to that point, had denied the humanity of black subjects, and the practices of the Freedmen's Bureau toward freedwomen were defined by these contradictions. On the one hand, freedwomen were seen as an essential source of labor in the southern economy, and vagrancy laws and mandatory labor contracts applied to freedwomen replaced slavery with a regime of forced labor that bears a striking resemblance to contemporary workfare programs. On the other hand, in a society where white women's roles as citizens had been understood primarily as maintaining the sanctity of domestic space and raising future citizens, entrance into citizenship also meant that freedwomen were expected to adhere to norms of domesticity. Freedwomen were frequently the targets of civilizing projects as the freedwoman's home was seen as the measure of freedpeople's preparedness for citizenship. State and nongovernmental efforts to prepare freedpeople for the responsibilities of citizenship emphasized teaching freedwomen how to be good wives and mothers, and the emphasis the bureau placed on marrying freedpeople reflected deep anxieties about controlling black women's sexuality in much the same way that marriage promotion within the welfare system does today.[7] Resonating strongly with contemporary welfare policy, the dual emphasis on forced labor and domesticity produced an impossible mandate for black women by defining their potential as citizens through contradictory obligations that were in practice impossible to meet.

The emphasis that the bureau placed on cultivating domesticity and marriage highlights the fact that for freedpeople entrance into citizenship

and freedom was simultaneously entrance into a regime of gender regulation in which compliance with heteropatriarchal family norms was the
measure of one's worthiness for inclusion in the nation (Franke 1999). The
American Freedmen's Inquiry Commission's report to the U.S. secretary
of war in 1863 strongly recommended marriage as vital to mediating the
transition from slavery to citizenship and stressed that entering into the
marriage contract carried with it gendered responsibilities that had to be
enforced amongst freedpeople. The commission argued that the marriage
ceremony, "while it legitimizes these relations, imposes upon the husband
and father the legal obligation to support his family" (American Freedmen's
Inquiry Commission 1863, 6). In addition, the commission noted: "This
obligation, and the duties connected with the family relation of civilized
life, should be carefully explained to these people, and, while they remain
under our care, should be strictly maintained among them" (6).

Heteropatriarchal family norms were frequently invoked to undermine
public assistance for freedpeople. The idea that providing material assistance to freedpeople would promote "pauperization" and "demoralization"
was a theme that surfaced repeatedly in debates about the Freedmen's
Bureau (Bentley 1974; Farmer 1999). Equating freedom with self-sufficiency and adherence to a masculine ideal of independence, the Freedmen's Bureau asserted that "no greater harm can be done to the negro,
than supporting those who can support themselves."[8] The purpose of the
Freedmen's Bureau was not to "create a race of paupers or to encourage
idleness" but rather, as the Virginia Freedmen's Bureau's assistant com-
missioner, Orlando Brown, argued, "to make the Freedmen into a self-
supporting class of free laborers, who shall understand the necessity of
steady employment and the responsibility of providing for themselves and
[their] families."[9] In these ways, marriage and the gender hierarchies inherent in it offered a vehicle for simultaneously constructing freedpeople as
in need of cultural reform (particularly reform of sexuality), restructuring
household economies, and rationalizing state austerity toward them. The
gendering of institutions of citizenship worked as a means of perpetuating
racial inequality in the post-emancipation period.

The bureau's promotion of marriage predicated entry into citizenship
on the performance of heteronormative gender roles while at the same
time reiterating the compulsion that black women work outside the home,
which made that performance in many ways materially impossible. While
marriage promotion was rooted in the belief that conforming to het-

eronormative gender roles was fundamental to freedpeople's entry into the nation, these beliefs did not extend into the realm of labor. Black women who chose caring for their families over wage work were cited as embodying the "evils of female loaferism" (J. Jones 1992, 45). Bureau officials expressed contempt for "lazy and idle" black women who "played the lady" by staying home and expecting their husbands to support them. For example, South Carolina Freedmen's Bureau agent John William De Forest wrote that "myriads of women who once earned their own living now have aspirations to be like white ladies and, instead of using the hoe, pass the days in dawdling over their trivial housework, or gossiping among their neighbors" (J. Jones 1992, 59).

Securing labor contracts in both agricultural and domestic labor for freedwomen was a regular practice of the bureau, and freedwomen who did not have labor contracts could be charged with vagrancy just as freedmen were (Frankel 1999). In a context in which freedpeople were forced into yearlong labor contracts and were paid at the end of their contract for the entire year's labor, payment was frequently withheld from women for labor time "lost" in caring for their families. In addition, as the vast majority of freedwomen worked as domestics or as agricultural workers, they did not even have access to privatized domestic space because of their labor conditions. Domestics most frequently lived in their employers' homes, while agricultural workers were often paid in the form of room and board on the plantation. In the absence of land redistribution, the ideals of domesticity were in practice unachievable, yet freedwomen were frequently held accountable as individuals and as a race for the impossibility of the obligations on which their citizenship was contingent.

Despite their very different contexts, there are many resonances between this historical example and the representations so fundamental to the restructuring of the U.S. welfare state in the mid-1990s. In the case of the Freedmen's Bureau, the crisis in the meaning of citizenship engendered by emancipation was in many ways resolved through the deployment of gendered definitions of citizenship that made citizenship for freedpeople always contingent on the performance of gendered norms that were materially contradictory and nearly unattainable. The bureau's definition of citizenship in terms of requirements both to work and to conform to domestic ideals created a structure of unachievable obligations for black women that was ultimately employed in the project of reinventing black subordination so that legal emancipation coincided with the persistence of black unfreedom. While discourses that linked the performance of domestic ideals to preparation for citizenship positioned black women as perpetually in need of state-sponsored cultural reform and surveillance, the emphasis on creating independent households justified a policy of state neglect when it came to redistributing social rights and resources.

Not only does the state discourse on marriage and compulsory labor during Reconstruction resonate eerily with the anti-welfare discourse mobilized to secure public consent for "welfare reform" in the mid-1990s, but the more recent promotion of marriage plays much the same role in constructing welfare recipients as culturally inadequate, promoting household economies organized around the rubric of self-sufficiency, and justifying state austerity. These two examples exhibit a striking articulation of race, gender, nation, and class into a circular and mutually reinforcing logic that justifies exacting the obligations of citizenship from black women without granting any of the privileges. Within this logic, gender difference posited as natural fact functions as the measure of civilization and the precondition for full incorporation into the nation. However, gender difference simultaneously operates as a marker of racial difference, with the failure to perform heteropatriarchal norms serving as a primary sign of racial inferiority. Ultimately, within this circular logic, black women are placed in a position in which they are simultaneously seen as racially inferior because they do gender wrong and as doing gender wrong because of their racial inferiority. As a result, the gendered forms of cultural reform that are often posited as the objectives of social policy efforts prove to be an impossible project in the face of the immutability of racial categories within particular contexts.

Returning to Omi and Winant, what are the implications of these two examples for thinking about racial formation theory and theories of intersectionality? First, the interplay between race and gender in these historical examples reveals a great deal about how race appears as an absent presence within contemporary debates about social welfare in the United States. The resonances between the discourse on marriage and citizenship during Reconstruction and contemporary discourse on marriage and citizenship suggests the ways that racism lives in the very language that we use to talk about political and cultural belonging (i.e., terms like *individual, responsibility, worker, wife,* and *mother*). While in more contemporary debates about welfare the explicit language of race is almost surgically excised from the discourse, the historically developed, racially stratified meanings that inhere in these terms remain. In particular, the case of the Freedmen's Bureau reveals the way that heteronormativity and gender difference signified and secured racial hierarchy. In the contemporary context of the ascendancy of colorblind discourses of race (Bonilla-Silva 2003b), the language of gender deviance often stands in for explicit discussion of racial inferiority. This shuttling between race and gender is one of the ways we continue to talk about race without explicitly talking about race and one of the reasons that racism in public discourse on welfare can be so difficult to pin down. The case of the Freedmen's Bureau also demonstrates how heteronormativity is itself a structure of racism and as such suggests the importance of critiquing state racism from a perspective that denaturalizes heteronormative ways of being. Significantly, the ways that the heteronormative family was employed as a mechanism of privatizing inequality in relation to freedpeople foreshadows the use of the discourse of family values to privatize inequality throughout society more generally in current neoliberal state practices.

Second, these two examples illustrate how the state negotiates its investment in structures of race, gender, and capitalism in contradictory ways suggesting that, to understand the workings of the racial state, it is necessary to recognize it as inseparable from the patriarchal and capitalist state. Rather than seeing these different dimensions of state power as developing in isolation from each other, it is necessary to center the processes by which divergent state interests become articulated alongside the displacements required to give state power its seeming coherence. In both the case of the Freedmen's Bureau and that of welfare reform, state interests in regulating women as wives and mothers through the institution of marriage diverged from the state's investments in maintaining women of color as a low-wage workforce. However, the contradictions inherent in policies that sought to do both at the same time remain obscured because they were articulated and made coherent through a racialized logic of state austerity. In effect, both marriage and forced labor became vehicles for ending state assistance to communities of color. As such, imperatives concerning racial exclusion worked to reconcile contradictory demands regarding work and marriage just as racial exclusion was itself effected through these demands.

Finally, and perhaps most importantly, these examples suggest some crucial insights as to why social movements were largely unable to challenge the basic premises of "welfare reform" successfully. Given the imbrication of race and gender in the examples put forth here, it is imperative to examine how social movements that seek to address gender inequality might participate in reinforcing racial hegemony in the framing of their claims and vice versa. Evidence of this can be seen in feminist efforts to draw attention to the impact PRWORA might have on victims of domestic violence. Citing research that documented that approximately 60 percent of welfare recipients had been victims of domestic violence and between 15 and 30 percent of welfare recipients were currently in abusive relationships, these activists argued that specific provisions of the welfare law such as time limits on aid, work requirements, family caps, and mandatory paternity identification would have excessively harsh effects on victims of domestic violence (Raphael 1996). However, instead of disputing the basic premises of welfare reform itself, anti-violence activists argued that domestic violence victims constituted a special category of welfare recipients who both needed and deserved special treatment. Their intervention resulted in the creation of the Family Violence Option (FVO), an amendment to the welfare law that allows individual states to screen and identify victims of domestic violence within the welfare population, to refer victims to appropriate services, and to grant temporary waivers to domestic violence victims in cases when the aforementioned TANF requirements might put victims at risk.

While seemingly a success in reforming the law, in practice, the FVO has done little to improve the situations of women on welfare. This is largely because the activists who fought for the provision developed an analysis of domestic violence and welfare receipt that focused exclusively on gender in isolation from other structures of oppression. Advocates of the FVO made their case by arguing that victims of domestic violence were innocent victims who wanted to work but were unable to do so because of their abusive partners. By stressing that domestic violence impeded the ability of women on welfare to work, advocates of the Family Violence Option, like supporters of the welfare reform law, uncritically accepted the assumptions that women on welfare did not already work and that entry into the low-wage labor market was the solution to women's economic inequality. In addition, in suggesting that domestic violence victims were innocent, they implicitly contrasted this group with other welfare recipients who were presumably guilty of all of the things that anti-welfare discourse charged them with and therefore deserved harsh treatment from the law (Kandaswamy 2010). This strategy was flawed because in practice victims of domestic violence did not appear as a distinct category of innocent victims but were in fact part of the same population as the rest of welfare recipients, who were depicted as undeserving within anti-welfare discourse.[10] As a result, the FVO, while successfully adopted, remains dramatically underutilized (Hearn 2000; Spatz and Katz 2005). I would argue that this underutilization has a great deal to do with the fact that the dominant discourse about welfare recipients as undeserving, promiscuous, lazy, and aggressively cheating the system makes it difficult for most women on welfare to qualify for a provision designed to help innocent victims.

I point to this example not simply to critique these feminist activists. In fact, similar observations might be made about other groups' efforts to challenge PRWORA, such as immigrant rights groups that often asserted their political claims by invoking their deservingness on the grounds of having a strong work ethic or strong family values. Instead, I think this example and others like it demonstrate that the constitution of hegemony through complicated and often contradictory articulations of race, gender, sexuality, and class makes it difficult to build political coalitions across these differences. The feminist activists discussed above chose to engage the state with a particular critique of patriarchy within the home but, in doing so, fell back on the language of compulsory work in an effort to make their political claims. Given the way that preserving the heteropatriarchal family structure and promoting compulsory labor outside the home for welfare recipients are articulated in the service of a larger project of racialized state austerity within anti-welfare discourse, it would appear that confining the political claims of oppositional groups to the language of work or family is one strategy by which state power insulates itself. In effect, the contradictions in state practices as they relate to work and marriage secure consent for policies such as welfare reform by enabling a structure in which even those who opposed the law end up supporting it.

These examples illustrate the importance of applying an intersectional lens to Omi and Winant's theory of racial formation, and of integrating an analysis of processes of racialization into intersectional approaches. Not only does such an approach provide greater insight into the working of the racial state, but it critically revamps how we approach contemporary racial politics. Drawing attention to how gender works to signify and constitute racial difference suggests one way colorblind discourse operates as a discourse on race that does not use the explicit language of race. Therefore, if gender is one of the languages through which we talk about race, engaging gender seems a vital course for racial politics. Rather than thinking about the racial state as developing in isolation from other modalities of state power, it is necessary to explore how racism is produced in and through other forms of differentiation such as gender and class. In particular, if it is the articulations of these sometimes contradictory structures that secures hegemony and insulates the state from critique, it seems that racial politics must take on the rearticulation not just of racial meanings but also of how race gains its meaning through reference to other forms of hierarchy.

NOTES

1. This is not to imply that women and gender studies is a homogenous field. Many scholars and departments within the field have certainly made race central to their work and, in doing so, engaged Omi and Winant. Rather, I seek to draw attention to the fact that concern with processes of racialization remains marginalized within the field as a whole.

2. For examples of this critique, see Moraga and Anzaldúa 1981 and Mohanty 1988.

3. For representative presentations of these arguments, see Piven and Cloward 1971; Quadagno 1994; and L. Gordon 1994.

4. Some notable exceptions that have looked at the welfare state from an intersectional perspective include Mink 1995; Chang 2000; and Roberts 1997.

5. For further discussion of the representation of the welfare queen, see Collins 1990, 67–90, and Roberts 1997, 202–245.

6. For an overview of these arguments, see Grace Chang, "Breeding Ignorance, Breeding Hatred," in Chang 2000, 21–54.

7. For discussion of the role the obligation to work and the obligation to marry played in defining black women's citizenship during Reconstruction, see Kerber 1998, chapter 2; Edwards 1997; Frankel 1999; and Hartman 1997, chapters 4 and 5.

8. Quoted in Farmer 1999, 165–166.

9. Quoted in Farmer 1999, 167.

10. For further discussion of the categorization of victims of domestic violence, see D. Davis (2006).

TWO

On the Specificities of Racial Formation

GENDER AND SEXUALITY IN HISTORIOGRAPHIES
OF RACE

Roderick A. Ferguson

Most commentators on Omi and Winant's groundbreaking book address it as a theory of racial processes within the United States, an analysis of how race as a mode of representation intersects with race as an articulation of social structure. As powerful as this thesis is, our attention to it has perhaps overwhelmed another observation about the text—that the text offered a way to frame race in the postwar and post–civil rights United States. Indeed, *Racial Formation* became a way of taking charge of that recent past shaped by civil rights and national liberation movements, and differentiating it from what had preceded it, those years before the civil rights movement that were characterized by Omi and Winant as the triumph of "the liberal ethnicity vision" of a "race-free society" (Omi and Winant 1994, 98). According to the authors, this vision of a race-free society gave way to a period of insurrectionary movements around racial identity and difference in the fifties and sixties, as well as the fragmentation and cooptation of those movements in the seventies and eighties. *Racial Formation* thus tried to produce historiographic frameworks by which we might understand race in the movement years and beyond. In doing so, *Racial Formation* helped to theorize U.S. national liberation movements as more than instances and outcomes of social agitation, showing that they were historiographic provocations that prodded folks in the United States to think differently about racial difference and identity.

But upon closer reading, we can see that the historiographic framework advanced by *Racial Formation* occludes anti-racist movements no less significant than the social formations around civil rights and national liberation. Those movements were initiated by women of color and queers of color within the United States. Indeed, reperiodizing anti-racist politics according to the emergence of those movements constituted by people of color who were marginalized by sexuality and gender allows us not only to observe the specificities of civil rights and national liberation movements but also to see how race and anti-racist politics were rearticulated in the very moments that Omi and Winant characterize as marked by anti-racist fragmentation.

PARADIGM SHIFTS AND GREAT TRANSFORMATIONS

In their chapter "Great Transformations," Omi and Winant argue that anti-racist movements were processes of articulation: "The racial upsurges of the 1950s and 1960s were among the most tempestuous events in postwar American history. The struggles for voting rights, the sit-ins and boycotts to desegregate public facilities, the ghetto rebellions of the mid-1960s, and the political mobilizations of Latinos, Indians, and Asian Americans, dramatically transformed the political and cultural landscape of the U.S." (Omi and Winant 1994, 95). As processes of articulation, the anti-racist movements were inserting themselves into and impinging upon the workings of U.S. society, revealing the contradictions between racial exclusion and democratic ideals, demonstrating how race shaped subordination and inequality, illustrating how the rearticulation of race's meaning could produce opportunities for intervention into state practices. As sites of articulation, the anti-racist movements were therefore both concerned with observing race and politicizing it. Theorizing articulation as an object for observation and a process of politicization, Jennifer Slack argues that articulation is "not just a thing (not just a connection) but a process of creating connections, much in the same way that hegemony is not domination but the process of creating and maintaining consensus or of coordinating interests" (Slack 1996, 114). Omi and Winant implied this understanding of articulation when they wrote, for example, "Racial *projects* do the ideological 'work' of making these links [between structure and representation]. *A racial project is simultaneously an interpretation, representation, or explanation of racial dynamics, and effort to reorganize and redistribute resources along particular racial lines*" (Omi and Winant 1994, 56; emphasis in original).

Indeed, for Omi and Winant, part of the ideological work done by the race-based movements was through effecting certain paradigm shifts in how we understand race and ethnicity. As they put it, "In the postwar period, minority movements, led by the black movement, radically challenged the dominant racial ideology. As a result of this challenge, the racial order anchored by the state was itself destabilized, and a comprehensive process of reform was initiated" (Omi and Winant 1994, 88). As the passage suggests, Omi and Winant were attempting to both demonstrate and assert a connection between the anti-racist movements and analytical transformations within U.S. society. What Omi and Winant did was to argue and demonstrate how the anti-racist movements in particular and student movements in general affected the interpretive worlds within and outside the American academy, making the race-based movements "the first new social movements—the first to expand the concerns of politics to the social, to the terrain of everyday life" (Omi and Winant 1994, 96).

THE DECLENSION HYPOTHESIS

Despite the undeniable power of the book's argument about the significance of the race-based movements as social formations, *Racial Formation* both obscures the specificity of those movements of the fifties and sixties and occludes the emergence of new definitions of race in the seventies and eighties, definitions articulated by women-of-color and queer-of-color organizations. Indeed, the book renders those histories invisible by erecting a historiography that overshadows the emergence of women-of-color and queer-of-color formations through the book's use of a narrative of historical decline. To begin with, while designating the fifties and sixties as moments of anti-racist upsurge, *Racial Formation* classifies the seventies and eighties as periods of anti-racist repression, fragmentation, and co-optation. "By the 1970s," the authors write, ". . . through repression, cooptation, and fragmentation these movements experienced a sharp decline, losing their vitality and coherence. In the ensuing context of the economic, political, and cultural crises of the period, even the moderate gains they had achieved came under attack by an alliance of right-wing and conservative forces" (Omi and Winant 1994, 95).

To be sure, the conservative attack on the gains inspired by the race-based movements is undeniable and well documented. As Omi and Winant argue, "Beginning in the 1970s, the forces of racial reaction seized on the notion of racial equality advanced by the racial minority movements and *rearticulated* its meaning. Racial reaction repackaged the earlier themes—infusing them with new political meaning and linking them to other key elements of conservative ideology" (Omi and Winant 1994, 117; emphasis in original).

A major force in that repackaging was the presidential administration of Ronald Reagan. Omi and Winant write:

> Reagan "civilized" the race issue by being quite adept at rearticulating the issues of race and racial equality. Drawing on themes derived from both new right and neoconservative currents, Reagan successfully assaulted the racial policies initiated in response to "the great transformation." Under his leadership, the federal government reversed itself and switched sides on racial policy. This was accomplished by rewriting recent history to suggest that discrimination against racial minorities had been drastically curbed and by radically transforming the state institutions which were previously mandated to "protect" racial minority interests. (Omi and Winant 1994, 135)

Reagan "civilized" race by making whites and American civilization the victim of the race-based movements and their anti-racist legacies in the realm of federal policy. Reagan and the new right were, hence, engaged in a hegemonic struggle against the paradigm shifts of the race-based movements, a struggle to produce state structures antagonistic to civil rights gains.

To the extent that *Racial Formation* understands the years after the "great transformation" as only ones overwhelmed by a conservative backlash, the text is caught up in an oedipalization that allows it to see the ensuing decades only as a time of struggle between national liberation/civil rights and the new right. In this sense, as the text is hyperfocused on the new right, it betrays an identification even in the midst of its antagonism. Such an oedipalization prevents the text from asking what progressive rearticulations of race were being evolved as well, an inquiry that would have led it to women-of-color and queer-of-color critical formations.

Omi and Winant's characterization of the seventies and eighties as "fragmented" and "co-opted" evokes national liberation movements' anxiety about feminism and queerness. Indeed, the historical record is rife with tales of anti-feminist and homophobic sentiments among civil rights advocates and revolutionary nationalists, sentiments marshaled against the threat of critiques of patriarchy and homophobia fragmenting various movements. In the context of the civil rights movement, for instance, Thaddeus Russell, in his article "The Color of Discipline: Civil Rights and Black Sexuality," shows that for the modern civil rights movement "the project of attaining citizenship was constructed upon heterosexuality and in opposition to nonheteronormative behavior" (Russell 2008, 103), a project that led to the disciplining of black queer subjects by civil rights leaders in the fifties. In the introduction to the anthology *Home Girls*, Barbara Smith cites as one of the myths that black nationalists used to divert black women from feminism the notion that "women's issues are narrow, apolitical concerns. People of color need to deal with the 'larger struggle'" (B. Smith 1983, 29). The narrative of fragmentation and co-optation used to describe the seventies and eighties repeats the dominant nationalist logic around gender and sexuality—that feminist and queer assertions of anti-racism are the disruptive and politically unintelligible others to civil rights and national liberation. But what happens to our understanding of articulation when this version of the anti-racist movements is raised to the level of historical periodization? What connections might we glimpse through such a maneuver? By doing so, we might gain a new understanding of the connections made in the period in which opposition was fragmented, absorbed, and co-opted.

THE GREAT TRANSFORMATIONS OF WOMEN-OF-COLOR AND QUEER-OF-COLOR FORMATIONS

However this narrative of the 1970s characterizes the U.S. nation-state's period of retrenchment, framing that period solely as one of decline, lethargy, and incoherence occludes the elaboration and diversification of anti-racist critique and practice, an oppositional diversification created by women-of-color and queer-of-color activists, artists, and scholars. The emergence of women-of-color and queer-of-color formations in the seventies and eighties challenges the notion that the periodization advanced by *Racial Formation* is "the best possible form of demarcation" (Foucault 1998, 280). Moreover, women-of-color and queer-of-color formations illuminate the constructed nature of a periodization that reads civil rights and national liberation as periods of upsurge and the years that followed as moments of decline and fragmentation. In discussing the constructed nature of historical periodization, Foucault argued, "Every periodization carves out in history a certain level of events, and, conversely, each layer of events calls for its own periodization" (Foucault 1998, 280). For Omi and Winant, the fifties and sixties as the moments of civil rights and national liberation within the United States carved out such events as mass protests, appeals to the state, and rearticulations of racial identity and difference. Periodizing according to the emergence of women-of-color and queer-of-color movements promotes other events and layers.

Indeed, feminist and lesbian-of-color activists and cultural workers had a very different sense of the seventies and eighties. In the introduction to *All the Women Are White, All the Blacks Are Men, But Some of Us Are Brave: Black Women's Studies,* Gloria T. Hull and Barbara Smith argued, concerning the decades immediately after civil rights and national libera- tion: "The core courses on Black women at colleges and universities has grown slowly but steadily during the 1970s. And increasing interest in Black feminism and recognition of Black women's experiences point to the '80s as the time when Black women's studies will come into its own" (Hull and Smith 1982, xvii). In addition, Asian American poet and *This Bridge Called My Back* contributor Mitsuye Yamada identifies the 1970s as the period that saw the emergence of Asian American feminism: "From the highly political writings published in *Asian Women* in 1971 (incisive and trenchant articles, poems, and articles [*sic*]), to more recent voices from the Basement Workshop in New York City to Unbound Feet in San Francisco, as well as those Asian Pacific Women showcased at the Asian Pacific Women's Conference in New York, Hawaii, and California this year, these all tell us we have been *active* and vocal" (Yamada 1983, 71–72; emphasis added). As Gloria Hull, Barbara Smith, and Mitsuye Yamada suggest, the decades after the sixties saw a burgeoning rearticulation of anti-racist politics and analyses.

To foreground intersectional organizing and critical production means that we must also provide a critical "addendum" to the narratives of the sixties and early seventies. Such a reperiodization would necessarily mean outlining and theorizing the political offshoots of civil rights and national liberation, offshoots that constituted women-of-color and lesbian-of-color organizations. For instance, Kimberly Springer writes, in *Living for the Revolution: Black Feminist Organizations,* "Black feminist organizations were rooted in the civil rights movement, and their dates of emergence coincided with the transition of the locus of black activism from key integrationist civil rights organizations to black nationalist groups" (Springer 2005, 8–9). Indeed, 1968 occasioned the birth of the first explicitly black feminist group—Third World Women's Alliance, "which formed as the Black Women's Liberation Committee . . . of the Student Nonviolent Coordinating Committee" (9). In 1974 black lesbians would found the black lesbian feminist organization Combahee River Collective; it too would be made up of members who hailed from civil rights organizations.

In reperiodizing anti-racist movements within the seventies and eighties, one is also confronted with the fact that the very definition of anti-racist politics began to expand. Because of the efforts of women-of-color feminists, issues concerning reproductive freedom, domestic violence, rape prevention, child care, welfare rights, nuclear proliferation, labor exploitation, war, homophobia, and apartheid became part of the universe of anti-racist opposition. In fact, one of the signature features of the years after the eighties is how deliberate women and lesbians of color were in pushing the boundaries of what counted as race-based politics. For instance, in a conversation between black lesbian feminists activists published in *Home Girls,* Barbara Smith referred to a demonstration against nuclear disarmament held at the United Nations: "To me, for somebody to come and present that issue [of nuclear disarmament] to a Black lesbian organization is not disruptive or divisive. But it's up to black lesbians to figure out how do we relate to it in such a way that we make it our issue. I think that's the answer" (B. Smith 1983, 309). In fact, we might locate the women-of-color feminist desires to broaden political identifications to the ties that organizations like Combahee River and Third World Women's International had to national liberation movements. As Amy Abugu Ongiri argues in her discussion of Huey Newton's 1970 speech on behalf of gay liberation, the Black Panther Party, in particular, attempted to develop models of identification that would "provoke a radical affiliation: across various communities of marginality" (Ongiri 2009, 70). But anti-racism in the period of women-of-color and queer-of-color rearticulations represented, in part, an explicit effort to build on the political breadth of nationalist organizations, using racialized gender and racialized sexuality to multiply political preoccupations.

Reperiodizing the seventies and eighties as moments of anti-racist mobilization also allows us to see an incitement to organize around intertwined issues of race, gender, sexuality, and class—organizing that took place at conferences and in various media. The year 1977 witnessed the appearance of the black lesbian magazine *Azalea* (B. Smith 1983, xxxvii–xxxviii). That same year *Sojourner: A Third World Women's Research Newsletter* was founded (Hull and Smith 1982, xxvii). In 1978 the Varied Voices of Black Women concert toured eight cities and the Association of Black Women Historians was started (Hull and Smith 1982, xxvii). In 1979 the Third World Lesbian Writers Conference was held in New York City, and the National Council of Negro Women's National Research Conference on Black Women convened in Washington, D.C. (Hull and Smith 1982, xxvii). In that same year, the National Third World Lesbian and Gay Conference was held in Washington, D.C. (B. Smith 1983, xxxvii). As these events suggest, contrary to the declension hypothesis of *Racial Formation,* the seventies represented an explosive rearticulation of race along the lines of gender and sexuality.

The 1980s were just as dynamic, becoming the period for elaborating anti-racist feminist critiques within and outside the United States. More to the point, periodizing women-of-color and lesbian-of-color formations in the eighties means also highlighting how international coalitions and conversations became layers in the historical formations around gender, sexuality, and race. In fact, Barbara Smith wrote in 1983, "To me the single most enlivening and hopeful development of the 1980s has been the emergence of so many Third World feminists" (B. Smith 1983, xlii). Hence, in 1980 and 1981, respectively, the first National Hui Conference for Black Women and the First Black Dyke Hui Conference convened in Auckland, New Zealand.

In addition, one of the "events" that emerge from this periodization is the development of cultural, intellectual, and activist work among queer men of color, a development that was an extension of the ways in which women of color and lesbians of color had activated the terrain of culture as a site of struggle. In fact, we might think of the publication of such black gay male anthologies as *In the Life: A Black Gay Anthology* (Beam 1986) and *Brother to Brother: New Writings by Black Gay Men* (Hemphill 1991a) as inheritors of such anthologies as *Home Girls, This Bridge Called My Black,* and *But Some of Us Are Brave.* The genre of the anthology seemed particularly adept at capturing the heterogeneity of interests, aesthetic forms, and racial subjectivities within women-of-color and queer-of-color formations (see Franklin 1997).

The 1980s were also the period in which black queer men, again inspired by black lesbian feminists, worked to theorize how anti-racist work necessarily meant confronting heterosexual masculinity as the taken-for-granted principle of oppositional politics. Such a confrontation would necessarily mean utilizing various cultural, social, and intellectual forms. As Essex Hemphill stated in the introduction to *Brother to Brother,* "Black Gay Men can consider the 1980s to have been a critically important decade for our literature" (Hemphill 1991b, xxiv). Indeed, during that period the black gay male writing collective Other Countries started; the L.A.-based African American gay and lesbian newsmagazine *BLK* released its first issue in 1988. In 1989 black British queer filmmaker Isaac Julien released his film *Looking for Langston;* that same year African American filmmaker Marlon Riggs released his film *Tongues Untied.*

The 1980s also occasioned the emergence of black gay male social and political organizations. Indeed, this period of black gay male organizing was to a large degree an extension and inheritor of black feminist organizing, particularly black feminism's critiques of sexism and homophobia within black communities and among black leaders. Discussing this time, Hemphill writes, "The 1980's also witnessed the emergence of black gay men's groups such as Gay Men of African Descent (New York), Adodi (Philadelphia), Unity (Philadelphia), and Black Gay Men United (Oakland)" (Hemphill 1991b, xxvi).

The incitement to cultural politics represented by the emergence of women-of-color and queer-of-color movements during the seventies and eighties is not a history that can be appreciated within a declension hypothesis like the one advanced by *Racial Formation.* That hypothesis can only occlude anti-racist feminist and queer formations. In its occlusion of those robust histories, the declension hypothesis bequeaths to U.S. anti-racist critique "hauntings, ghosts, gaps, muted absences and seething presences" (A. Gordon 1997, 21)—traces of the insurgent histories of racialized gender and sexuality. As these "ghosts" nag the declension hypothesis, they remind us that the age of modern anti-racist critique is simultaneously the era of feminist and queer contestations. If truth be told, the contemporary study of race was, therefore, born out of heterosexist and masculinist rigors *as well as* the feminist and queer formations that disturbed them. By reperiodizing the study of race to apprehend the feminist and queer insurgencies of the seventies and eighties, we become more fully aware of this contradiction and our place within it.

If the histories of women-of-color and queer-of-color critical formations are historiographic provocations, they also compel us to investigate how race-based movements were not simply governed by identity politics but compelled by the limits and critique of identity as well. For Omi and Winant, one of the "events" produced by the race-based movements of the fifties and sixties is the emergence of anti-racist identity formations. Discussing those formations, they write,

> The depth and breadth of "the great transformation" can hardly be exaggerated. The forging of new collective racial identities during the 1950s and 1960s has been the enduring legacy of the racial minority movements. Today, as gains won in the past are rolled back and most organizations prove unable to rally a mass constituency in racial minority communities, the persistence of the new racial identities developed during this period stands out as the single truly formidable obstacle to the consolidation of a newly repressive order. Apparently, the movements themselves could disintegrate, the policies for which they fought could be reversed, their leaders could be co-opted or destroyed, but the racial subjectivity and self-awareness which they developed had taken permanent hold, and no amount of repression could change that. The genie was out of the bottle. (Omi and Winant 1994, 97)

As "events" the racial identities developed in this period are monumental in significance, promising to outlast the ups and downs of historical change and assault. They are thus constructed as part of the inheritance of the movements toward civil rights and national liberation, the indissoluble and last remaining weapons against conservative attacks. The periodization presumed by Omi and Winant—one that constructs the fifties and sixties as moments of anti-racist surge and that narrates the eighties as anti-racist decline—tells the story of the absolute necessity of identity in anti-racist politics. More to the point, the periodization within *Racial Formation* naturalizes identity politics as the basis of anti-racist action.

But a periodization of the seventies and eighties as the moment of women-of-color and queer-of-color emergences tells a different story about identity. This periodization promotes the historical and *contingent* importance of identity in anti-racist struggles as well as identity's limitations with regard to those struggles. In *Queer Latinidad: Identity Practices, Discursive Spaces,* Juana Maria Rodriguez delineates specific instances in which the limitations of identity politics became "events" in women-of-color/queer-of-color organizing, instances involving splits because of political divergences, linguistic differences, bisexual practices among group members, and the use of pornographic media, as well as ethnic and racial distinctions within various organizations. Rodriquez writes, "Identity politics' seeming desire to cling to explicative postures, unified subjecthood, or facile social identifications has often resulted in repression, self-censorship, and exclusionary practices that continue to trouble organizing efforts and work against the interests of full human rights, creative individual expression, and meaningful social transformation" (J. Rodriguez 2003, 41). The Combahee River Collective statement also includes a record of how identity politics produced tension within that group. "In the fall [of 1975]," the collective noted, "when some members returned [after a summer in which membership had declined], we experienced several months of comparative inactivity and internal disagreements which were first conceptualized as a Lesbian-straight split but which were also the result of class and political differences" (Combahee River Collective 1983, 280).

Similarly, in "The Theoretical Subject(s) of *This Bridge Called My Back* and Anglo-American Feminism," Norma Alarcón critiques Anglo-American feminism as a form of identity politics. For her, that version of feminism idealizes "an autonomous, self-making, self-determining subject who first proceeds according to the *logic of identification* with regard to the subject of consciousness, a notion usually viewed as the purview of man, but now claimed for women" (Alarcón 1990, 357). According to Alarcón, this logic of identification becomes part of the drama of Anglo-American feminism's identity politics: "This 'logic of identification' as a first step in constructing the theoretical subject of feminism is often veiled from standpoint epistemologists because greater attention is given to naming female identity, and describing women's ways of knowing as being considerably different than men's" (Alarcón 1990, 358). In other words, Anglo-American feminism's focus on identifying and articulating female identity, ironically, prevents Anglo-American feminism from seeing its identifications with the patriarchal archetype of the rational individual.

We might say that Alarcón points to the workings of a kind of repressive hypothesis within Anglo-American feminism, one that sees patriarchal power solely as a repressive force weighing upon women. Alarcón uses the notion of a logic of identification to point to the ways in which patriarchy does not simply repress women but actually activates Anglo-American feminism, convincing feminists to take patriarchy as the basis of the movement's models of agency and being. In this way, Alarcón revises patriarchy away from being a strictly negative mode of power and reexamines it as a positive system in the development of Anglo-American feminism. This version of feminism and its presumptions about female identity—as the domain of absolute difference from patriarchal cultures, as the fort that promises to keep patriarchy out—are thus revealed to be new jurisdictions for the expansion of patriarchal power.

Of course, Anglo-American feminism is not the only social movement to have invested in a repressive hypothesis. Indeed, the race-based movements also engaged in their own narratives of repression, narratives that usually understood racial exclusion as the repression of heterosexual masculinities of color. The repression hypothesis of those movements would therefore become the context and reason for the affirmation of minority identity, an affirmation that—like Anglo-American feminism—helped to popularize the patriarchal individual as the paradigm of agency.

Women-of-color and queer-of-color organizing and cultural production were often sites for disrupting narratives of identity. For example, as many women-of-color and queer-of-color activists and cultural workers pointed to the disagreements, disruptions, and conflicts within progressive organizations, this was more than airing dirty laundry or refusing to tow the line. We can think of the archiving and recording of those moments of dissensus as critically historiographical maneuvers, efforts by women-of-color and queer-of-color artists and critics to turn their attention away from the presumed unities of identity and toward the reality of dissension, conflict, and heterogeneity within anti-racist formations.

In his discussion of historiography, Michel de Certeau states, "Since the sixteenth century—or, to take up clearly marked signs, since Machiavelli and Guichardi—historiography has ceased to be the representation of a providential time, that is, of a history decided by an inaccessible Subject who can be deciphered only in the signs that he gives or wishes. Historiography takes the position of the subject of action—of the prince, whose objective is to 'make history'" (de Certeau 1988, 17). The historiography formalized by the race-based movements of the fifties and sixties and theorized by *Racial Formation* is one that takes racial identity as the subject of action. But the histories and critiques of women-of-color and queer-of-color formations in the seventies and eighties suggest that identity is not the most efficient intelligence for mobilizing against power and the conditions within which we find ourselves.

If we approach Omi and Winant's powerful book not as a canonical object whose theorizations and pronouncements we must obey, but as a field of investigation that is still alive and beating, then we may come to appreciate the current moment as one in which we are faced with one of the most strenuous tasks of all—the discovery and education that lie in our most foundational and well-traveled texts. Indeed, the limits of its periodization notwithstanding, *Racial Formation* has taught us that to study race is to intervene in periodization. In this way, the text reacquaints us with a question that covers one of the simplest acts of our existence: "What does it mean to read and then read again?"

The Transitivity of Race and the Challenge of the Imagination

James Kyung-Jin Lee

In the end, this may be what enlightened social maturity is: accepting the world for what it is, and learning to speak of it in its particular, differential details—without denying anything, without leaving oneself out, no matter how painful it might be to be there.

CHARLES LEMERT, *Sociology after the Crisis*

Our work begins with an engagement with the past, out of which we imagine, create, and dare to secure a future.

LISA LOWE, *Immigrant Acts*

While sociologists generally do not deign to assume such a rhetorical mantle, Michael Omi and Howard Winant suffuse the first edition of *Racial Formation* with the language of prophecy that they at once fear to articulate and hope to imagine otherwise. "What does the immediate future hold?" they anxiously wonder. "It is unlikely that we shall experience a period of racially based mobilization such as 'the great transformation.' The conjuncture in which the 1960s racial upsurge occurred was almost certainly unique. The sophistication of the contemporary racial state and the transformed political landscape as a whole seem to thwart any short-term radical political initiative based in opposition to the racial order" (Omi and Winant 1986, 143). This "great transformation" is nothing less, they argue earlier, than the painful movement away from a "racial dictatorship" that characterized much of the United States' path to a tentative "racial democracy," which in turn provided the social space and political will to forge human collectivities other than what the impossible imperative of assimilation would allow. This great transformation is now pejoratively dismissed as "identity politics." In 1986, Omi and Winant foresaw the dismissal, and, less than a decade later, ambivalent clairvoyance turned to resigned revelation in their 1994 edition. Gone is the question about the future: the future was here and "clear": "the great transformation would not recur" (1994, 143).

Those of us who became practical, if not professional, sociologists in the intervening years of the two editions of *Racial Formation* know and, more important, feel why the authors replaced inquiries with clarity, fear and hope with settled understanding. And for those of us who became practitioners of the study of language and literature, the analytic key to how we feel about this interregnum is best found in the penultimate paragraph of the two versions, in both the tense and transitivity of race. In the first edition: "The Reagan administration's attempt to create a 'colorblind society' will instead initiate a vicious cycle of political and economic inequality" (1986, 143). In the second edition: "The Reagan administration's attempt to create a 'colorblind society' certainly exacerbated already wide disparities between whites and non-whites in economic and political terms" (1994, 144). Omi and Winant make their most significant theoretical contribution to the study of race when they argue both for race's centrality and dynamism in the United States and against race as ontological essence, arguing for it instead as a subjectivity in formation, "the sociohistorical process by which racial categories are created, inhabited, transformed, and destroyed" (1994, 55). In other words, race is better described as a verb than a noun, as production rather than destiny. But compare the two editions, side by side, and notice the transitive agent of race. Notice also how the previous paragraph is almost identical in both editions, and one cannot help wondering at the stasis that emergent groups of color—in this case, Asian Americans and Latinas and Latinos—seem to suffer from. (Granted, the second edition takes note of the emergence of different subsets of Latinas and Latinos, but the line suggests ethnic, not necessarily racial, difference.) Tense and transitivity mark Omi and Winant's important but reluctant revision: it is Reagan and his followers who are the agents of change, who have turned the ominous future into the sad past.

In 1986 few of us in the humanities picked up *Racial Formation*, but many of us had by 1994. It wasn't for the resignation of the second edition's conclusion, which confirmed Omi and Winant's suspicions in the first. Rather, what compelled us to read their work was the decade of feelings that characterized not a future anterior but the always already present of our intellectual and political development, a thick tableau of complex experience that we still wrestle with, even as we reside in the names of the eras that suggest race's displacement: post–civil rights, postmodern, transnational, multicultural. Invoking Avery Gordon's notion of haunting, Grace Hong refers to this complex of feelings as race's "remainder," a ghost: "We are today the inheritors of this violently repressed history, and as such, we are left with both presence and absence as our object of study; we are left with the overwhelming sense of our loss, which is a paradoxical state. . . . Race is one of the names for what has been rendered unknown and unknowable through the very claim of totalizing knowledge" (Hong 2007, 34–35).

Omi and Winant's work is that rare sociological endeavor that takes seriously the materiality of our melancholy, individually felt but collectively determined, which we are at pains to displace but can't help embracing—affect without target or with multiple objects but whose effects are as consequential as the social death of incarceration and genocide or the decision to wear blue contact lenses. We picked up *Racial Formation* in 1994 because it provided a language for what seemed either too deterministic or too inchoate, because it taught us that knowing the world of race as it is might, against prevailing evidence, help us in the humanities disrupt the assumption that race's remainder was only negativity and loss. "In just eliciting the question, What's it for?" Marianne Hirsch, a former editor of *PMLA,* claims, "literary/humanistic study disrupts received ideas" (2005, 326). We picked up *Racial Formation* because the question that the sociologists ask—What happened?—is, its authors argue, the same question that we in the humanities ask, sometimes in whispers but increasingly out loud: Why do I feel this way? and, What's it for? And we picked up the second edition of *Racial Formation* because it makes visible the racial ghost through the figure of an Italian man writing while sitting in a prison cage.

If he haunts the fourth chapter of the first edition, Antonio Gramsci materializes explicitly in chapter 4 of the second edition, and it is this brief inclusion that, I would suggest, is at the heart of the reason why so many of us turned to *Racial Formation* in the 1990s and why even more of us return to it today. Indeed, apart from the last two pages of the conclusion and the addition of the epilogue, no other chapter received such substantial revision in the 1994 edition as "Racial Formation." We hear echoes of Gramsci when Omi and Winant schematize race as organizing social principle at both micro and macro levels, only to caution that these two levels "are only analytically distinct. In our lived experience, in politics, in culture, in economic life, they are continuous and reciprocal" (1986, 67). And how does race occupy our lives in a continuous and reciprocal way? "The effort," they explain, "must be made to understand race as *an unstable and 'decentered' complex of social meanings constantly being transformed by political struggle*" (1986, 68; emphasis in original). Curiously, in the first edition, Omi and Winant locate two kinds of "struggle" in the determination of the ongoing significance of race. Race itself is a process of constant and transforming political struggle, but there must also be "effort" to remind ourselves of race's significance through political struggle; in other words, an epistemological struggle that itself requires constant and transforming labor. Why this fetter that demands such a double effort? What is it about racial meaning and racial attachment that requires such vigilance, despite Omi and Winant's invocation of postmodern instability in this definition of race as a process? Whither this anxiety?

When Gramsci firmly appears in 1994, Omi and Winant have already gone through pages describing both the ideology and the material consequences of what they call the long era of "racial dictatorship" in the United States, a tragic but easy enough story to tell. It is more difficult to explain why, despite the "successes of the black movement and its allies," race and particularly the inequalities that race produces remain "stubborn and persistent" (1994, 66). They introduce Gramsci by way of his consideration of the term *hegemony*, one stripped of its thick meaning by our overuse of its adjectival form, and they foreground not the modes of domination that the term might conventionally suggest but rather the ways in which the rule of society depends on the consent of subordinated groups. Yet this is not simply assent to domination, as the phrase most attributed to hegemony—"a combination of coercion and consent" (1994, 67)—might suggest. Omi and Winant extend Gramsci's delineation of hegemony as permeating not only our willingness to be ruled but also the seeds of our resistance to such rule. Consider their prime example of how consent operates:

> It is possible to locate the origins of hegemony right within the heart of racial dictatorship, for the effort to possess the oppressor's tools—religion and philosophy in this case—was crucial to emancipation (the effort to possess oneself). . . . In their language, in their religion with its focus on

the Exodus theme and on Jesus's tribulations, in their music with its figuring of suffering, resistance, perseverance, and transcendence, in their interrogation of a political philosophy which sought perpetually to rationalize their bondage in a supposedly "free" society, the slaves incorporated elements of racial rule into their thought and practice, turning them against their original bearers. (1994, 67)

If you are like me, on rereading this passage, you would have immediately picked up your well-worn copy of *This Bridge Called My Back* and turned to Audre Lorde's often cited but less often read presentation "The Master's Tools Will Never Dismantle the Master's House." And sure enough, there in the middle of her reflection Lorde utters the famous statement and asserts that the "master's tools" will never bring about genuine change. But read on, see how Lorde concludes her remarks, and go back to Omi and Winant: "*I urge each one of us here to reach down into that deep place of knowledge inside herself and touch that terror and loathing of any difference that lives there. See whose face it wears*" (Lorde 1983, 101; emphasis in original). Omi and Winant's invocation of Gramsci's understanding of hegemony has less to do with race as an explanatory term for society's protocols than with race as astonishment, a startling capacity that helps us imagine anew. Sometimes, however, this surprise leaves us with terror and loathing as much as freedom and possibility.

Omi and Winant offer us a sociological vision that instructs us to look for race across scale, from the micro processes of "everyday experience" and "common sense" to the macro dimensions of social structure and political economy—what Gordon calls moving "within and between *furniture without memories* [from Toni Morrison's *The Bluest Eye*] and Racism and Capitalism" (A. Gordon 1997, 4). We in the humanities have heeded this directive and found traces of the master's tools in much of what we call culture in the United States. The emergence of the contemporary subject, lodged in the democratic discourses of citizenship, depends on the constant displacement of others, often racially marked and thus rendered vulnerable to premature death. The very liberal (even sometimes liberatory) impulse of cultural politics in the United States is governed by the absent presence of imperial desire and of the coded but very visible effects of empire: reservations, ghettos, military bases in Seoul, nursing schools in the Philippines. We learned that the American Adam was indeed a myth that we might need to dispense with, once and for all, and that we might offer instead Lazarus—someone who dies but still manages to live on—as a better story through which to gauge the discontinuities that threaten to tear us asunder as a community and to struggle to make new meanings to survive, individually, collectively. Since the publication of both editions of *Racial Formation,* we have taken on in ways unimaginable the question of how power—and, in this case, power as racial hegemony—continues to impose modes of identity that we are loath to inhabit. But somewhere along the way, in the midst of this enormous intellectual and political effort, we missed the opportunity to do what the humanities is meant to do best: to imagine otherwise and then try to live there. We looked for resistance in the form of figures of agency jin our texts, not as a relentless life practice, a practice toward life, which sometimes exceeds the tools we've been given in our analytic labor. And we conceived of racial power as an object that could be grasped and therefore could be countered by another object that became known as multiculturalism. And then we wondered, even after we won that "war," why the world still looked so awful.

What Omi and Winant refer to through Gramsci as "consent" and what Lorde invokes as "terror and loathing," Judith Butler articulates this way: "The power imposed upon one is the power that animates one's emergence, and there appears to be no escaping this ambivalence. . . . [T]here is no ambivalence without loss as the verdict of sociality, one that leaves the trace of its turn at the scene of one's emergence" (Butler 1997, 198). That is, plumb the recesses of your collective racial soul, and you'll find that the tools and technologies that caused and causes so much damage are ones that you're holding too. Then look in the mirror, and you'll see reflected back at you what is often called subjectivity. This is in part what W. E. B. DuBois calls the veil. Certainly, Asian American literary studies, my primary field, has wrestled with the emergence of our subject as deeply ambivalent, sometimes so much so that we assert subjectlessness or melancholy as our theoretical starting point. Model minorities for almost half a century, Asian Americans hew too closely to social structures that have produced such racial misery for others. Our emergence in force onto the United States cultural stage is troublesome, not because we have historically suffered but because we haven't suffered enough, and our relative lack of suffering provokes the anxiety of our complicity in the wide disparities that Omi and Winant sigh over at the end of *Racial Formation.* "Is this my assimilation, so many years in the making?" muses Henry Park, Chang-Rae Lee's narrator in *Native Speaker* (1995), written three years after the Los Angeles uprisings that resurrected the image of the model minority, this time in the construction of Korean immigrants besieged by black and brown looters. Min Song takes a cue from Lisa Lowe when he writes that we have "turned to the terrain defined by culture to experiment, conceive, and put into practice what has been denied other opportunities for expression," but even this cultural expression as the "political place of last resort" is at best liminal and, for Song, ultimately pessimistic (Song 1992, 16).

Asian American culture has emerged as one of fundamental ambivalence, enabled by what Butler calls power; is this not the ambivalence that the humanities feels toward racial transformation? All we have to work with are the master's tools, and we dream for other ones; we look for resistance but settle for multiculturalism; we critique the power that power imposes on us, and this intellectual work leaves us breathless at the end of the day.

Omi and Winant remind us, between the first and second editions of their volume, that ambivalence doesn't prevent action: Reagan and the neoconservative movement show us as much. At the brink of death, Lee Atwater expressed deep ambivalence in 1991 for his mobilization of racial and sexual fear of black men during the 1988 presidential campaign, but the damage was already done. Omi and Winant foresaw in 1986 that the political right in the United States remembered what the left somehow had forgotten, that the racial imagination, like power, is not something that is seized, but an act, many acts in fact, of creativity. Or, as Ruth Wilson Gilmore hypothesizes, "power [and the imagination] is not a thing but rather a capacity composed of active and changing relationships enabling a person, group, or institution to compel others to do things they would not do on their own (such as be happy, or pay taxes, or go to war)" (Gilmore 2007, 248–249). Lorde's proclamation about the "master's tools" is not about finding different tools, and her injunction to face the "terror and loathing" of our difference is not about waiting to come to terms with the ambivalence that racial power imposes on us to create our consent. Rather, in thinking through Gilmore and Lorde together, we might think of the vocational plea of *Racial Formation* in this way: instead of asking the perennial question of the post–civil rights era (Does race still matter?), maybe a less brittle question might be, How can we make race matter so that it attends to the "exile of our longing" (thank you, Patricia Williams) (P. Williams 1991, 49) and invites others to imagine resistance as a life's work and power as acts of making and remaking? How might the humanities reclaim the transitivity of race, despite or even because of the terror and loathing that passive ambivalence evokes?

The literary archive that I read, teach, and write about (which I suspect might be your archive too) gives us many examples, scenes, and passages that remind us that race is an activity that must be reproduced over and over, every day, across all scales, to maintain its power to make us do things we might not otherwise do. But this archive also offers us the potential to put that reproduction into crisis, not out of the belief in or certainty of our work's or crisis's outcome, but in the simple commitment of never saying no to the utopian impulse that lives alongside our terror and loathing and of being, in the words of Toni Cade Bambara, "totally unavailable to servitude" (1977, 77). Mrs. Kim in Paul Beatty's *The White Boy Shuffle* pleads with her black neighbors to "burn my fucking store down" in the wake of the Rodney King verdict, and then looks for the police to place her under arrest (Beatty 1996, 133). Almost fifty years earlier, John Okada throws Ichiro, the Japanese American protagonist in *No-No Boy*, a lifeline through the voice of Rabbit, the black shoeshiner who, unlike everyone else in the story, says to Ichiro of his decision to refuse the draft, "Good boy. If they'd a come for me, I would have told them where to shove their stinking uniform" (Okado 1976, 238). In our contemporary parlance, we might refer to these scenes as prime examples of comparative-race studies, of the mutually constitutive nature of racial formation. But they're more than that. They're certainly more than what we've exhaustingly but often fruitlessly been calling coalitional politics and more than the recognition of both differential and relational racialization. Rather, the archive that responds to the transitivity of race is more like what Fred Moten describes as "blackness," most commonly but not exclusively applied to black people, the "special site and resources for a task of articulation where immanence is structured by an irreducibly improvisatory exteriority that can occasion something very much like sadness and something very much like devilish enjoyment" (Moten 2003, 255). Or, to put it more succinctly, the archive represents the deep traditions that appear as encounters that point to the "needs and aspirations of an ineluctably differentiated humanity" (Singh 2004, 224).

It is in this archive, in these encounters that we might help Omi and Winant write a new chapter of *Racial Formation*, a sociology of race's transitivity, its "recognition of something more" (A. Gordon 1997, 206), a chapter that displaces the narrative of a future that is already a past, sad prophecy fulfilled. In taking seriously the question, What is literary study for? In the struggle over race and its transformation, the disruption of received ideas, we build an archive of feeling that might become the capacity to compel you and others to do things you and they would not do on their own. For me, commitment to these encounters in the books we read and the people we meet when we put our books down—the commitment to discover relentlessly, both in our present, through our pasts, and into a dim future—is what it means to become Asian American rather than simply to be called one. But whatever you call yourself or become through this encounter with terror and loathing and the exile of your longing, it is perhaps this encounter that is the basis on which we dare to imagine a racial future worth securing.

NOTE

I'm grateful to my colleague Erin Ninh, who introduced me to the term *transitivity* and helped me think through it; her work on transitivity and power was quite important in my reflection, as it will be for others when her forthcoming book is published. I'd also like to thank Joanna Brooks, David Kamper, Gaye Theresa Johnson, and Jane Iwamura for reading drafts and offering insight, suggestions, and most of all, support.

FOUR

Indigeneity, Settler Colonialism, White Supremacy

Andrea Smith

Many scholars in Native studies have argued that the field has been co-opted by broader discourses, such as ethnic studies or postcolonial studies (Cook-Lynn 1997; Stevenson 1998). Their contention is that ethnic studies elides Native claims to sovereignty by rendering Native peoples as ethnic groups suffering racial discrimination rather than as nations undergoing colonization. These scholars and activists rightly point to the neglect within ethnic studies and within broader racial justice struggles of the unique legal position Native peoples have in the United States. At the same time, because of this intellectual and political divide, there is insufficient dialogue between the two that would help us understand how white supremacy and settler colonialism intersect, particularly within the United States. In this chapter, I examine how the lack of attention to settler colonialism hinders the analysis of race and white supremacy developed by scholars who focus on race and racial formation. I then examine how the lack of attention to race and white supremacy within Native studies and Native struggles hinders the development of a decolonization framework. I conclude with a brief look at emerging intellectual and political projects that point to new directions in addressing the intersecting logics of white supremacy and settler colonialism.

FROM MULTICULTURALISM TO WHITE SUPREMACY

Before I begin this examination, however, it is important to challenge the manner in which ethnic studies has formulated the study of race relations,

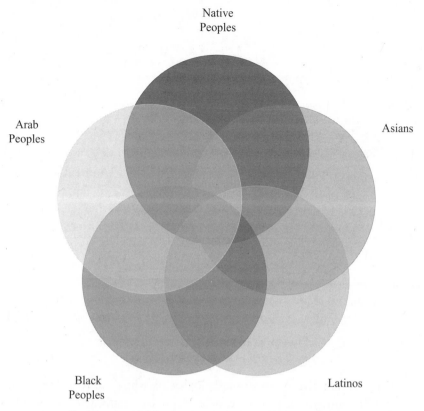

Native
Peoples

Arab
Peoples

Asians

Black
Peoples

Latinos

FIGURE 4.1. Traditional model for people-of-color organizing or ethnic studies.

as well as how people-of-color organizing within the United States has formulated models for racial solidarity. As I have argued elsewhere, the general premise behind "people of color" organizing, as well as behind "ethnic studies," is that communities of color share overlapping experiences of oppression that they can compare and organize around (see figure 4.1) (A. Smith 2006). The result of this model is that scholars or activists, sensing that this melting-pot approach to understanding racism is eliding critical differences between groups, focus on the uniqueness of their particular history of oppression. However, they do not necessarily challenge the model as a whole—often presuming that this model works for all groups except their own. Instead, as I have also argued, we may wish to rearticulate our understanding of white supremacy by not assuming that it is enacted in a singular fashion; rather, white supremacy is constituted by separate and distinct, but still interrelated, logics.

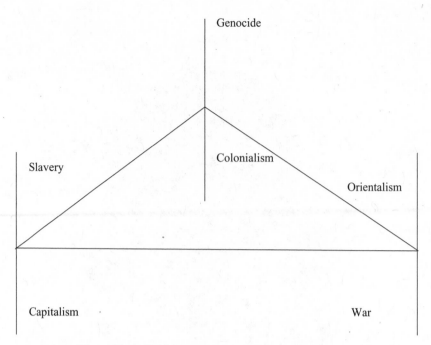

FIGURE 4.2. Three pillars of white supremacy.

I argue that the three primary logics of white supremacy are (1) slaveability/anti-Black racism, which anchors capitalism; (2) genocide, which anchors colonialism; and (3) orientalism, which anchors war (see figure 4.2).

One pillar of white supremacy is the logic of slavery. As Sora Han, Saidiya Hartman, Jared Sexton, and Angela P. Harris note, this logic renders Black people as inherently slaveable—as nothing more than property (Han 2002; Hartman 1997; Sexton 2008; A. Harris 2000). That is, in this logic of white supremacy, Blackness becomes equated with slaveability. The forms of slavery may change—whether through the formal system of slavery, sharecropping, or systems that image Black peoples as permanent property of the state, such as the current prison industrial complex (whether or not they are formally working within prisons).[1] But the logic itself has remained consistent. It is the anchor of capitalism. That is, the capitalist system ultimately commodifies all workers: one's own person becomes a commodity one must sell in the labor market while the profits of one's work are taken by someone else. To keep this capitalist system in place, the logic of slavery applies a racial hierarchy to this system. This racial hierarchy tells people that as long as you are not Black, you have the opportunity to escape the commodification of capitalism. Anti-Blackness enables people who are not Black to accept their lot in life because they can feel that at least they are not at the very bottom of the racial hierarchy: at least they are not property; at least they are not slaveable.

The second pillar of white supremacy is the logic of genocide. This logic holds that indigenous peoples must disappear; in fact, they must *always* be disappearing, in order to enable nonindigenous peoples' rightful claim to land. Through this logic of genocide, non-Native peoples then become the rightful inheritors of all that was indigenous—land, resources, indigenous spirituality, and culture. The pillar of genocide anchors colonialism—it is what allows non-Native peoples to feel they can rightfully own indigenous peoples' land. It is acceptable to singularly possess land that is the home of indigenous peoples, because indigenous peoples have disappeared.

The third pillar of white supremacy is the logic of orientalism. Edward Said defined orientalism as the process of the West defining itself as a superior civilization by constructing itself in opposition to an "exotic" but inferior "Orient" (Said 1994). (Here, I am using the term *orientalism* more broadly than to solely signify what has been historically identified as the "Orient" or "Asia.") The logic of orientalism marks certain peoples or nations as inferior and deems them to be a constant threat to the well-being of empire. These peoples are still seen as "civilizations"—they are not property or "disappeared"—however, they are imagined as permanent foreign threats to empire. This logic is evident in the movements within the United States that target immigrants of color. Regardless of how long any particular group of immigrants of color reside in the United States, they generally become targeted as foreign threats, especially during wartime. Consequently, orientalism serves as the anchor for war, because it allows the United States to justify being in a constant state of war to protect itself from its enemies. Orientalism allows the United States to defend the logics of slavery and genocide, as these practices enable the it to stay "strong enough" to fight these constant wars. What becomes clear, then, is, as Sora Han has put it, that the United States is not *at* war; the United States *is* war (Han 2006). For the system of white supremacy to stay in place, the United States must always be at war.

Under the old but still-dominant model, people-of-color organizing was based on shared victimhood. In this model, however, we see that we not only are victims of white supremacy but are complicit in it as well. Our survival strategies and resistance to white supremacy are set by the system of white supremacy itself. What keeps us trapped within our particular pillars of white supremacy is that we are seduced with the prospect of participating in the other pillars. For example, all non-Native peoples are promised the ability to join in the colonial project of settling indigenous lands. All Non-Black peoples are promised that if they comply, they will not be at the bottom of the racial hierarchy. And Black and Native peoples are promised that they will advance economically and politically if they join U.S. wars to spread "democracy." Thus, people-of-color organizing must be premised on making strategic alliances with one another, based on where we are situated within the larger political economy. Coalition work is also based on organizing not just around oppression but also around complicity in other peoples as well as our own oppression.

These pillars are best understood as logics rather than categories signifying specific groups of people. Thus, the people that may be entangled in these logics may shift through time and space. Peoples may also be implicated in more than one logic simultaneously, such as people who are Black and Indigenous. This model also destabilizes some of the conventional categories by which we often understand either ethnic studies or racial justice organizing—African American, Latino, Asian American, Native American, Arab American. In the case of Latinos, these logics may impact peoples differently depending on whether they are Black, Indigenous, Mestizo, or other. Consequently, we may want to follow the lead of Dylan Rodriguez, who suggests that rather than organize around categories based on presumed cultural similarities or geographical proximities, we might organize around differential impacts of white supremacist logics. In particular, he calls for a destabilization of the category "Asian American" by contending that the Filipino condition may be more specifically understood in conjunction with the logics of genocide from which, he argues, the very category of Filipino itself emerged (D. Rodriguez 2010).

In addition, these logics themselves may vary depending on the geographic or historical context. Obviously, these logics emerge from a U.S.-specific context and may differ greatly in other places and times. However, analyzing white supremacy in any context may benefit from not presuming a singular logic but assessing how it might be operating through multiple, varied logics.

With this framework in mind, I now explore how the failure to address the logics of genocide and colonialism negatively affects the work of scholars who focus on racial theory. Of course, the most prominent work would be that of Michael Omi and Howard Winant's *Racial Formation*. This groundbreaking work speaks to the centrality of race in structuring the world. The authors demonstrate that race cannot simply be understood as epiphenomenal to other social formations, such as class. They further explain that race is foundational to the structure of the United States itself. As I discuss later, their work makes important contributions that those engaged in Native studies will want to take seriously. At the same time, however, this work generally ignores the importance of indigenous genocide and colonialism in its analysis of racial formations.

The one instance in which Omi and Winant discuss colonialism at length is in their critique of the "internal colonialism" thesis—that communities of color should be understood as colonies internal to the United States. In rejecting this thesis, they do not differentiate Native peoples from "racial minorities." Interestingly, they state that the internal colonialism thesis "as applied to the contemporary U.S. with significant exceptions such as Native American conditions . . . appears to be limited" (Omi and Winant 1994, 47). But then they do not go on to discuss what the significance of this "exception" might mean.

One possible reason for not fully exploring the "exception" of Native genocide is that it is relegated to the past. Omi and Winant explain that the United States has shifted from a racial dictatorship characterized by "the mass murder and expulsion of indigenous peoples" to a racial democracy in which "the balance of coercion began to change" (1994, 47). Essentially, the problem of Native genocide and settler colonialism today disappears. This tension is further reflected in some contradictory impulses in Omi and Winant's analysis. On the one hand, they note that "the state is inherently racial" (1994, 82). Their analysis of an inherently racial state echoes Derrick Bell's notion of racism as permanent to society. However, they do not necessarily follow his implications. Bell calls on Black peoples to "acknowledge the permanence of our subordinate status" (1995, 306). He disavows any possibility of "transcendent change"; to the contrary, he argues that "it is time we concede that a commitment to racial equality merely perpetuates our disempowerment" (307). The alternative he advocates is resistance for its own sake—living "to harass white folks," or short-term pragmatic strategies that focus less on eliminating racism and more on simply ensuring that we do not "worsen conditions for those we are trying to help" (308). While Omi and Winant similarly argue that the United States is inherently racial, they clearly do not want to adopt Bell's pessimism. Consequently, they argue that a focus on institutional racism has made it "difficult to see how the democratization of U.S. society could be achieved, and difficult to explain what progress has been made. . . . The result was thus a deep pessimism about any efforts to overcome racial barriers" (Omi and Winant 1994, 70). Now, if one understands the state to be inherently racial, it would then follow that one would not expect racial progress, but rather shifts in how racism operates within it. Under this racial realism framework, either one is forced to adopt a project of racial progress that contradicts the initial analysis of the United States as inherently racist, or one must forego the possibility of eradicating white supremacy. The analysis leading to these two equally problematic options presumes the permanency of the United States. Because many racial theorists lack an analysis of settler colonialism, they do not imagine other forms of governance not founded on the racial state. When we do not presume the givenness of settler states, it is not as difficult to recognize the racial nature of nation-states while simultaneously maintaining a nonpessimistic approach to ending white supremacy. We can work toward "transcendent change" by not presuming it will happen within the confines of the U.S. state.

This tendency for theorists of race to presume the givenness of the settler state is not unique to Bell or Omi and Winant, and in fact appears to be the norm. For instance, Joe Feagin has written several works on race that focus on the primacy of anti-Black racism because he argues that "no other racially oppressed group has been so central to the internal economic, political, and cultural structure and evolution of American society" (Feagin 2001, 3). He does note that the United States is formed from stolen land and argues that the "the brutal and bloody consequences of the European conquests do indeed fit the United Nations definition of genocide" (39). So if the United States is fundamentally constituted through the genocide of Native peoples, why are Native peoples not central to the development of American society? Again, the answer is that Native genocide is relegated to the past so that the givenness of settler colonialism today can be presumed.[2] Jared Sexton in his otherwise brilliant analysis in *Amalgamation Schemes,* also presumes the continuance of settler colonialism. He describes Native peoples as a "racial group" to be collapsed with all non-Black peoples of color (Sexton 2008, 246, 249). Sexton goes so far as to argue for a Black/non-Black paradigm parallel to a "Black/immigrant" paradigm, thereby rhetorically collapsing indigenous peoples into the category of immigrants and effectively erasing their relationship to this land and hence reifying the settler colonial project (253). Similarly, Angela Harris argues for a "Black exceptionalism" that defines race relations in which Native peoples play a "subsidiary" role (A. Harris 2000, 444). To make this claim, she similarly lumps Native peoples into the category of a racial minority and even that of "immigrant" by contending that "contempt for blacks is part of the ritual through which immigrant groups become 'American'" (443–444).

Of course, what is not questioned in this analysis is the idea that "America" itself can exist only through the disappearance of indigenous peoples. Feagin, Sexton, and Harris fail to consider that markers of "racial progress" for Native peoples are also markers for genocide. Sexton contends that the high rate of interracial marriages for Native peoples again indicates racial progress, rather than reflecting part of the legacy of U.S. policies of cultural genocide, including boarding schools, relocation, removal, and termination. Interestingly, a central intervention made by Sexton is that the politics of multiculturalism depends on anti-Black racism. That is, multiculturalism exists to distance itself from Blackness (since difference from whiteness, defined as racial purity, is already a given). However, with an expanded notion of the logics of settler colonialism, his analysis could resonate with indigenous critiques of *mestizaje,* whereby the primitive indigenous subject always disappears into the more complex, evolved mestizo subject. In doing so, these signs of "racial progress" could then be rearticulated as markers of indigenous disappearance and what Denise da Silva terms as racial engulfment by the white self-determining subject (da Silva 2007). Thus, besides presuming the genocide of Native peoples and settler society, these analyses also misread the logics of anti-indigenous racism (as well as other forms of racism).

As mentioned previously, it is important to conceptualize white supremacy as operating through multiple logics rather than through a single one. Otherwise, we may misunderstand a racial dynamic by simplistically explaining one logic of white supremacy through another logic. In the case of Native peoples, those who may have lighter-skin privilege may to some extent have more "independence" than Black peoples, reflecting their position on the color hierarchy. However, if we look at the status of Native peoples also through a logic of genocide, this "independence that accrues through assimilation" is in fact a strategy of genocide that enables the theft of Native lands (Feagin 2001, 39). Andrew Jackson justified the removal of Cherokee peoples from their lands on the basis that they were now really "white," and hence not entitled to their lands.[3] It is important to complicate how proximities to whiteness can enable different kinds of white supremacist projects. Andrew Shryock has argued that because Arab Americans are classified as "white" in the U.S. census, that they cannot be properly understood as "racialized" (Shryock 2008). Essentially, they are sufficiently distant from Blackness and close to whiteness on the Black-white binary that they cannot qualify as racialized. But again, if we understand Arab Americans as racialized through a white supremacist logic of orientalism, it is in fact their proximity to whiteness that allows this logic of orientalism to operate. That is, while their proximity to whiteness may bestow some racial privilege, it is also what allows them to be cast as a "civilization" that, while "inferior," is still strong enough to pose a threat to the United States. This privilege, then, does not signal that they will be assimilated into U.S. society, but that they will always be marked as perpetual foreign threats to the U.S. world order. Similarly, in the case of indigenous peoples, it is the proximity to whiteness that allows them to disappear into white society. Cheryl Harris has brilliantly articulated how whiteness is constructed as "property" withheld from people of color (C. Harris 1995). George Lipsitz similarly argues that white people have a "possessive investment in whiteness" (Lipsitz 1998). However, these characterizations of whiteness as property generally fail to account for the intersecting logics of white supremacy and settler colonialism as they apply to Native peoples. In this intersection, whiteness may operate as a weapon of genocide used against Native peoples in which white people demonstrate their possessive investment not simply in whiteness but also in Nativeness. The weapon of whiteness as a "scene of engulfment" (da Silva 2007) ensures that Native peoples disappear into whiteness so that white people in turn become the worthy inheritors of all that is indigenous.

To be clear, I am *not* arguing against a Black-white binary. Nor am I arguing that lighter-skinned Native peoples are more oppressed than those who are darker skinned. Recently, with the growth of "multiculturalism" there have been calls to "go beyond the black-white binary" and include other communities of color in our analysis. There are a number of flaws with this analysis. First, it replaces an analysis of white supremacy with a politics of multicultural representation: if we just *include* more peoples, then our practice will be less racist. This model does not address the nuances of white supremacy's structure, such as through these distinct logics of slavery, genocide, and orientalism. Consequently, scholars who challenge the so-called Black-white binary do not address settler colonialism any more than do scholars who focus on anti-Black racism. As Candace Fujikane, Dean Saranillio, and Sora Han note, these calls to go beyond the Black-white binary often rely on an immigrant paradigm of "exclusion" from the settler state that does not challenge the conditions of the settler state itself.[4]

Second, the call to move beyond the Black-white binary obscures the centrality of the slavery logic in the system of white supremacy, which is *based on a Black-white binary.* The Black-white is not the *only* binary that characterizes white supremacy, but it is still a central one that we cannot go "beyond" in our racial justice organizing efforts or critical analyses. It also imposes a color hierarchy that impacts all peoples of color. However, I am suggesting that in addition to the Black-white binary, there are other binaries that intersect with this one, such as an indigenous-settler binary, that are distinct but mutually reinforcing. These logics position peoples in multiple and sometimes contradictory positions within the larger settler colonial/racial state.

In addition, I presume that Angela Harris and Jared Sexton's interventions are primarily to call attention to the anti-Black implications behind the call to go beyond the Black-white binary rather than to render a full account of the dynamics of white supremacy. Thus, my point is not to invalidate the importance of those interventions. Rather, I think these interventions can be strengthened with some attention to settler colonialism. The consequence of not developing a critical apparatus for intersecting all the logics of white supremacy, including settler colonialism, is that it prevents us from imagining an alternative to the racial state. Our theoretical frameworks then simultaneously consolidate anti-Black racism rather destabilize it. This tendency affects not only the work of race theorists but that of Native studies as well. I next focus on some of the work emerging in Native studies as it grapples with white supremacy.

As mentioned previously, many Native studies scholars have refused engagement with ethnic studies or critical race theory because they think such engagement relegates Native peoples to the status of racial minorities rather than as members of sovereign nations. Yet, even as Native studies articulates its intellectual framework around sovereignty, some strands within it also presume the continuance of settler colonialism. Glen Coulthard sheds light on this contradiction in noting that in the name of sovereignty, Native nations have shifted their aspirations from decolonization to recognition from the settler state (Coulthard 2007). That is, they primarily articulate their political goals in terms of having political, economic, or cultural claims recognized or funded by the settler state within which they reside. In doing so, they unwittingly relegate themselves to the status of "racial minority," seeking recognition in competition with other minorities seeking the same thing.

One example can be found in the work of Ward Churchill. Churchill offers searing critiques of the United States' genocidal policies toward Native peoples and calls for "decolonizing the Indian nations" (Churchill 1983, 202). Nevertheless, he contends that we must support the continued existence of the U.S. federal government because there is no other way "to continue guarantees to the various Native American tribes [so] that their landbase and other treaty rights will be continued" (Churchill 1983, 1). Thus, in the name of decolonization, his politics are unwittingly grounded in a framework of liberal recognition whereby the United States will continue to exist as the arbiter and guarantor of indigenous claims. In such a framework, Native peoples compete with other groups for recognition. For instance, in some of his work Churchill opposes a politics that would address racism directed against nonindigenous peoples, arguing that Native peoples have a special status that should take primacy over other oppressed groups (Churchill 1983, 419). Such analyses do not take into account how the logics of settler colonialism are enabled through the intersecting logics of white supremacy, imperialism, heteropatriarchy, and capitalism. Consequently, when Native struggles become isolated from other social justice struggles, indigenous peoples are not in a position to build the necessary political power to actually end decolonization and capitalism. Instead, they are set up to be in competition rather than in solidarity with other groups seeking recognition. This politics of recognition then presumes the continuance of the settler state that will arbitrate claims from competing groups. When one seeks recognition, one defines indigenous struggle as exclusively as possible so that claims to the state can be based on unique and special status. In contrast, if one seeks to actually dismantle settler colonialism, one defines indigenous struggle broadly in order to build a movement of sufficient power to challenge the system. (As I discuss later, indigenous peoples' struggles in Latin America that are based on a politics of decolonization have articulated indigeneity as an expansive rather than an exclusive category.)

Churchill's analysis is similar to that of many other scholars who replace a Black-white binary with an indigenous-settler binary. While, as argued previously, this binary certainly exists, our analyses of this binary is insufficient if not intersected with other logics of white supremacy. In particular, we need to look at how "settlers" are differentiated through white supremacy. In much of the rhetoric of the Red Power movement, scholars and activists did not necessarily question the legitimacy of the U.S. state, arguing instead that the United States just needs to leave Native nations alone.[5] As Native activist Lee Maracle comments: "AIM did not challenge the basic character, the existence of the legitimacy of the institutions or even the political and economic organization of America, but rather, they addressed the long-standing injustice of expropriation" (Maracle 1988, 128). Native studies scholars and activists, while calling for self-determination, have not necessarily critiqued or challenged the United States or other settler states themselves. The problem that arises from this analysis, as Maracle notes, is that if we do not take seriously the analysis of race theorists such as Omi and Winant and Bell who define the United States as fundamentally white supremacist, we will not see that it will never have an interest in leaving Native nations alone. Also, without a critique of the settler state as simultaneously white supremacist, all "settlers" become morally undifferentiated. If we see peoples in Iraq simply as potential future settlers, there is no reason not to join the war on terror against them, because morally, they are not differentiated from the settlers in the United States who have committed genocide against Native peoples.

Native studies scholar Robert Williams does address the intersection of race and colonialism as it impacts the status of Native peoples. Because Williams is both a leading scholar in indigenous legal theory and one of the few Native scholars to substantially engage critical race theory, his work demands sustained attention.

Williams argues that while Native nations rely on the Cherokee Nation cases as the basis for their claims to sovereignty, all of these cases rely on a logic based on white supremacy in which Native peoples are racialized as incompetent to be fully sovereign. Rather than uphold these cases (decided under the John Marshall court and understood as articulating Native nations as domestic, dependent nations), he calls on us to overturn them so that they go by the wayside like the Dred Scot decision:

> I therefore take it as axiomatic that a "winning courtroom strategy" for protecting Indian rights in this country cannot be organized around a set of legal precedents and accompanying legal discourse that views Indians as lawless savages and interprets their rights accordingly. . . . I ask Indian rights lawyers and scholars to consider carefully the following question: Is it really possible to believe that the court would have written *Brown* the way it did if it had not first explicitly decided to reject the "language in *Plessy v. Ferguson*" that gave precedential legal force, validity, and sanction to the negative racial stereotypes and images historically directed at blacks by the dominant white society? (R. Williams 2005, xxxiii)

This intervention demonstrates the extent to which Native peoples, by neglecting the analytics of race, have come to normalize white supremacist ideologies within the legal frameworks by which they struggle for "sovereignty." What this illustrates is the manner in which Native peoples can themselves unwittingly recapitulate the logics of settler colonialism even as they contest it, as long as they do not engage the analytics of race. Williams points to the contradictions involved when Native peoples ask courts to uphold these problematic legal precedents rather than overturn them: "This model's acceptance of the European colonial-era doctrine of discovery and its foundational legal principle of Indian racial inferiority licenses Congress to exercise its plenary power unilaterally to terminate Indian tribes, abrogate Indian treaties, and extinguish Indian rights, and there's nothing that Indians can legally do about any of these actions" (R. Williams 2005, 151).

However, Williams's analysis also tends to analytically separate white supremacy from settler colonialism. That is, he argues that addressing racism is a "first step on the hard trail of decolonizing the present-day U.S. Supreme court's Indian law" by "changing the way that justices themselves talk about Indians in their decisions on Indian rights" (R. Williams 2005, xxix). The reason for this first step is that direct claims for sovereignty are more politically difficult to achieve because claims based on sovereignty challenge the basis of the United States itself.[6] As a result, Williams articulates a political vision that contains many of the contradictions inherent in Omi and Winant's analysis. That is, he cites Derrick Bell to assert the permanency of racism while simultaneously suggesting that it is possible to address racism as a simpler "first step" toward decolonization. "I believe," Williams writes, "that when the justices are confronted with the way the legalized racial stereotypes of the Marshall model can be used to perpetuate an insidious, jurispathic, rights-destroying form of nineteenth-century racism and prejudice against Indians, they will be open to at least considering the legal implications of a postcolonial nonracist approach to defining Indian rights *under* the Constitution and laws of the United States (R. Williams 2005, 164; emphasis mine). If Williams were to take seriously the implications of Bell's analysis of the permanency of racism, it would be difficult to sustain the idea that we can simply eliminate racial thinking in U.S. governance in order to pave the way for "decolonization." Consequently, Williams seems to fall back on a framework of liberal multiculturalism that envisions the United States as a fundamentally nonracial democracy that is unfortunately suffering from the vestiges of racism. According to Williams, the Supreme Court is not "a helplessly racist institution that is incapable of fairly adjudicating cases involving the basic human rights [and] cultural survival possessed by Indian tribes as indigenous peoples. I would never attempt to stereotype the justices in that way" (R. Williams 2005, xxvii). He implies that the Court is not an organ of the racial state, but simply a collection of individuals with personal prejudices.

In addition, the strategy of addressing race first and then colonialism second presupposes that white supremacy and settler colonialism do not mutually inform either other—that racism provides the anchor for maintaining settler colonialism. In the end, Williams appears to recapitulate settler colonialism when he calls for "decolonizing the present-day U.S. Supreme Court's Indian law" in order to secure a "measured separatism for tribes in a truly postcolonial, totally decolonized U.S. society" (R. Williams 2005, xxix, 172). He holds out hope for a "postcolonial nonracist approach to defining Indian rights *under* the Constitution and laws of the United States" (164; emphasis mine), as if the Constitution is itself not a colonial document. Obviously, if the United States and its highest court were "totally decolonized," they would not exist. In the end,

Williams's long-term vision does not seem to go beyond state recognition within a colonial framework.

That said, this critique is in no way meant to invalidate the important contributions Williams makes in intersecting Native studies with critical race theory. The apparent contradictions in his analysis may well be based less on his actual thinking than on a rhetorical strategy designed to convince legal scholars to take seriously his claims. In addition, while conditions of settler colonialism continue to exist, short-term legal and political strategies are needed to address current conditions. As Michelle Alexander notes, reform and revolutionary strategies are not mutually inconsistent. Reformist strategies can be movement-building if articulated as such (Alexander 2010). In this regard, Williams's provocative call to overturn the precedents established in *Johnson v. McIntosh* and the Cherokee Nation cases speaks to the manner in which Native sovereignty struggles have unwittingly built their short-term legal strategies on a foundation of white supremacy. And as Scott Lyons's germinal work on Native nationalism suggests, any project centered on decolonization begins with the political and legal conditions under which we currently live, and so our project is to make the most strategic use of the political and legal instruments before us while remaining critical of how we can be co-opted by using them (Lyons 2010). But in the end, as Taiaike Alfred and Coulthard argue, we must build on this work by rethinking liberation outside the framework of the white supremacist settler state (Alfred 1999; Coulthard 2007).

FUTURE DIRECTIONS

Scholars are wrestling with how to address the intersecting logics of empire, white supremacy, and settler colonialism. As a means to explore possibilities for future directions, I focus on the debate about whether to term nonindigenous communities of color as "settlers of color." The arguments on all sides of this debate provide building blocks for both politically and intellectually engaging the intersections of white supremacy and settler colonialism.

A critical contribution made by scholars and activists who adopt the terminology of "settlers of color" is to highlight how nonindigenous peoples of color are set up to take part in a politics of genocide regardless of their intentions or historical circumstances, because their displacement onto indigenous lands simultaneously erases the indigenous people who previously occupied those lands. At the same time, this intervention has been sharply critiqued on a number of grounds. This section of the chapter engages these critiques through Nandita Sharma and Cynthia Wright's germinal essay to explore what these disagreements might tell us about future intellectual and political possibilities (Sharma and Wright 2009).

According to Sharma and Wright, the "settlers of color" argument presumes indigenous nationhood as an inherent good that cannot be questioned (2009, 130). While Sharma and Wright do note that not all articulations of indigenous nationhood are based on statist models of sovereignty, they nonetheless conclude that decolonization must entail an end to nationhood itself. They contend that nationhood necessarily defines a group of people against others in a manner that facilitates capitalism and empire rather than challenging it. Of course, many indigenous scholars critique this approach because disclaiming all projects of nationhood when your nation is not subject to genocide sounds highly suspicious. However, even as Sharma and Wright note, just because an argument may seem suspicious does not mean the argument has no validity. Certainly, as I discuss later, there is much debate about and critique of the efficacy of terms like *sovereignty, nationalism,* and *nationhood* within Native studies and Native communities (see, for example, Womack 1999; A. Smith 2008; Alfred 1999). These terms could have such baggage attached to them that they may not be politically efficacious. At the same time, because of this baggage, we may presume that indigenous peoples' articulations of these terms are always equivalent with their use in mainstream discourse. This presumption is often based on western epistemological understandings of the subject as individualized self who connects with others through a fiction of nationhood that then positions itself over and against others who are not part of the nation. However, as we can see particularly with the development of indigenous struggles in Latin America, not all forms of nationhood derive from this sense of self. If one understands oneself as fundamentally constituted through relationship with all of creation and other peoples, then nationhood is not defined as being against other peoples, but through radical relationality. Nationhood is by definition expansive rather than insular. Consequently, the desire to liberate Native peoples from nationalism can reinstantiate what Elizabeth Povinelli describes as a tradition-free and nation-free liberal subject free from past encumbrances. The liberal subject articulates itself, she suggests, as an autological subject completely self-determining over and against the "genealogical" subject (i.e., the indigenous subject) that is trapped within tradition determined by the past and the future (Povinelli 2006). Essentially, then, this call for "no nationalism" can rely on a primitivizing discourse that positions a simple, premodern indigenous subject locked in history as a foil against the complex cosmopolitan diasporic subject.

Sharma and Wright further contend that the "settler of color" paradigm falsely equates the migration of peoples through enslavement, war, and so forth with the processes of settler colonialism. Such an approach, they contend, pits one oppressed group against the other (Sharma and Wright 2009, 121). Their critique reminds us that white supremacy operates through multiple logics. As previously argued in this article, if we focus only on the logic of settler colonialism without looking at how migration is racially differentiated, we may neglect how Native peoples are sometimes complicit in these processes of forced migration.

Sharma and Wright further contend that this "settler of color" critique presumes a moral innocence to indigeneity in which migrants are marked as "enemies of the nation" (Sharma and Wright 2009, 123). The ultimate problem of settler colonialism, they argue, is thus migration itself. Of course, some proponents of "settler of color" politics implicitly or explicitly base their analysis on such an assumption. However, I would contend that this assumption is not inherent in the critique. The central program presumed in such a critique is not migration, but the relationship between peoples and land. According to Wright and Sharma, indigenous nationhood is defined ethnically or racially by which one group has claim to a land based on prior occupancy. This rationale certainly does exist within Native communities, but the claim occludes alternative visions of indigeneity articulated by many scholars and organizers. As Glen Coulthard and Patricia Monture-Angus demonstrate, this politics of recognition co-opts decolonization struggles by reshaping the relationship between indigenous peoples and land. Indeed land claims are often made on the basis of a temporal framework of prior occupancy rather than on a spatial framework of radical relationality to land. This temporal framework of prior occupancy is then easily co-opted by state discourses that enable Native peoples to address land encroachment by articulating their claims in terms of landownership. Essentially, it is not "your" land; it is "our" land because we were here first. Following this line of thinking, land must then become a commodity that can be owned and controlled by one group of people.

If we understand Native identity as spatially rather than temporally based, claims to land are based not solely on prior occupancy (a temporal framework) but based also on radical relationality to land. As Patricia Monture-Angus (1999) argues, indigenous nationhood is not based on control of territory or land, but on relationship with and responsibility for land.

> Although Aboriginal Peoples maintain a close relationship with the land . . . it is not about control of the land. . . . Earth is mother and she nurtures us all . . . it is the human race that is dependent on the earth and not vice versa. . . . Sovereignty, when defined as my right to be responsible, . . . requires a relationship with territory (and not a relationship based on control of that territory). . . . What must be understood then is that the Aboriginal request to have our sovereignty respected is really a request to be responsible. I do not know of anywhere else in history where a group of people have had to fight so hard just to be responsible. (Monture-Angus 1999, 36)

Unfortunately, Sharma and Wright's analysis overlooks those Native scholars and organizers who are reconceptualizing the relationship between land and peoples. In doing so, they fail to consider how the capitalist conception of land forces all peoples (including indigenous peoples) who migrate (whether it be through enslavement, migration, or relocation) to become "settlers." However, the issue is not migration per se, but the construction of land as property. If land is property, then migration, for whatever reason, relies on a displacement and disappearance of indigenous peoples that emerge from that land. The processes of settlement can be undone when we rethink our relationship to land.

Fortunately, there are many Native scholars and activists who articulate an indigenous politics that centers on relationality to land. One example would be the statements issued by indigenous peoples' organizations at the 2008 World Social Forum. These groups contended that the goal of indigenous struggle was not simply to fight for the survival of a particular people, but to transform the world so that it is governed through principles of participatory democracy rather than through nation-states. The nation-state has not worked for the past five hundred years, they argued, so it is probably not going to start working now. Their vision of nationhood requires a radical reorientation toward land. All are welcome to live on the land, they asserted, but we must all live in a different relationship to it. We must understand ourselves as peoples who must care for the land rather than control it. Because they articulate indigeneity within the context of global liberation, their understanding of indigeneity becomes expansive and inclusive. Their politics is not based on claims for special status to be recognized by the state, but on a commitment to liberation for all peoples that depends on dismantling the state.

Essentially, then, indigeneity in this framework becomes a praxis rather than a static identity that focuses on the building of relationships between peoples and all of creation. Consequently, the "migrant" is not the problem—the problem is commodification of land such that migration can happen only through the processes of land commodification.

Such a politics addresses the critique made by scholars such as Sharma and Wright that indigenous claims to land rest on essentialized notions of Native peoples having a "natural" connection to land. Muscogee scholar and language revitalization activist Marcus Briggs-Cloud argues that indigenous relationships to land happens through the *practice* of ceremony and of living in right relationships to land. The fact that many indigenous peoples have suffered relocation, loss of language, and historical discontinuities in the transmission of ceremonies does not preclude them from reestablishing relationships through prayer and ceremony. Tradition is not static—it is the historical accumulation of communications with the land. These traditions may have been severed, but communication can always begin again (Briggs-Cloud 2010). And as Scott Lyons argues in his brilliant *X-Marks,* we must critically examine "the genocidal implications that are always inherent in the notion of Indian identity as timeless, stable, eternal, but probably in the minds of most people still 'vanishing.' Being vanishes. Doing keeps on doing" (Lyons 2010, 60).

In addition, many Native scholars and activists are doing political and organizing work that questions what Sharma and Wright see as a presupposition in "settler of color" politics that indigenous nationhood presumes a moral superiority. This work focuses on organizing against the complicity of indigenous peoples themselves in empire, anti-Black racism, and heteropatriarchy.

Julia Good Fox and Michael Yellow Bird have called for a rearticulation of indigenous nationhood that identifies the complicity of indigenous peoples in the forced migration of peoples to this land through their involvement in the military. Good Fox has been active in organizing Native peoples against military recruitment, combat the war on terror, and challenge the Israeli apartheid state. Yellow Bird similarly calls on indigenous people to withdraw from U.S. imperial ventures based on a framework of radical relationality. In his critique of Native involvement in the Iraq War, Yellow Bird asserts:

All people and beings are related to us, so we are being asked to make war on our relatives.

We value all life, so war truly must be a last resort.

We value Mother Earth as a living being, and the United States military is contaminating the lands, waters, trees, plants and people in Iraq through the use of biowarfare, landmines and depleted uranium.

We believe in the great circle of life, and we are doing to the Iraqi people what the US did to our ancestors.

All of the killing, maiming, poisoning, and torturing will have drastic effects upon our people, especially on the psychic and cosmological levels.

The US has mistreated us in the past and the present, and it has conscripted our minds and hearts so that we are participating in their oppressive behaviour towards another race of humans. (Yellow Bird 2006)

Currently, indigenous and immigrant groups are collaborating to fight Senate Bill 1070, passed into law in Arizona in 2010, which essentially gave police officers carte blanche authority to arrest "suspected" undocumented immigrants. Indigenous groups in Arizona point to the fact that anti-immigration policies have the simultaneous impact of both reinforcing the legitimacy of the U.S. state while liquidating the claims of indigenous nations within the settler state, particularly those nations that cross U.S. borders. According to the O'odham Solidarity Across Borders Collective,

Border security is needed to ensure neo-liberal projects (NAFTA), and really should be read for what it is: border "regulation/militarization" of indigenous land to ensure capital exportation of people and resources.

. . . It must be clear that the immigration struggle is also an indigenous struggle. In order for the state to pass immigration reform, it has called for the "securing" of the borders first, in order to manage the flow of migration. This securing includes and is not limited to a physical wall to be made on indigenous land (Tohono O'odham/Lipan Apache to name a few). The state's power to waive pre-existing laws (such as NEPA, NAGPRA) in the name of security, directly attacks indigenous autonomy/sovereignty. . . . If others cannot acknowledge the indigenous people of the land, and call for policies that attack them (O'odham! Yaqui!), such as Berlin Wall–like barriers, in the name of "reform/security," then we will witness the cycles of capitalist imperialism continue long into the 21st Century! . . . Attack the root, not each other. (O'odham Solidarity Across Borders Collective 2010)

On May 21, 2010, Native activists occupied the Border Patrol office to protest SB 1070. Among their demands were the following:

On this day people who are indigenous to Arizona join with migrants who are indigenous to other parts of the Western Hemisphere in demanding a return to [the] traditional indigenous value of freedom of movement for all people. Prior to the colonization by European nations (Spaniards, English, French) and the establishment of the [E]uropean settler state known as the United States and the artificial borders it and other [E]uropean inspired nation states have imposed; indigenous people migrated, traveled and traded with each other without regard to artificial black lines drawn on maps. U.S. immigration policies dehumanize and criminalize people simply because [of] which side of these artificial lines they were born on. White settlers whose ancestors have only been here at most for a few hundred years have imposed these policies of terror and death on "immigrants" whose ancestors have lived in this hemisphere for tens of thousands of years, from time immemorial.

. . . .

The protestors are demanding:

An end to border militarization
The immediate repeal of SB1070 and 287g
An end to all racial profiling and the criminalization of our communities
No ethnic cleansing or cultural genocide
No border patrol encroachment/sweeps on sovereign native land
No Deportations
No Raids
No ID-verification
No Checkpoints

Yes to immediate and unconditional regularization ("legalization") of all people
Yes to human rights
Yes to dignity
Yes to respect
Yes to respecting Indigenous People[']s inherent right of migration.[7]

As the occupiers' statement indicates, they identify as the problem not migration, but the nation-state and its reliance on control and ownership of territory.

The Taala Hooghan Infoshop in Flagstaff, Arizona, which was central to the anti–SB 1070 organizing, similarly subscribes to an expansive understanding of indigenous politics. Here are the ground rules for this organization: "This community space maintains agreements which are based on respect and mutual aid. They include, but are not limited to, . . . No drugs, alcohol, racism, heteropatriarchy, colonialism, neoliberalism, hierarchy, capitalism, drama." The Infoshop also attempts to build a politics around decolonization rather than recognition through its critique of the nonprofit industrial complex: "This is not an office. Please refrain from any activities that may be related to or are directly connected to the nonprofit industry, vertical administration (hierarchy), organizational capacity building (and not community building), foundation brown nosing, free market capitalism, and/or just plain capitalism."[8]

Many scholars have spoken out against injustices (including anti-Black racism, homophobia, sexism, and imperialism) committed within Native communities, such as Jennifer Denetdale (2008),[9] Waziyatawin (2008),[10] and Scott Lyons. Lyons encapsulates this work in Native studies in his call for Native scholars to engage broader leftist struggles:

> A . . . pressing danger in my view is the use of Native nations and indigenous sovereignty for purposes that can be just as harmful and retrograde as anyone else's oppression. When gays and lesbians, workers, black people— or anyone—are harmed in the name of travel sovereignty, then discourses other than nationalism are called for in the name of justice. . . . It is always the job of intellectuals to "look also at racism, political and economic oppression, sexism, supremacism, and the needless and wasteful exploitation of land and people," *no matter who perpetuates the injustice.* (Lyons 2010, 163; emphasis in original)

These projects of decolonization are achieving a mass scale in Latin America. As I have described elsewhere, these projects are based on the concept of taking power by making power. That is, they are trying to build the world we would like to live in now, proliferating these alternative forms of governance, and in doing so, challenging the state and capitalism indirectly. Consequently, they attend to the local needs of communities, while positioning themselves as part of a global struggle for transformation (A. Smith 2005). While further discussion is beyond the constraints of this chapter, many intellectual and political projects pursued by nonindigenous peoples are also making these critical links between settler colonialism and white supremacy in the areas of immigration, militarism, environmental racism, queer politics, and gender justice.[11]

CONCLUSION

What is at stake for Native studies and critical race theory is that without centering the analytics of settler colonialism, both intellectual projects fall back on the presumptiveness of the white-supremacist, settler state. On one hand, many racial justice theorists and activists unwittingly recapitulate white supremacy by failing to imagine a struggle against white supremacy outside the constraints of the settler state, which is by definition white supremacist. On the other hand, Native scholars and activists recapitulate settler colonialism by failing to engage how the logics of white supremacy may unwittingly shape our visions for sovereignty and self-determination such that we become locked into a politics of recognition rather than a politics of liberation. We are left with a political project that can do no more than imagine a kinder, gentler settler state founded on genocide and slavery. Nonetheless, a growing number of scholars and activists (indigenous and nonindigenous) are building theoretical and political projects that address the intersections of settler colonialism *and* white supremacy simultaneously, and that thus engage a politics of liberation that engages us all.

NOTES

1. For works that trace the lineage of slavery and Jim Crow to the prison industrial complex, see Alexander 2010; Ignatieff 1978; and A. Davis 2003.

2. Feagin acknowledges that the United States is fundamentally built on indigenous genocide and Black labor. However, he contends that contemporary society is organized along a Black-white binary (along which other communities of color are placed). Here Native nations whose genocide is foundational to the United States disappear, only to reappear as part of the collection of "Latinos . . . and Asian Americans [who] have been able to make some use of these civil rights mechanisms to fight discrimination" (Feagin 2001, 32) Again, with the presumption of settler colonialism, the question of Native nations as nations no longer exists;

Native peoples are simply racially discriminated minorities who can be collapsed with all other people of color. Feagin argues that Native peoples were privileged because they were allowed "more independence, albeit . . . as individuals, only if assimilated" (2001, 39). Assimilation is read then as a relatively benign marker of racial progress rather than as a process of genocide (as I explain in greater detail later in this article).

3. During the Trail of Tears, in which the Cherokee Nation was forcibly relocated to Oklahoma, soldiers targeted for sexual violence Cherokee women who spoke English and had attended mission schools. They were routinely gang-raped, prompting one missionary to the Cherokee, Daniel Butrick, to regret that any Cherokee had ever been taught English (Evans 1977, 259).

4. For strong critiques of this multiculturalist approach to racism and its inability to address settler colonialism, see Han 2006; Saranillio 2009; and Fujikane and Okamura 2008.

5. For example, prominent Native studies scholar Vine Deloria Jr. once argued that there was nothing particularly problematic with the U.S. political or economic system (Deloria 1970, 61). "It is neither good nor bad, but neutral" (Deloria 1969, 189). Prominent AIM leader Russell Means further argued that Native sovereignty could be guaranteed by "free market capitalism" and "the Constitution" (Means 1995, 482, 542).

6. Sovereignty is "inherently problematic for the dominant non-Indian society and its judges in a way that the more general types of minority individual rights at the center of the struggle for racial equality represented by *Brown* were not. It's much harder, in other words, to secure recognition and protection for highly novel forms of Indian group rights to self-determination and cultural sovereignty in American society than for the far more familiar types of individualized rights that most other minority groups want protected" (R. Williams 2005, xxxv–xxxvi).

7. No Borders, "Occupation of Border Patrol Headquarters, Davis-Monthan Air Force Base, Tucson, AZ, *Arizona Independent Media Center,* http://arizona.indymedia.org/news/2010/05/76990.php, accessed May 21, 2010.

8. Photocopy of ground rules in author's possession.

9. In her critique of anti-Black racism, homophobia, and U.S. patriotism within Native communities, Denetdale argues that Native communities support Christian Right ideologies, often in the name of tradition. She calls for a critical interrogation of the politics of "sovereignty," arguing that present-day tribal governance structures are themselves a by-product of colonialism. As such, tribes' welfare is then tied to the well-being of the U.S. settler state. She suggests that these formations in turn inhibit the political imaginaries of Native peoples to envision what true sovereignty and self-determination outside the confines of settler colonialism might look like. She suggests that such a vision not entail self-determination for Native peoples at all costs, but would be tied to a politics dedicated to the end of capitalism, anti-Black racism, imperialism, and heteropatriarchy.

10. Waziyatawin similarly articulates an intellectual and political project of decolonization that specifically involves the dismantling of both capitalism and

the settler state. Like Williams, she does suggest short-term strategies to promote indigenous peoples' survival, including truth commissions, dismantling the icons of U.S. imperialism, land reparations, and language revitalization. However, unlike Williams, she makes it clear that all of these strategies must be part of a larger project for decolonization that transforms the current political and economic status quo. This project of decolonization necessarily demands the involvement of all peoples in solidarity with those fighting for indigenous struggle. As she notes, the capitalist and colonial world order is an unsustainable system that eventually oppresses everyone. "Decolonization requires the creation of a new social order but this would ideally be a social order in which non-Dakota would also live as liberated peoples in a system that is just to everyone, including the land and all beings on the land. Those clinging to traditional Dakota values are not interested in turning the tables and claiming a position as oppressor, as colonizer, or of ruthlessly exploiting the environment for profit" (Waziyatawin 2008, 174).

11. For a few examples, see the work of the Audre Lorde Project (alp.org), Incite! Women of Color Against Violence (incite-national.org), and the Sylvia Rivera Law Project (srlp.org).

PART TWO

Racial Projects and Histories of Racialization

The concept of "racial projects" represents one of the most generative and influential theoretical contributions of *Racial Formation in the United States*. If racial formation itself is fundamentally a sociohistorical *process*, then racial projects represent the historically specific political, social, and cultural developments—including laws, social movements, political initiatives, and cultural phenomena—that shape or direct this process. Omi and Winant stress that racial projects operate at two levels: they attempt to interpret, represent, or explain the meaning of particular racial dynamics and also to reorganize and redistribute resources on the basis of race (Omi and Winant 1994, 56). Racial projects link structures and representations within specific historical contexts; they perform the ideological labor known as racialization—the extension or elaboration of racial meaning to particular relationships, social practices, or groups.

The contributors in this section all utilize racial projects and racialization as conceptual touchstones to engage a wide range of topics. The essays demonstrate that the contours of racialization often exceed a rudimentary white-nonwhite binary; racial projects operate most powerfully through the elaboration and specification of multiple categories of difference.

For example, in "The Importance of Being Asian: Growers, the United Farm Workers, and the Rise of Colorblindness," Matthew Garcia explores the racialization of Japanese and Armenian immigrants in California. While both groups were racialized as "Asian" when they arrived in the San Joaquin Valley in the late nineteenth and early twentieth centuries and attempted to challenge "the boundaries of citizenship and whiteness," only Armenians succeeded in crossing the racial divide between white and Asian. To explore these varying trajectories, Garcia considers the experiences of grower Harry Kubo and the ways he deployed his public identity as a Japanese American to defeat a labor rights initiative led by César Chávez and the United Farm Workers in the 1970s.

Similarly, in "The Unbearable Lightness of Being (Black): Legal and Cultural Constructions of Race and Nation in Colonial Latin America," Michelle A. McKinley examines the complex logics and political forces that shaped racial formation in early colonial Lima. By interrogating the complicated ways that legal categories and socially constructed identities of race interact, she offers a fresh perspective on notions of hybridity, multiculturalism, and racial democracy within contemporary Latin America.

The historical forces explored in McKinley's essay also find expression within Tomas Almaguer's "Race, Racialization, and Latino Populations in the United States." Almaguer considers the ways that racial formation during the colonial era shapes patterns of racialization between and among Latino ethnic groups today. He investigates the changing meaning of race and racial categories for Mexican Americans and Puerto Ricans in particular, especially as they are mediated by categories of gender, sexuality, and indigeneity. Almaguer argues that while Latinos do not fit neatly within American racial categories, they often "have far less trouble racializing one another," as evidenced in the pejorative stereotyping that Mexican Americans and Puerto Ricans often apply to each other's racial identities.

The final two essays in this section explore the ways that contemporary discourses of "racial colorblindness" discipline and restrict political and legal efforts to challenge racial inequities. Scholar-activist Gary Delgado begins his chapter, "Kill the Messengers: Can We Achieve Racial Justice without Mentioning Race?" by assessing the many ways that racial subordination becomes naturalized and reproduced through a framework of racial colorblindness. As a result of this process, he argues, "racial justice advocates have largely been cowed into avoiding explicit discussion of race and racist messages, for fear of alienating whites whose support they have been convinced they need and will not otherwise obtain." This move, Delgado demonstrates, ignores the central insight of Omi and Winant's work, "that individuals' political attitudes are not set in stone and that simple human interaction (organizing, advocacy, education, discussion) may affect people's views and actually change minds."

In the section's concluding essay, "The New Racial Preferences: Rethinking Racial Projects," Devon W. Carbado and Cheryl I. Harris consider how the end of affirmative action in California functions as a racial project. By reinterpreting the meaning of race through veneration of colorblindness, these efforts redistribute resources along racial lines. Harris and Carbado demonstrate this process through an inventive analysis of hypothetical personal statements written by Barack Obama and Clarence Thomas in their law school applications, suggesting that bans on the explicit use of race in law school admissions reorder, rather than abolish, racial preferences. Their analysis demonstrates Omi and Winant's argument that "racial projects come in all ideological stripes," suggesting important questions about the ways in which "good" (anti-racist) and "bad" (racist) racial projects become distinguished.

Collectively, these essays remind us of the continuing ways that a complex array of racial projects modify and rearticulate the meaning of race, and the particular role they play in contesting or legitimating complex relations of power and authority.

FIVE

The Importance of Being Asian

GROWERS, THE UNITED FARM WORKERS, AND
THE RISE OF COLORBLINDNESS

Matthew Garcia

The rise in popularity of "food studies" has produced renewed interest in the history of agriculture and U.S. agrarian reform movements, including a virtual renaissance in the study of the United Farm Workers and the farm-worker movement of the 1960s and 1970s.[1] These studies have contributed attention to the much overlooked subject of labor, offering a view from below that explores the diversity of workers and activists who struggled for farmworker justice, often with limited success. What is still evolving in the literature is a nuanced look at the growers that these workers and activists faced. Like workers, the growers harbored a significant degree of racial and class diversity that shaped the direction of the movement.

During the early years of California agribusiness, the cultural divisions among growers impeded organizing among some producers. Cooperation suggested sameness in modes of production, when in reality growers often raised a variety of crops using culture-bound methods on farms located within ethnic-specific colonies. Although the image of the wealthy Anglo-Saxon grower predominates in current literature on California farming, producers were actually a rather ethnically heterogeneous bunch that often harbored suspicions about their fellow growers. In their early days, agriculture communities encompassed native Mexican Californios, white colonists from the East and Midwest, and large numbers of Italian, Slavic, Armenian, and Japanese immigrants. Later, as specialty crops took shape and industries matured, immigrants remained important participants. According to Marshall Ganz, former strategist for the United Farm Workers, "agriculture itself was a mosaic of ethnic groups" divided into "tightly knit clumps."[2] Like the rest of society throughout the first half of the twentieth century, communities in rural California participated in a process of racial formation, determining the racial fault lines among them.[3]

In this chapter, I explore a process of racial formation among owners of grape farms in rural California during the twentieth century. My attention to the histories of two immigrant groups—Armenians and Japanese—considered "Asian" when they arrived in the San Joaquin Valley in the late nineteenth and early twentieth centuries, demonstrates the divergent paths some immigrants took in pursuing acceptance from peers of European descent. While Armenians succeeded in crossing the racial divide from Asian to white during World War II, Japanese Americans found themselves the victims of increased state oppression in the form of Executive Order 9066, which required the evacuation of all people of Japanese descent on the West Coast to internment camps in the interior of the country. Over time, however, Nisei (or second-generation Japanese Americans) small farmers earned their way into the grower class, especially during the height of the labor wars with the United Farm Workers in the 1970s. Unlike the Armenians, Nisei farmers gained acceptance not by pursuing a white identity, but rather by mobilizing their nonwhiteness in the service of all growers, regardless of race.

The career of Harry Kubo, a fifty-three-year-old Nisei small farmer and grower activist in 1975, best illustrates how the importance of being Asian in rural California changed during the second half of the twentieth century. His acceptance by white growers as a spokesperson for agribusiness in the mid-seventies signaled their embrace of a colorblind ideology that championed the heroic efforts of Japanese Americans to overcome internment and succeed in California agriculture. Under these new beliefs, growers accepted a history of racial discrimination not as evidence of the government's obligation to right the wrongs of the past, but rather as proof that American capitalism enabled anyone, regardless of race, to overcome hardships and succeed. Kubo's self-promotion as an antidote to Mexican and Filipino farmworkers and the black urban poor aided the growers' position and strengthened the belief that race had little to do with one's success.

A study of racial formations in rural California provides a useful test for Omi and Winant's assertion that "racial theory is shaped by actually existing race relations in any given historical period" (Omi and Winant 1994, 11). I contend that the different trajectories of assimilation and cultural adjustment experienced by Armenians and Japanese reflect, in part, the paradigmatic shifts in racial thinking that occurred in the United States from the 1960s to 1990s. According to Omi and Winant, the first shift occurred in the 1960s, when participants in racial minority movements rejected the prevailing premise inherent in the *ethnicity model*: that racial minorities could be incorporated into American life in the same way white ethnic groups had, and that equality and social justice defined the experience for all Americans, regardless of race. Pressure from civil rights groups, such as the United Farm Workers, forced a reconsideration of these assumptions and produced public policy that accounted for the prevalence of racial hostility. By the 1970s and 1980s, Omi and Winant argue, a white "backlash" against this approach led to the resurgence of ethnicity theory under the guise of "neoconservatism" (Omi and Winant 1994, 11). The story of Harry Kubo's life, in particular, parallels these developments, and offers a useful example of how one man of color shaped the neoconservative agenda that emerged during this period.

ARMENIANS AND JAPANESE IN THE FOUNDING OF GRAPE CULTURE

From the beginning in the late nineteenth century, through the boom years of the 1970s, immigrants played a significant role in determining the culture of grapes in California. Many immigrants flocked to grape country, drawing on knowledge from their homelands and solidarity with coethnics. Armenian, Slavic (specifically Croatian), Italian, and Japanese growers were among the leading ethnic groups.

The participation of Armenians in the world of the grower challenged the boundaries of citizenship and whiteness. Armenians came to the United States in waves, often in response to ethnic and religious persecution from Turks in their homeland. Between 1915 and 1923 the Ittihad Party in the Turkish capital of Constantinople attempted to exterminate two million Armenians living within the Ottoman Empire. Of this total, one million were massacred and another 500,000 escaped to become part of a worldwide Armenian Diaspora (Jendian 2001, 46–51).

Throughout this period, Armenians migrated to the United States in search of "Yettem," or an "Eden" away from the religious and ethnic persecution at home. Although Armenian immigrants established communities elsewhere during the nineteenth century, few claimed to have found paradise until hearty pioneers traveled across the country to the Central Valley of California during the 1880s. By 1920 Armenians accounted for 25 percent of Fresno County's foreign-born population, enough to establish Yettem, the only all-Armenian town in the United States (Jendian 2001, 62; Minasian 1983).

Most Armenians found Eden elusive in the San Joaquin Valley. Often labeled "Dirty Armenians" and "Fresno Indians" by their neighbors, Armenians found themselves the subject of restrictive covenants and hostile, racist attitudes from white residents. Discrimination in housing made clear the racial dimensions of this harassment. The San Joaquin Abstract Company maintained restrictions in its sales contracts for property barring "any person born in the Turkish Empire [or] any lineal descendent of such person" from buying land in a new, upscale portion of north Fresno. Such restrictive deeds against Armenians remained in contracts through 1944 (Jendian 2001, 67).

The debate concerning Armenians' racial identity went beyond Fresno realtors to U.S. courts. During the first quarter century, Armenians played a prominent role in determining the boundaries of whiteness in the United States in two federal immigration cases: *In re Halladjian* in 1909 and *United States v. Cartozian* in 1925. In *Halladjian*, four Armenian immigrants challenged a U.S. Bureau of Naturalization decision to bar their application for U.S. citizenship on the basis of their "Asiatic" origins. The Massachusetts court not only overturned the bureau's decision but also established a definition of whiteness in the course of its decision. On the question of Armenians' "Asiatic" origins, the court held: "They are no darker than many west Europeans, and they resemble the Chinese in feature no more than they resemble the American aborigines" (M. Jacobson 1998, 231–233).

By the 1920s, court decisions undermined skin color and origins as the primary criteria for determining the boundaries of whiteness. In 1922 Japanese immigrant Takao Ozawa questioned his exclusion by arguing that Japanese people had a white complexion and therefore should be granted U.S. citizenship on the basis of their whiteness. The court denied his request, finding that Ozawa "is clearly of a race which is not Caucasian." When a federal district court in Oregon granted Indian immigrant Bhagat Singh Thind U.S. citizenship in 1920 on the premise that he was a Caucasian and thus should be eligible for citizenship, government lawyers succeeded in convincing the court that even an "average man" in the United States could see that Thind was not white. According to legal scholar Ian Haney López, the *Thind* decision established a "common knowledge" test for determining the racial status of immigrants based on "popular, widely held conceptions of race and racial divisions" (López 1996, 5).

The new "common knowledge" litmus test created by *Thind* forced Armenians back into a racial gray zone given the everyday discrimination against them in places like Fresno, California. Having achieved success in reversing the naturalization of Ozawa and Thind, the United States went after the citizenship eligibility of Armenian applicant Tatos O. Cartozian in 1925 on the grounds that he was "not a free white person within the meaning of the *naturalization* laws of Congress."[4] In *United States v. Cartozian* (1925), the court ruled in favor of Cartozian, holding "that the *Armenians* are of the Alpine stock" and therefore must be considered white by law. To establish this fact, the defendant called in famed anthropologist Franz Boas to explain away the Asian identity of a people whose origins resided well within the "Asian" territory of the Turkish empire. Boas testified: "The evidence is so overwhelming that nobody doubts any more their early migration from Thrace across the Hellespont into Asia Minor."[5] The Christianity of Armenians in a Muslim world provided perhaps the strongest argument for their European ways. Cartozian's lawyers also claimed that Armenian men, upon their arrival in the United States, commonly married "American wives." Embracing the logic of "white is what white does," the court saw such behavior as a sign of the whiteness of Armenians and, thus, their eligibility for citizenship.[6]

The court's verdict flew in the face of the treatment of Armenians in the grape-growing regions of California. In 1930 Stanford researcher Richard Tracy LaPiere conducted a survey of the 474 non-Armenian residents of Fresno County concerning their impressions of Armenians. LaPiere conducted his studies in the tradition of the Chicago School, a research group started by University of Chicago sociologist Robert Park concerned with the attitudes of the dominant white population toward immigrants and minority groups. True to his training, LaPiere directed most of his questions toward a deeper understanding of the racial tension within society. For Fresno and its Armenians, LaPiere's results were not encouraging. When asked "What do you find are the principal characteristics of Armenians?" respondents listed a total of 1,119 derogatory traits, including "dishonest" (16%), "undependable" (12%), "arrogant" (11%), and "tricky" (9%). For at least half of LaPiere's respondents, Armenians reminded them of Jews, while 92.5 percent refused to accept marriage between Armenians and their kin. A majority of respondents also rejected Armenians as neighbors or playmates for their children and advocated barring Armenians from becoming U.S. citizens. The Christian backgrounds of Armenians did not convince at least 42.5 percent of respondents to accept them as members of their church. Although the courts considered Armenians white in 1925, that whiteness remained "of a different color" for those who policed racial boundaries in grape country throughout the 1930s and forties (M. Jacobson 1998).

LaPiere described the divisions between non-Armenians and Armenians as "racial-cultural" given the racial language used by some of his respondents. A banker who provided credit to many Armenian businessmen in the county told LaPiere, "The Armenians are, as a race, the worst we have to deal with." Claiming that they "steal, lie and do everything to save a penny," the man compared them to "the nigger who steals his dinner on the way home from church" (LaPiere 1930, 380). In the raisin industry, fellow growers accused Armenians of opposing the organization of the California Associated Raisin Company, though the number of Armenians resisting the CARC did not substantiate their claims. According to LaPiere, at the time of the association's attempts to organize a cooperative of between 60 and 80 percent of the growers in the industry, Armenian growers produced between 10 and 15 percent of the raisin crop (Jendian 2001, 64–65; LaPiere 1930, 383–385; M. Jacobson 1998). It should come as no surprise that some Armenians were wary of joining a cooperative made up of people who opposed their presence in the valley.

Eventually, however, Armenians' "European origins" and Christian beliefs opened the door for them to secure white privilege through a performance of whiteness, especially in the realm of business. Krikor Arakelian of Fresno County provides perhaps the earliest and best example of how business acumen translated into acceptance among the elite members of society. Born in Marsovan, Turkish Armenia, in 1871, Arakelian moved with his parents to Fresno County in 1883, where he spent a substantial portion of his youth. In 1892 Arakelian returned to Marsovan for college and became an outspoken critic of the Ottoman Empire and an advocate for Armenian independence. The Islamic government imprisoned him for revolutionary activities, though he quickly gained his release on account of his U.S. citizenship.

Arakelian sought refuge from political persecution in Fresno, where he invested all of his savings in a forty-acre melon farm. Within a short time he became known as the "Melon King of America," based on the sale of his Mission Bell brand of watermelons and cantaloupes. In 1919 Arakelian again tempted fate when he retired from melons and bought two of the largest vineyards in California at severely discounted prices after the specter of Prohibition dampened investments in the wine industry. Although Prohibition became law in 1920, Arakelian foresaw a robust raisin and table grape market he could exploit. Marketing his raisins and grapes under the same Mission Bell brand that he had used for his melons, he enjoyed success that earned him the respect of his Anglo peers, who admired his ability to expand within the limits of his personal credit during the Great Depression. Despite the economic crisis, Arakelian built six packing-houses in the San Joaquin Valley and purchased property in Fresno, Kings, Madera, Stanislaus, and San Joaquin Counties. In 1933, when Prohibition ended, Arakelian parlayed his good fortune into wine production, developing the Madera brand used for sacramental, medicinal, and manufacturing purposes across the United States (Winchell 1933, 291–292).

As subsequent generations of Armenians settled in California, the tendency to marry non-Armenians gradually became more common. Krikor Arakelian's marriage to Rose Agamian, a fellow Armenian immigrant from Constantinople, in 1899 would have placed them among the 90 percent of Armenian couples who chose a spouse of the same ethnic background during that period. By 1980, however, Armenians were as likely to marry a non-Armenian as an Armenian, an act that made it harder to deny them their whiteness. While too much can be made of these marriage patterns, they suggest that assimilation *and* a retention of ethnic identity occurred among Armenians in Fresno at a time when grapes dominated the agricultural landscape of rural California.[7]

If the grower culture somehow could forget the Asian identity of Armenians and bring them into the fold over time, it could not do the same for Japanese growers. Several Japanese immigrants (Issei) arrived in California during the late nineteenth and early twentieth century with the ambition of owning their own farms. By 1920, 5,152 Japanese residents had achieved this goal on 361,276 acres, producing crops valued at $67 million (Matsumoto 1993, 31). This fortunate class of horticulturalists constituted a minority among Japanese immigrants, most of whom never transitioned from laborer to owner. Nevertheless, the few who succeeded as farmers mirrored the successful among Armenians, if not in outcome, at least in approach. Under the assistance of Japanese businessman Kyutaro Abiko, Japanese farmers established three colonies in the San Joaquin Valley: Livingston (known as Yamato), Cressey, and Cortez.

Local resistance to Japanese farmers proved to be too strong for their assimilation into San Joaquin Valley society. By 1919, rural opposition to Japanese settlement had become more pronounced as Abiko established the two-thousand-acre Cortez Colony in Merced County on the heels of creating the Yamato colony in 1907 and Cressey colony in 1918 (Matsumoto 1993, 30). Journalists writing about the "hordes of nonassimilable" Japanese in the local newspapers prompted the Merced County Farm Bureau directors to form a special committee to oppose further Japanese colonization. Elbert G. Adams, editor of the *Livingston Chronicle,* sounded an ominous tone in the pages of his daily beginning in 1919. Differentiating between the original inhabitants of Yamato and the new arrivals, Adams opined that "we could not blind our eyes or deaden our senses to the fact that more Japanese were coming in here; Japanese not of the type of the original twenty-one families." Although the first Yamato colonists tended to be better educated and have more money than later settlers, the increased hysteria over the "Japanese Problem" signaled the strength of anti-Japanese sentiments among members of the dominant culture, and was not precipitated by new or unusual actions by more recent Japanese immigrants. By 1920 Merced County maintained one of the most aggressive Anti-Japanese Associations, one that routinely posted signs stating, "No more Japanese wanted." The association also circulated cards among landowners requesting a "morally binding" agreement not to sell land to Japanese buyers. When these measures did not work, exclusionists in the state assembly passed the California Alien Land Law, barring the transfer or lease of land to Japanese nationals and preventing the ownership of land by any corporation in which Japanese held a majority of the stock. In 1924, as a part of that year's Immigration Act, the federal government imposed a quota on Japan that limited the number of new immigrants to a mere 2 percent of the current population of Japanese immigrants in the United States and prohibited the entry of any "alien ineligible to citizenship." This legislation essentially cut off all further immigration from Japan (Matsumoto 1993, 32, 42).

This was the world Harry Kubo entered on December 4, 1922, in Sacramento, California. As a son of Japanese immigrant tenant farmers in Placer County, Kubo came of age at the height of anti-Japanese sentiments. Such discrimination intensified after Japan attacked Pearl Harbor on December 7, 1941. Kubo had been attending community college when the raid happened, on a Sunday. Kubo recalled, "The first thought that came to mind was . . . I do not particularly care to go to school [on Monday,] knowing the climate that already existed among these few people." His parents refused to allow him to stay home as an act of defiance against such racism. "When we entered the bus the following morning," Kubo remembered, fellow riders peppered the family with insults; "why don't you Japs go home, you dirty Japs." Although Kubo and other Japanese American students felt tension throughout the winter and spring, few incidents occurred. Kubo attributed the absence of conflict to the "docile" and "quiet" nature of Japanese Americans, and prided himself on being one among a people who "were non-reactionary and were able to take abuses . . . because it doesn't solve anything to get in confrontations with people who don't understand the situation."[8]

In spite of his demeanor, Kubo, like other Japanese Americans, fell victim to Executive Order 9066. The authorities came for the Kubos on May 12, 1942, and told the family they had forty-eight hours to prepare to relocate to an assembly center in Arboga, California. Kubo saw the internment as "one of the darkest days amongst the people of Japanese ancestry." Kubo reflected: "Can you imagine ordering a citizen without due process—you are going to be uprooted from your home; we don't know when you are going to get back, but in the meantime we want you to settle your business; we don't know where we are going to take you, but be prepared to leave for anyplace that we may wish you to go?" Local whites whom Kubo referred to as "vultures" in his 1978 oral history offered to buy appliances at severely discounted prices from the family, adding insult to injury. "It took a lifetime to buy those things," Kubo explained, "and they were offering my parents for the refrigerator and the washing machine two dollars, a dollar and a half, five dollars, and my father said, 'well, even if we had to throw it away, we wouldn't give it to them.'"[9] Fortunately for the Kubos, the Leak family, which owned the property the Kubos sharecropped, stored their possessions and even sent them their portion of the profits after they moved to the internment camp at Tulare Lake in Modoc County, California. Still, the threat of losing everything and watching other Japanese American families have their private property appropriated by the state inspired in Kubo a distrust of government.

Following their release from the camp, the Kubos landed in Sanger, just outside Fresno, where the entire family worked as field hands for seventy-five cents an hour. By 1949 they had pooled their earnings into one bank account and purchased a forty-acre grape and tree-fruit farm in the neighboring town of Parlier. While the family worked the homestead, Kubo and his brothers continued as farmworkers to pay off the mortgage and raise money to buy another 60 acres from a neighbor in 1954. By the mid-1950s, the Kubos had accumulated 110 acres in the Parlier-Sanger section of the San Joaquin Valley and eventually acquired 210 acres in 1976. Kubo took great pride in the ability of Japanese Americans like himself to recover from the trauma of internment. In 1971 he joined with fellow Japanese American farmers Abe Masaru and Frank Kimura to organize the Nisei Farmers League. The league's defense of private property rights and vigorous opposition to United Farm Workers attempts to unionize field laborers drew both Japanese and non-Japanese growers into the organization. The league began with 25 neighboring farmers; under Kubo's leadership, it grew to 250 members within a year. By 1976 the league had swelled to more than 1,400 members, of which, surprisingly, only 43 percent were of Japanese descent.[10]

Kubo served as the league's first president and emerged as an outspoken critic of UFW president César Chávez. The two first butted heads in 1970, when the UFW attempted to corral a small group (15%) of independent family farms that had escaped signing the grower-union accord on July 29. Chávez and UFW cofounder Gilbert Padilla directed United Farm Workers pickets against eight packinghouses handling the fruit picked on seventeen farms in Tulare and Fresno Counties. Japanese Americans owned fourteen of the seventeen fields picketed, including the Kubos' small farm.[11] During the conflict, tension erupted into occasional acts of vandalism, including slashed tractor tires, nails and spikes left in driveways, arson, and yearling trees cut down at the trunks. Larry Kubo, Harry's son, remembered one incident in which a number of young UFW picketers entered the Kubo farm at night. "I was fourteen," Larry recalled, "and they ran on to our property and started screaming and yelling at us, and they were not much older than me." In their exuberance, the group vandalized the Kubo tractor, though Harry kept his family inside and told his son to "stay where you're at" until the group left. Such incidents alarmed the Japanese grower community and precipitated the formation of the league and inspired Kubo's activism.[12]

Kubo's star rose in 1976 when the United Farm Workers attempted to strengthen the Agricultural Labor Relations Board (ALRB). In 1975 California passed the Agricultural Labor Relations Act, which established the board and a number of regional offices to regulate farm labor disputes and conduct union elections. During the first five months of the law's existence, these offices oversaw hundreds of union elections. The flurry of activity reflected the pent-up demand for justice; however, it also quickly exhausted agency budgets. The UFW won a majority of the elections, prompting growers to appeal to state senators to block an additional appropriation to keep the ALRB functioning through the year. When the agency ran out of money in February 1976, the United Farm Workers turned to the voters by sponsoring Proposition 14, an initiative that, among other things, would secure year-round funding for the ALRB.

The United Farm Workers also designed Proposition 14 to address the thorny issue of union access to workers on California farms. Although ALRA recommended equal access to unions, in practice, this provision was honored more in the breach than in the observance by farmers and agents. The UFW experienced difficulty in gaining entry to farms before and after working hours in order to campaign for votes, and struggled for time equal to that permitted the Teamsters. The initiative sought to write into the law an "access rule" that required growers to permit union representatives on their property one hour before work, one hour after work, and at lunchtime. Marshall Ganz, head of the "Yes on 14" campaign, simplified the union's argument for the rule change as "an access to information" issue. "If you are going to have free union elections," he explained, "the workers must be fully informed."[13]

The growers responded first by organizing an Ad Hoc Committee composed of many organizations, including the Nisei Farmers League, to determine how to fight Proposition 14. At the meeting, Kubo distinguished himself as a credible voice on farm labor issues and earned the grudging praise of his peers as the chair of the committee. "[Kubo's] not polished and he's not a professional," one unidentified leader of a statewide farm group told a reporter, "but he knows what he's talking about and he knows how to tell it to the people." The local newspaper took note of Kubo's rags-to-riches story in 1976, deeming him "the ineloquent speaker-turned-spokesman" for all farmers.[14] His handling of labor issues facing a wide spectrum of the agricultural community, from large-scale farmers to small family farmers like himself, provided useful cover to corporate entities that had become easy targets for derision in this David-and-Goliath struggle. Seeking a more focused, sustained campaign, the Ad Hoc Committee formed a "No on 14" organization known as Citizens for a Fair Farm Labor Law and named Harry Kubo as its president.

Chávez and the "Yes on 14" advocates viewed Kubo's involvement as a cynical ploy by wealthy growers to hide behind a small farmer, and discounted his concern for private-property rights violations. Throughout the campaign, Chávez emphasized the $2.5 million budget of his opponents, used to hire "experienced manipulators of public opinion" who tried to "persuade a lot of people that passage of Proposition 14 will give the right to Mexican farm workers to enter their homes without permission." Such allusions to white fears of home invasion never directly entered into Kubo's vocabulary; however, others disseminated these ideas to the public on behalf of growers.[15] In his public speeches and published commentaries, Kubo remained focused on the consequences of the rules change for farmers and farmworkers. For farmers, he worried, "you kick an organizer off the farm for being disruptive, . . . and the next day the guy is back on your farm and you have to let him enter and he can disrupt things all over again." For workers, Kubo argued, "under '14' the worker would just about lose his right to work or not work under a union contract." He added, "the union could bring such pressure on him . . . he'd have to join even if he didn't want to."[16] In his rebuttal, Chávez ignored nuances in the anti-14 position, inserting a not-so-subtle gibe at Kubo's credibility by asserting that agribusiness had "started a slick campaign with . . . a small grower as a front, presenting Proposition 14 as a violation of property rights."[17] Kubo rarely, if ever, criticized Chávez's character in public, though in his oral history, he shared his impressions of the labor leader after they met for the first time in 1974 at a debate held at the Hilton Hotel in Fresno. "My first impression of him," he told his interviewer, "was [of] a person that was very arrogant, very arrogant in his statements, but I also found that he was a very intelligent man, a person with total dedication to the cause that he was pursuing." Kubo maintained an abiding respect for Chávez, acknowledging that their "roots are the same" and that they shared a commitment to improving farmworkers' lives, though by different means.[18]

The cities became the battleground for Proposition 14, with both the UFW and Citizens for a Fair Farm Labor Law investing much time and money in winning the war of ideas among the large blocs of voters. Kubo traveled more than thirty thousand miles in 1976, engaging Chávez in a number of debates and becoming what one newspaper called the "focus of Chávez's wrath."[19] He organized highly visible "No on 14" rallies in Los Angeles, the San Francisco Bay Area, and San Diego in the week prior to the election, drawing as many as four thousand participants at each event.[20] In each location, he orchestrated successful door-to-door campaigns that rivaled the UFW's supremacy in grassroots outreach, and conducted media events, complete with a country-and-western concert, throughout the state. Kubo honed the growers' position to an easily digested message, "Protect Private Property—*No* on 14," that the public understood and that the editorial boards of several urban newspapers and television and radio stations picked up and incorporated in their opinions on the subject.[21] These efforts gave the growers an unprecedented voice in the cities and helped raise political contributions that supported campaign ads on the airwaves.[22]

The union countered these events with an aggressive grassroots campaign of its own, which included community groups that communicated their message via leaflets and door-to-door appeals. In Los Angeles, for example, the Coalition for Economic Survival (CES) worked on behalf of the union to challenge the private-property argument as "the old 'big lie' campaign." "They have poured millions into a demagogic 'vote no' campaign," CES's steering committee wrote to its members, "using the phony 'private property' slogan."[23] As the election neared, Chávez's attack on the validity of the private-property argument became more urgent. In a speech to eight hundred supporters in National City, Chávez implored the partisan crowd not to take victory for granted and asked everyone to take individual responsibility for challenging the growers' attempt to confuse voters. "We've got to tell the people that [the private-property argument] is a phony issue," he warned, "or we're in trouble."[24] In many posters and fliers that appeared in the months leading up to the election, the UFW routinely drew attention to Kubo's private-property argument as "the Big Lie" and republished articles naming the wealthy growers who contributed to Citizens for a Fair Labor Law.[25] The union also highlighted the many politicians whom it counted as allies, including President Jimmy Carter, Governor Jerry Brown, San Francisco mayor George Moscone, and Los Angeles mayor Tom Bradley.[26]

In the end, none of these endorsements helped the union. Voters handed the UFW a crushing defeat, rejecting Proposition 14 by a better than 3–2 margin on November 2, 1976. The "No on 14" forces garnered more than two million more votes than advocates for the initiative, and carried fifty-six of the state's fifty-eight counties, with Alameda and San Francisco the only two counties voting in favor.[27] Although the growers' newsletter interpreted the outcome as "a repudiation of the naked power grab of César Chávez" and "a major defeat for Governor Gerald Brown," Kubo offered a more sanguine evaluation, highlighting the importance of the organizing drive: "[It was] amazing to see the grassroots response from agriculture. People we didn't know were out there came to the front and pitched into the effort to defeat this bad initiative. It was this all-out support that made the victory possible. . . . Every grower—all of agriculture—can be proud of this accomplishment."[28] Union organizers tried to attribute the outcome to the $2.5 million budget that fueled the growers' intense media campaign, though in the end the UFW spent a substantial sum of its own, $1.3 million.

Support for Kubo's message manifested common ground between growers like him and voters concerning the sanctity of private property in California. The electorate's decision was consistent with an entrenched preoccupation with the rights of property owners, perhaps most clearly articulated in 1964 in the repeal of the fair housing law known as the Rumford Act. Amidst the civil rights movement, the California State Assembly had passed the law, named for William Byron Rumford, the first African American elected official in Northern California. It prohibited discrimination in most privately financed housing and outlawed racial discrimination by home lenders. In response, a coalition consisting of the California Real Estate Association, Home Builders Association, and Apartment Owners Association organized a successful campaign to overturn the law by way of an initiative—coincidentally, also Proposition 14—that passed by a two to one margin. Racism clearly played a role in the vote, though many voters also expressed their opposition to what they perceived as the state interfering in the management of private property (Lipsitz 2006, 114; Elinson and Yogi 2009, 148–149; HoSang 2010, 70–71).

Kubo's role as spokesman also signaled an important turn in the growers' political strategy. Prior to their victory, they had attempted to discredit Chávez as a false prophet, the UFW as a social movement rather than a union, and the Teamsters as the superior choice for workers. None of these strategies worked. In Kubo, however, they found a life story and a sympathetic character whose experience successfully countered the appeals of the UFW on behalf of poor farmworkers. By 1976 much of the public accepted the internment of Japanese Americans during World War II as an injustice and saw Kubo as a victim of the misguided Executive Order 9066. Indeed, within two years, the Japanese American Citizens League believed it had enough public sympathy to launch a reparations movement. In 1983 a congressional committee issued the report *Personal Justice Denied,* recommending compensation to the victims, and in 1988 President Ronald Reagan signed the Civil Liberties Act, offering $20,000 in redress to surviving detainees. Kubo's personal history and the growing sentiment in society regarding the mistake of internment gave him increased credibility with the public and enabled him to articulate a political position that questioned the state's right to determine who could enter private property. Perhaps the most enduring and effective image of the "No on 14" campaign was a poster of Kubo standing in front of his home with the following message in bold letters: "34 years ago, I gave up my personal rights without a fight . . . IT WILL NEVER HAPPEN AGAIN."[29] Such an evocation of the internment paid tremendous dividends for large and small growers alike who, ironically, now relied on a man of color and an act of racial injustice to stem the momentum the UFW had gained since ARLA's passage.

In the wake of the growers' success, Kubo enjoyed a level of celebrity unique among Japanese Americans that provided him a platform to advance his conservative viewpoints. In the same election in 1976, Mill Valley resident, former San Francisco State University president, and fellow Japanese American S. I. Hayakawa won a seat in the U.S. Senate as a Republican candidate and appealed to Kubo to run for public office. Kubo declined, though he continued to serve the Nisei Farmers League as an effective lobbyist for growers in Sacramento and became a member of the Parlier school board, happily leaving the responsibility of farming to his brothers and children. As a public figure, he espoused a political message of racial uplift consistent with an emerging colorblind ideology that challenged racial minorities to avoid making excuses for their problems and to take responsibility for their own lives.[30] In his oral history, Kubo shared his philosophy: "If you have a chip on your shoulder and you're going to feel sorry for yourself, you will never get ahead in this life. . . . I've seen too much of that, because you are an ethnic minority, you have lived under poverty, the government owes you a living, that is not an attitude Japanese-American people have; we're going out and trying and this is what we did."[31]

Kubo identified both farmworkers and African Americans as the largest and most significant groups carrying such a "chip." He labeled farmworkers a "unique" people whose unpredictable nature made them undeserving of anything more than the minimum wage. According to Kubo, "some come early, some won't show up at all," but on average, "they're not responsible enough in a lot of instances to call up and say I won't be there tomorrow." Kubo reserved his harshest criticism for African Americans, whom he called a "handicapped people" for their presumed dependence on welfare. According to Kubo, in providing African Americans welfare, "you destroy any incentive or desire [for them] to work on their own and to persevere."[32] Kubo contrasted these groups and others interested in government subsidies with Japanese Americans, who, he testified, pooled their resources and labor to become successful farm owners. Kubo believed that "if the Japanese-American can do it under these handicaps, the alien land laws, the fact that our parents couldn't be naturalized and the incarceration during the war years, and they could still come back and have enough perseverance and determination to try, then anybody in this country could own a piece of land if they really wanted to."[33]

Such beliefs went well beyond the property rights position advocated by the growers, though Kubo's thoughts on a range of issues, from worker responsibility to welfare and the assumed culture of poverty among many racial minorities, provide a window on the conservative politics of a grower class that now made room for Japanese Americans. For former detainees of the internment camps, the postwar shift in racial attitudes did not earn them an immediate spot among their grower peers, though Kubo fondly remembered those in the San Joaquin Valley who assisted them in their reintegration into society. When the Kubos left the camp at Tulare Lake, they landed as tenant farmers with an Armenian family, the Peters, living just outside Fresno. Kubo appreciated the "similarity between the Armenian[s] and Japanese," though this perception of belonging to what George Lipsitz called "a family of resemblance" had more to do with the sharing of food, child care, and the duties of farming than with a consciousness about the two groups' parallel histories of pursuing whiteness in U.S. courts during the early twentieth century (Lipsitz 1990, 150). Kubo acknowledged how instrumental the kindness of others had been in his family's road back to society, at one point emphatically stating, "I don't ever recall any acts of discrimination, prejudice, [or] uncomfortableness" after the war.[34]

Kubo's focus on his own story of triumph and the generosity of neighbors, however, fostered an ignorance concerning the differences between the period of his ascendancy in the late 1940s and 1950s, and the 1960s and 1970s, when Mexican and Filipino workers butted up against new challenges such as undocumented immigration, stagflation, the growth of corporate farms, and the continued upheaval in the Mexican and Philippine economies, which fed the postwar stream of poor itinerant workers into California fields. These blind spots did not stop Kubo from comparing his struggles to those of contemporary farmworkers. In a speech to a local seventh-grade class, for example, Kubo told his mostly Mexican audience, "I'm one of you, too," referring to his life as a son of immigrants, though he could not help but broaden the comparison to "Indians," "Germans," "Armenians," and "probably thirty or forty ethnic groups in this country."[35] For Kubo, the struggles of farmworkers in the 1970s represented an earlier version of his own life, albeit without the corrosive power of the state restricting their movement and ownership of property.

Kubo's thoughts manifested the shift toward "neoconservativism" during the late 1970s that Omi and Winant identify in *Racial Formation* (1994, 128–132). Their description of this political philosophy, however, relies primarily on an analysis of the backlash against the black civil rights movement and President Reagan's repeal of civil rights legislation in the 1980s. Ethnic studies scholarship since the publication of *Racial Formation* allows us to evaluate the particular experiences of ethnic minorities in this moment of transition, including the life of Harry Kubo.

It is tempting to see Kubo's history as an example of the familiar model minority, which frequently casts Asian Americans as the alternative to other minority groups that demand that the government play a more serious role in leveling the societal playing field. While elements of Kubo's story correspond with this interpretation, Vijay Prashad has recently observed that a mélange of racial theories existed throughout the twentieth century, especially after the Immigration Act of 1965, when immigration from all corners of the globe increased the diversity of U.S. society. The model minority concept, Prashad argues, stood alongside competing theories of liberal pluralism and multiculturalism, all designed to manage and incorporate this diversity within a nation now clinging to white supremacy (Prashad 2006). In many respects Kubo served this purpose, though seeing him primarily as a model minority denies him agency in the construction of his own message of racial uplift. Moreover, Kubo spoke not only for Japanese Americans but also for growers, a largely non-Asian group that chose him as its spokesperson.

More recently, Peggy Pascoe has argued that the period after the 1967 Supreme Court case *Loving v. Virginia,* ending the ban on interracial marriage, initiated another shift in thinking about race that is relevant to Kubo's success (Pascoe 2009). Pascoe's careful tracing of the erosion of racial classification prior to the *Loving* decision and the rise of a colorblind ideology in the years following it provides a powerful context for understanding Kubo and his appeal. Although it took fifty-four years—from the prosecution of boxer Jack Johnson in 1913 for his sexual relations with white women, to the *Loving* decision—the majority of Americans eventually adopted the position advocated by those Pascoe calls "culturalists," social scientists who challenged the biological foundations of race. As her study of the 1921 Arizona Supreme Court case *Kirby v. Kirby* shows, these scholars held "not that there was no such thing as biological race but that race was nothing more than biology" (Pascoe 2009, 125). This intellectual precursor to colorblindness gained acceptance among many, if not most, Americans by the mid-1960s, Pascoe tells us, after Martin Luther King Jr. shared "his famous dream of being judged not by the color of his skin but by the content of his character" (301). Ironically, during the 1970s, conservatives, who had been among the most stubborn on this issue, became the strongest advocates for a meritocracy in which people in the United States would be measured by their abilities. Colorblindness, in other words, did not ignore racial difference; it simply disregarded its importance and wanted social policy to follow (302–303).

Kubo and his fight for property rights demonstrate colorblind politics in process of formation—what we might call proto-colorblindness. As a public figure, he espoused a political message of racial uplift consistent with an emerging colorblind ideology that challenged racial minorities not to make excuses for their problems and to take responsibility for their own lives. In the years following his victory, Kubo criticized both farmworkers—

including by extension Mexicans and Filipinos—and African Americans as two groups who, he argued, asked for government handouts and assistance based on their racial identities. He labeled farmworkers a "unique" people whose unpredictable nature made them undeserving of anything more than the minimum wage (cf. Pascoe 2009, 23).

Kubo assumed his right to speak as a man of color and for people of color, and reveled in the credibility he assumed his identity gave him to address such issues as welfare, immigration, property ownership, and labor. Although he did not disavow the harsh experience of internment or slavery and discrimination, he argued that a colorblind American system based on merit in the postwar period allowed anyone, regardless of race, to succeed. Rather than deny the importance of their identities, Japanese Americans like Kubo drew on those identities both to extend their reach over society and to appeal to people with whom they felt an affinity. Thus, during the anti-14 campaign, Kubo frequently honored Chávez's hard work by admitting "César Chávez has done some good things," but he saw Chávez's request for state intervention in managing labor relations as unacceptable.[36]

The paths toward assimilation and acceptance from white peers differed among Armenians and Japanese Americans due to the relative "Asian-ness" of each group and the usefulness of their identities to the wider grower community. Both Armenian and Japanese immigrants attempted to challenge "the racial state," as Omi and Winant termed it (1994, 81), by proclaiming their whiteness in court; however, only Armenians succeeded. Armenians retained their whiteness by claiming not that Armenia falls within the boundaries of Europe, but rather that their "homeland," northeast of Baghdad and north of Tehran, became such after their migration from the West. The establishment of the "common knowledge" litmus test for Asians with the *Thind* decision placed South Asians and Japanese Americans on the outside of whiteness. Such ideologies influenced their access to U.S. citizenship, which remained off-limits until passage of the McCarran-Walter Act of 1952 allowed for their naturalization.

In the end, the acceptance of Japanese Americans by white growers depended on the activism of Nisei farmers who, like Harry Kubo, espoused political positions useful to all growers regardless of race. By the time Kubo initiated his "No on 14" campaign in the name of private-property rights, the racial ideology of California society had shifted from a belief in skin color as a determinant of intellect and ability, to a notion that these markers had little consequence in the trajectory of "minority" groups. Kubo served as the ideal representative of this idea, having overcome the internment to become a successful farmer and a valued member of the agribusiness community. His value was partly predicated on his willingness to articulate a "model minority" perspective that challenged Mexicans, Filipinos, and African Americans to be more like Japanese Americans and allowed growers not to take responsibility for the poor health and inadequate education of their workers. His embrace of colorblind conservatism, according to which anyone could succeed in the United States regardless of race, offered Kubo an additional ideological pillar that propped up not only his fortunes but also those of white growers much richer than him. Ultimately, Kubo's life illustrates how, at least for Japanese Americans, the path of acceptance by society now came by way of identifying with a history of racialized oppression. For many who profited from agriculture and whiteness, Kubo's personal success in the face of such injustice proved the inherent equality of the U.S. system and the perseverance of the American dream.

NOTES

1. Pawel 2009; Ganz 2009; Shaw 2008. Recent books on the topic include Bardacke 2011; Pawel 2009; and Garcia, forthcoming.

2. Marshall Ganz, interviewed by author, March 26, 2008.

3. See Almaguer 1994. Almaguer draws on Omi and Winant (1986) for analysis of California's racial history.

4. *United States v. Cartozian*, 6 F.2d 919 (U.S. District Court, D. Oregon, 1925).

5. Ibid.

6. Ibid.; Tehranian 2000.

7. Jendian 2001, 176. Matthew Jendian, in his interesting study of Armenians in Fresno entitled "Assimilation *and* Ethnicity" (italics in the original), makes the important point that assimilation and the retention of ethnicity are processes that are not mutually exclusive.

8. Harry Kubo, interviewed by Sam Suhler, Fresno County Library, October 13, 1978, p. 6.

9. Ibid., 10.

10. "Who Is Harry Kubo?" *Fresno Bee*, February 22, 1976; Harry Kubo interview, 32–33. With additional satellite groups in Stockton, Los Angeles, and San Diego County, the total membership of the league topped out at 2,200 in 1976.

11. Harry Kubo interview, 29; Gilbert Padilla, interviewed by the author, January 11, 2010.

12. Larry Kubo, interviewed by the author, January 6, 2010.

13. *Los Angeles Times,* April 15, 1976.

14. Ibid.

15. *Los Angeles Times,* October 24, 1976.

16. Ibid.

17. César Chávez to Supporters, September 1976, UCLA Political Literature Collection.

18. Harry Kubo interview, 33, 36.

19. "Who Is Harry Kubo?"

20. Harry Kubo interview, 36.

21. *Council of California Growers Newsletter,* September 20, 1976; October 4, 1976, in Scrapbook April 16, 1975–August 20, 1976, Table Grape Negotiating Committee Papers, Fresno State University.

22. *Council of California Growers Newsletter,* September 13, 1976; November 1, 1976.

23. Coalition for Economic Survival to CES Members and Friends, November 2, 1976, UCLA Political Literature Collection.

24. *National City Star-News,* September 19, 1976, UCLA Political Literature Collection.

25. Flyers, n.d., UCLA Political Literature Collection.

26. *Fresno Bee,* September 6, 1976.

27. *San Francisco Chronicle,* November 4, 1976; *Fresno Bee,* November 3, 1976; *Council of California Growers Newsletter,* November 8, 1976.

28. *Council of California Growers Newsletter,* November 8, 1976.

29. Poster, n.d., UCLA Political Literature Collection.

30. For the emergence of a colorblind ideology, see Pascoe 2009, 287–306.

31. Harry Kubo interviewed by Sam Suhler, Fresno, CA, October 13, 1978, 18.

32. Ibid., 27–28.

33. Ibid. 23.

34. Ibid., 2–3, 18–19.

35. Ibid., 44.

36. Flyer for Citizens for a Fair Farm Labor Law, n.d., UFW Information and Research Collection, Box 26–11, Archive of Labor and Urban Affairs, Wayne State University, Detroit.

SIX

The Unbearable Lightness of Being (Black)

LEGAL AND CULTURAL CONSTRUCTIONS OF RACE AND NATION IN COLONIAL LATIN AMERICA

Michelle A. McKinley

This chapter offers readers an insight into the colonial legacies of Latin American racial formations. In particular, it traces the legal construction and development of mixed racial categories in early colonial Lima in both ecclesiastical courts and enumeration procedures. Interrogating the theme of "racial democracy" and its associated racial projects of *mestizaje, indigenismo,* and contemporary multiculturalism in Latin America, the case studies included here examine the constitutive nature of "race" itself in Iberian thought as reflected in the legal recognition of *mestizo* categories.

The terms *racial formation* and *racial project* are specifically drawn from Michael Omi and Howard Winant's influential volume *Racial Formation in the United States* (1986). Like many scholars of contemporary racial politics, I adopt the racial formation framework as a useful optic for examining the interplay between structural/institutional politics and quotidian interpersonal relationships. I am aware that the racial formation framework travels south with the imprimatur of U.S. racial history. But in adopting Omi and Winant's terminology, I am not attempting a critique of its contemporary transnational application. In other words, I hope that the inclusion of terminology does not signal the unreflective (or ethnocentric) application of one racial paradigm to all contexts. This chapter is about historically and geographically distinct racialized practices and discourses that drew upon ideas of blood, nature, climate, language, temperament, and religion to instantiate racial hierarchy.

Iberian flexibility in incorporating miscegenation is a source of controversy regarding Latin American "racial democracy" and those who discount the significance for, or determinative influence of race—as opposed to class—on sociopolitical condition in Latin America. Iberian flexibility is often contrasted with the more rigid Anglo-American parochialism that subjected peoples of mixed racial descent to bipolar racial thought and discrimination. As Cuban nationalist José Martí proclaimed in *Nuestra América*: "A Cuban is more than white, black or mulatto . . . there can be no racial animosity because there are no races." Following Martí's logic: how could there be legally segregated theaters or water coolers if one could claim mixed ancestry across the spectrum? The argument is deceptively simple: the law could not officially enforce racial segregation while simultaneously proclaiming a national creed of racial fusion. Although the law could not underwrite segregation, the degree to which darker-skinned people "knew their place" according to internalized racial cartographies was extralegally enforced.

How does the legal regime augment, or contradict, the ways in which race is—and has been—lived and experienced? What role does the law play in elaborating racial projects? How do racial democracies deal with multicultural political movements that demand legal remedies to ameliorate racial disparities? What are the implications for hybridity when race gets politicized, implicitly using a model of agitational politics? How has the politicization of race in Latin America affected countries' assessment of themselves as racial democracies?

The role of jurists in creating racial categories (as opposed to enforcing racial hierarchy) is particularly salient in North American critical race theory scholarship (Crenshaw 1991b; Gotanda 1995; Ngai 2005; Volpp 1996; Carbado 2009). Critical race theorists have illuminated our thinking about the ways that the U.S. legal system determines the rights, status, and privileges of citizenship by drawing upon the social meanings of race (Haney-López 1996). However, the role of courts in constructing race or enforcing segregation is not an element that is studied in Latin American law. This lacuna has been attributed to the distinction between civil and common law systems, to the "buffer" provided by the Church between weak states and slaveholders, and also to distinct racial logics and historical experiences (Watson 1989; Baade 1996; de la Fuente 2004). All are valid observations. They pose challenges for hemispheric conversations about race in the Americas. But they also present opportunities for a rich discussion about the potentialities of comparative work, especially in light of new thinking about transnationalism, migration, borders, and diaspora. These have all opened up new entryways and points of investigation into belonging, nationhood, and identity in a global context.

Mestizaje is a term widely used to denote racial hybridity; it was coined in the nineteenth century when independent Latin American republics appropriated a discourse of inclusive citizenship to fortify their nation-building projects. Eighteenth-century elite republicanism had barely encompassed the metropolitan liberals, conservatives, and intellectuals who comprised the political body, making this a shaky foundation on which to build a cohesive national community. Commentators have noted that despite Latin America's early wars of independence, the republics floundered for decades as states without nations. The appeal to a nation, *patria,* and an imagined community would come a century later—reversing the chronology of Anderson's otherwise evocative schema on nationalism (Anderson 1983; Castro-Klarén and Chasteen 2003). Hence, the emergence of *mestizaje*: a convivial hybrid amalgamation of black, white, and Indian in the liberal *imaginaire.* But why hybridity when racial purity, white supremacy, and scientific racism were available racial paradigms of the nineteenth century?[1] We intuit that these choices were politically instrumental, but they also responded to erstwhile notions of identity and nation held by their proponents. In thinking about race, Latin American statesmen drew upon ideologies of nation and identity rooted in Iberian taxonomies of blood purity and elaborate hierarchies of caste based on fractions of blood *mixing. Mestizaje's* roots in Iberian diversity and Catholic humanism are the subjects of centuries of intellectual scrutiny. Indeed, miscegenation is an enduring preoccupation in Latin American thinking about race. It is continually posed in dialogue with, and in opposition to, the hegemony of North American racial thought, which has traditionally demonstrated a particular discomfort with racial mixing.

Before we retreat into early medieval racial thinking, two things should be clear. First, this chapter historically situates the twentieth-century Latin American racial project of *mestizaje* and twenty-first-century multiculturalism within their origins in medieval hierarchies of *blood mixing.* But as critical scholars remind us, "*mestizaje* should not lead to a mistaken assumption that a happy commingling of different bloodlines and ways of life underlies Latin America's unique identity" (Mignolo 1995, 179). Just as contemporary multiculturalism acknowledges postcolonial realities of migration, shifting and hardening borders, and tense negotiations of identity, language, and nationality, I do not separate *mestizaje* from the historical realities of genocide, domination, and sexual violence that brought about multiracial beings.

Second, we need to confront the tensions that surround comparative conversations about race. Although this chapter aims precisely to avoid reductive comparisons, invariably, any endeavor purporting to analyze Latin American laws of slavery and their concomitant effects on racial formations is formulated with the U.S. experience of race and slavery in mind. This is due undoubtedly to the intellectual legacy of comparative historical research in the 1960s that drew sharp contrasts between U.S. and Latin American laws of slavery. Comparative slavery scholars in the 1960s launched a long-lasting debate about where on the mild-abusive continuum Latin American slavery belonged, with the United States and Brazil as the basis for evaluation. Scholars also argued about the degree to which various societies in the Americas had "transcended" race as a result of their laws of slavery and the correlation between manumission and citizenship in post-emancipation racial formations. Given the political volatility of the time for race relations in the United States, and the legal remedies subsequently developed to ameliorate the effects of discrimination, the comparative effort grew even more contentious.

Today, most scholars would agree that the dichotomy between North and South is increasingly pointless. North American legal scholars grapple with colorblind constitutionalism and its impact in a putatively "post-racial" era. Ironically, as race has become more politicized in Latin America, strict adherence to the racial democracy thesis has given way to calls for legal remedies like affirmative action and reparations—policies associated with the racial tyranny of the North. Conversely, the ultimate enforcer of hypodescent and one-drop rules—the U.S. Census Bureau—recently offered more than twenty categories for Hispanic and Asian Pacific American preferences on the 2010 census. We all agree on the constructedness of race and recognize that racial identities are situational, fluid, and relational (Reid Andrews 2009). For the sake of brevity, this chapter assumes that while scholars agree on the social constructedness of race, debates continue regarding ways that racial mixing (miscegenation, *mulataje, mestizaje*) has been accepted, theorized, vilified, or celebrated throughout the hemisphere. The problem I sense is that the comparative debate continues to rely on a U.S. model as the universal racial formation, rendering other ways of "doing race" as variations on a theme (Ferreira da Silva 1998). Thus, Afro-Latinos are hindered by the lack of an agitational black power movement (Winant 1992) or by the existence of an unresponsive, elitist judiciary, or simply—and perhaps most damningly—are the victims of false consciousness in asserting that Latin America has no racial problem. In other words, the excursions of U.S. racial theories beyond the southern border have explicitly endorsed a set of *prescriptive responses and solutions* as a model for Latin American racial justice in contexts that have historically been entwined with *mestizaje* and transculturation (Ortíz 1942; García Canclini 1995).

Given the tremendous intellectual effort that has been expended on these discussions, this chapter proposes a slightly different twist on exploring the existence of Latin America's "racial democracy" as compared with North America's "racial tyranny." My concern is to explore the way that ideas of blood purity were worked out (retained, shaped, transformed) in a slaveholding, colonial milieu in which extensive race mixing occurred. I examine the development of categories of race and caste in seventeenth-century Lima, Peru, as they were informed by both the ecclesiastical law and Iberian sensibilities of religious difference. In particular, I trace the effect of the enumerative responsibilities of the clergy on the elaboration of racial categories. To this end, the chapter uses three distinct historical sources: annulment petitions alleging "notorious inequality"; seventeenth-century parish records of birth, baptism, marriage, and death within the Archbishopric of Lima; and a census (*padrón*) undertaken in 1613 by the Church and Crown to enumerate the urban indigenous population living in Lima's multiethnic parishes. Because my primary goal in using both parish records and ecclesiastical litigation is to trace the intersection of race, gender, and status, these historical sources highlight the complex nature of mapping racial formations in a society with slaves. Although colonial historians more commonly use these sources, they enable us to critically evaluate multicultural affirmations of racial politics in contemporary Latin America—a point I touch on briefly at the end of the chapter.

The choice of the 1613 *padrón* is relatively straightforward: censuses are widely used by scholars to examine racial categorization and demographic patterns (Nobles 2000; Cahill 1994; Cook 1968). Although censuses are undertaken for specific administrative purposes, they interject a putatively neutral, objective approach to racial categorization often at odds with the situational understandings (or the social meanings) of race. Census takers purport to merely "record" racial categories, not to create them.

Conversely, parish records—a particular form of enumeration—powerfully highlight the plasticity of race and status throughout an individual's life cycle. Racial categories could be manipulated at birth or during certain moments of interaction with the ecclesiastical bureaucracy (e.g., making a will, petitioning for a license, being accused of adultery), and could be reinvented at death. It is not uncommon to see litigants appearing in one category at birth and classified in another at death, according to the ebb and flow of their life circumstances. These records thus provide an invaluable source for mapping the early legal constructions of race, and beautifully complement the implacable reductionism of the census. Mixed-status annulment cases reveal the more complex relationship between race and freedom in a society with significant numbers of freed people of color and people coded as white (given their ambiguous phenotype and uncertain parentage) but who remained enslaved. Most important, these cases show the court's regulation of those who inhabited racial borderlands (Gross 2008; Dudziak and Volpp 2006; McKinley 2010) and reinstated racial hierarchies, when, arguably, non-legal strategies broke down.

These three sources together demonstrate how racially mixed identities were constructed by courts operating within the context of an Iberian ideal of blood purity (*pureza de sangre*). Iberian sensibilities framed difference within an encompassing yet tense accommodation and quiescent suspicion of religious otherness. The discourse is one of accommodation (universal humanism) with the goal of conversion (potential inclusivity). Accommodation was always at the grace of the sovereign—whether papal or regal—and on his absolute terms. Although scientific racialist discourses emerged in the nineteenth century, they were profoundly intertwined with previous ideas about blood and heredity (Martínez 2008). While I recognize that sixteenth- and seventeenth-century racialism cannot be neatly cordoned off historically,[2] my focus here is on the idea that cultural and religious traits (which would later be naturalized as "race") were transmissible and heritable through commingled blood (Stocking 1994). We cannot fully appreciate the political allure of *mestizaje/mulataje* without understanding its historical roots in the early colonial period. I now turn to a discussion of emergent *mestizaje* within the political, institutional, and rhetorical practices of a society with slaves.

Many years ago, Frank Tannenbaum called our attention to the importance of slave law in creating distinct racial hierarchies and identities in the Americas (Tannenbaum 1946). According to Tannenbaum, the influence of Roman law on the *Siete Partidas*, combined with the pervasive authority of the Catholic Church, gave rise to a more benign system of slavery than the "Virginia" variant that prevailed in the North American colonies. The *Partidas* retained Roman law's liberal provisions for manumission and, consequently, favored the presumption of freedom whenever personal status was contested. As the official source for private law in the colonies, the *Partidas* governed litigation and legislation involving slaves and was particularly influential in determining manumission cases. Following this, Tannenbaum reasonably concluded that the civil law created greater paths to manumission than the common law. But he controversially claimed that this legal transition from slavery to freedom created more harmonious post-emancipation societies than did chattel slavery systems marked by hostile racial segregation and rigid exclusion.

Tannenbaum's claim that the civil law tradition endowed slaves with a moral and legal personality provided much grist for the scholarly mill, especially in tandem with the publication of Gunnar Myrdal's *An American Dilemma* (1944) and Gilberto Freyre's *The Masters and the Slaves* (1946). Although Tannenbaum was unduly sanguine about the salubrious effects of the civil law of slavery on Latin American racial inclusion, his observations invite further inquiry into the ways that laws of slavery influenced racial projects in the aftermath of emancipation and independence. Clearly, legal categories that were developed within a slaveholding society would influence the way that peoples of the Americas thought about racial stratification in the independent republics.

Although slavery was a predominant mode of coercive labor organization throughout the New World, not all post-emancipation racial projects followed the same trajectory. Francophone colonies assumed a race-blind, universalizing discourse of citizenship, premised on the assimilability of *civilizés* and the unifying power of the French language, culture, and republican political ideology. Although this republican assimilationist strain privileged *white* hybridity, it was directly fashioned in opposition to the Germanic blood-based understandings of racial purity and national belonging (Camiscioli 2009). North America adopted a discourse heavily steeped in racialized criteria for citizenship. Before and after emancipation, white supremacy fortified the exclusion of nonwhites from legal personhood, citizenship, and naturalization and from geographic spaces—all on the basis of race (Gómez 2010).

Somewhat in contrast, the Latin American racial project of *mestizaje* was one rooted in syncretic hierarchies of blood mixing. José Vasconcelos, the Mexican educator, lawyer, and legislator celebrated the alchemy of Latin American race fusion among indigenous, African, and Spanish peoples that produced what he called "the cosmic race" (*la raza cósmica*) (Vasconcelos 1967). This cosmic race was a vibrant product of the best biological and cultural traits, whose cross-fertilization would overcome social and ethnic divisions and transform Mexico into a modern progressive nation. Vasconcelos argued vociferously against the scientific racism that had pronounced negative views on the effete "mongrelization" and degeneracy of race mixing. Moreover, Vasconcelos reveled in the debunking of "race" and the emphasis on "culture" that emanated from the Boasian-inspired anthropological school in the 1920s. Though deeply wedded to essentialist notions, Vasconcelos used the *raza cósmica* to dispel the eugenicist goals of racial purity that had dominated political and academic discourse across the Americas and Europe (Stepan 1991).

A distinct, though related, racial project emerging in twentieth-century Latin America that celebrated *mestizaje* was the "racial democracy" thesis. The myth/ideal of "racial democracy" is attributed to the Brazilian anthropologist Gilberto Freyre, who underscored a Luso-Iberian tolerance of miscegenation that developed in the Portuguese and Spanish colonies. In comparison to the more virulent forms of white supremacy and hypodescent instituted in North America, miscegenation created a racial democracy and a society supposedly free from racial tension (Freyre 1986). Like Vasconcelos, Freyre argued that Brazil's strength lay in the mixing of its African, indigenous, and Portuguese peoples.

Freyre's ideas have been vigorously contested—often excoriated—over the years by feminists, indigenists, anthropologists, comparative scholars of race and slavery, and contemporary scholars of Afro-Brazilian studies. It is neither my intention nor my interest to enter the debate over the merits of Freyre's decidedly idiosyncratic corpus here. Despite his problematic cultural nationalism and his suspect gender politics[3] (Fêo Rodrigues 2003), Freyre was nonetheless correct in looking at Brazil's slave past to account for patterns of socialization about race that were grounded in taxonomies of racial mixing. Scholars of race and slavery have long pondered whether racism legitimated or predated slavery, or whether material exigencies created the need for racist doctrines that subsequently legitimated the enslavement of Africans (Sweet 1997; Viotti da Costa 1985; Russell-Wood 1978; Thornton 1992; Fredrickson 1988). However we choose to synchronize racism and slavery, the relations among people whose legal status was categorized as free, freed, indentured, or enslaved clearly shaped the racial landscape that preceded and followed formal declarations of emancipation and independence (Cooper, Holt, and Scott 2000). Let us now turn to a detailed review of these processes in the annulment petitions of Inés de Escobar and María de Alcala.

MAPPING HIERARCHIES OF RACE, CASTE, AND STATUS IN ANNULMENT PETITIONS

On August 9, 1670, Inés de Escobar, a *mulata* slave, sought an annulment of her marriage on the grounds of "notorious inequality." Inés alleged in her pleadings that "I understood that my husband Antonio was *mulato,* but it turns out he is *morisco* of Berber parents, and a slave, and for this reason he is so depraved and of poor habits and condition." Inés came to court with a slew of witnesses who attested to Antonio's violent behavior and his habitual drunkenness—attributing these unseemly traits to his *morisco* (Muslim convert to Catholicism) heritage. Many witnesses alleged that Antonio was skilled in the arts of sorcery and black magic. Others corroborated Inés's claim that Antonio portrayed himself as a "*moreno*" (darker-skinned man), and at times as a *mulato,* to cover-up his Moorish background.[4] Inés was granted an ecclesiastical divorce on the basis of the unequal status that existed between Catholics and *conversos* (Muslim converts to Catholicism). Inés, a *mulata* slave, differentiated herself from her "depraved" Moorish husband by claiming a preferential place on the racialized religious scale distinguishing Catholics and infidels.

On December 13, 1688, María de Alcala, *cuarterona de mulata* (one-quarter mulatto), filed a petition to annul her marriage to Agustin de Llanos. According to María, she had entered into marriage with Agustin when she was fourteen years old at the behest of his mother, who thought a young wife would calm her son's fiery temper. Agustin's mother never disclosed her son's enslaved status, and María entered into the marriage believing that Agustin was a free *mulato*. Indeed, Agustin had all the trappings of freedom. He lived independently in a rented room. He participated in all the military marches of the *mulato* militia, and he bore arms. María later discovered that Agustin was in fact enslaved and in the service of a military official. Soon thereafter, María separated herself from Agustin, and a decade later (in 1688), she sought a formal dissolution of their marriage. María requested an annulment on the basis of fraud, inequality of condition, and *error de persona* (mistaken identity over Agustin's enslaved status).

These petitioners—Inés, Antonio, Agustin, and María—inhabited lower rungs of a colonial society that was stratified on the basis of race, status, and gender. Yet Inés—herself an enslaved *mulata*—depicted her *morisco* husband with images of debauchery, sloth, and violent temperament, images shared by an ecclesiastical judiciary with predisposed hostility toward Moors. Inés's portrayal of her *morisco* husband worked with a racial grammar whose equivalent today could conjure up notions of black criminality and delinquency for a crime fighting prosecutor to secure a conviction in court. For at least four centuries, the Iberian Moor had been marginalized, enslaved, and expelled on the peninsula. By the late fifteenth century, *moriscos* were forced to either convert to Catholicism or leave Spain. Most chose conversion over expulsion, but their faith and allegiance were always in question. As a prominent chronicler proclaimed in 1615: "All Moors are unfaithful, ill-intentioned thieves and drunkards, filled with sensual desires and capable of committing innumerable crimes" (Dominguez Ortiz 1952, 371). *Moriscos* were perennially regarded with these sentiments of distrust and fear.

María similarly appealed to elite *criollo* (Creole) and viceregal anxieties about armed and dangerous *mulato* slaves in order to underscore her domestic plight. The Crown, fearful of rebellion, flight, or insurrection, repeatedly inveighed against arming free or enslaved *mulatos*.[5] These fears of maroonage and rebellion were used pretextually to control the mobility of *mulatos*—who were constantly declaimed as the source of social unrest, vice, and crime. Black men were forbidden to ride horseback, deliberately limiting any visible demonstration of equestrian virility to Spaniards. In sum, perhaps no two images would have effectively triggered the alarms of the viceroyalty as groups of unsupervised slaves bearing arms, or decadent *moriscos* undermining the conversion efforts of the Catholic kings. María and Inés confirmed the worst fears of Church and Crown and, in so doing, validated their institutional patriarchal and protective roles vis-à-vis vulnerable colonial subjects (Premo 2005; Bennett 2003).

Clearly these women's petitions strategically invoked racialized stereotypes to gain the desired result—dissolution of their marital ties. Annulment was a difficult legal undertaking in an ecclesiastical court, given the Tridentine rule of marriage as a sacrament. Both Inés and María alleged severe cruelty (*sevicia*) as one of the grounds for seeking annulment. But church officials were particularly reluctant to grant annulments solely on the basis of domestic cruelty, and more inclined to dissolve the marriage in the case of marital inequality (Mannarelli 1993; Nazzari 1996). Given the close surveillance of status and caste in colonial society, a more plausible explanation of these "surprise discoveries" of unseemly characteristics was that they were strategically mobilized to compel the sought-after annulment (McKinley 2010). Notwithstanding this speculation, the fact still remains that the parties alleging racial inequality were themselves located at the lowest rungs of colonial society. True, these expressions must be filtered through the pens of notaries and cannot be said to represent a "true" subaltern voice (if one exists), given the context of litigation and the elite interests that prevail in recording and privileging certain viewpoints. These limitations aside, legal proceedings do provide a lens through which to examine the ways that racial inequality as an organizing principle among elites was also contingent on inequalities among lower castes and enslaved peoples (Johnson and Lipsett-Rivera 1998; Lavallè 2001).

A common theme in colonial studies is precisely this essentialist manipulation of elite discourses by subaltern subjects for instrumental ends. Here, I want to press a bit further than the patently instrumental. What happens when these labile identities are given life by the law? How did Inés differentiate herself as an honorable person from her "degenerate" *morisco* husband, and how was that difference manifested within her complaint so that petitioner and prosecutor articulated a mutual language of inequality? If we shape our inquiries into the constructed nature of race as a dialogic process, we see how people actively traffic in, and ultimately end up reifying, these discriminatory ideologies (de la Cadena 2000).[6] Elite and subaltern views of "race" thus become consensual rather than oppositional, with room for negotiating individual positions within the agreed-upon contours of the racial structure. I do not want to suggest complete consensus—clearly, the overarching contours are always disputed and redrawn. But given the plasticity of race, any racial system must leave room for individual social relocation. Inés's case reveals an early phase of geocultural distinction between and among Creole (i.e., Peruvian-born) blacks, African-born black slaves, and Iberian-born blacks. The brown-skinned *mulato/moreno* category became a New World racialized identity, mutating from the suspect Old World *morisco*. In effect, local notions of color became a proxy for caste, nation, and character.[7]

For the period under review, other forms of social categorization such as *calidad* (class or social condition), status, and gender also interacted powerfully with racialized identities. These interactions afforded individuals a measure of autonomy in choosing among permissible racial identities—between the ascribed and the self-imposed. Rather than accepting the givenness of María's and Inés's identities as they were inscribed, a more nuanced inquiry would scrutinize the ways in which these women came to identify themselves—and came to be identified—women who left abusive husbands and who sought relief in court. Unless we peel back the layers of the proverbial onion using a class, gender, and race analytical knife, we lose a nuanced, multifaceted understanding of these processes. Inés de Escobar's story is simultaneously a battle against an abusive husband, the Church, and her enslaved condition. She may have "played a race card" to win her case, but it is impossible to tell whether she shared in or disputed the position she articulated before her notary. I suspect the answer lies somewhere in between. Yet we can glean clues about the legal and social construction of race through a retrospective look at the cases in which slaves, free blacks, and lower-castes fought. This is not a study about the invocation of state force to police interracial relationships; rather our analytical concern is to understand how men and women's experience of inequality affected their intimate relationships.

MAPPING RACE, CASTE, AND *CALIDAD*

At this point, it behooves the inquiry to briefly set out some of the ideas of race, caste, and *calidad* that developed in tandem with the consolidation of Iberian slavery in Latin America. Indeed, it is difficult to grasp the legal rationale for these annulment petitions based on marital inequality without understanding how race, caste, and *calidad* emerged in a slaveholding society. Ideas about race were inextricable from the ideas that legitimated the enslavement of Africans and Moors and that exempted indigenous peoples from servitude. As medieval ideas of "race" were defined in religious and "cultural" terms, we need to examine the deep implication of the Church in the process of enumerating categories of race and caste.

In its original Iberian form, blood purity symbolized the absence of Jewish or Moorish ancestry. Blood purity distinguished Old Christians from converts (*conversos*) and restricted the domains of nobility and rank to Christians while enveloping converts in the Catholic fold. The incorporation of *conversos* fluctuated between the poles of brutal inquisition, invidious discrimination, and expulsion on the one hand and peaceful accommodation (*convivencia*), juridical autonomy, and multicultural pluralism on the other (Benton 2002). Blood purity, primarily a way of hierarchically ordering religious difference on the Iberian peninsula, assumed new racialized forms when transported to the Americas (Martínez 2008). In the Americas, the imprimatur of blood purity as a symbol of nobility was reoriented toward developing elaborate hierarchies of caste based on fractions of blood *mixing*. Colonial caste categories were premised on flexible taxonomies that shuttled between racial mixing and racial whitening. Concurrently, racial mixing reinforced the notion of whitening (*blanqueamiento*) as critical to social ascendancy. Contaminated blood would, through interracial procreation, become progressively "sanitized" until it was no longer traceable. Note that this vision of whiteness was not premised on blood purity, as was the case with North American theories of hypodescent. Rather, it located blackness and indigeneity on a steady trajectory toward whiteness (Wade 1993; 1997). There is no neat correlation between peninsular ideals of blood purity and colonial realities of social mobility through whitening. Indeed, those who were nearly white—and thus closest to white privilege—were precisely those who were most compromised in terms of blood purity (Estenssoro Fuchs 2000). The stakes for the nearly white (including *cuarteronas* like María de Alcala) were the highest in terms of their potential assimilation or their demotion in their trajectory toward whiteness.

As shown in the following chart, the mixed offspring of European, indigenous, and African parents, known as *castas,* were classified in sixteen categories on the basis of fractions of blood mixing. This enumerative schema also established the legal and social distinctions that formed the basis of the colonial caste system (Cahill 1994; Lau 1997). Presuming a stable racial order at the founding of the Peruvian colony (itself a negligible proposition given the internal diversity of the racial trinity of black, white, and Indian),[8] the trinity dissolved into seemingly infinite equations based on quotients of blood mixture in the seventeenth and eighteenth centuries.

1. español + negra = mulato
2. mulato + española = tercerón
3. tercerón + española = quarterón
4. quarterón + española = quinterón
5. quinterón + española = blanco *or* español común
6. negro + mulata = zambo
7. zambo + mulata = zambaigo
8. zambaigo + mulata = ténte en el aire
9. ténte en el aire + mulata = salta atrás
10. español + india = mestizo
11. mestizo + india = cholo
12. cholo + india = ténte en el aire
13. ténte en el aire + india = salta atrás
14. indio + negra = chino
15. chino + negra = rechino/criollo
16. criollo + negra = torna atrás[9]

Humanist scholars have long been struck by the dizzying array of categories of caste that emerged in Latin America during the seventeenth and eighteenth centuries. Magnus Mörner noted that "the almost pathological interest in genealogy characterized by the baroque age created a series of almost mathematical permutations and combinations that sought to exhaust all possible racial couplings, . . . which according to such logics was almost infinite" (Mörner 1967, 58). The *casta* chart above portrays the naturalist monogenecist racial thought of the early modern period, in which all humankind was thought to emerge from a common family (Stocking 1994). Difference was a question of rationality, reason, and intellect: barbarians were located *within* the human species but considerably more childlike, scantily clad, and pre-social and less exposed to God's word (Pagden 1982; Quijano 2000).

Scholars have argued that these *casta* charts reflect Iberian approaches to racial mixing (Frederickson 2002) and serve as a precursor for Latin America's racial democracy. It is true that enumeration schemes provide a lens for examining the social construction of race. Clerics—charged by Tridentine decree to receive and register all Catholic souls—struggled to freeze identity at the moment of birth, devising such ambiguous categories as *ténte en el aire* ("suspended in the air"), *no te entiendo* ("I don't understand you"—an obvious phenotypical anomaly), and *salto atrás* ("children darker than their mothers"). This was an attempt to forge "caste" out of phenotype, maternal identity, and whatever evidence about possible paternity was proffered by the newborn's mother and witnesses. When paternal identity was known, clerics could determine the caste of an infant depending on the degree of blood admixture of both parents.

Racial categorizations of mixed Indian-and-negro/*español* offspring varied over time, showing the greatest diversity and social mobility. Juan Pérez, *salto atrás* (John Doe, darker than his mother), did not remain in this caste category throughout his life. At certain key moments of contact with the administrative state, Juan would be classified as a *zambo* (half Indian–half black), with his age, marital status, residency, and occupation. Juan's status as enslaved or free would also be recorded. If apprenticed in his youth to someone of higher caste, Juan could assume the caste of his master (*maestro*) rather than that of his darker-skinned, perhaps unknown father. If he prospered in the trade and established his own business, in his application for a license, he could be simply registered as Juan Pérez, *mestizo*—a capacious and more upwardly mobile category. If he floundered as a young apprentice and fell into the hands of criminal prosecutors, Juan would revert to *zambo, mulato, negro criollo,* or *chino.*[10]

Given what we know of census taking, the processes of ascription and identification are important indices of other racialized hierarchies and can be easily performed, subverted, and even ascribed in collusion with witnesses and the enumerator. Thus for tax purposes, enumeration as a *natural* (Indian) carried onerous tribute obligations—a point I discuss at length in the following section. Indigenous identification also implied some leniency in criminal sentencing and the ability to secure ecclesiastical immunity, given the "childlike" status accorded Indians (Premo 2005). Court officials during this period developed the pejorative category of *mestizo en hábito de indio*: literally, the cultural defense of a "deracinated" Indian passing as an "authentic" Indian to avail himself of a lighter sentence. As such, none of these enumerations were "value free, objective descriptions of phenotype" or complexion. Juan Pérez, *zambo,* was a priori illegitimate—a product of illicit sexual relations between black and Indian parents. Juan Pérez, *mulato,* was also presumptively the off-spring of lower-class white men and black women. For the most part, *casta* was a racialized designation vested with the opprobrium of illegitimacy and lower social status. Granted, this arrangement reflects an elite perspective, but it undoubtedly influenced the way *castas* viewed themselves. In other words, caste was not merely a designation of blood lineage or phenotype; it was indicative of one's status, descent, occupation, condition at birth, and networks of patronage. *Calidad*—a broader barometer of one's social location—encompassed reputation, prestige, family connections, and honor. Caste categories, like *calidad,* were negotiable both in terms of the law and the broader community, but they were closely monitored and upheld by the parties themselves.

Thus, María de Alcala, the petitioner in the second vignette, was identified in the annulment proceeding as a *cuarterona de mulata* (one-quarter mulatto). But how was that category applied—given that María may not have identified herself as a *cuarterona?* Court officials customarily ascribed the racial identity of colonial litigants. María may have proffered evidence of her *cuarterona* status, but she was alleging freedom—not race—as the basis for her annulment. Moreover, how was the one-quarter fraction derived? The possibilities were encumbered only by María's appearance and her racial performance, which presumably were Hispanicized enough for her to credibly claim belonging to a higher *calidad* or status.

If we look closely at parish records, we see that the racial categorizations change according to life circumstances. Shortly after her petition for annulment in 1688, María de Alcala reappears in the archival record. In 1691 she returned to court to give her consent to marry Juan de Toribio.[11] In his declaration of intent, Juan de Toribio identified himself as an *español oficial de botonero* (an independent Spanish proprietor of his own button-making establishment, licensed by the Crown). Since María had to prove the annulment of her previous marriage to Agustin, the couple had numerous witnesses who could substantiate the absence of impediments to marriage. Curiously, none of the six witnesses alluded to María's *cuarterona* status, and all seemed only remotely aware of the previous marriage to Agustin (which presumably had taken place a decade before these current witnesses knew her). In her marriage petition, María was simply *española*—incontrovertibly white (Kuznesof 1995). Her final will and testament (drawn up in 1734) attested to an even higher, more genteel category: doña María de Toribio, *mujer legítima del difunto don Juan de Toribio* (legitimate wife and widow of the late don Juan de Toribio). In that document, doña María made significant testamentary bequests to religious orders in the parish of San Marcelo—including donations of two female slaves. This beatific act is fully consonant with the last wills and testaments of pious Catholic slaveowners, but María's bequest prompts further reflection given her early marriage to an enslaved man. Why would she not have opted for a testamentary bequest of manumission of her slaves? The record is inscrutably silent as to sentiment, and we can only speculate about María's motivations in facilitating her ascent into heaven.

INVENTING INDIANS

In 1607 the Count of Montesclaros, Juan de Mendoza de Luna, was appointed viceroy of the colony of Peru. His promotion to the highest rank of the colonial administration, though prestigious, was particularly challenging. Faced with a growing need for colonial revenue to finance Spain's militaristic campaigns in Europe and its mercantile expansion in the East Indies (Kamen 2003), the Crown had imposed severe fiscal policies on its overseas territories. These demands for increased taxation generated a great deal of local resistance from *criollo* elites. Besides his impending battles with Creole magnates, Montesclaros faced a diminished tax-evading indigenous population.

Peru had been the largest producer of silver in the Americas, converting the colony into a source of unprecedented wealth for the Hapsburg monarchy (Andrien 1985). Montesclaros's eminent predecessor, Viceroy Francisco Toledo, had instituted a series of reforms during his lengthy reign (1569–1581) to centralize the tax and tribute structure according to residence and chieftaincies. Under the Toledan reforms, all Indians were relocated in *reducciones* (nucleated Indian settlements or towns), conforming closely to their pre-conquest *allyus* (traditional communities). They continued to pay tribute to their *caciques* (Indian chiefs), who in turn were obligated to Spanish *encomenderos*—noblemen who had been granted lands and allotments of resident indigenous peons by the Crown. In effect, these reforms transferred rent-seeking rights from indigenous Inca elites to the Spanish. *Encomenderos* then remitted silver from the mines to the Crown, while reserving a healthy profit for themselves. This provided a great deal of income for diversifying the colonial economy, created local sources of wealth for the growing Creole elite, and fueled opportunities for economic expansion within Peru.[12]

In the rural valleys and upper montane regions of the Peruvian colony, Montesclaros's enumerative efforts were performed with the aid of local priests and *caciques* (Andrien 1985). As mentioned earlier, the clergy were required by Tridentine decree to register their parishioners. It should be pointed out that parish priests recovered fees for carrying out the enumerative function and justified their budgets on the numbers of souls in their flock. They were therefore highly motivated to collaborate in census taking.[13] But the underlying objective of the bureaucratic census—as an instrument of taxation—understandably led to resistance on the part of the indigenous population to be enumerated as Indian (*natural*).

By 1613 the indigenous population had migrated outside the central and southern highlands and valleys. Removed from their land base, these *naturales* became wage earners or landless laboring peasants on large agricultural estates (*yanaconas*). Landless Indians remitted their tributary obligations in cash, rather than in kind.[14] *Naturales* living in urban areas were also exempt from communal tribute, which was a reciprocal arrangement that provided land in exchange for subsistence and independent production. And presumably more worrisome to the clergy, urban Indians were not under the tutelage of a priest or religious order.

Montesclaros's census sought to determine whether urban Indians had ties to their communities of origin and, hence, owed tribute to their *caciques* (traditional leaders). This census was not a phenotypic exercise: rather, it was a way of discerning who was culturally (and thus racially) Indian. Besides the veritable wealth of demographic information collected in the *padrón*, the herculean efforts of the indefatigable enumerator show us in surprising ways the plasticity of "racial" identity and the extent of interethnic relationships in Lima.

Juan Contreras, the sole enumerator, personally visited 3,163 households, commercial establishments, workshops, and taverns in a seemingly relentless search of Indian residents. The entire enterprise took 140 days and encompassed the city of Lima, as well as the two multiethnic parishes of San Lázaro and Santa Ana. Despite knocking on the doors of more than three thousand households, Contreras found "Indians" in only 685 establishments willing to be enumerated as such. In other words, less than one-third of the people Contreras encountered could identify the name of their *cacique,* let alone their *encomendero.* A representative entry illuminates these points:

> In the market and Plaza of Santa Ana, I found an Indian married woman, who gave her name as Cecilia and whose husband was absent. She has been in the city for about three years, and she could not tell me her age, but she seemed to be about 24 years old. She named Your Majesty as her *encomendero,* because the creoles of this city belong to the Crown and they do not have *caciques.* She is childless and rents a room from a brown-skinned woman (*morena*) named Luisa. She has never paid tribute and claims to have no obligation to do so. (de Contreras, Cook, and Gamboa 1968)

Reading these entries, we are justifiably suspicious of such repeated ignorance of key facts—birthplace, age, spousal or parental whereabouts. Revealing these facts would have implied accumulated tributary obligations, or at least ongoing obligations for adult males. Undoubtedly frustrated by his small sample, Contreras broadened his definition of "Indian." At the end of the *padrón,* we are introduced to 115 "Indians" who originally came from Manila (the Philippines), Portugal, Japan, and China.[15] Here, according to Contreras, is a representative entry for an "Indian" household: "On Tambillo Street, in the house of Francisco de Toro, Spanish shoemaker, I found an Indian who said he had been brought to Lima when he was very young from China. His name is Francisco Jimenez, and [he] is married to a brown slave named Juana Angola. This Indian is of the Zaguey caste, 24 years of age, and is the father of four children: Antonio (3), Marcelo (6 months), María (7) and Juliana (4)" (de Contreras, Cook, and Gamboa 1968, 237). Marriage records for both the couple appear in the archbishopric book of slave marriages, and the birth of their children is also duly recorded. In those records, however, they are simply registered as "*chinos.*" According to the *casta* chart presented earlier, we could plausibly have counted these children as black (*chino* being a category ascribed to the offspring of black and Indian parents). On the basis of the surnames of the couples alone, we could also have classified the marriage as involving enslaved African-born women with free Indian men.[16] But these men were not in fact "Indian" in the Andean sense. Not only do Contreras's methodical efforts highlight the plasticity of race, but the *padrón's* details show extensive intermarriage and rapid generational assimilation. Indeed, the *padrón* vividly describes the accelerated process of creolization and racial drift through enumerative practices and terminologies.

Contreras was not alone in using a visual assessment of phenotype to arrive at his conclusions.[17] His exercise in racial mapping rendered the visual intelligible with the "racial." He assimilated difference into one "Indian" category—the fungible category of alterity for the "Oriental"—by relying on what George Stocking has called "the perceptual fact" of *difference*. Like Columbus, Contreras saw the "Indians" he encountered as a group "quite distinct from his own, but the criteria of their distinctiveness was not clearly differentiated, and his description of them lumped together physical, linguistic and cultural characteristics" (Stocking 1994, 8). This "undifferentiated differentness" was pivotal to seventeenth-century naturalist racial thought, which was still firmly within the grasp of creationism, common human ancestry, and divine design. Naturalist racial thought blended various ideas of similarity of appearance to establish a relationship of direct heredity that resonated with popular understandings of crossbreeding and animal husbandry. We begin to see glimmers of the emerging distinctions in the *casta* charts, based on the observable and "perceptual fact," and in individual interpretations of racial hierarchies— what today we might call the "common sense" or social meaning of race (Gross 2008). And we see how this was acted upon to produce a desired result in court.

CONCLUSION: FAST FORWARD TO THE FUTURE

Do these cases and enumerative practices act as a mirror in which we can scrutinize our present "post-racial" twenty-first-century projects? Do they merit close analysis (beyond the constant invocation of the historian's mantra that it is important to understand the present by looking at the past?) My concern has been to outline the continuities between the foundational fictions of racial democracy and contemporary multiculturalism, given that the latter grows out of this particular context of racial manipulability. More important, this retrospective inquiry allows us to trace the cultural zoning of black (Afro-Latino) and indigenous (*indio*) that reemerged in the contemporary discourse of Latin American multiculturalism.

In an effort to increase the visibility of the black population and to combat racial drift, Afro-Colombian activists began to reincorporate a range of skin-color identifiers like *triguena, raizal, mulato,* and *zambo* in regional census taking. Ironically, this draws upon visual markers that Afro-Colombians traditionally use to identify themselves as darker-skinned and that adhere to the phenotypical logic of the seventeenth- and eighteenth-century *casta* charts. And it seems from recent journalistic reports that the term *mulatto* is making a comeback among those who identify as "multiracial" in the United States.[18] Although these are modern variations of erstwhile census-taking projects, they are borne out of different political contexts. Afro-Latinos need visibility to substantiate their claims for greater political representation and social inclusion. Multiracial subjects in the United States want something besides the binary of black-white identity that is the legacy of hypodescent. These efforts may share vocabulary with the colonial and nineteenth-century enumerative projects, but they have completely distinct political goals. In sum, racial enumeration depends heavily on who's counting and for what political purposes.

An interesting question for modern Latin American racial formations is how Afro-Latino social movements challenge and expand the racial democracy ideal. As we might expect, contemporary scholars of race in the Americas have hotly contested the racial democracy thesis since its inception. The "democratic promise" encompasses everyone, provided that they are en route to racial whitening. "Democracy" accounts for the tense coexistence of racial discrimination and tolerance, racial exclusion and inclusion, *mestizaje* and whitening in Latin American societies. Perhaps not surprisingly, the tensions inherent in the racial democracy closely mirror those within the medieval and early modern discourse of universal humanism.

No one contests the incongruities between the region's official, racially inclusive discourse and the social realities of discrimination and exclusion that persist in Afro-Latino communities. In addition to the prickliness of the hemispheric debate, a substantial body of literature deals exclusively with particularities of indigeneity, regionalism, and patron-clientelism, a literature I am not able to do justice to here.[19] Finally, the success of *mestizaje* in forging inclusive polities was negligible. Indeed, most Latin American historians of the "long nineteenth century" have painstakingly described how authoritarian and exclusionary most regimes were despite the egalitarian rhetoric of *mestizaje, indigenismo,* and liberalism (Mallon 1995; Larson 2004).

Scholars of race can either deride or celebrate the foundational myth of racial democracy for particular political purposes. Thus, in defiance of the growing power of scientific racism, the rise of eugenics, and Anglophone geopolitical ascendancy, Latin American *indigenistas* could promote hybridity as evidence of positive racial production—not sterile mongrelization, but a sturdy, dynamic, cosmic race. This could allow a racial order that simultaneously promoted incorporation, encouraged assimilation, and ultimately validated whitening. Hybridity-as-official-discourse allowed the descendants of the cosmic race to celebrate the regal indigenous past and idolize the sensuality/maternalism of the *mulata,* while keeping everyone on the road to whitening.

This would be the pragmatic or even cynical assessment of the racial democracy. Those who repudiate racial democracy bring up empirical data about discrimination, enduring poverty, low levels of educational achievement, poor self-esteem, deliberate historical annihilation, and outright rejection from the national family. But a more generous assessment would take its endorsement of hybridity seriously. As an official identity, *mestizaje/mulataje* proclaims the desirability of forging a nation (or imagining community) out of heterogeneity. It is attentive to aesthetic production of borderlands and hybrid culinary and literary "traditions," poetically proud of indigeneity and blackness, nostalgically romantic about the Indian past, and schizophrenically jittery/celebratory of black ancestry. Indeed, the plasticity of the discourse of *mestizaje* shows that it can be molded to fit liberal, radical/confrontational, or conservative ideologies depending on the political landscape and aspirations of modern Latin American states and social actors. Both Martí and Freyre insisted on the value of multiracial societies that transcended race: perhaps not coincidentally, they were concerned with citizenship in countries that had abolished slavery very late in the nineteenth century. The imperative for Cuban statesmen and scholars was to forge a modern nation out of racially diverse and hitherto unequal groups. For Martí, the preference for a racially transcendent, universalist notion of citizenship was clear (Bronfman 2004; Ortíz 1942). In rejecting "race" and exalting class as an organizing political strategy, twentieth-century leaders also responded to the allure of the Soviet revolutionary left, whose presence in Latin America at the time was formidable. (We are mindful also of the rhetorical power of the 1910 Mexican revolution for progressive political parties and social reformers during the period). Scholars of early-1900s Cuban racial politics have also pointed out that the racial democratic ideal was not just an elite project, but that Afro-Cubans strategically used the rhetoric of inclusion to mobilize in other areas for social mobility, particularly that of worker rights (de la Fuente 1999).

If we then fast-forward to the 1990s—the apogee of constitutional revaluations of multiculturalism—we see an agitational political discourse that prompted new visions of the racial democracy. Fin-de-siècle multi-culturalism was launched in the context of a "return" to democracy, with globalized and diasporic sensibilities and an avid embrace of neoliberalist economic policies. Neoliberal multiculturalism demanded a new version of the racial democracy. Critics indicted the multicultural turn of the 1990s in their rejection of neoliberalism and globalization—claiming the uni-versal multicultural subject was a homogenized MTV-world-musicalized/ Benetton-ized amalgamation that was neither too indigenous nor too black (Feldman 2006; Warren and Twine 2002). In this vein, multiculturalism was seen as the result of a Faustian bargain in which newly elected demo-cratic governments accepted a neoliberal program that imposed draco-nian structural reforms while celebrating cultural rights. These economic agendas disarmed the "culturally authentic subjects" of any possibility of controlling the material conditions or resources that would really enable them to function as independent autonomous subjects (Hale 2002). In other words, as other aspects of the economy and society open up to global penetration, the "cultural" or the "domestic" closes off and represents the "authentic elements of the nation." As of this writing (2012), Afro-Latino social movements are pressuring their governments to distribute the eco-nomic gains of neoliberal investments: we now see a vigilant demand for social inclusion with cultural recognition, equitable income redistribution, and respect for difference.

So where does this leave our fragile racial democracies—halfway between multicultural aspirations and racial democratic myths? Juliet Hooker has argued convincingly that the multicultural model has worked more effec-tively for indigenous people than it has for Afro-Latinos (Hooker 2005; Greene 2006). Hooker maintains that the efficacy of indigenous communi-ties in arguing for multicultural rights depends on the way that they have been racialized throughout the colonial and republican periods. Obviously, we have to allow for vast regional variation here, but the "indigenous" subject has always been a cultural subject in need of tutelage and segrega-tion, the bearer of an enviable civilization (Flores Galindo 1986). When codifiers and constitutional writers sit down to draft a citizenship regime to address inequality, they automatically think in terms of indigenous cultural autonomy in the trinity of language-territory-ethnicity. Afro-Latinos have already been presumed to be on the road to assimilation, with no recognizably distinct language apart from the national official one, and no demonstrably significant regional dominance; thus they have a difficult time making a multicultural claim, because these claims rest on a politics of regionalism rather than a politics of difference.

There are also valid points about the ways in which elites perceive Afro-Latino mobilization as opposed to what they see as a less threatening indigenous cultural validation. This has fewer valences now with Evo Morales's election to the Bolivian presidency, but black mobilization historically has been insurrectionary, criminalized, and shrouded in a Jacobin fear—to be contained either through assimilation or deracination (Rolph-Trouillot 1995). Indigenous peoples are "rooted," while Afro-Latinos are uprooted, to be rerooted through a process of acculturation and their unbearable blackness lightened until rendered invisible. Black multicultural claims seem to work most effectively when there is visible regional dominance (maroon communities, coastal demographic concentration)—signifying sufficient territorial rootedness and cultural authenticity to be able to stake political claims (Escobar 2008).

In closing, I point out the obvious: like globalization, multiculturalism takes on local and regional forms. It comes into communities through Western Union giros, Telemundo/Univisión, and *reggaetón*—is smuggled in with migratory bodies and imaginations. What is patently wrong in much of the discussion on multiculturalism is that it assumes importation and imitation rather than locating it as a process within regional spaces that are already unique environments of racial-cultural hybridity. Thus the dominant opposition between indigenous and Afro-Latino— ever present in the colonial and contemporary literature—overlooks the historical relationships between the groups that gave rise to the *mestizo,* the *chino,* and the *zambo.* These children would have navigated between their mothers' communities and the slave community, always already cultural mediators and newly minted racialized subjects. Most important, today's opposition projects expunge hybridity even as the earlier racial democratic predecessors embraced it. Cultural/racialized subjects can only be "*indígenas*" or "*afros*": no "cultural rights" accrue to *cholos* (urban migrants from the Andean provinces) or nonfolkloric blacks who live in cities, participate in the workforce, or visibly have lost their authentic way. But as the experiences of Juan Pérez, *salto atrás,* and Antonia Jiménez Angola, *zamba,* tell us, there is more than one way to "be multicultural."

NOTES

1. Note that hybridity and *mestizaje* were not unanimously celebrated in the early twentieth century. Indigenist thinkers like Luis Valcárcel, for instance insisted on the purity of the Indian—rejecting the assimilationist policies promoted by Peruvian *criollos* (see Larson 2004). Equally important, some Latin American social reformers embraced the eugenicists' concern with genetic makeup and heredity to frame ideas about racial fitness and national identity (Stepan 1991).

2. As historian George Stocking has pointed out, nineteenth-century racial thought was not coherently "scientific" or limited exclusively to biological ideas. There was a fair amount of confusion among racial science proponents about ideas of "blood" as transmitting sociocultural traits as opposed to physical heredity. This confusion was doubly fueled by Latin American elites arguing for "constructive miscegenation" and a culturalist view of "race" (see also de la Cadena 2000).

3. Most problematic in Freyre's analysis of libidinal democracy is that sexual unions were not benign evidence of tolerance and uninhibitedness, but often acts of power and coercion. Indeed, Freyre completely overlooks the violence of interracial sex by highlighting love in the cross-cultural encounter: "The encounter between the Portuguese and the Tropics has almost always had another configuration, that of convenience tied with love. . . . Rarely were these unions without love: love between a man and a woman of color and love of a man for the hot tropical land" (Freyre 1967, 50.)

4. Where possible, I have retained the racial descriptors of the time, both in the interest of historical accuracy and to foster thinking about how these ascriptions informed people's self-identities.

5. These laws also sought to regulate the dress and behavioral codes of enslaved and free black women. Sumptuary codes prohibited black and *mulata* women—regardless of status—from wearing silk, gloves, laced veils, and pearls (see Konetzke 1958, 183).

6. As anthropologist Marisol de la Cadena perceptively notes: "Elites and commoners eventually came to share beliefs in the power of 'culture' to legitimate discrimination. . . . Moreover, the taxonomy deriving from a definition of race was particularly ductile, as it included both the perception of rigid hierarchies and an unequivocal fluidity to position individuals within it. Although the ranking of racial groups was consensually accepted and class related, the definition of what label adhered to which person left room for negotiation" (de la Cadena 2000, 9).

7. Although we commonly think of African slavery in terms of the massive forced transfer of Africans to the Americas, the enslaved population was a

significant—albeit on a much more modest scale—community on the Iberian peninsula. Historian Ruth Pike noted that travelers to the port city of Seville described a city "teeming with Negro, Moorish and Morisco slaves," leaving the impression of a "giant chessboard containing an equal number of white and black chessmen" (Pike 1967, 348). Initially, the Catholic monarchs Ferdinand and Isabella insisted that those slaves sent to the Americas should be Christian—"that they should have been born in Spain or have resided there long enough to have been baptized." Subsequent legislation revealed the ambivalence about sending Iberian-born blacks, since the Crown prohibited "*negros ladinos*" with questionable criminal backgrounds from embarking on ships headed for the Americas. Apparently, the Crown feared that these Iberian-born *ladinos* spread seditious and slovenly customs among the pacific, hardworking African-born blacks, and sought to limit passage to Iberian blacks who had been on the peninsula for only one year (Konetzke 1956, 80). These fears encompassed the heretical beliefs of Jews and Moors as well, who were prohibited in the sixteenth century from settling in the Americas (Silverblatt 2004). In sum, slaves and free blacks from the Iberian continent occupied an ambiguous social position in the militarized expedition and quest for adventure, wealth, and power that characterized the Peruvian Conquest. They were both cultural interlocutors for Spanish efforts and henchmen in the sexualized and military exploits of conquest. To paraphrase Matthew Restall, they were voluntary expeditionaries and involuntary colonists (Restall 2000).

8. José Piedra, whose work examines African influences in the forging of Iberian identity, cleverly refers to Spain as "the darker child of Christian Europe and the lighter child of Islamic Africa" (Piedra 1993, 824). Indigenous groups at the onset of conquest were similarly diverse; many communities were loosely affiliated (and unhappy) with the centralizing ambitions of Inca rulers. And the African population obviously came from widely different ethnic groups and nations. As a result, there was considerable diversity between and among Creole, Iberian, and African-born blacks during this period.

9. Cited in Cahill 1994, 339. This list is representative of many of the caste classification systems. According to this enumerative scheme, it is the higher-status male who reproduces offspring with a "racially inferior" female.

10. Patricia Seed traces the links between "race" as a social category and the division of labor, and shows how racial labels shifted according to occupation and the individual's ability to accumulate capital. Building on James Scott's influential thesis about the administrative "gaze" and Foucauldian theories of governmentality, archival scholars are increasingly drawn to studying the formulaic structure of bureaucratic writing. According to colonial historian and anthropologist Brian Axel, the record as it is procedurally rendered should not be viewed "as repositories of facts of the past, but as complexly constituted instances of discourse" that produced and posited racialized subjects as part of the colonial administrative enterprise (Axel 2002).

11. According to canon law, all couples had to testify as to their consent to marry, as well as to prove the lack of impediments to enter into the proposed mar-

riage. Such impediments included consanguinity, previous matrimonial promises, and existing spouses. After these statements were noted, banns would be posted, in every parish where either petitioner had lived for more than six months, for three consecutive Sundays, thereby giving anyone who opposed the marriage an opportunity to voice his or her objection.

12. The *reducciones* were nucleated settlements that involved the uprooting of many Andean communities and their subsequent consolidation into one *pueblo* or *reducción*. To meet the seemingly cavernous need for tax revenue, the Indian population not only had to be physically located but also had to be counted. The enumeration, assimilation, and regulation of the colonial population became a priority for all incoming viceroys. On the surface, the census was a cadastral tool primarily used for tax revenues—a statistical tool of human inventory. But it was also a deeply racialized tool: the viceroy had to know who was an "Indian" and where he owed tribute (and where he could logically be transported into a consolidated *reducción*).

13. The motivation of priests to register their flocks does not detract from the opposition of some to the Crown's fiscal policies regarding indigenous taxation, who often cooperated with mothers to enumerate their children as non-Indians or to avoid registering births altogether (Jackson 1999).

14. Tax rates were assessed twice a year, according to the wealth of the community and its population. All adult men who worked the communal lands were taxed at a higher rate. At the same time, local elites, resentful of the fiscal demands of the metropolis that diverted revenue from colonial investment, resisted or at least evaded tax remittance as best they could.

15. All 115 entrants were brought to Lima either enslaved or in servitude—attached primarily to the households of Portuguese and Castilian merchants and tradesmen.

16. African born slaves were identified by their surname according to the region of Africa where they were born, or where they were procured. Thus Ana Biafra and Juana Angola bore common surnames for West African born slaves.

17. Indeed, Columbus did a similar calculation in conferring Indianness onto Amerindian peoples. If birthplace is even remotely correlative with "racial" origins, Contreras was arguably more correct in assigning Indianness to those born in the East Indies rather than conferring the category onto indigenous Americans.

18. Susan Saulny, "Counting By Race," *New York Times,* February 9, 2011.

19. Here, I call particular attention to the regionalism inherent in Peruvian *indigenismo* that excludes—through deliberate omission or historical erasure—the Amazonian indigenous population. Peruvian indigenists were typical of their continental counterparts, in that educated (mostly urban) intellectual elites examined Andean indigenous realities from their privileged, outsider perspectives (Coronado 2009).

SEVEN

Race, Racialization, and Latino Populations in the United States

Tomás Almaguer

The racial and ethnic landscape of the United States has been rapidly transformed in the twenty-five years since the initial publication in 1986 of Michael Omi and Howard Winant's *Racial Formation in the United States*.[1] Since that time scholars have built upon Omi and Winant's powerful theoretical approach in order to perceptively remap how the long-standing "black-white" binary in this country has been rapidly transformed. Some have argued that this framework has morphed into a "nonwhite-white" binary, while others have argued that our racial and ethnic landscape has taken a decidedly "Latin Americanization" form in recent years.[2] In both cases, overpowering demographic trends and formidable structural factors have moved the United States away from a two-tiered racial hierarchy to a more complex and variegated, multitiered structure.

The chapter explores some of these recent demographic and structural changes, with a specific focus on the Latino population. My goal is to assess the impact that the precipitous increase in the Latino population in the United States has had on this racial topography in two specific ways. First, I explore the vexing conundrums that Latinos have posed for how we think about race and ethnicity in this country. The accelerated growth of an increasingly diverse Latino population has profoundly complicated Latinos' placement in both the evolving racial hierarchy and the popular imagination in the United States. Second, I assess the troubling ways that Latinos have increasingly come to racialize one another and that could not have predicted twenty-five years ago. Briefly stated, Latinos have taken the way that racial lines were drawn and given meaning both in the Spanish colonial world and in the United States to reracialize one another in disturbing ways. Recent ethnographic studies have perceptively documented this process and provide valuable insights into this unexplored aspect of the racial formation process. I explore both of these nettlesome issues in turn and, in so doing, draw on a variety of primary and secondary sources to support the analysis.

THE RACIALIZATION OF LATINOS
IN THE UNITED STATES

The Latino population has historically occupied a unique position in the racial and ethnic hierarchy of the United States. It is important to assess how Latinos have been racialized over time and the various ways that they have complicated how we think about race. When *Racial Formation in the United States* was published in 1986, the federal government's standards for defining racial and ethnic groups had recently been reformulated. In 1977 the Office of Management and Budget's Statistical Policy Division and Office of Information and Regulatory Affairs issued "Directive 15: Race and Ethnic Standards for Federal Statistics and Administrative Reporting." That decree standardized the governmental collection and use of "racial" and "ethnic" statistics in the United States. It provided new operational definitions for the OMB's racial/ethnic cartography of the United States. Directive 15 clearly specified the codification of four major "races"— "American Indian or Alaska Native," "Asian or Pacific Islander," "Black," and "White"—and the delineation of two "ethnic" groups—"Hispanic origin" and "not of Hispanic origin." According to Ruben Rumbaut, "Since that time, in keeping with the logic of this classification system, census data on Hispanics have been officially reported with a footnote indicating that 'Hispanics may be of any race'" (Rumbaut 2009, 24).

These race and ethnic standards were revised in 1977 in response to mounting criticisms of the way these categories were deployed in implementing Directive 15. In that year, the federal government adopted a new set of standards for defining racial/ethnic categories, which led to the formalization of five "racial" groups rather than four. In essence, the "Pacific Islander" population was disaggregated from the "Asian American" population and placed in a separate racial category. Census 2000 offered respondents for the first time the option of selecting more than one racial designation and reworded the two existing "ethnic" categories as "Hispanic or Latino" and "not Hispanic or Latino." In so doing, the census formally defined an individual of "Hispanic or Latino" background as "a person of Cuban, Mexican, Puerto Rican, South or Central American, or other Spanish culture or origins, regardless of race."

The revisions to Directive 15 in 1977 were the product of intense political contestations and vociferous criticisms from various quarters. In this regard, as Rumbaut discovered, the announcement reporting these changes in the *Federal Register* candidly noted: "The categories in this classification are social-political constructs and should not be interpreted as being scientific or anthropological in nature. . . . The standards have been developed to provide a common language for uniformity and comparability in the collection and use of data on race and ethnicity by Federal agencies" (Rumbaut 2009, 25). In his perceptive assessment of these OMB changes, Rumbaut concludes: "The classification of 'Hispanic' or 'Latino' itself is new, an instance of a panethnic category created by law decades ago. But the groups subsumed under that label—Mexicans, Puerto Ricans, Cubans, Dominicans, Salvadorans, Guatemalans, Colombians, Peruvians, Ecuadorians, and the other dozen nationalities from Latin American and even Spain itself—were not 'Hispanics' or 'Latinos' in their countries of origin; rather, they only became so in the United States. That catchall label has a particular meaning only in the U.S. context in which it was constructed and is applied, and where its meaning continues to evolve" (16–17).

Yet many Latinos continue to base their racial identities on the way that the various nationalities were racialized in their country of origin when it was part of the Spanish colonial empire.[3] However, this highly variegated and nuanced racial system clashes with the way racial categories are more starkly drawn and defined in the United States. It appears that Latino immigrants are racialized in one particular way in the Spanish colonial context and then reracialized under the cultural logic of another racial order when they come to this country.

This difficulty in unambiguously racializing the Latino population has a long and complex history in this country that dates back to at least the middle of the nineteenth century when the United States seized control of the American Southwest through the U.S.-Mexico War of 1846–48. For example, it was principally as a result of the annexation of the Southwest that the Mexican population was formally granted U.S. citizenship and, in effect, deemed an "honorary white" population. The nearly 110,000 Mexicanos who remained in the territory ceded by Mexico one year after the ratification of the Treaty of Guadalupe Hidalgo (1848) became U.S. citizens with formally recognized claims to the prerogatives and privileges of whiteness. (Whether they were ever fully or meaningfully extended in the various territories and eventual states is quite another matter altogether).[4]

Clear codification of the racial status of the Mexican population can be seen in the 1850 decennial U.S. census; when the newly conquered Mexican population in the American Southwest was enumerated as "White," as it remained until 1930. In that year, they were summarily removed from the white category and placed in a separate racial designation as "Mexican." By the Great Depression, the number of Mexican people in the United States had grown to more than 1.5 million and had become the source of intense anti-immigrant xenophobia.

By 1940, however, the Mexican population was once again redefined as part of the "white" population and marked as speaking the "Spanish mother tongue." In that year, the federal census classified "persons of Mexican birth or ancestry who were not defined as Indian or some other nonwhite race . . . as white." The federal censuses of 1950 and 1960 continued to enumerate Mexicans as "white persons of Spanish surname."[5]

When one spoke of the Latino/Hispanic population in the late 1960s, before the publication of *Racial Formation in the United States,* one still referred primarily to Mexicans. This was at a time before widespread and sustained Puerto Rican, Cuban, or Central American immigration to the United States. After 1960, however, things changed dramatically and quickly. The explosive rise in Latino immigration after 1965 led to the exponential increase in the pan-Latino population in the United States, one not only far larger but also more racially diverse than it had been in prior years.

In 1970 the federal census relied on the category "Hispanic" to capture the tremendous internal diversity of the various Latino nationalities in the United States. It underscored their common "Hispanic" (i.e., Spanish) ethnicity and former status as part of the Spanish colonial world. Having a "common culture" rooted in the Spanish language and Catholic religion was the key ethnic signifier that bound these diverse nationalities into one category.[6] This shared ethnic background is something that none of the other racialized populations have in common that are placed in the discrete racial categories deployed in the United States. None of the groups racialized as "White," "Black," "Asian," "Hawaiian/Pacific Islander," or "American Indian" share a common culture solidly anchored in one particular language or religious background. Latinos are thus a unique population in this regard.

By 1970 there were more than 10 million "Hispanics" in the United States. Mexicans were still the largest Latino population, numbering 4.5 million and accounting for nearly 45 percent of Hispanics in the United States at the time. In that year there were also 1.5 million Puerto Ricans; 550,000 Cubans; 1.5 million Central and South Americans; and another million designated as some "Other Spanish" population.

By 1990, a mere twenty years later, the Hispanic population had more than doubled to nearly 22 million. By the time Census 2000 was taken, the Hispanic/Latino population had dramatically risen to 35.2 million and accounted for nearly 12.5 percent of the total U.S. population. Mexicans still remained the largest Latino nationality, comprising 60 percent of the Latino population in that year. They were followed by Puerto Ricans (9.7%), Central Americans (3.5%), South Americans (4.0%), Dominicans (2.3%), and the "Other Hispanic" category (15.7%).

By the time Census 2000 was taken, Latinos had actually surpassed African Americans as the largest racial-ethnic group in the United States. Each accounted for 35 million individuals that year, or approximately 12.5 percent of the total U.S. population. However, by 2007 the number of Latinos in the United States had dramatically swelled to nearly 45 million, or 15 percent of the total population. In the fifty-year period from 1950 to 2000, the Latino population had dramatically increased from approximately 4 million to over 35 million individuals. Census 2010 data has documented that the Latino population grew from 35.3 million in 2000 to over 50 million in 2010 (U.S. Bureau of the Census 2010). Current population trends suggest that by the year 2050 Latinos will have increased in number to an estimated 128 million people, or 29 percent of the total U.S. population. Demographers predict that they will significantly exceed the total number of all other racial/ethnic groups combined. African Americans, for example, are projected to continue to account for only 13 percent of the national total; while Asian Americas will account for another 9 percent of the U.S. population in 2050 (Rumbaut 2009, 17).

This monumental population increase has been accompanied by a number of profound structural changes that have powerfully impacted our perceptions of race and race relations in the United States. Among these changes worth noting here have been the momentous change in U.S. immigration policy in 1965 (which shifted the focus away from Western

Europe and toward Latin America and Asia), the hard-won victories of the Civil Rights Movement (which arguably extended meaningful, first-class citizenship rights to African Americans and other people of color), and the overturning of anti-miscegenation laws, through *Loving v. Commonwealth of Virginia*. That 1967 Supreme Court decision put an end to more than three hundred years of legal prohibitions on interracial marriages in the United States and directly contributed to the recent rise of a growing "multiracial" population. This mixed-race population grew by nearly 30 percent in the from 2000 to 2010 and now comprises approximately 3 percent of the total U.S. population (U.S. Bureau of the Census 2010). If one were to combine this "multiracial" population with the Latino population, approximately 18 percent of the total U.S. population is arguably mixed-race. This is clearly a very recent historical development that has had profound implications for how we understand the meaning of race and for the changing nature of race relations in the contemporary United States.

THE CONUNDRUMS OF RACIAL IDENTITY
AMONG THE LATINO POPULATION

We know from the way that Latinos responded to both the race and ethnic questions in Census 2000 that many had difficulty placing themselves in the discrete racial categories used in the federal census. It appears that many Latinos resorted to constructions of racial categories and identities drawn from the Spanish colonial world or simply used their nationality as the basis of their racial identity. In 2000, more than half (52.3%) of the pan-Latino population racially defined themselves as "White." Despite the central role that the Indigenous and African populations played in the Spanish racial regime, it is surprising that so very few Latinos actually identify as either Indian or black. Less than 1 percent defined themselves in 2000 as "American Indian" or "Alaska Native, Asian, or Native Hawaiian or other Pacific Islander." Only 1.4 percent of Latinos racially defined themselves as "Black," while another 3.9 percent claimed to be of "two or more races" (Candelario 2007a, 345). It is significant that less than 2 percent of the total U.S. population indicated that they were of more than one race. But of those who did, Hispanics were more than three times as likely to report being of "two or more races" than non-Hispanics (Rumbaut 2009, 26–27).

In Census 2000 a person who ethnically identified as "Hispanic" or "Latino" was, in essence, separated from the other five racial categories and then asked to racially define him- or herself based on the OMB's newly reformulated racial categories. Nearly half of the Latino populations when asked to give their racial identity in Census 2000 provided answers that led to their being placed in the "some other race" category. Many Latinos simply used their nationality as a proxy for race by indicating that they were "Chicano," "Cuban," "Puerto Rican," "Dominican," or some another Latino nationality. Others invoked the nuanced racial categories or skin-color designations used in their countries of origin to racially identify themselves.

What is significant here is the large number of Latinos who do not see themselves as falling into any of the discrete racial categories deployed on the federal census. Over 40 percent (41.2%) of Latinos opted to define themselves as belonging to "some other race." For many of these individual, intermediate racial categories such as "mestizo" and "*mulato*" or color designations such as "*trigueño*" or "*moreno*" were written into the space provided.[7]

There are, of course, significant differences among the pan-Latino population in how the different nationalities racially identify themselves. The vast majority of people from Cuba, Uruguay, Argentina, and Chile see themselves as white (75–88%). Panamanians claim the highest percentage of individuals who self-define as black (40.1%), followed by Dominicans, Costa Ricans, and Hondurans (9.4%, 7.2%, and 5.3%, respectively) (Candelario 2007a, 345).

People from the Dominican Republic, El Salvador, and Guatemala are among the most likely to define themselves as being of "some other race." Dominicans, on the other hand, often racially self-identify by invoking the intermediate categories "Indio blanco" and "Indio oscuro," which are among the core racial designations in the Dominican Republic. In Haiti, only the Francophone immigrant population is seen as being black.[8]

Given the prerogatives and entitlements of whiteness extended to both Mexicans and Puerto Ricans as a result of U.S. colonial conquest (the Treaty of Guadalupe Hidalgo in 1848 and the Jones Act in 1917), it is not surprising that both of the two largest Latino groups generally see themselves as a white population.[9] In 2000, approximately 47 percent of both Mexicans and Puerto Ricans racially defined themselves as white.

"Some other race" was the second-largest category enumerated by Mexicans (45.4%) and Puerto Ricans (38.4%) when they were asked to racially identify themselves. Another 10.7 percent of Mexicans and 14.3 percent of Puerto Ricans did not answer the race question. Once again, only a very small number of Mexicans define themselves as "Black" (0.7%). Despite the growing number of indigenous people from Mexico now in the United States, only about 1 percent of Mexicans racially self-define as "Indian." A smaller number of Puerto Ricans identified themselves as "Indian" (0.5%), while a significant number (5.8%) racially defined themselves as "Black." Both groups made significant use of the "two or more races" category. However, given their mixed-raced ancestry, it is surprising that only 5.2 percent of Mexicans and 7.8 percent of Puerto Ricans claimed more than one racial background.[10]

THE RERACIALIZATION OF LATINO POPULATIONS IN THE UNITED STATES

While this ambiguity in how Latinos racially identify themselves is understandable given that they have straddled two very different racial regimes, they apparently have far less trouble racializing one another. Nowhere is this more apparent than in the ways that the two largest Latino populations have increasingly come into conflict in ways that can be traced to how each group racializes the other. In other words, Mexicans and Puerto Ricans have increasingly come to racially define each other through the lens and logic of the Spanish racial regime that previously ensnared them. They apparently rely on this cultural logic after immigrating to the United States.

Growing evidence of this pattern can be seen in a number of recent ethnographic studies that have explored the often contentious relationship between the two Latino populations. Let us now explore the curious way that this reracialization unfolds and how it complicates the forging of a pan-Latino identity among the various Latino nationalities in the United States.

Some of the most interesting, and troubling, research in Latino studies has produced superb ethnographic studies of multiple Latino populations in areas where they have converged in recent years. Nicolas De Genova and Ana Ramos-Zayas' *Latino Crossings* (2003), De Genova's *Working the*

Boundaries (2005), Gina Perez's *The Near Northwest Side Story* (2004), Arlene Davila's *Barrio Dreams* (2004), and Robert Smith's *Mexican New York* (2006) are a few examples of this sophisticated ethnographic research. While each of these scholars addresses a distinct set of issues, all have in the process also documented the increasing tensions between recent Mexican immigrants and Puerto Rican migrants in Chicago and New York City.

De Genova and Ramos-Zayas's powerful book *Latino Crossings* offers the following troubling summary of this contentious intergroup conflict:

> What emerge are competing visions of each group's "civilized" or "modern" qualities in juxtaposition to the other's purported "rudeness" or "backwardness." . . . Mexican immigrants often generalized from the allegation that Puerto Ricans were "lazy" to posit variously they were like-wise untrustworthy, deceptive, willing to cheat, disagreeable, nervous, rude, aggressive, violent, dangerous, and criminal. In constructing these racialized images of the character of Puerto Ricans as a group, Mexicans were implicitly celebrating themselves as educated, well-mannered, and civilized. In contrast, Puerto Ricans frequently elaborated further upon their perceptions of Mexicans as uninitiated into the workings of the sociopolitical system in the United States and inclined to sacrifice their dignity in a desperate quest for work. Puerto Ricans commonly coupled these judgments with allegations that Mexicans, as a group, were submissive, obliging, gullible, naïve, rustic, out-moded, folksy, backward, and predominantly "cultural," in contrast to a vision of themselves as political, principled, sophisticated, stylish, dynamic, urban, and modern. Remarkably, these parallel discourses on the parts of both groups served to sustain their own divergent claims of civility or modernity, in ways that implied their differential worthiness for the entitlements of citizenship. (De Genova and Ramos-Zayas 2003, 83)

While there is considerable merit in De Genova and Ramos-Zayas's characterization of this ethnic tension, I suspect that there is something far more fundamental taking place here than a cultural conflict between two Latino populations. At the core of these tensions are the different ways that each group constructs the meaning of race in its country of origin and how each group reracializes the other in the United States. It is the distinct constructions of race in the Spanish and U.S. colonial contexts that leads to each group viewing the other through the eyes of the two colonial regimes that have largely structured their historical experiences. In other words, Mexicans appear to view Puerto Ricans principally through the lens of how "blackness" is constructed in both Mexico and in the United States. Puerto Ricans, on the other hand, essentially come to view Mexicans through the lens of how "Indianness" is given meaning in Puerto Rico and in the United States. While notions of "civilization" and "modernity" undeniably play a role in these racialized constructions, they do so through the way that blackness and Indianness have been infused with racialized cultural meaning in their distinct historical experiences.

These racialized constructions are the product of the ways that each group has internalized its Spanish colonial world's view of the African and Indigenous populations subjugated in Mexico and Puerto Rico. Added to that foundation, these groups then reracialize each other under the discursive logic that structures the meaning of race in the United States. Mexicans take what they learned from their Spanish colonizers and fuse that with what they quickly learn about the meaning of race in the white supremacist United States. The negative constructions of blackness that Mexican immigrants bring with them from Mexico are exacerbated by the way in which African Americans and black Latinos are racially constructed by the white population in the United States. Puerto Ricans, and also many African Americans, tend to immediately mark and position Mexicans as a largely backward population that they view as fundamentally "Indian."

MEXICAN VIEWS OF RACE IN MEXICO AND THE UNITED STATES

Racial categorization and self-identity among ethnic Mexicans in the United States generally crystallizes along lines of racial difference that position them within a skin-color hierarchy, or pigmentocracy. Those at the very top are usually the most fair-complexioned and light-skinned Mexicans who can claim some Spanish ancestry. This status is generally marked by use of terms such as *guero* and *guera* (light-skinned) or *blanco* and *blanca* (white). This has been, and remains, a privileged racial status with a profound impact on the life chances and mobility opportunities of the Mexican population.

Mexicans have had long and deep investments in claiming whiteness in the United States. From the mid-nineteenth century, when they were first granted an "honorary white" status after the U.S.-Mexico War, through the mid-twentieth century, Mexicans struggled for equal rights by vigilantly claiming the rights and entitlements of whiteness. It was not until the late 1960s, at the height of the Chicano Movement, that Mexicans began to redefine themselves as a "brown" population and, in the process, explicitly claim and celebrate their Indian ancestry. In so doing, they systematically devalued any claims to European ancestry and completely denied any African ancestry.[11]

The superordinate status of "whiteness" among ethnic Mexicans is generally followed by the large intermediate racial category that the vast majority of the population occupies. The most commonly used term designating this status is *mestizo* (mixed-race; typically of Spanish and Indian ancestry) or the skin-color referent *moreno* (medium brown). It is generally acknowledged that most ethnic Mexicans have a mixed-race ancestry and are largely *mestizo* in origins.

Recent ethnographic research in Mexico has documented that in areas where Mexicans with palpable African ancestry reside, individuals often invoke skin color distinctions to distinguish them from the *blanco/a* and *moreno* populations. These shades of difference are made with reference to individuals seen as either *moreno claro/a* (light brown) or *moreno oscuro/a* (dark brown) (Sue 2009, 115). This strikingly parallels the way that Dominicans designate those mixed-race individuals of African ancestry into *Indio claro* or *Indio oscuro* categories.

There are, however, other racial categories and skin color referents invoked among ethnic Mexicans to mark other phenotypical distinctions made among them. Racial categories such as *negro* (black), *Chino* (Chinese, or Asian more generally), and *Indio* (Indian) are widely used by ethnic Mexicans to designate individuals with African, Asian, or Indian phenotypical features. It was very common in the Southern California world in which I was raised to find individuals with strong African, Asian, or Indian features who were referred to in these terms. They were generally ranked below *mestizos* (because they were less white) and placed near the bottom of the racial hierarchy. But it is very clear that the most derisive term and devalued racial category invoked was the term *Indio*. It signified the very bottom tier of the Mexican gradational racial hierarchy or pigmentocracy.

In its most common usage throughout Mexico (and much of Latin America) *Indio* is not just a neutral term for being "Indian" or "*Indigena*." Instead, it is most often used as a derogatory epithet synonymous with being "rude," "uncouth," or generally "backward." Other anthropologists suggest that the term *Indio* went hand in hand with the notion of Indians as lazy, idle, or shiftless, as in the phrase laboring "*como Indio*" (Stephen 2007).

The way in which Spanish-Indian relations in Mexico clearly elevated the white Spanish population and summarily subordinated the Indigenous population to the bottom of that racial regime has a long and sordid history. To call a fellow Mexican an *Indio* was to invoke a derisive racial epithet that connoted being ugly, dumb, and primitive. The term *Indio* was a derisive racial slur that conveyed an image of a dark-complexioned, low-class, and ill-bred person.

It comes as no surprise, therefore, that other Latino groups (such as Puerto Ricans) would paint the Mexican population—especially recent undocumented individuals with indigenous ancestry from Oaxaca or Chiapas—as essentially Indians. This is probably the most offensive thing one could possible say to a Mexican *mestizo*. It captures and reflects the negative status of the Indian population under the Spanish colonial dominion of Mexico and in the American Southwest prior to U.S. annexation.

Blackness, however, is also marked in a derisive way by recent Mexican immigrants as well as by second- and third-generation Mexican Americans and Chicanos. While it may be true that *negrito* is often used as a diminutive term of endearment, it is nonetheless an inherently problematic construction. This is clearly seen when the base term *negro* is used to describe an adult black person: *"un negrote"* (a huge, menacing black person). The diminutive construction of blackness is marked as unthreatening, while the latter construction is unambiguously marked as threatening with troubling sexual connotations.[12]

There can be little doubt that ethnic Mexicans have systematically devalued and denied the full extent of their African ancestry, while simultaneously valorizing either their Spanish or Indian ancestry. The full extent of this negrophobia is clearly seen when one considers that the Mexican national census in 1646 documented that there were slightly more people of African descent then Spaniards enumerated in that year (Menchaca 2001, 61). From this fact, it seems clear that ethnic Mexicans actually have far more African ancestry than they have been willing to acknowledge. This troubling denial and negrophobia has curiously affected the way blackness has been constructed by both native-born Mexican Americans and the recent immigrant population.

In the case of Chicago, for instance, De Genova has discussed how blackness carries racial significance in the Mexican immigrant's description of the African American population in that city. The most common and benign constructions were made with reference to their being dark-complexioned, such as references to them as *"Negros"* (blacks), *"Morenos"* (dark brown or dark-skinned), or *"Prietos"* (dark or swarthy). However, the most common of these terms used by Mexicans to refer to African Americans was *"morenos,"* which De Genova maintains was often used as a way of avoiding the use of the term *Negroes* or the n-word. According to him:

> What is remarkable in the ubiquitous usage of the term moreno in place of negro, however, is that many Mexicans (perhaps the majority) would have been most commonly inclined to describe themselves in Mexico (before migrating) as morenos, and—excluding diminutive uses that are always relative and highly contextual—would have tended to reserve the category negro for Mexicans considered to be of recognizable African ancestry. In the course of reracialization in the United States, however, the two were conflated as markers of Blackness, and the term moreno was displaced onto African Americans as a generic and collective (racial) category. . . . Thus, the fairly ambiguous, highly contextual, sweeping middle term moreno—the color category that brushes the broad mass of "brown" Mexicans within Mexico's distinct and relatively fluid racial order—is deflected altogether from Mexicans as a group in the United States and tends to be fixed unequivocally upon African Americans as a rigid generic racial category. (De Genova 2005, 196–197)

However, both recent Mexican immigrants and Chicanos or Mexican Americans find common ground in making widespread use of the same racialized term in referring to African Americans. In this regard, *El Libro de Calo: The Dictionary of Chicano Slang* offers an insightful confirmation of this convergence in the way that both groups racialize African Americans (Polkinhorn, Velasco, and Lambert 2005). This dictionary affirms that the most commonly used term to designate blackness among ethnic Mexicans is *mayate* or *pinacate*. Both terms refer to a black beetle (a Mexican dung beetle in the first case and, in the second, a smaller black beetle commonly found in the Southwest). The term *mayuco*, which is also widely used, appears to be a variant of *mayate*. These designations foreground the blackness of these insects while also providing a sweeping, dehumanizing move in the racialization process. Other zoomorphic terms such as *changos* or *chanates* (monkeys) are also used and share disturbing commonalities with the way African Americans have been historically racialized in the United States.

Interestingly, the majority of the other terms Chicanos use to designate blackness are less inflected by these zoomorphic referents and, instead, foreground dark complexion. For example, disparaging references to African-Americans as *prietos* (blackish, dark), *tintos* (dyed, stained), *oscuros* (dark), *tostados* (toasted, dark brown), *quemados* (burned, very dark), or simply *negros* (black, swarthy) all focus on their dark complexion as the key signifier in this racialization.

But the term *mayate* is clearly the most commonly used racial epithet invoked by ethnic Mexicans and is always used in a disparaging way. The term appears to have taken on particular significance in various subcultural worlds among ethnic Mexicans. It was often used in the 1940s to describe a hip African American zoot-suiter who donned the same stylized garb that the Mexican pachuco wore. Despite their shared sense of style and affinities in music and dance, it was always used as a disparaging racial slur.

Alternatively, it was also used in a more sexually explicit way by queer Latino men to describe virile, heterosexual African American men who anally penetrate sexually passive homosexual men. These black men were never stigmatized as being homosexual because they assume the active, inserter role (i.e., *"activo"* as opposed to *"pasivo"*). In this particular usage of *mayate,* the association between homosexuality and anal sex—and its simultaneous use to refer to a big black beetle that feasts on dung—does not require too much imagination to see the racialized sexualization of African Americans.[13]

PUERTO RICAN VIEWS OF RACE IN PUERTO RICO AND
THE UNITED STATES

Like ethnic Mexicans, Puerto Ricans in both the United States and the island also invoke a gradational racial hierarchy to mark lines of racial difference among themselves. In his interesting analysis of racial identity among Puerto Ricans, anthropologist Jorge Duany has documented at least nineteen different ways in which Puerto Ricans have racially define themselves on the island. Among these racial categories and skin-color referents are *blanco* (white), *trigueño* (wheat-colored or brunette; usually light mulatto), *moreno* (dark-skinned; usually dark mulatto), *mulato* (mixed-race; rarely used in public); *Indio* (literally, Indian; brown skin with straight hair); *prieto* (dark-skinned; usually derogatory); *negro* (black; rarely used as a direct term of reference); and *negrito* (literally, little black) (Duany 2002b).

Duany maintains that "racialized images of Indians and Africans have dominated how Puerto Ricans imagined their ethnic background" (Duany 2002b, 276). "Puerto Rican identity," he contends, "reveals the systematic overvaluation of the Hispanic element, the romanticization of Taino Indians, and the underestimation of the African-derived ingredients" (280). Like Mexicans, Puerto Ricans also have long and deep investments in their claims to whiteness. For example, in response to the Census 2000 question on race, approximately 48 percent of Puerto Ricans in the United States claimed to be "white," while another 38 percent gave responses that led to their being categorized as belonging to "some other race" (Jung and Almaguer 2004, 72). Despite the widespread racial mixing in their Spanish colonial history, very few Puerto Ricans actually claim to be either "Black" or "Indian" in any significant numbers. Only 5.8 percent of Puerto Ricans identified as "Black," and less than 1 percent as "Indian" in Census 2000 (Jung and Almaguer 2004, 72). Curiously, Duany has shown that the actual number of Puerto Ricans on the island—known as "the whitest of the Antilles"—who identify as "White" has actually grown over the years and was calibrated at over 80 percent in Census 2000 (Duany 2002b, 248).

What is so interesting about the racial classifications deployed among Puerto Ricans is the particular way in which Indianness is socially marked. The preconquest indigenous Taino population has taken on importance in the way that Puerto Ricans have come to racialize Mexicans. Being of Taino ancestry assumes certain social associations that capture the way in which Indianness is infused with racial meaning in Puerto Rico. The dominant characterizations of the Taino, according to Duany, constitute the prototype of Rousseau's "noble savage" (in which these indigenous people are seen as "docile, sedentary, indolent, tranquil, and chaste") (Duany 2002b, 268).

In terms of skin color, the most relied-upon racial descriptions of the Taino is "neither white nor black but brown or 'copper like' and that their intermediate phenotype placed them between Europeans and Africans in moral and ascetic terms" (Duany 2002b, 270). Duany contends that few "standard descriptions of the Taino Indians fail to mention their skin color, physical stature, bodily constitution, hair texture, and facial features. . . . For example, one third-grade textbook widely used in Puerto Rico today lists the following 'characteristics of the Taino race': medium build, copper-tone skin, black and straight hair, prominent cheekbones, slightly slanted eyes, long nose, and relatively thick lips. These features are sharply contrasted with the phenotypes of both Spaniards and Africans" (270).

In Chicago, Puerto Ricans are quick to acknowledge that Mexicans have a much closer and deeper association with Indianness than do Puerto Ricans. As one informant told De Genova and Ramos-Zayas: "Mexicans have real Indians. We (Puerto Ricans) have Indian blood in our heritage, be we are not *Indian* Indian" (2003, 192). According to sociologist Robert Smith, the racial mapping of Mexican bodies in Indian terms also occurs in New York City (R. Smith 2006).

Arlene Davila also underscores this point in her book *Barrio Dreams*. Therein she acknowledges that Herman Badillo, the Puerto Rican chairman of the board of trustees at the City University of New York and unsuccessful candidate for mayor in 2001, articulated the commonly held view among Puerto Ricans that Mexicans " 'came from the hills,' from countries with little tradition of education, and were mostly short and straight haired Indians. These racist comments exposed stereotypes of Mexicans as less educated or unsophisticated 'newcomers,' as opposed the 'urban savviness' of Puerto Ricans" (Davila 2004, 173).

This perception that Mexicans are racially "more Indian" than Puerto Ricans occasionally finds expression in how these Latino groups explicitly racialize one another's gendered bodies. A conversation among young Puerto Rican informants in *Latino Crossings* offers an insightful example of this racialization: "You can tell if someone is Mexican or Puerto Rican by looking at their asses. . . . Yeah, you see, Puerto Ricans have an ass and Mexicans are flat-assed—they have an Indian ass. . . . Yeah, Selena was real pretty. She looked Puerto Rican, you know. She had an ass . . . Women who have big tits have flat asses. If you really want to know if a woman has a flat ass, you look at her chest. That's why you have a lot of Mexican women who are big on top and have no ass" (quoted in Davila 2004, 193).

This ethnographic data documents the troubling way that Latino populations previously ensnared by the Spanish colonial empire have come to view one another in the United States. This brings us back to how Puerto Ricans view the Mexican immigrant population in Chicago as essentially "Indians." It is their construction of the Taino that provides a window on how they have come to construct recent Mexican immigrants. This is, in one respect, just the other side of the way Puerto Ricans are have been constructed as "black" by the Mexican population in Chicago.

CONCLUSION

This chapter explores the unique way in which the Latino population has been racialized in the United States and situated within its racial and ethnic landscape. I argue that Latinos stand alone among communities of color in the United States in that they are principally defined in ethnic—rather than racial—terms. It is fundamentally on the basis of their common culture (based on the Spanish language and Catholic religion) that they are placed in the "Spanish/Hispanic/Latino" category rather than one discrete racial category. In other words, it is the cultural logic of ethnicity, rather than that of race per se, that leads to placing the multiracial Latino populations in the "Spanish/Hispanic/Latino" ethnic category.

In addition to the unique way that Latinos are located within the racial and ethnic landscape of the United States, I attempt to make sense of the equally curious and troubling way that Latinos have come to racialize one another in areas where they have increasingly settled in the United States. There is mounting ethnographic evidence that Latinos have resorted to stigmatizing one another by using the ways in which racial categories were infused with meaning in the Spanish colonial world. It is in the disparaging ways that Indianness and blackness are given cultural meaning in the countries of origin that we are able to better understand the documented tensions between the two largest Latino populations in the United States. Both Mexicans and Puerto Ricans, both of whom have valorized and made direct claims to the privileges and entitlements of "whiteness," resort to racializing each another by drawing on the most stigmatizing ways that race is defined in both Mexico and Puerto Rico. Mexicans largely denigrate Puerto Ricans on the basis of their African ancestry, while Puerto Ricans denigrate Mexicans based on their putative Indianness.

The complex meaning of race and the particular way that racialization unfolds in the United States is an ever changing sociohistorical process. Nowhere are the ambiguities and vagaries of racial formation in this country more starkly evident than in the case of the Latino population. Making sense of the unique way that race and racialization has been given cultural meaning among Latinos provides yet another window on a process that has been most eloquently articulated in Michael Omi and Howard Winant's seminal work. *Racial Formation in the United States* has enabled us to clearly see that race is fundamentally a sociohistorical category at once fictional and yet also profoundly real in its profound sociological implications.

One of these implications is the particular way that the United States has given cultural meaning to racial designations and attempts to locate various populations within the logic of the racial categories deployed in the United States. It is here that the Latino populations continue to complicate the very logic of the racial formation process in this country. As I show here, there is also mounting ethnographic evidence that Latinos often resort to the way that race was given specific meaning in the Spanish colonial context to racialize one another. It is here, in the troubling convergence of two distinct racial regimes in the lives of the Latino population, that we may illuminate the conundrums and contestations inherent in the racial formation process in the United States.

NOTES

1. The second edition of the book was published in 1994 under the slightly revised title *Racial Formation in the United States: From the 1960s to the 1990s.*

2. See, for example, O'Brien 2008; Bonilla-Silva 2003a; Murguia and Forman 2003; and Forman, Goar, and Lewis (2002).

3. In this regard, see the canonical study by Ramón Gutiérrez on the way these racial lines were initially drawn in Spanish colonial New Mexico (Gutiérrez 1991). Also see his classic essay "Hispanic Identities in the Southwestern United States" (Gutiérrez 2009).

4. A number of scholars have explored the racialization of the Mexican population after the U.S.-Mexico War. See, for example, Menchaca 2001, 2007; Haas 1995; Almaguer 1994; Foley 1997, 2007; Montejano 1987; Guglielmo 2006; Ruiz 2004; Gómez 2007, 2009.

5. A number of scholars have written about the historical and contemporary ambiguities in the placement of Latinos in the decennial census. See, for example, C. Rodríguez 2000, 2009; and Tienda and Ortiz 1986.

6. See, for example, Portes 2007.

7. For example, I answered the ethnic question on both Census 2000 and Census 2010 by indicating that I was of "Spanish/Hispanic/Latino" origin (I ethnically self-identify as "Chicano"). I then indicated in response to the race question that I was "mestizo" when asked "What is this person's race?" As a result, that particular response led to my being summarily placed in the "Some other race" category.

8. See, in this regard, Candelario 2007b and Torres-Saillant 1998, 2007.

9. The scholarly literature on the claims to whiteness by both Mexicans and Puerto Ricans continues to increase over time. On the Mexican population, for example, see Almaguer 1994; Foley 1997, 2007; Guglielmo 2006; and Menchaca 2007. On Puerto Ricans, see Duany 2002a, 2003, and 2007; Loveman and Muniz 2007; Landale and Oropesa 2002; and Vidal-Ortiz 2004.

10. These figures are based on the use of U.S. Census Public Use Microdata Samples (PUMSs) for 2000 that are gathered in Jung and Almaguer 2004, 72.

11. See, for example, the compelling book on this topic by Haney-Lopez (2004).

12. See, for example, Vaughn 2005 and Lewis 2000.

13. See, for example, the discussion of the politics of active and passive sexual roles among Latino gay men in Vidal-Ortiz et al. 2010. See also the use of the term *bugarron* among Dominicans as a parallel term for *mayate* in Padilla 2007 and among Puerto Ricans in Guzman 2005.

EIGHT

Kill the Messengers

CAN WE ACHIEVE RACIAL JUSTICE WITHOUT
MENTIONING RACE?

Gary Delgado

The election of Barak Obama in 2008 led the mainstream media to immediately proclaim the arrival of a new, "post-racial" era. As one pundit observed, "The post-racial era, as embodied by Obama, is the era where civil rights veterans of the past century are consigned to history and Americans begin to make race-free judgments on who should lead them."[1]

However, as Obama's term progressed, it became increasingly evident that victory over racism had been declared prematurely. For example, in February 2010 a fraternity-sponsored "Compton Cookout" at the University of California, San Diego (UCSD), encouraged students to attend a party "celebrating" Black History Month, with male guests urged to wear bling and baggy clothes and female guests urged to dress as "ghetto chicks" with gold teeth, nappy hair with cheap weaves, and "bad colors—such as purple or bright red."[2] Shortly after the event a noose was found hanging in the UCSD library. According to writer Tim Wise, parties with stereotypically racial themes, including "Tacos and Tequila" and "Cowboys and Indians," have been held at more than thirty college campuses, including the University of Chicago, Swarthmore, the University of Virginia, Emory, MIT, Dartmouth, Cornell, and the Universities of Colorado, Tennessee, Arizona, Alabama, Delaware, and Mississippi (Wise 2007). In addition:

- In the political sphere, Congressman John Lewis was called a "nigger" by furious Tea Partiers as he walked to the Capitol with his colleagues to vote on health care reform in April 2010—on the forty-fifth anniversary of the march from Selma to Montgomery, no less—and his fellow representative Andre Carson was spat upon.[3]

- In a 2009 case of "flying while Muslim," a group of nine Muslim passengers were removed from an AirTran flight and prevented from flying after another passenger heard a "suspicious remark."[4]
- In 2008, the homes of Filipino immigrants who were either citizens or permenent residents were invaded and searched by Immigration and Customs Enforcement (ICE) agents in Idaho. That same year, an ICE raid in Postville, Iowa, cost the town one-third of its population. Agriprocessors responded by importing homeless people from Texas to work.[5]

Do these seemingly disparate events have a common denominator? One has to conclude that race is more prominent than ever in our political culture but operates differently than in the last half of the twentieth century—which is the frame through which mainstream culture encourages us to analyze it.

These not-so-isolated incidents might be dismissed as rare and aberrant were it not for an accompanying full-scale legislative push to ensure that disenfranchised and discriminated-against groups stay that way. Between 1997 and 2004 more than one hundred resolutions and laws to ban affirmative action were introduced in states, municipalities, and institutions of higher learning. For immigrants, the post-9/11 era emerged with a brazenly racist edge: "special registration" efforts targeting South Asians, Arabs, and Muslims; renewal of the Patriot Act, ensuring the continued suspension of due process and the rule of law; stepping up of workplace raids by the newly minted ICE; and laws proposed in twenty-two states to stop and request identification from anyone who might be in the United States without papers.[6] For some Americans it's hard to understand, digest, and assess the impact of these actions. Conservatives gleefully defend them, while progressives vacillate between horror and disbelief.

Two interrelated dynamics are operating in the racial arena. The first is the unbridled ascendance of racism in the guise of colorblindness. The media anoints the neocolonial empire with a new stage of post-racialism; a magic wand is waved, and the effects of five centuries of murder, economic exploitation, and racial privilege are wiped out. Moreover, not only are people of color suddenly equal, but the only racism that *does* exist is reverse discrimination against Whites. Anyone who claims differently, as former President Jimmy Carter did when he commented that opposition to national health care legislation was rooted in racism directed at President

Obama, will see the claim rejected (as Obama rejected Carter's observation) or be accused of "playing the race card," as conservative pundits charged. We have reached a point in racial discourse where our values have been turned upside down. Racist acts or speech by White students, politicians, or media personalities, despite their volume, are usually successfully interpreted as "mistakes," "misspeaking," "lapses," or speaking up in opposition to the overreaction of an "overly sensitive" constituency of people of color. The accompanying dynamic is that racial justice advocates have largely been cowed into avoiding explicit discussion of race and racist messages, for fear of alienating Whites whose support they have been convinced they need and will not otherwise obtain.

White college students in blackface and the public display of nooses on college campuses, ongoing reports of racially motivated police violence, anti-immigrant legislation, and multistate raids on immigrant workplaces—it's difficult to imagine that these things are all related. But they are.

RACIAL FORMATION AS THE STAGE
FOR RACIAL MESSAGING

In 1986, Michael Omi and Howard Winant's *Racial Formation in the United States* offered an explicit analysis of the changing racial terrain in the United States. Not only did they challenge what was, at the time, the reductionist trend that viewed race as a subset of class, ethnicity, or nation; they also used historical examples and current political debate to challenge the "continuous temptation to think of race as an *essence,* as something fixed, concrete, and objective," by showing how a changing, evolving, and even mutating racialized social structure is immediately linked to the meaning of race (Omi and Winant 1986, 57). *Racial Formation* has since become a standard text for race relations, social science, and ethnic studies courses nationally, giving a new generation of racial justice advocates, organizers, and pundits an unusually nuanced lens through which to assess and address issues of racial justice. Thus, while it is never easy to chart the dynamics of the *"unstable and 'decentered' complex of social meanings constantly being transformed by political struggle"* that is Omi and Winant's changing racial terrain (68; emphasis added), the very fluidity that the book's construct offers has enabled activists to analyze and adjust how they do their work.

I contend here that racial justice advocates must not lose sight of the fundamental truth highlighted in *Racial Formation:* that the notion of race in U.S. political culture is always predominant and always evolving. At the same time, we must forge new frameworks for understanding and communicating the reality of race in the twenty-first century. I write from the perspective of a racial justice practitioner. As a strategist, political organizer, and writer exposed to early Black and ethnic studies courses, and then excited by the historical parallels offered by the theoretical construct of internal colonialism, I was, truthfully, not eager to embrace a new, more comprehensive, *and more complex* theoretical model. However, as I illustrate in this chapter, the notions of the racial state and the idea that social meanings in the area of race are transformed by political struggle are extremely useful in understanding the thinking behind and the use of racial messaging in ballot initiative campaigns.

This essay is divided into three parts. First, I examine framing and messaging as applied to ballot initiatives that anticipate racially potent outcomes. Second, I focus on the advice of and results from professional communicators in racially charged ballot initiative campaigns. Finally, I explore key questions for future campaign initiative work from the perspective of a racial justice advocate.

SHAPING RACIAL DISCOURSE THROUGH BALLOT INITIATIVES

One arena in which the contradiction articulated earlier has played out, wherein proponents of colorblindness use racial messaging while racial justice advocates fear to do so, is the struggles over state ballot initiatives. In his recently published *Racial Propositions: Ballot Initiatives and the Making of Postwar California,* scholar-activist Daniel Martinez HoSang focuses on the messages and frames used by conservative forces in California's racially biased ballot initiative campaigns between 1946 and 2003. HoSang suggests a number of reasons why the study of these campaigns is important. Naming them "racial propositions," he argues not only that ballot measures that were focused on fair employment (1946), housing discrimination (1964), school desegregation (1972, 1979), and English-only instruction in public schools (1984, 1986), among other policies, produced the *political products* of new rules of law, but also that "these measures as they unfolded within the media, at public debates, neighborhood meetings, and through campaign advertisements have made [these political products] a central site for Californians to deliberate the meaning of race, rights, and authority." HoSang's study further posits that these ballot initiatives, shaped and organized by assertions of "colorblindness," were actually "propositions about the meaning of race and racism" (HoSang 2010, xvi, 8).

No ballot initiative in the last fifteen years more clearly tested the limits of racial tolerance and the meaning of both race and racial justice than the series of anti–affirmative action measures that began with the infamous Proposition 209, California's 1996 "Civil Rights Initiative," and continued through similar efforts in seven other states. To understand the significance and meaning of the actual messages used to advance both pro– and anti–affirmative action positions among the electorate, we must first explore the concept of framing and how current approaches may help or hinder the work of racial justice advocacy.

CREATING A FRAME

Much of the understanding of the significance of public messaging in the past decade is based on the thinking and writing of George Lakoff, professor of cognitive science and linguistics at the University of California, Berkeley. According to Lakoff, "We think, mostly unconsciously, in terms of systems of structures called 'frames.' Each frame is a neural circuit, physically in our brains. We use our systems of frame-circuitry to understand everything, and we reason using frame-internal logics. Frame systems are organized in terms of values, and how we reason reflects our values, and our values determine our sense of identity" (Lakoff 2009). In Lakoff's view, "framing is critical [to winning a public debate] because a frame, once established in the mind of the reader (or listener, viewer, etc.), leads that person almost inevitably towards the conclusion desired by the framer, and it blocks consideration of other facts and interpretations" (Kennedy, Fisher, and Bailey 2010, 409).

Lakoff's work is useful in pointing out both the existence and the importance of framing and in presenting models representing liberal and conservative values and belief archetypes. Lakoff asserts that the core values of most U.S. residents align with either the model of the "strict father"—a patriarchal figure who teaches his children the difference between right and wrong, protects his family in a dangerous world, and supports his family in a difficult world—or the model of the "nurturant parent"—a gender-neutral figure who believes in empathy, responsibility, freedom, cooperation, service, trust, and open, two-way communication (Lakoff 2004, 12–13). Lakoff elaborates further on these approximations of conservative and liberal icons to explain why conservatives believe that it is only the "deserving"—for example, the obedient, disciplined investors—who merit society's rewards (and tax breaks), while the do-gooders and those dependent on a bloated government are both immoral and undeserving. Conversely, Lakoff describes six subcategories of liberals, each with a separate "progressive" focus—socioeconomic, identity politics, environmental, civil liberties, spiritual, and antiauthoritarian—all of whom, he says, share progressive values and "nurturant parent" morality.

Lakoff's ideal types are rough constructs, useful to understand but of limited value in predicting how people might act and react to a discourse that is explicitly racially polarized. For example, these iconic constructs don't capture everyone—both of Lakoff's archetypes are clearly White. For me, some of the protectionist tendencies of the strict father are clearly recognizable in the practices of my first-generation, matriarchal, Afro-Caribbean family, while as a Black male adult, I'd observe that the value of "open communication between equals" is a power dynamic that may not apply where one is routinely compelled to speak truth to power and live with the consequences.

However, the simple fact that I can't "see myself" in the iconic constructs is not the only reason that I find the model troubling and unconvincing. Lakoff's description of the "identity politics" subcategory of "progressives"—where he'd no doubt place me—has us saying "it is time to get our share now" (Lakoff 2004, 14). (How impatient we are!) Despite his patronizing characterization of the "identity politics" group, on this point Lakoff is correct: we are not accorded the same level of legitimacy, resources, acceptance, or power as the other groups of progressives. Attacks on us are virulent, public, and more numerous. Far from a post-racial nirvana, this society as we experience it is regressing to its shameful history—and we're angry. The content of our character is at a rolling boil.

In *The White Racial Frame* (2009) Joe Feagin offers a much more pessimistic but racially realistic iconic construct. He argues that the White racial frame is ingrained in most Whites' character structure and that the frame automatically shapes the meaning of events, both guiding and rationalizing discriminatory behavior (2009, 15–16). He further asserts that the White racial frame is "more than one significant frame among many; it is one that has routinely defined a way of being, a broad perspective on life, and provides the language and interpretations that help structure, normalize, and make sense out of society" (11). I offer Feagin's analysis not because I concur with all aspects of it, but as a contrast to Lakoff's work, which many analysts take quite seriously though it has almost nothing of substance to say about race, gender, or sexuality. Indeed, Lakoff apparently rejects such a focus when he writes that "each [of the six progressive types] thinks that theirs is the only way to be a true progressive. This is sad. We have to get past that harmful idea. The other side did" (Lakoff 2004, 15).

A final problem is that Lakoff's iconic constructs seem static and hard-wired. In urging us to appeal to existing ways of thinking, he accepts as a fundamental principle that *we do not have the same transformative capacity as our opponents—we can't change people's minds.* This approach, which many liberal communications professionals adhere to as well, offers very little hope for an epiphany, a change—a transformation in the public's thinking. The "groupthink" environment of focus group "science" clearly reinforces this position.

BALLOT INITIATIVES AND RACIAL FRAMING

Lakoff's archetypes are one building block in message development; a second consists of common myths in U.S. culture; and a third, of commonly held beliefs about race. Table 8.1 is drawn from an article by members of the Race Equity Project of Legal Services of Northern California (Kennedy, Fisher, and Bailey 2010, 412, 414, 417), which contends that advocates must change the way they talk about the issues affecting low-income communities, and offers examples of how to do so. The article illustrates how communications experts have used U.S. cultural myths, race-specific beliefs, and framing approaches geared to mobilize public support and action for racial equity initiatives.

In campaign settings, these theoretical constructs and frames have produced noteworthy outcomes. All of the state-based anti–affirmative action

TABLE 8.1 Myths, Racial Beliefs, and Frames

American Myths	Common Racial Beliefs among Whites	Recommended Messaging Frame
• Land of equality • Americans play by the rules. • Rags-to-riches (self-made man) • Rugged individualism • America as a meritocracy	• Racism is individual action • To achieve racial justice, we must be colorblind. • Racist attitudes socially unacceptable and rare.	• Opportunity for all
• Americans are ingenious and innovative.	• Individuals are personally responsible for their fate.	• American ingenuity: "We fix what's broken."
• America is different from other nations.	• Racially, matters have improved dramatically in the past fifty years.	• We are a nation of shared fates.

SOURCE: Kennedy, Fisher, and Bailey 2010.

initiatives have been championed by former University of California regent Ward Connerly, a California-based Black businessman and self-described "disciple of the Reagan revolution." Connerly's anti–preference and quota message is generally compatible with the mainstream beliefs that racism is not structural, that it is a phenomenon of the past, and that institutions within the United States operate without racial bias. Indeed, public perception has swung so far in this direction that a 2011 study found that Whites believe that anti-White racism is now a bigger problem than anti-Black racism.[7]

Clever use of language from the Reverend Dr. Martin Luther King's "I Have a Dream" speech—wherein King expressed his hope that his children would be "judged not by the color of their skin but by the content of their character"—have been appropriated and co-opted by anti–affirmative action advocates like Connerly to deflect criticism. Doubly packaged as promoting mainstream meritocracy and continuing the King legacy, anti–affirmative action "Civil Rights Initiatives" in California, Michigan, Washington, Arizona, and Nebraska all claimed a substantial (and winning) portion of those states' electorates.

As with the earlier ballot initiatives HoSang examined in California, the success of these measures was, at least in part, a tribute to the nearly universal acceptance of the doctrine of colorblindness. In its simplest articulation, adherents argue that they "do not see race" and that race is not an important factor in understanding how U.S. society metes out

TABLE 8.2 Contesting Racial Ideologies

Contested Questions	Colorblind Perspective	Racial Justice Perspective
Does racism exist?	Racism against people of color is mostly past, except for rare, extreme cases; reverse discrimination exists against whites. Social inequalities are based on income, not race.	Racism routinely results in current and vast racial inequalities. Race is a major determinant of income and life opportunities.
What is racism?	Racism is bias, prejudice, bigotry, or hatred between individuals of different races. Racism involves willful, prejudicial intent.	Grounded in the ideology of white supremacy, racism in the U.S. is an institutionally reinforced system of inequity that advantages whites, while disadvantaging and excluding people of color, regardless of individual intent.
Who's responsible?	Extreme bigots and "bad apples" (KKK, rogue cops). People of color act like victims and "play the race card."	Inequitable institutions and policies in a system of white supremacy; individuals who use racial privilege, consciously or not, for advantage at the expense of others.
What's to be done?	"Colorblindness" is needed. People of color need to "get over it" and "get on with it." Slavery was abolished long ago, and discrimination is now illegal.	Ongoing racial justice initiatives including policy and institutional changes are needed to produce and measure racial equity.

SOURCE: Terry Keleher, Racial Justice Leadership Initiative, Applied Research Center, http://www.arc.org (printout in author's possession)

rewards, privileges, and punishment. Terry Keleher, senior researcher at the Applied Research Center, suggests that the "real assumptions about color-blindness are actually hidden in the answers to four usually unarticulated questions: (1) Does racism exist? (2) What is racism? (3) Who's responsible for its persistence? (4) What's to be done?" In table 8.2, Keleher compares how these questions are answered by advocates of two contesting racial ideologies—colorblindness and racial justice (Keleher 2005).

The differences between the assumptions and beliefs of colorblindness versus racial justice advocates suggest two radically different frames for understanding and explaining racial meaning. For those working to end affirmative action, the messaging task was relatively simple: instead of focusing on the stark reality of racial discrimination against people of color and the need for equitable racial outcomes, colorblindness proponents directed the focus to "quotas" and "preferential treatment," thereby triggering notions of the idealized norms of *meritocracy, rugged individualism,* and *the level playing field* and attracting wide and *guilt-free* support.

Examining anti–affirmative action websites reveals a number of trends. First, in line with the assumption that the only remaining discrimination is reverse discrimination against Whites, many sites do not even mention historical racial discrimination. Second, although the term "Civil Rights Initiative" was the frame of choice on every website, when Missouri secretary of state Robin Carnahan proposed changing the description of that state's initiative to read, "amend the state's constitution to ban affirmative action programs designed to eliminate discrimination against, and improve opportunities for, women and minorities in public contracting, employment and education"—*which was the actual effect of the initiative*—a county circuit court judge overruled that language.[8] In addition, the trumpeting of these notions by the most potent symbols of those racially discriminated against—Black men like Ward Connerly and Thomas Sowell—made it easy to build political momentum. The initiative prohibited the government "from giving preferential treatment or discriminating against any person based on his or her race or gender in public education, public hiring and public contracting." Thus, one could be colorblind; that is, *against* people of color hurting themselves by accepting preferential treatment, *for* meritocracy, *against* quotas—and cool!

On the pro–affirmative action side of the debate, the messaging dynamic was more complex. Because of the campaigns' relatively short length and goal of winning a simple majority of the electorate (50 percent plus 1, in the lingo of electoral campaigns), message professionals viewed their task as influencing a predominately White electorate to vote for a policy that many were predisposed to think was unfair to Whites. This approach purposefully avoided *challenging the electorate's beliefs about race and racism,* because such a challenge was perceived as a sure way to trigger White antagonism and thereby to lose.

In March 2008, before the votes in Colorado, Nebraska, Oklahoma, Missouri, and Arizona, FrameWorks Institute, a well-funded and influential communications organization with a stated mission of framing public discourse about social problems, issued an eleven-page document entitled *Framing Race.*[9] The document briefly analyzed U.S. residents' views on race and concluded with a brief list of messaging do's and don'ts (see table 8.3).

TABLE 8.3 Dos and Don'ts of Framing
Public Discourse about Social Problems

Do . . .	Don't . . .
Invoke the deeply embedded American value of Ingenuity/Can Do spirit with respect to solving tough problems.	Engage in a rhetorical debate about the intentionality of discrimination.
Show people where systems that we all rely upon break down and specify how they might be fixed.	Focus on problems and disparities to the exclusion of solutions.
Remind people of our common belief in Opportunity for All and how failures in the system hurt everyone.	Talk about fairness or the historical legacy of racism.

In the memo's three-page analytical section, authors Lynn Davey and Susan Bales argue that advocates should not talk about White privilege, because "the default belief that life chances are determined by the individual trumps the idea that certain groups may have stored 'credit' that gives them an advantage." And, according to the memo's authors, because that dominant model "is rooted in individual 'little picture' thinking, people cannot acquire a 'big picture' perspective on how bias in the system accounts for racial disparities." Because Americans can't understand the cumulative nature of racism, they can't be reasoned out of it. Thus, the authors conclude: "The more explicit the racial cue in communications, the greater the opposition to race-based public policies. . . . This is consistent across policy domains (e.g., welfare, immigration, affirmative action, health disparities, social determinants of health)."

This, by and large, has been the same losing advice given to affirmative action advocates in every state since the series of ballot initiatives was launched in California in 1996. In every subsequent battleground, White communications and messaging "experts" were hired—often with funding from national foundations—who seem to have ignored the dismal track record of the strategies they promoted.

Until recently, the immigration reform debate was shaping up to follow the same road followed by anti–affirmative action ballot initiatives: the "anti" forces use explicit and subliminal racial messaging, while the racial justice side is browbeaten into avoiding race. A full-page June 8, 2007, ad in the *Washington Times,* under the banner headline "Immigration Reform Must Address Race Preferences," proclaimed, "When they give 'undocumented' or illegal aliens a 'way to earn their citizenship,' they will give them all that comes with citizenship *including* the entitlement to race/ethnic preferences if they are designated as part of an 'underrepresented minority' group."[10]

Politicos, pundits, and publicists continue to urge immigrant rights activists *not* to address the underlying racist xenophobia and instead to tackle the "play by the rules" myth by focusing on *illegality.* "Undocumented immigrants should apologize for their presence in the U.S.," writes American Environics messaging expert Pamela Morgono. "Every day that an illegal immigrant stays in the U.S., s/he is repeating the lawbreaking behavior . . . not only repeating the offense, they are 'thumbing their noses' at remorse and restitution, and they certainly are not repenting and changing their behavior." Morgono's conclusion? "Because Americans love to be generous and love a story of redemption, . . . undocumented immigrants should humbly request a second chance." Her suggested message? "I'm sorry; I was wrong; I promise never to do it again. How can I make it up to you? Will you give me a second chance?" Finally, she writes, "if ALL of the accompanying speech acts are not spoken—*the person does not deserve a second chance*" (emphasis added).[11]

Recent anti-immigrant state legislation or ballot initiatives in place in six states—and proposed in an additional five—require law enforcement officers to attempt to determine the immigration status of a person they suspect is not authorized to be in the United States.[12] These measures typically also make it a criminal offense to transport or provide housing to an illegal immigrant. The vitriolic nature of these laws has coalesced civil liberties, immigrant rights, and traditional civil rights organizations in an effort to explicitly attack the legislation as racist. According to the National Network for Immigrant and Refugee Rights, the legislation "follows a long history of racist persecution of undocumented people and communities of color" (Coalicion de Derechos Humanos 2011).

Despite the dismal track record so far, I concede that it is possible (though unlikely) for racial justice advocates to defeat a racially charged ballot initiative without mentioning race. I would argue however, that by omitting any mention of race, this approach does not challenge the fundamentally racist frames that undergird the initiative, whether the terrain be affirmative action, immigration reform, health care, or criminal justice. Yet this approach has become standard operating procedure in many policy fights in which the likelihood is high of a damaging outcome for individuals and communities of color. Although much of the advocacy for this position has come from communications professionals who may or may not have a personal stake in the outcome of their work, activists and advocates from across the racial spectrum have embraced it, in part because looking for success at the ballot box by challenging the White voting majority seems counterintuitive. California, for instance, has had eight racialized policy battles in the past twelve years over issues ranging from three-strikes criminal penalties, bilingual education, and affirmative action ballot initiatives to service cuts, refusal of driver's licenses to immigrants, and the so-called racial privacy initiative.

Although these fights have played out in an increasingly racially polarized political climate, the political discourse—apart from that over the 2003 Racial Privacy Initiative, which would have banned the collection of racial information in public education, contracting, and employment—has largely avoided any *explicit* racial reference. In every circumstance the advice offered by foundation-supported messaging experts has been the same: "Don't mention race."[13]

The *implicit* discourse, though, has been all about race, intimated through coded language and images. For instance, although the explicit discussion was about the morality of "zero tolerance" and "public safety" (that catchphrase of White fear), the subliminal imagery undergirding the three-strikes initiative was that of imprisoned African American males. The affirmative action discourse, ironically, was about fairness for Whites. Anti-immigrant initiatives are discussed primarily in terms of public safety and "responsible expenditures" in an era of scarcity, but the public's—and, especially, the voters'—image of immigrants is heavily racialized (the image conjured up, after all, is not of immigrants from Ireland or Canada). Not only do juvenile predators, personal responsibility, welfare queens, illegals, and the like evoke racial images, but those who use such terms know exactly what they're doing and do so intentionally. But advocates are cautioned that explicit racial cues trigger opposition to racial justice policies, and so they seldom confront the racial messaging of supposedly "race-neutral" language.

This explicitly "race-neutral" approach has been legitimated by academics, supported by philanthropic institutions, and delivered by professional communications organizations to activists engaged in state and local fights all over the country. Harvard sociologist Theda Skocpol, ignoring the many examples of economic and educational policies that are theoretically designed to "lift every boat" but that nonetheless bypass communities of color, has long argued that only universal policies that lack an explicitly stated racial outcome will attract broad public support for changes that will benefit people of color. Some racial justice advocates argue the opposite, pointing out that "universal programs are very likely to exacerbate inequality rather than reduce it. . . . Treating people who are situated differently as if they were the same can result in much greater inequities" (powell, Menendian, and Reece 2009). Clearly, if we are not explicit about the racial outcomes we seek, we are unlikely to achieve them.

THE COSTS OF RACIAL SILENCE

Away from the immediacy and heat of a political campaign, other foundational questions about the racially silent approach emerge, especially when the racial justice stakes—stated or not—are high. For example, what are racial justice advocates' long-range objectives? The conventional wisdom is that one is *only* trying to win the initiative, to get 50 percent plus one. The method for determining how to do that is the focus group, with messaging experts honing in on the answer to this question: "What can we say to convince an already defined, usually white, frequently voting majority that they should vote in favor of a racial justice initiative?"

Thus far, messages crafted in such a manner to sway this constituency have been largely unsuccessful. California's anti–affirmative action initiative passed in 1996 by 54 to 46 percent, and although similar initiatives were knocked off of the ballot due to either court or signature challenges in Florida (2000) and Oklahoma, Missouri, and Arizona (2008), anti–affirmative action measures passed in Washington State in 1998, Michigan in 2006, and Nebraska in 2008, all by margins of approximately 58 to 42 percent. The only state where the initiative did not pass was Colorado in 2008, where it lost 51–49.[14]

HoSang's historical examination of racially charged ballot initiatives in California illustrates how conservative forces have used that process to preempt control of political discourse and test ideas for consolidating a political base, while defining their interests as beneficent and egalitarian and their opponents as narrow-minded and whiney. In both the anti–racial equity and anti-immigrant attacks, the right has used ballot initiatives as a tool to shift the terrain of political discourse, while the progressive response has been largely defensive and shortsighted. Progressives who run ballot initiative campaigns (usually, these days, in opposition to right-wing initiatives) see them as one-shot, "beat back" efforts.

This defensive posture does not strive to educate or reorient people. Rather, it attempts to reframe the initiative's core meaning in a manner that appeals to a narrowly defined self-interest of the electoral majority. The key difference between this mobilization strategy for winning ballot initiatives and other kinds of organizing work is that community and racial justice organizers view the challenge of educating their constituents as an important prerequisite to moving into action. From an organizer's perspective, while "50 percent plus one" may be *a* goal of a campaign, it may not be the only or even the most important goal.

CRAFTING AN EFFECTIVE APPROACH TO FRAMING
RACE AND PUBLIC POLICY

Racial justice advocates must reclaim racial discourse, understand the electorate's evolving demographics, and demand leadership from those in positions of authority. This work should be explicit, should directly challenge the underlying assumptions of colorblindness as well as its policy manifestations, and should be proactive and ongoing. Examples that meet these criteria include the passage of anti–racial profiling legislation in twenty-four states,[15] racial impact legislation passed in Iowa and Connecticut to reduce the overrepresentation of people of color in the criminal justice system, and the introduction in Illinois, California, Minnesota, Nevada, and Washington of racial justice report cards that assess how specific pieces of legislation affect African American, Native American, Latino, and Asian American communities.[16]

Polling and focus groups aside, it is important to remember that social science research supports the notion that human interaction, education, and political campaigning can change people's minds. Political scientist Paul Kellstedt's quantitative study *Mass Media and the Dynamics of American Racial Attitudes* (2003) describes interactions with researchers that changed political responses. Citing the work of political scientist Jennifer Hochschild, Kellstedt observes that "political attitudes are often not defined in straightforward 'liberal' or 'conservative' ideological terms."

Hochschild spent many hours interviewing twenty-eight adults and learning how they formed their political beliefs. She found that most people do not hold simplistic, Black-or-White beliefs. Rather, people tend to be ambivalent about important political issues: "Given the opportunity, people do not make simple statements, they shade, modulate, deny, retract, or just grind to a halt in frustration" (Kellstedt 2003, 56–57). Kellstedt also refers to a study by social psychologists Irwin Katz and R. Glen Hass, who found that many of their subjects simultaneously held racist and anti-racist ideas. In a clever experiment, Katz and Hass discovered that subjects were more likely to express "pro-black sentiments" when primed with a values scale that represented egalitarian values, and anti-Black sentiments when presented with a scale that represented individualism (60).

These findings suggest that individuals' political attitudes are not set in stone and that simple human interaction (organizing, advocacy, education, discussion) may affect people's views and actually change minds. Over the long term, of course, one can see many indicators of significant shifts in public attitude. In 1942, 32 percent of Americans favored integration; in 1995 the proportion had tripled to 96 percent. While integration has proven somewhat anemic as a strategy for ending racial discrimination, segregationists' best efforts were defeated not by focus group researchers and professional messengers but by the strident persistence of the civil rights movement. Racist ideology and practice lost to activists' willingness to challenge the existing political terrain and overturn the way things had "always been."

ARE RACIAL JUSTICE EFFORTS TARGETING THE RIGHT
PORTION OF THE ELECTORATE?

Given the electorate's changing demographics, racial justice advocates may want to reconsider whom to target in a high-stakes campaign having explicit racial outcomes. Campaign methodology has been geared toward a majority-White electorate. What happens when the majority tips? Since 1996, racial justice advocates have won electoral majorities in two ballot initiative campaigns. The more recent is the slim, 51-to-49 percent victory in Colorado in 2008. However, another Ward Connerly proposal in 2003—California's Proposition 54, the so-called Racial Privacy Initiative, aimed at prohibiting government agencies from collecting or tracking racial data—was defeated by a resounding 64 to 36 percent. Political analysts cite a number of reasons for this overwhelming defeat, including fears that diseases closely associated with particular racial or ethnic groups would not be identified and treated, lack of funding, opposition by key corporate players and the medical establishment, and voter confusion. However, ballot architect Connerly had a different observation: "I could not understand why certain interests, such as the health-care industry, the gay/lesbian community, and the environmentalists, had joined labor unions, Indian Tribes, trial lawyers, 'educrats,' and race advocates to oppose an initiative that had no obvious effect on them. As the campaign evolved, I began to understand . . . by threatening certain members of that cartel, Prop. 54 had unwittingly declared war on all of them."[17]

Connerly was right. In California, the state that has passed more racially biased ballot initiatives than any other, each initiative has targeted a slightly different group. For instance, Proposition 187 was aimed at undocumented immigrants, while the anti–bilingual education initiative was aimed at both immigrant and permanent-resident Latinos. Three-strikes and the anti-affirmative action initiatives were perceived to be more "Black-focused." While each affected all California residents, the net effect has been to erode trust and, in many cases, to compound racial tension within the new demographic majority of people of color. However, Proposition 54 was indeed roundly opposed by all communities of color. Derisive language aside, Connerly's observation that he was "declaring war on all of them" in a state that had just tipped to a majority of people of color may have radically redefined the meaning of race—and the political potential of a new majority.

Connerly's point was made in a different arena by several political commentators in the last presidential election when they noted that Lyndon Johnson was the last Democratic presidential candidate to win the White vote. Jimmy Carter, Bill Clinton, and Barak Obama were able to gain the support only of a minority of White voters. They won *only* when those votes were added to the sizeable majorities they received from people of color. Obama got 43 percent of the White vote, 95 percent of the Black vote, 67 percent of the Latino vote, and 62 percent of the Asian vote.[18] The point goes beyond a simple "look who's in charge." Although people of color in California are a numerical majority, they are not yet a voting majority. And, aside from their collective response against the Connerly proposal, the political beliefs of people of color about racial meaning or racial justice do not necessarily converge. Significant and meaningful electoral participation, and the development of a collective political vision and agenda, will require ongoing education and organizing.

HOW DO WE DEFINE POLITICAL LEADERSHIP?

A final political consideration is how these racially based electoral contests address issues of agency and leadership. The Obama victory demonstrates a priori that the leadership of a person of color in a significant political effort in the United States not only shapes the effort itself, as the appearance of various racist images of the president during the health-care debate demonstrated, but also affects the campaign outcome and concretely demonstrates leadership possibilities both to Whites and, more important, to other people of color. The political leadership of these ballot initiative campaigns, both visible and invisible, is similarly important because political victories—real and symbolic—are not always won by those with a numerical majority. As the Tea Party activists demonstrate, a vocal minority with significant resources can affect public discourse and influence policy priorities. A movement for racial justice that does not just react to attacks must set the tone for future initiatives and eschew the strategy that messaging experts recommended to the Michigan African American pro–affirmative action groups: let White women who benefited from affirmative action be the face of the campaign. Not only was this a dishonest tactic that fooled no one; but it was a dead loser. The White electorate may not favor affirmative action, but it knew the ballot initiative was about race. In a 2009 interview, activist scholar Matthew Countryman summed up his experience in the Michigan Affirmative Action campaign this way: "The campaign had so many layers of nuance that we were never really able to discuss what was at stake. We lost without ever being able to put our real concerns on the table."[19]

In contrast, the right has never been shy about leading with unpopular ideas. Jean Hardisty and Deepak Bhargava's examination (2005) of the reasons for the right's success point to a number of key practices including (1) a willingness to adopt, project, and organize around unpopular ideas until those ideas are perceived to be the beliefs of the majority, and (2) the ability to recruit constituents through a hodgepodge of issues—resistance to taxes and government; opposition to gay/lesbian, racial, or reproductive rights—and build a base that can be mobilized for both local actions and national campaigns.[20]

This level of organization and intentionality has made conservative political efforts highly successful. Progressives, on the other hand, have neither the same level of infrastructure nor the ability to coordinate on such a massive scale. If we take to heart Omi and Winant's assertion that the racial state "is defined and redefined in relationship to the emerging patterns of conflict and accommodation which take place over time between racially based social movements and the policies and programs of the state" (Omi and Winant 1986, 58), then racial justice advocates have an additional barrier: we have not put forth our own proactive initiatives. Although "winning" a ballot initiative without being explicit about its racial implications may stave off an immediate threat, the right's efforts have demonstrated that questions of racial equity will reemerge in the next campaign. Until we define a political initiative that both challenges existing race-specific beliefs and galvanizes action across communities of color, and among progressive Whites, racial meaning in the electoral arena will be defined by episodic campaigns to beat back racist legislation and periodic symbolic victories of candidates of color—some of whom may even claim that they are evidence that race is no longer an issue, and all of whom may be used as fodder for that colorblind canon.

In addition to rethinking our assumptions and strategies in light of what has actually worked and what has not—rather than what focus groups deem desirable and communications professionals claim as strategic—people with a personal and political stake in advancing racial justice must reclaim both the moral high ground and the strategic leadership of these political campaigns. Unless we lead with principle rather than opportunism, proactively aiming to break the myth of colorblindness while asserting the essential value of racial justice, the problem of the twentieth century will remain the problem of every century to come.

NOTES

1. Daniel Schorr, "A New 'Post Racial' Era in America," *National Public Radio,* January 28, 2008, http://www.npr.org/templates/story/story.php?storyId=18489466 (accessed January 12, 2012).

2. "The 'Compton Cookout,'" on Resist Racism, February 18, 2010, http://resistracism.wordpress.com/2010/02/18/the-compton-cookout/ (accessed January 12, 2012).

3. "Tea Party Protests: 'Ni**er,' 'Fa**ot' Shouted at Members of Congress," *Huffington Post,* March 20, 2010, http://www.huffingtonpost.com/2010/03/20/tea-party-protests-nier-f_n_507116.html (accessed January 12, 2012).

4. Matthew DeLong, "'Flying While Muslim' the New 'Driving While Black,'" *Washington Independent,* January 2, 2009, http://washingtonindependent.com/23578/flying-while-muslim-the-new-driving-while-black (accessed January 12, 2012).

5. Spencer S. Hsu, "Immigration Raid Jars a Small Town," *Washington Post,* May 18, 2008.

6. Fred Lucus, "Nearly Half of the United States Considering Arizona-Style Immigration Legislation," *CNS News,* August 18, 2010, http://www.cnsnews.com/node/71294 (accessed January 12, 2012).

7. A 2011 study by Michael I. Norton and Samuel Sommers in the journal *Perspectives on Psychological Science* found that whites believe that anti-white racism has increased and is now a bigger problem than anti-black racism. The authors write that "not only do whites think more progress has been made toward equality than do blacks, but whites also now believe that this progress is linked to a new inequality—at their expense." See "Whites Believe They Are Victims of Racism More Often Than Blacks," *TuftsNow,* May 23, 2011, http://now.tufts.edu/news-releases/whites-believe-they-are-victims-racism-more-o (accessed January 12, 2012).

8. Harry Stein, "Racial-Preference Ballots Go National," *City Journal,* April 16, 2008, http://city-journal.org/2008/eon0416hs.html (accessed January 12, 2012).

9. Lynn Davey and Susan Bales, "FrameWorks Message Brief: Framing Race," *FrameWorks Institute,* March 7, 2008 (version as of this date in author's files).

10. "Immigration Reform Must Address Racial Preferences," *Adversity.Net News,* http://www.adversity.net/supertuesday2008/immigration-reform-01.htm#01-ad-text (accessed January 12, 2012).

11. Pamela Morgono, Memorandum titled "Immigration Frames: Lawbreakers," *American Environics,* December 17, 2007 (in author's files).

12. States that have adopted such anti-immigrant measures at the time of this writing are Alabama, Arizona, Georgia, Indiana, South Carolina, Oklahoma, and Utah. Similar bills are currently pending in Virginia, Mississippi, Missouri, and Tennessee.

13. These same foundations are increasingly pushing community organizations to produce measurable results in their struggles for racial justice. Unfortunately, the same "outcome" standards do not apply to messaging experts.

14. Affirmative Action Ballot Initiatives Ballotpedia, http://ballotpedia.org/wiki/index.php/Affirmative_action_on_the_ballot (accessed February 10, 2012).

15. "Racial Profiling Policies," Open Congress, http://www.opencongress.org/wiki/Racial_profiling_policies (accessed February 10, 2012).

16. See, for example, Julianne Hing, "Washington Groups Deliver Racial Equity Report Card," *Colorlines: News for Action*, January 20, 2010, http://colorlines.com/archives/2010/01/washington_groups_deliver_racial_equity_legislative_report_card.html (accessed January 12, 2012).

17. Ward Connerly, "Not a Chance: The Electoral Journey of Proposition 54," *Adversity.Net*, October 15, 2003, http://www.adversity.net/RPI/rpi_mainframe.htm (accessed January 12, 2012).

18. Roger Simon, "What Happened to Post Racial America," *NBC New York*, August 7, 2009, http://www.nbcnewyork.com/news/politics/What_happened_to_post-racial_America_-52638552.html (accessed January 12, 2012).

19. Matthew Countryman, personal interview with author, April 2009.

20. Hardisty and Bhargava 2005.

NINE

The New Racial Preferences

RETHINKING RACIAL PROJECTS

Devon W. Carbado and Cheryl I. Harris

INTRODUCTION

Among the central contributions offered by Omi and Winant's now classic work is their theory of racial formation—the process by which racial categories are "created, inhabited, transformed and destroyed" (Omi and Winant 1994, 55)—and the related concept of racial projects—roughly, how race is represented, deployed, and institutionalized. Because race is a technology that links social and political struggle to different human bodies—bodies whose racial meanings are constructed and constantly under pressure and transformation—our task, as Omi and Winant illustrate, is less to search for lasting characteristics that define race in a once-and-for-all sense than to attend to how race is constructed and formed—a process of installing various racial projects. Racial projects connect an interpretation of race in a given historical moment or context to the organization of social structures and everyday practices. Thus, a racial project *is simultaneously an interpretation, representation, or explanation of racial dynamics, and an effort to re-organize and redistribute resources along particular racial lines* (Omi and Winant 1994, 56; emphasis in original).

Under this formulation, anti–affirmative action initiatives, such as Michigan's Proposal 2 and California's Proposition 209, are both racial projects. These measures *represent* affirmative action as a racial preference in order to *reorganize and redistribute resources*—admissions spaces, government contracting, employment opportunities—*along particular racial lines*. This reorganization is then explained as the restoration of a distribution that is objective, neutral, and meritorious, rather than as a return to a racial preference baseline that primarily benefits whites.

Given the many years that have passed since the original publication of *Racial Formation* and the emergence of these anti–affirmative action initiatives in the mid- to late 1990s, the concept of racial projects has demonstrable durability. It illustrates that racial meanings are neither inherent nor fixed, but rather are contested political projects that individual and institutional actors mobilize to do organization and redistribution work. This racial work need not be conservative in its ideological orientation. As Omi and Winant conceive them, racial projects come in all ideological stripes. Indeed, racial projects include efforts to install and secure a range of race-conscious interventions, such as affirmative action and voting rights remedies that create majority-minority districts.

This does not mean that Omi and Winant make no distinctions among racial projects or that they do not make assessments about their value, power, or desirability. Precisely because racial projects pursue any number of ideological objectives, Omi and Winant draw a line between racial projects we should embrace and nurture and those we should vigorously reject and oppose. Thus, we have little doubt that had Proposition 209 or Proposal 2 been part of the political backdrop against which *Racial Formation* was written, Omi and Winant would have criticized and condemned both measures. Our conclusion in this respect is based in part on the fact that they expressly contest the conceptualization of affirmative action as a racial preference. They ask: "Is the allocation of employment opportunities through programs restricted to racially defined minorities, so called 'preferential treatment' or affirmative action policies, racist?" Their answer is "We think not."[1] With this response, Omi and Winant both disaggregate "preferential treatment" from "affirmative action" and repudiate the dominant characterization of affirmative action as reverse discrimination. Through these discursive moves, they enact a racial project of their own, a counterhegemonic one. In so doing, they help to make clear the point we articulate above—that racial projects hail from all ideological corners.

But how exactly does one separate the good racial projects from the bad? For Omi and Winant the answer resides in the distinction between racism and racial awareness. A racial project is racist "if and only if it creates or reproduces structures of domination based on essentialist categories of race" (Omi and Winant 1994, 71). Drawing on Diana Fuss's influential *Essentially Speaking*, they define essentialism as "the belief in real true human essences, existing outside or impervious to social and historical context" (181n6). Building on this idea, Omi and Winant distinguish between racial awareness, on the one hand, which they do not condemn, and efforts to "link essentialist representations of race and social structures of domination," on the other, which they reject (72). Their reasoning is that only the latter is necessarily racist. To make this point more concrete, they apply their theory to the following two statements: (1) "Many Asians are highly entrepreneurial" (which they conclude is neither essentialist nor racist), and (2) "Many Asians are naturally entrepreneurial" (which they conclude reflects both essentialism and racism) (71–72).

They develop this argument further by offering a more complex account of racism that rejects a transhistorical and quixotic search for its inherent or "essential" characteristics. They vigorously reject, for example, claims that only those with social power can be racist. To their way of thinking, racism can take many forms. At the same time, they are careful to point out that not all racial projects characterized as racist have the same normative valence or distributional consequences. The harms imposed by different forms of racism have to be assessed relative to their role in entrenching "the dominant hegemonic" framework on race (Omi and Winant 1994, 73). By way of a (well-worn) example, they invoke Louis Farrakhan's reliance on essentialist arguments about the inherent constitution of black people (as good) and white people (as evil). Under their framework, Farrakhan's claims are not situated outside racism; they are a form of racism. But this form of racism is less harmful than that espoused by white supremacists, they reason, because the latter coheres so readily with the dominant discourse on race that undergirds white racial domination (73–74).

Still, one may query whether Omi and Winant, in rendering this more nuanced account, important though it was—and still is—went far enough. Recall again their express repudiation of the conservative line on affirmative action. Yet at the same moment, they also, at least in part, reproduce a liberal consensus that affirmative action is problematic because it imposes costs on innocent whites. Thus they assert, "It should be acknowledged that [affirmative action] programs often do have deleterious consequences for whites who are not personally the source of the discriminatory practices the programs seek to overcome" (Omi and Winant 1994, 73). If one were to modify this quote slightly so that it states that affirmative action programs *have*, not simply *often do* have deleterious consequences for whites," it lines up squarely with what Omi and Winant call a "neo-conservative racial project" and, more particularly, with the idea that whites are innocent victims of affirmative action, while blacks and Latinos are preferred beneficiaries.

To be clear, we are not arguing that Omi and Winant and neoconservatives are similarly situated in terms of their framing of affirmative action. We only mean to suggest that even a text as brilliant, progressive, and paradigm-shifting as *Racial Formation* seems at times to acquiesce in the view that race-conscious remediation like affirmative action harms innocent white victims. This formulation of affirmative action as a racial project that produces distributional costs on those who have not caused or benefited from the injury not only makes the policy more difficult to defend but also blurs the analytical distinction they previously attempted to draw between a racial preference and affirmative action.

Omi and Winant's discomfort with the costs of particular racial remediation efforts is even more pronounced with respect to majority-minority districts. These districts are a race-conscious voting rights mechanism that attempts to ensure the effective political participation of racial groups historically excluded from political power and office. According to Omi and Winant, the establishment of majority-minority districts is a form of gerrymandering. They maintain that that while this gerrymandering is preferable to the outright denial of the right to vote, it is "vulnerable to charges of essentialism," "tokenism," and "racial lumping" and does not achieve the act's purpose of promoting electoral equality within and across racial lines (Omi and Winant 1994, 74). Presumably because majority-minority districts are predicated on the essentialist view that all blacks have common political interests or a particular political/social voice, fighting for more majority-minority districts is a form of racism, albeit a mild one. This mild racism freezes inequality and "subverts . . . political processes through which racially defined groups could otherwise negotiate their differences and interests" (74).

This analysis is somewhat confounding. While the question of whether majority-minority districts increase democratic power and accountability is certainly debatable, Omi and Winant's argument disaggregates the remedy from two significant racial injuries that majority-minority districts were intended to cure: vote dilution (the dispersal of minority voters to thwart their efforts to select political representatives of their choice) and white bloc voting (the historical practice of whites voting as racial blocs to limit black political participation and representation). Were racially subordinated groups able to negotiate their differences both within and across groups through "normal" (and presumably "racially clean") politics, there would be no need for race-conscious intervention.

Omi and Winant's argument is that majority-minority districts constitute a form of "racial lumping" predicated on the view that blacks think alike—a view that "creates or reproduces structures of domination based on essentialist categories of race" (Omi and Winant 1994, 71). This critique bears a striking similarity to conservative complaints about voting rights remedies more generally. The conservative U.S. Supreme Court majority in *Shaw v. Reno*, for example, questioned the constitutionality of a majority-minority redistricting plan in a region where there had been no black representatives since Reconstruction, in significant part because the alleged assumption underlying this remedy—that all blacks had the same political views—was both wrong-headed and racist. According to Justice Sandra Day O'Connor, writing for the majority:

> A reapportionment plan that includes in one district individuals who belong to the same race, but who are otherwise widely separated by geographical and political boundaries, and who may have little in common with one another but the color of their skin, bears an uncomfortable resemblance to political apartheid. It reinforces the perception that members of the same racial group—regardless of their age, education, economic status, or the community in which they live—think alike, share the same political interests, and will prefer the same candidates at the polls.[2]

While Omi and Winant do not adopt overwrought analogies to apartheid, their argument reproduces the complaint about essentialist conceptions of race—a logic frequently employed by the Court's conservative majority to strike down race-conscious remediation. This "anti-essentialism" is often tethered to arguments that more generally conflate racial awareness and racism, a conflation that Omi and Winant caution against.

The foregoing illustrates a tension in the underlying framework Omi and Winant offer to determine which racial projects can be fairly described as racist: in tying the metric to essentialism, Omi and Winant risk both over- and underidentifying racism. To name all essentialist projects as racist elides the distinction that Fuss herself elucidates between lapsing into essentialism and deploying essentialism. To condemn all essentialist projects as problematic is to "essentialize essentialism" (Fuss 1989, 21).[3] In fact, essentialism is neither inherently progressive nor reactionary. (Similarly, the idea that race is not a natural but a socially constructed category is not ineluctably tied to either progressive or conservative racial projects; many conservatives argue that it is precisely because race is socially constructed that it should be ignored.[4])

Essentialist conceptions of race as a natural hierarchy might well operate to reinforce subordination, but anti-essentialist arguments like those deployed against race-conscious voting rights remedies or affirmative action can in fact operate to reinforce subordination by undermining the idea of race as a cognizable and legally significant social reality. The problem, then, is neither essentialism nor anti-essentialism per se, but rather the normative and political work we mobilize these discursive practices to perform. After all, to speak of black people as such is always already to engage in essentialism. As Omi and Winant acknowledge, invoking "Black people" or "the Black community" does not in and of itself create or reproduce "structures of domination based on essentialist categories of race" (Omi and Winant 1994, 71–72).

As we make clear below, we are not arguing that the theory of racial formation necessitates a liberal understanding of affirmative action. Nor do we intend to conflate Omi and Winant's analysis with the conservative colorblind perspective, as there are important distinctions. Rather, our point is that Omi and Winant's concerns about "racial lumping" in the voting rights context and innocent white victims in the affirmative action context are not necessary entailments of racial formation theory but reflect a normative ambivalence that Omi and Winant can—and indeed should—jettison. To the extent that they do not do so, one of their political aims—to expose and contest the racial project of colorblindness—will remain unfulfilled.

This brings us to our own contribution to this volume, which is precisely to take up Omi and Winant's challenge to expose and contest colorblind racial projects. We pursue this goal by offering an alternative framework through which to conceptualize race-conscious remedies in general and affirmative action programs in particular. More specifically, our intervention is to disrupt not only the description of such remedies as preferences but also the characterization of their absence as racially neutral. Amplifying Omi and Winant's theoretical insights—particularly their claim that "it is not possible to represent race discursively without simultaneously locating it, explicitly or implicitly, in a social construct . . . context" (Omi and Winant 1994, 60)—we reveal the malleability of two terms that overdetermine our racial "common sense": racial preferences and racial neutrality (60).

Our context for this engagement is admissions. As best we can, we step outside the question of how we align ourselves in the affirmative action debate (we are proponents of affirmative action policy) and interrogate the premises of anti–affirmative action initiatives like Proposal 209 and Proposal 2. Our interrogation takes the form of a seemingly simple and straightforward thought experiment: what, concretely, does it mean to make institutional processes or decision-making colorblind or race neutral? How might admissions officials implement colorblindness or race neutrality in the context of admitting a university's entering class?

In addition to an evaluation of "objective" measures of academic achievement, such as standardized test scores and grade point averages, college and university admission requirements also include an assessment of letters of recommendation and personal statements. The personal statement plays a particularly important role in an applicant's file; admissions officers read these statements to ascertain whether an applicant's potential contributions to the school extend beyond the numerical scores, while applicants employ the personal statement as a way to quite literally inscribe themselves into and personalize the application. Because personal statements play such a critical role, it is important to consider the question, What do "anti-preference" mandates require with respect to personal statements?

Focusing on the personal statement, we demonstrate that excising race from admissions is far from simple. Indeed, so long as the personal statement is part of the admissions process, implementing the colorblind imperative of Proposition 209 and Proposal 2 might not even be possible.

First, an applicant's file can contain not only direct or explicit racial signifiers (e.g., "As a young Latina . . .") but also indirect or implicit racial signifiers (e.g., "My name is Maria Hernandez and I have lived all my life in East Los Angeles," or even, "I have lived all my life in East Los Angeles"). Because race can be embedded in an applicant's name, geographical connections, and other non-race-specific references, eliminating explicit and direct references to racial categories or racial group membership is not the same thing as eliminating race altogether.

Second, the fact that an admissions officer understands that she is not supposed to take race into account does not mean that she is in a cognitive position to comply with that command. Studies in social psychology suggest that, notwithstanding efforts to ignore race, race remains salient— an elephant in the mind. How this impacts the admissions officer's reading of any given file is hard to know. The broader point is that preventing the explicit consideration of race is not the same thing as preventing any consideration of race.

Third, even assuming that an admissions file contains no racial markers whatsoever (i.e., no implicit or explicit racial signifiers), at least one line of research in social psychology provides a basis for concluding that an admissions officer's default presumption will be that the applicant is white. To the extent that this is the case, race remains a part of the admissions process.

Significantly, our claim that it is unlikely that race can be excised from the admissions process—and that elimination of the express consideration of race is not *the* elimination of race *tout court*—is only half of the story. As we show in what follows, prohibiting explicit references to race in the context of admissions does not make admissions processes race neutral. On the contrary, employing the standard definition of "preferential treatment" (the " 'giving of priority or advantage to one person over . . . others' "[5]), we argue this racial prohibition installs what we call a *new racial preference*.

From the applicant's perspective, colorblind admissions regimes that require applicants to exclude references to race in order to comply with the ban on considering race create an incentive for applicants to suppress their racial identity and to adopt the position that race does not matter in their lives. This incentive structure is likely to be particularly costly to applicants for whom race is a central part of their social experience and sense of identity. The life stories of many people—particularly with regard to describing disadvantage—simply do not make sense without reference to race. Their lives may become unintelligible to admissions officials and unrecognizable to themselves.

Of course, how one presents oneself in the context of any admissions process is ultimately a question of choice: applicants can ultimately choose whether to make their racial identity essential or inessential, salient or insignificant. Our point is simply that a formally colorblind admissions process exerts significant pressures and incentives that constrain that choice and inhibit the very self-expression that the personal statement is intended to encourage. This is at least one sense in which, in a colorblind admissions process, applicants are neither similarly situated nor competing on a level playing field. The dissimilarity among applicants and the unevenness of the field is a function of the racial preference colorblind admissions regimes produce. This racial preference benefits applicants who (a) view their racial identity as irrelevant or inessential and (b) make no express mention of it in the application process. These applicants are advantaged vis-à-vis applicants for whom race is a fundamental part of their sense of self.

The racial preference enacted by colorblind admissions regimes is also discernible from the institutional side of the application process. Should an applicant describe herself in explicitly racial terms because her racial identity and experiences are an important part of who she is, she is disadvantaged in a colorblind admissions process in two ways. First, readers of admissions files who encounter a personal statement from an applicant who asserts her racial identity confront the dilemma of whether they can legitimately consider the statement as it stands, whether doing so would constitute "cheating," or whether the statement can or should be racially cleansed. Whichever option is pursued, the reader must wrestle with whether and how this racial information can be processed. Because of uncertainty about the way racially marked information should be managed, the file risks being classified as problematic; files without explicit racial references do not pose such difficulties.

Second, to read the file in a "colorblind" way, the admissions officer would likely have to ignore highly relevant information, without which the applicant's personal statement might not make sense. Candidates whose personal statements avoid references to race do not face these risks. This is another sense in which colorblind admissions processes are tilted to prefer applicants who subordinate or suppress their race.

As should already be apparent, the new racial preference that formally race-free admissions processes create is not a preference for a racial category per se. Nor is this a preference "on the basis of skin color," which is how opponents of affirmative action characterize the policy. The new racial preference gives a priority or advantage to applicants who choose to suppress, or are perceived as suppressing, their racial identity over those not (or perceived as not) so choosing.

One might think of this preference as a kind of racial viewpoint discrimination, analogous to the viewpoint distinction or preference that the First Amendment prohibits. Race is the "content," and colorblindness and racial consciousness the competing "viewpoints." Just as the government's regulation of speech must be content neutral and cannot be based on the viewpoint expressed, a university's regulation of admissions should be content neutral and should not burden or prefer applicants based on the racial viewpoint their personal statements express.

To be clear, we are not employing the terms *content* and *viewpoint* in their strict First Amendment sense. We employ them here as heuristics to make the point that racial viewpoints are expressed not only at the level of explicitly articulated ideas but also at the level of identity. In this respect, it bears mentioning that most people believe that race exists as a social relation, but they differ as to its meaning, its social and legal significance, and how it should be expressed and embodied. They would agree that race has "content" (at least in the minimalist sense of racial categorization), but disagree about the "viewpoint" race should express.

Note that in the context of any given admissions pool, black students could be in the category of students for whom race is not an essential part of their identity, and white students could be among the students for whom race is central to their self-definition. This is not to say that whites and nonwhites are likely to be equally represented in both categories. The effects of the colorblind racial preference may well be racially disproportionate. In other words, as an empirical matter, it could be that a greater proportion of racial minorities as compared to whites consider race to be a salient and constitutive part of who they are (Robinson 2008, 1127, 1124; see also R. Friedman and Davidson 1999, 213). While this disparate impact is important, it is not the focus of our critique. Our primary objective is to highlight the role the personal statement plays in the context of admissions in order to demonstrate that Proposition 209 and Proposal 2 neither eliminate race from admissions nor make admissions processes racially neutral. Both initiatives produce a new racial preference that has gone largely unnoticed.

To develop these arguments more fully, we draw on the life experiences of two public figures as relayed in their autobiographies: Barack Obama, president of the United States, and Clarence Thomas, a Supreme Court justice.[6] First, we draw on these accounts to construct personal statements as if each subject were a hypothetical candidate for admission to a selective college, university, or graduate program. We then examine these statements from the university's perspective. Here we ask, Can an admissions committee read race out of the personal statement, and what are the consequences of doing so? Our hope is to demonstrate the persistence of race even in formally race-free admissions regimes such as those implemented in response to Proposition 209 and Proposal 2.

THE APPLICANT: CONSTRUCTING THE PERSONAL STATEMENT

While the specific question can differ from school to school, the personal statement generally calls on applicants to provide a personal narrative in which they describe something unique about themselves. Others call on applicants to provide information regarding "disadvantage overcome."

In this section, we take autobiographical statements from President Barack Obama to construct a hypothetical personal statement. We do so for four principal reasons: (1) to identify the burdens imposed on applicants by "anti-preference initiatives" like Proposal 2 and Proposition 209 that are interpreted to require that applicants not include references to race in their personal statements; (2) to explain how racial erasure does not make the application process racially neutral; (3) to illustrate some of the subtle but significant ways in which racial advantages and disadvantages can persist in formally race-free admissions environments; and (4) to reveal that racial formation occurs not only at the level of social structures but also at the level of identity expression. This last point is particularly important given Omi and Winant's definition of racial formation as a "the sociohistorical process by which racial categories are created, inhabited, transformed and destroyed" (Omi and Winant 1994, 55).

In a way, our interest lies in demonstrating how the discursive self-representational choices an individual makes in the context of writing her personal statement can *create* a particular racial persona, signal specifically how she *inhabits* her racial identity, effectuate a *transformation* of that identity, and effectively *destroy* core parts of her racial sense of self. Understood in this way, the personal statement becomes a significant site for the enactment or performance of race, which is to say, a site for racial formation.

The foregoing raises the question of whether Omi and Winant recognize the performative dimensions of race. And indeed they do. They rightly observe that "we expect people to act out their apparent racial identities; indeed, we become disoriented when they do not" (Omi and Winant 1994,

59). Yet Omi and Winant do not explore the implications of this insight for their theory, perhaps because their analysis is largely superstructurally oriented. In this respect, one might read our engagement with how applicants inscribe themselves in their personal statements as an effort to broaden the theoretical terms on which racial formation is understood. We begin this engagement with a "personal statement" based on Barack Obama's *Dreams from My Father: A Story of Race and Inheritance.*[7]

Dreams from My Father: Pieces of a Story of Race and Inheritance

That my father looked nothing like the people around me—that he was black as pitch, my mother white as milk—barely registered in my mind.

In fact, I can recall only one story that dealt explicitly with the subject of race. . . . According to the story, after long hours of study, my father had joined my grandfather and several other friends at a local Waikiki bar. Everyone was in a festive mood, eating and drinking to the sounds of a slack-key guitar, when a white man abruptly announced to the bartender, loudly for everyone to hear, that he shouldn't have to drink good liquor "next to a nigger." The room fell quiet and people turned to my father, expecting a fight. Instead, my father stood up, walked over to the man, smiled, and proceeded to lecture him about the folly of bigotry, the promise of the American dream, and the universal rights of man. "This fella felt so bad when Barack was finished," Gramps would say, "that he reached into his pocket and gave Barack a hundred dollars on the spot."

[Multiracial.] "I am not black," Joyce said. "I'm multiracial. . . . It's not white people who are making me choose [one part of my identity]. Maybe it used to be that way, but now they are willing to treat me like a person. No—it's black people who always have to make everything racial. They're the ones making me choose."

They, they, they. That was the problem with people like Joyce. They talked about the richness of their multicultural heritage and it sounded real good, until you noticed that they avoided black people. It wasn't a matter of conscious choice, necessarily, just a matter of gravitational pull, the way integration always worked, a one-way street. The minority assimilated into the dominant culture, not the other way around. Only white culture could be neutral and objective. Only white culture could be nonracial, willing to adopt the occasional exotic into its ranks. Only white culture had individuals. And we, the half-breeds and the college-degreed, take a survey of the situation and think to ourselves, Why should we get lumped in with the losers if we don't have to? We become so grateful to lose ourselves in the crowd, America's happy, faceless marketplace; and we're never so outraged as when a cabbie drives past us or the woman in the elevator clutches her purse, not so much because we're bothered by the fact that such indignities are what less fortunate coloreds have to put up with every single day of their lives—although that's what we tell ourselves—but because we're wearing a Brooks Brothers suit and speak impeccable English and yet have somehow been mistaken for an ordinary nigger.

[Community organizing.] In 1983, I decided to become a community organizer. . . . That's what I'll do. I'll organize black folks. At the grass roots. For change. . . . [I] wrote to every civil rights organization I could think of, to any black elected official in the country with a progressive agenda, to neighborhood councils and tenant rights groups. When no one wrote back, I wasn't discouraged. I decided to find more conventional work for a year, to pay off my student loans and maybe even save a little bit.

Eventually a consulting house to multinational corporations agreed to hire me as a research assistant. . . . As far as I could tell, I was the only black man in the company, a source of shame for me but a source of considerable pride for some of the company's secretarial pool. They treated me like a son, those black ladies; they told me how they expected me to run the company one day. . . . [A]s the months passed, I felt the idea of becoming a community organizer slipping from me. . . . I turned in my resignation at the consulting firm and began looking in earnest for an organizing job. . . . In six months I was broke, unemployed, eating soup from a can.

[Divided soul?] When people who don't know me well, black or white, discover my background (and it's usually a discovery, for I ceased to advertise my mother's race at the age of twelve or thirteen, when I began to suspect that by doing so I was ingratiating myself to whites), I see the spilt-second adjustments they have to make, the searching of my eyes for some telltale sign. They no longer know who I am. Privately, they guess at my troubled heart, I suppose—the mixed blood, the divided soul, the ghostly image of the tragic mulatto trapped between two worlds. And if I were to explain that no, the tragedy is not mine, at least not mine alone, it is yours, sons and daughters of Plymouth Rock and Ellis Island, it is yours . . . well, I suspect that I sound incurably naive. . . . Or worse, I sound like I'm trying to hide from myself.

Does This Statement Violate the Mandate for Colorblindness?

Let's imagine that Barack Obama sat down and wrote the foregoing account as his personal statement for the law school application process. And let's assume that he believes that the above narrative best captures who he is as an individual and his normative commitments about family, community, and nation.

Assume further that Obama is interested in the University of California, Berkeley, School of Law as his second choice. He believes that the history of student activism at Berkeley suggests that the law school will be a good fit for a person who is interested in community organizing. However, he is concerned about Proposition 209 because since its implementation, the number of black law students at the law school has diminished. Indeed, in 1997, the very first year that Proposition 209 took effect, Berkeley Law enrolled only one black student. Although numbers at Berkeley Law have improved since then, they are not nearly as high as they were in the pre-209 days.[8]

Nor is Obama's concern just about how the demographics of a law school's student body might impact that school's institutional culture and environment, though this is certainly on his mind. Indeed, he has read Claude Steele's work on stereotype threat and its impact on groups like black students that are subject to negative societal stereotypes. According to Steele, black students tend to underperform on academic assessments like high-stakes tests because of a concern that their performance might confirm negative stereotypes about black intellectual inferiority (Steele 1997). Obama queries whether this "threat in the air" (Steele 1997) might actually be heightened as a function of small black enrollment. But, again, his worries do not end here. He is deeply concerned about the application itself. His questions, specifically, are these: Does the fact that his personal statement is explicitly racialized violate Proposition 209? Should he strike all references to race from his personal statement? Would any reference to race in his background violate the norm of colorblindness that Proposition 209 purportedly instantiates?

Obama searches Berkeley Law's admissions materials for an answer to this question. The admissions policies state simply that "race . . . [is] not used as a criterion for admission." On the other hand, there is no clear direction in the admissions material that prohibits any mention of race. Indeed, the school invites applicants to relate how they may have overcome disadvantage including "a personal or family history of cultural, educational, or socioeconomic disadvantage." Shouldn't this include racial disadvantage? Or would even these racial references be impermissible?

A number of options are available to Obama. He could decide not to apply to Berkeley Law. He could believe that doing so would require him to suppress an important sense of himself: his racial identity and experiences. But let's suppose that Obama decides to apply. He then asks:

"What if I simply removed all references of race from my personal statement? Presumably that would satisfy Proposition 209's investment in colorblindness." He proceeds to do precisely that, producing the personal statement below.

Redacted Statement

That my father looked nothing like the people around me ~~that he was black as pitch, my mother white as milk~~ barely registered in my mind. ~~In fact, I can recall only one story that dealt explicitly with the subject of race....~~ According to the story, after long hours of study, my father had joined my grandfather and several other friends at a local Waikiki bar. Everyone was in a festive mood, eating and drinking to the sounds of a slack-key guitar, when a ~~white~~ man abruptly announced to the bartender, loudly for everyone to hear, that he shouldn't have to drink good liquor ~~"next to a nigger."~~ next to my father. The room fell quiet and people turned to my father, expecting a fight. Instead, my father stood up, walked, walked over to the man, smiled, and proceeded to lecture him about ~~the folly of bigotry,~~ the promise of the American dream, and the universal rights of man. "This fella felt so bad when Barack was finished," Gramps would say, "that he reached into his pocket and gave Barack a hundred dollars on the spot."

[Multiracial.] "I am not black," Joyce said. "I'm multiracial. . . . It's not white people who are making me choose [one part of my identity]. Maybe it used to be that way, but now they are willing to treat me like person. No—it's black people who always have to make everything racial. They're the ones making me choose."

They, they, they. That was the problem with people like Joyce. They talked about the richness of their multicultural heritage and it sounded real good, until you noticed that they avoided ~~black~~ people. It wasn't a matter of conscious choice, necessarily, just a matter of gravitational pull, the way integration always worked, a one-way street. ~~The minority assimilated into the dominant culture, not the other way around. Only white culture could be neutral and objective. Only white culture could be nonracial, willing to adopt the occasional exotic into its ranks. Only white culture had individuals.~~ And we, ~~the half-breeds and~~ the college-degreed, take a survey of the situation and think to ourselves, Why should we get lumped in with the losers if we don't have to? We become so grateful to lose ourselves in the crowd, America's happy, faceless marketplace; and we're never so outraged as when a cabbie drives past us or the woman in the elevator clutches her purse, not so much because we're bothered by the fact that such indignities are what less fortunate ~~coloreds~~ people have to put up with every single day of their lives—although that's what we tell ourselves—but because we're wearing a Brooks Brothers suit and speak impeccable English and yet have somehow been mistaken for an ordinary ~~nigger~~ person.

[Community organizing] In 1983, I decided to become a community organizer. . . . That's what I'll do. I'll organize folks. At the grass roots. For change. . . . Wrote to every civil rights organization I could think of, to any ~~black~~ elected official in the country with a progressive agenda, to neighborhood councils and tenant rights groups. When no one wrote back, I wasn't discouraged. I decided to find more conventional work for a year, to pay off my student loans and maybe even save a little bit.

Eventually a consulting house to multinational corporations agreed to hire me as a research assistant. . . . As far as I could tell, I was the only ~~black~~ man in the company, a source of shame for me but a source of considerable pride for some of the company's secretarial pool. They treated me like a son, those ~~black~~ ladies; they told me how they expected me to run the company one day. . . . [A]s the months passed, I felt the idea of becoming a community organizer slipping from me . . . I turned in my resignation at the consulting firm and began looking in earnest for an organizing job. . . . In six months I was broke, unemployed, eating soup from a can.

[Divided Soul?] When people who don't know me well, ~~black or white,~~ discover my background (and it's usually a discovery, for I ceased to advertise my mother's identity at the age of twelve or thirteen, when I began to suspect that by doing so I was ingratiating myself ~~to whites~~), I see the spilt-second adjustments they have to make, the searching of my eyes for some telltale sign. They no longer know who I am. Privately, they guess my at my troubled heart, I suppose ~~— the mixed blood,~~ the divided soul, the ghostly image of the tragic ~~mulatto~~ person trapped between two worlds. And if I were to explain that no, the tragedy is not mine, at least not mine alone, it is yours, sons and daughters of Plymouth Rock and Ellis Island, it is yours . . . well, I suspect that I sound incurably naive. . . . Or worse, I sound like I'm trying to hide from myself.

Upon examining the statement, Obama notes that even if he endeavors to eliminate only explicit references to race, the statement sounds completely unlike his actual experience. Simply excising specific references to his race or the race of his parents renders his life story unintelligible. For example, deleting explicit references to race changes the statement "As far as I could tell, I was the only black man in the company" to "As far as I could tell, I was the only man in the company," which is simply inaccurate. The story about his father sounds like just another barroom brawl; the references to interracial marriage are incomprehensible. In the absence of any reference to Obama's race, his reluctance to speak about his mother to others and his sense that people speculate about his tragically divided soul read like symptoms of mental imbalance or paranoia. Of course, Obama could eliminate these passages and substitute others. But this alternative also presents problems. Exactly what constitutes a racial reference? Subtle references to knowledge about particular practices (like multiracial identity) also betray a racial basis of knowledge that can be a proxy for a person's racial identity.

Obama decides to revisit the question of whether he can transcribe his life in nonracial terms, not by editing what he has already written or by substituting race with some other social category, but by starting again from scratch. After spending several hours on this project, he can't seem to come up with a meaningful account of his life without referencing race. In a state of identity fatigue, he decides, at least for the moment, to suspend his application to Berkeley Law.

The Costs of Restricting Race

The foregoing hypothetical suggests that applicants who wish to make race salient—what we call race-positive applicants—face a number of burdens. First, even after learning that the admissions policies provide that race cannot be considered in the process, it is not altogether clear precisely what that means. Does this prohibit any mention of race, or specify simply that race qua race cannot be taken into account as a plus on behalf of the applicant? The uncertainty about the racial restrictions that anti-preference regimes impose on applicants could compel the expenditure of extra time and ultimately extra effort. Applicants for whom race is not a salient aspect of their identity, "race-negative applicants," do not have to perform this extra work.[9]

Indeed, race-positive applicants have to struggle with whether they can represent themselves without reference to their race or, even if they elect to include race-specific information, have to evaluate how much information will be seen as "going too far," and hence will become counterproductive. Just thinking about this is work, particularly in the context of a broader concern about making oneself competitive in an extremely competitive process . Time and energy spent thinking about how to present one's racial identity could be reallocated to other parts of the application process, which even absent these questions is demanding.

Should race-positive applicants believe that too many references to race will be seen as an inappropriate effort to solicit prohibited racial consideration, there is the work of actually rewriting the personal statement. In a world where there are both affirmative action and non-affirmative-action law schools, race-positive prospective law students likely will be applying to both. This may require that an applicant rewrite his personal statement to satisfy what he perceives to be the dictates of Proposition 209. Assuming an applicant believes he can do this, it entails serious intellectual and emotional work—work that colorblind admissions processes do not require of race-negative applicants.

If a race-positive applicant determines that he is not able to reimagine˙ himself in colorblind terms, and therefore decides not to apply to a non-affirmative-action law school, (a) his access to legal education (and quite possibly his options in the legal profession) has been diminished, and (b) he must accept the notion that there is something about his racial experiences and sense of identity that is negative. More than that, he must accept that within anti-preference and ostensibly colorblind institutional settings, his race-conscious identity is quasi-illegal—something that must remain undocumented.

Moreover, if the race-positive applicant finds that he is able to reinscribe himself in race-neutral terms, and is ultimately accepted to a law school that does not practice affirmative action, he will likely wonder whether that law school will expect him to embody his race neutrality in his everyday interactions and overall identity as a law student. Moreover, he might worry whether at such a law school most, if not all, of the nonwhite law students will be race-neutral, which would diminish his ability to form at least some identity-specific communities.

Any one of the foregoing costs is meaningful. Cumulatively, they are substantial. While we are not making an empirical argument, there is at least a strong theoretical basis for thinking that the costs we enumerate above are real. Although these costs are likely to disproportionately affect people of color, there are race-positive white people who would experience these costs as well.

THE INSTITUTION: READING THE PERSONAL
STATEMENT

Thus far, we have focused on how applicants might racially form themselves in their personal statement in response to the requirement of colorblindness in Proposition 209 and Proposal 2. We now shift the discussion from individuals to institutions. Here, we ask, How do non-affirmative-action colleges and universities operationalize the mandate of anti-preference initiatives? What, concretely, does it mean to not take race into account when deciding which applicants to admit? What institutional form does this racial project take? To answer this question, we draw on the life and jurisprudence of Supreme Court justice Clarence Thomas. Our aim is to show that while Thomas has extolled the value of colorblindness, his own life story reveals why, in the context of admissions, compelling a colorblind approach is both impracticable and normatively unsatisfying.

Against Race? Justice Thomas's Affirmative Action Jurisprudence

Justice Thomas has been a vocal critic of race-conscious remedies on the ground that they violate the legal and moral mandate of colorblindness.[10] What distinguishes his opinions from those of other justices who share his views, such as Justice Antonin Scalia, is that Justice Thomas frequently invokes black cultural references or adopts a specifically black subject position.[11]

Consider, for example, *United States v. Fordice,* a case in which the Supreme Court explored the constitutionality of desegregation mandates in higher education and the tension between dismantling a dual system (i.e., one in which whites and blacks are formally racially segregated) and the existence of historically black colleges and universities. Thomas begins his concurrence in that case with a quotation from W. E. B. DuBois: "We must rally to the defense of our schools. We must repudiate this unbearable assumption of the right to kill institutions unless they conform to one narrow standard."[12]

Similarly in *Missouri v. Jenkins,* a case in which a lower court had ordered the school district to make major financial investments to address inequalities under the idea of increasing "desegregative attractiveness," Thomas, along with the majority, struck down the remedial measures and declared the Kansas City school system to be unitary—that is, not de jure racially segregated into black and white schools. Thomas adopted this approach, notwithstanding pervasive de facto segregation and inequality.[13] More relevant for our purposes, he denounced the lower court's intervention, stating, "It never ceases to amaze me that the courts are so willing to assume that anything that is predominately black must be inferior."[14] In these and other cases Thomas either implicitly or explicitly marks himself as black, or draws upon black culture, history, or intellectual traditions, to argue for colorblindness. And it is precisely the fact that he is black that makes his commitment to colorblindness particularly productive (in the Foucauldian sense).

While Thomas vehemently eschews government policies like affirmative action that rely on or take cognizance of race, even if those policies seek to enhance equality, his autobiography explicitly articulates the role race played in shaping his life experiences and achievements. Of course, to say that one is opposed to the state engaging in practices that rely on race and yet assert a specific racial identity as an individual is not inherently contradictory. Yet for Thomas, the repeated assertion of racial identity belies any notion that he sees himself as a person for whom race was irrelevant, despite his conservative commitments. In his autobiography, *My Grandfather's Son*,[15] he relates the story of his beginnings in rural Georgia in the late 1940s and his experience as one of only a handful of blacks attending schools with whites in the early days of desegregation. It is a story of poverty, perseverance—and race.

Pieces of My Life as My Grandfather's Son

Imagine that Clarence Thomas has applied to the University of Michigan Law School and that he offers the personal statement below in support of his candidacy.

> I am descended from the West African slaves who lived on the barrier islands and in the low country of Georgia, South Carolina, and coastal northern Florida. In Georgia my people were called Geechees, in South Carolina, Gullahs. They were isolated from the rest of the population, black and white alike, and so maintained their distinctive dialect and culture well into the twentieth century. What little remains of Geechee life is now celebrated by scholars of black folklore, but when I was a boy, "Geechee" was a derogatory term for Georgians who had profoundly Negroid features and spoke with a foreign-sounding accent similar to the dialects heard on certain Caribbean islands. . . . Pinpoint [where I was born] is a heavily wooded twenty-five acre peninsula on Shipyard Creek, a tidal salt creek ten miles southeast of Savannah. A shady quiet enclave full of pines, palms, live oaks, and low-hanging Spanish moss, it feels cut off from the rest of the world and it was even more isolated in the fifties than it is today. Then as now, Pinpoint was too small to properly be called a town. No more than a hundred people lived

there, most of whom were related to me in one way or another. Their lives were a daily struggle for the barest of essentials, food, clothing and shelter. Doctors were few and far between, so when you got sick, you stayed that way, and often you died of it. The house in which I was born was a shanty with no bathroom and no electricity except for a single light in the living room. Kerosene lamps lit the rest of the house [x].

[After I began school, the house where my family and I lived was destroyed in a fire started accidentally by my cousins.] After that [my mother] took my brother and me to Savannah, where she was keeping house for a man who drove a potato-chip delivery truck. We moved into her one-room apartment on the second floor of a tenement on the west side of town. . . . Overnight I moved from the comparative safety and cleanliness of rural poverty to the foulest kind of urban squalor. The only running water in our building was downstairs in the kitchen. . . . The toilet was outdoors in the muddy backyard. . . . I'll never forget the sickening stench of the raw sewage that seeped and sometimes poured from the broken sewer line [6].

[After that winter, my mother decided to send my brother and me to live with our grandparents.] The main reason must have been that she simply couldn't take care of two energetic young boys while holding down a full-time job that paid only ten dollars a week. . . . Since she refused to go on welfare, she needed some kind of help, and I suspect that my grandfather told her that we would either live with him permanently or not at all [8–9].

The family farm and our unheated oil truck became my most important classrooms, the schools in which Daddy passed on the wisdom he had acquired in the course of a long life as an ill-educated, modestly successful black man in the Deep South. Despite the hardships he had faced, there was no bitterness or self-pity in his heart. As for bad luck, he didn't believe in it. Instead he put his faith in his own unaided effort—the one factor in his life he could control—and he taught [my brother] Myers and me to do the same. Unable to do anything about the racial bigotry and lack of education that had narrowed his own horizons, he put his hope for the future in "my two boys," as he always called us. We were his second chance to live, to take part in America's opportunities, and he was willing to sacrifice his own comfort so that they would be fully open to us [26–27].

What's Race Got to Do with It?

Imagine that the dean of admissions at the University of Michigan Law School, Michelle Philips, picks up Thomas's file as one of many that she will read as part of the admissions process. She instantly encounters the way in which race is prominently noted in Thomas's personal statement and worries that this might create a problem in light of Proposal 2. Given that Proposal 2 is a very recent legal mandate, she has virtually no institutional memory to draw on. After reading Thomas's file several times, she explores four approaches, none of which is satisfying.

Literally Removing All References to Race. Philips could begin by striking all references of race from the personal statement.[16] Imagine that she endeavors to do just that. There is no question in Philips's mind about whether the terms *black* and *white* should be stricken; thus, she is comfortable removing both. However, she is not at all clear about whether nonconsideration of race requires her to strike a number of other terms, among them *Caribbean, slave, Geechees,* and *segregation.* She worries that race might be embedded in each term, even though none of them explicitly signifies a particular racial identity. Moreover, somewhat familiar with recent studies in social psychology, she knows that striking this information from the file will not erase Thomas's racial identity from her mind or the minds of other reviewers.[17] Her efforts to suppress what she already knows—that Thomas is black—likely will be ineffective.

Philips now considers excising references to race from Thomas's statement and then passing his file on to another reader. Perhaps that reader—one without her personal knowledge of Thomas's original racially infused statement—would be able to read Thomas's file in a "race-free" manner. However, she worries that her editing will not prevent another reader from reading race into Thomas's statement, because it is likely that in the absence of explicit nonwhite racial references, her colleagues will presume that Thomas is white. This presumption is not illogical, since empirically, the majority of applicants to graduate school are white.[18] But even beyond that fact, a line of research in social psychology suggests that in the absence of an indication that a person is not white, the default presumption is that the person is white. Philips is troubled by this. She is now not at all sure that Thomas's file can be race-neutrally read. She comes to realize that, if Thomas's statement is considered as written, he is racially marked as black, while if it is successfully purged, he is presumptively white. Under neither condition is the process truly race-free. In both scenarios Thomas is explicitly or implicitly racially marked. Stumped by this, Philips decides to adopt another approach.

Imagining That Clarence Thomas Is White. Philips is aware that, in the context of admissions, colorblindness is sometimes formulated in terms of whether whites and nonwhites are treated the same. To ensure that no unfair consideration is given to Thomas because he is black, one might ask the counterfactual question, Would the applicant have been admitted if she were white? Philips tries to operationalize this standard with respect to Thomas's personal statement. To do so, she treats the statement as if a white person had written it. Upon doing so, she quickly realizes two things. First, significant parts of Thomas's story are incomprehensible from the racial subjectivity of a white person. Consider Thomas's statement of his origins: "I am descended from the West African slaves who lived on the barrier islands and in the low country of Georgia, South Carolina, and coastal northern Florida." Here, the statement makes little sense if Philips imagines Thomas as a white person. Indeed, it renders much of the statement unintelligible.

Philips's other reaction to this identity-switching approach is that it might not be race-neutral or colorblind at all. Reading Thomas's statement as though he were white simply substitutes one racial identity frame (white) for another (black).

Evaluate the Quality of the Writing—Not the Experience. Another way Philips might try to process Thomas's personal statement is to read his story for its prose, not its content—for its form, not its substance. But there are several problems with this approach.

First, to the extent that Philips is not evaluating other personal statements in this way, she is treating Thomas differently; for some, that alone might be cause for concern, particularly if the difference in treatment is framed as a process failure. Second, this different treatment substantively disadvantages Thomas. This is because personal statements are read primarily as a window on the applicant's character, experiences, and aspirations. They are read chiefly (though not entirely) for substance, not form. Third, such an approach would systematically disadvantage race-positive applicants. Because it is reasonable to assume that nonwhites are more likely to have a race-positive sense of identity than whites, reading personal statements for prose could have a disparate impact that would be far from race-neutral.

No Race-Neutral Way Out: Risk, Anger, or Indecision. Because of the difficulties of each of the foregoing approaches, Philips ends up feeling rather flustered about Thomas's file. What exactly is she to do? On the one hand, she could argue that there is an important difference between considering race as a plus factor in making a decision about whether to admit Thomas—that is, considering Thomas's black racial identity—and considering Thomas's life under pervasive racial segregation—that is, considering Thomas's black racial experiences. Proposal 2 arguably prohibits only the former, not the latter.[19] However, she notes that advocates of Proposal 2, like Ward Connerly, contend that any mention of race anywhere in the application invites a violation of the law and that applicants whose files reflect any racial information should be denied admission.[20] While empathic with Thomas's application, Philips may worry that any decision on his behalf will be subject to particular scrutiny and may invite litigation.

She may even feel angry about the fact that Thomas has put her in this position. Surely, given the language of the application for admissions, he knows that Proposal 2 forbids the school from taking race into account in the context of admissions? Why, then, would he write a statement that is so explicitly racially infused? Is he hoping that the school will cheat or, put more bluntly, violate the law? Is he providing a means by which the school might do so? Was he simply too lazy to spend the time to write a race-neutral application?[21] Or is he too racially invested to conceive of himself outside of race?[22]

Assuming that Philips is not angered or annoyed by Thomas's application, she might be inclined to categorize this file as a "hold"—a file difficult to process—leading Philips to make no decision as she tries to sort through whether or how to consider Thomas's statement. Thomas's file has now been placed in an ambiguous status and possibly in a negative light all because race is salient to his self-perception. Thomas's file would not raise any of these questions if race did not figure explicitly in his personal statement.

Many schools invite applicants to relate aspects of their background. Sometimes schools expressly invite applicants to relate personal or family history, including details about cultural, educational, or socioeconomic disadvantage. In Thomas's case, that history of disadvantage is also racial. Without reference to race, Thomas's story would be both incomplete and incomprehensible. The difficult position Thomas finds himself in here exposes the problem of formally removing race from an admissions process against a social backdrop in which race both matters and is cognizable. Under the colorblind hegemony of Proposition 209 and Proposal 2,

Thomas remains black and his racial experiences remain real, but neither can be expressly articulated.

CONCLUSION

Our project in this chapter is to reveal how the ideology of colorblindness obscures the racial preferences of "anti-preference" initiatives like Proposition 209 and Proposal 2. To borrow from Omi and Winant, Proposition 209 and Proposal 2 are racial projects that their proponents mobilize—employing the language of colorblindness and race neutrality—to produce the very thing against which both initiatives are ostensibly positioned—racial preferences.

The question then becomes, Why do these regimes continue to have standing as colorblind and race-neutral processes? This is an issue we explore more fully elsewhere. There, we note that a central problem lies in our tendency to conflate the normative assertion that "race *should not* matter" with the empirical assertion that "race *does not* matter." In that other work we also endeavor to clarify the debate by more fully challenging the notion that colorblindness is a mechanism through which race neutrality can be achieved. This conception of colorblindness (as a technology for race neutrality) is part of the same discursive field from which a related racial idea has grown: race consciousness leads ineluctably to racial preferences. These conceptual predicates are deeply flawed. We contest them to clear the ground for an understanding of "anti-preference" initiatives as racial preferences.[23]

Our intervention in this essay focuses almost entirely on the personal statement. Part of what we have attempted to show is that not formally removing race from an applicant's narrative preserves the individual's prerogative to assert (or not assert) what meaning race holds in her life. This is not a preference but rather a fair and open process that permits colleges and universities to take account of something that has been constitutive of an applicant's life and experiences: race. Applicants remain free to racially inscribe themselves in any way they see fit—or not at all. This strikes us more racially neutral than a system in which only colorblind personal statements are permissible. The latter system not only enacts a racial preference but also effectively creates a racially exclusive admissions criterion in which only colorblind personal statements can "get in."

Both Thomas's and Obama's narratives—in their rich *racial* detail—are important windows on their lives and accomplishments. Their respective narratives suggest that each individual would make a vital contribution to colleges or universities, which, after all, are venues for diverse ideas, perspectives, and experiences.[24] These benefits, and the stories themselves, are potentially lost if Proposition 209 and Proposal 2 are read to preclude the articulation and consideration of race in the admissions process. And new burdens are added, the burdens incidental to being forced to excise race from one's articulation of one's experiences and sense of community and identity.

Proponents of Proposition 209 and Proposal 2 would likely agree with the claim that the state should not force the individual to racially define herself in any particular way. They would also likely agree with the idea that people should have the right to freedom of racial expression, and that the state should not coerce people into occupying particular racial subject positions. Yet "anti-preference" initiatives are being interpreted to do just that—that is, to force individuals to be silent about their racial identity and experiences, a silence that implies the idea that race does not matter. Applicants who break that silence and explicitly inscribe themselves and their experiences in racial terms are disadvantaged.

We think that the implications of this insight extend beyond the structure and consideration of the personal statement. For example, one can easily apply the analysis to the workplace. In that context, as well, the colorblind imperative coerces individuals to downplay if not completely suppress their racial identity.[25] And certainly our analysis is applicable to the political arena, as demonstrated by the discussions that raised the question of whether Barack Obama could afford to be "too black" from the perspective of white people.

Both of the foregoing examples make clear that racial identity can be expressed in different ways and that some expressions are more racially palatable than others. Moreover, the examples illustrate that racial formation occurs at the level of identity performance, not just that of social or political structure. While Barack Obama cannot express himself "out of" the social category of blackness, he can express himself as less racially black. Some voters expected him to do just that. Proponents of Proposition 209 and Proposal 2 would have him do more—to not express himself as black at all, and to racially cleanse himself in the context of his personal statement. Imposing this new racial preference is tantamount to asking

Barack Obama to "pass." The state should not be permitted to do so—and certainly not under the legitimizing guise and false pretense of colorblindness and race neutrality.

Of course, one could take a stronger normative position about why formally excising race from personal statements is problematic. It legitimizes the idea that the way to avoid racism, and more specifically reverse discrimination, is to formally ignore race. We agree with Omi and Winant that this view of race is both wrongheaded and dangerous. Moreover, it limits our ability to eradicate racism. For Omi and Winant, formally paying attention to race is a necessary precondition to eliminating racism: "By noticing race we begin to challenge racism, with its evermore-absurd reduction of human experience to an essence attributed to all without regard for historical or social context. By noticing race we can challenge the state, the institutions of civil society, and ourselves as individuals to combat the legacy of inequality and injustice inherited from the past. By noticing race we can develop the political insight and mobilization necessary to make the U.S. a more racially just and egalitarian society" (1994, 159).

Proposition 209 and Proposal 2 restrict our ability formally to notice race and, in so doing, have made the admissions scales even more racially imbalanced for students of color. The racial asymmetry reflected in and produced by the operation of these initiatives betrays the presumptions behind racial neutrality as a flawed yet powerful racial project. The apparatus crafted by Omi and Winant offers critical analytical tools for continuing to excavate and expose such projects and the racial preferences they instantiate.

NOTES

1. Omi and Winant 1994, 72–73. The full answer is "We think not, with certain qualifications."

2. *Shaw v. Reno*, 509 U.S. 630, 647 (1993).

3. Indeed, Omi and Winant acknowledge this distinction as they affirm the notion of "strategic" essentialism (Omi and Winant 1994, 188n61).

4. For a juridical example of this conservative logic, see *Regents of the University of California v. Bakke*, 438 U.S. 265, 290–97 (1978), challenging the idea of an essential "white majority" and observing that the status of this group was constantly shifting.

5. *Hi-Voltage Works, Inc. v. City of San Jose,* 12 P.3d 1068, 1082 (Cal. 2000), citing *Webster's New Dictionary* (3rd College Ed., 1988).

6. In an extended version of this argument, we also include constructed personal statements based on autobiographical accounts written by Dalton Conley, a white male sociologist, and Margaret Montoya, a Chicana law professor. See Carbado and Harris 2008.

7. New York: Times Books, 1995.

8. See C. Harris 2002, 1236, app. A, noting a similar pattern at UCLA.

9. Note that "race-positive" does not mean that the applicant has a positive view about race. It simply means that race shapes that applicant's sense of herself. Likewise, "race-negative" does not mean that the applicant has negative views about race, but simply that the applicant does not believe that race figures meaningfully in her life.

10. See, e.g., *Adarand Constructors, Inc. v. Pena,* 515 U.S. 200, 240 (1995), Thomas, J., concurring in part and dissenting in part.

11. One of the authors has been exploring the extent to which Thomas's jurisprudence draws upon and invokes black cultural, historical, and political references. See Cheryl I. Harris, "Doubting Thomas and the Anti-Identity Identity" (draft manuscript on file with authors).

12. *United States v. Fordice,* 505 U.S. 717, 745 (1992).

13. *Missouri v. Jenkins,* 515 U.S. 70 (1995).

14. Ibid., Thomas concurrence, at 114.

15. New York: Harper, 2007. Bracketed page numbers in the following refer to this edition.

16. In so doing, Phillips might be emulating the efforts of Ward Connerly in California to erase the box indicating race from the application in order to avoid using the information in making admissions decisions. See Douglass 2007, 205, noting university administrators' resistance to Connerly's proposal on the grounds that it eliminated needed data on the effects of admissions changes, and the ultimate compromise, in which the data were electronically erased from applications before they were read by admissions staff.

17. See Wegner et al. 1987, 6. "Whether people are instructed to ignore the information before they encounter it . . . or are told to disregard it afterwards . . . , they tend to incorporate it into subsequent judgments nonetheless."

18. This presumption derives from the normativity of whiteness and the fact that it operates as a default identity. See Pratto, Korchmaros, and Hegarty 2007, 223: "White Americans generally presume that being White and male is normative." See also Stroessner 1996, 248–249: "Thus, when a racial identity is unspecified the 'cultural expectation' is that the person is white." See Devos and Banaji 2005, 449: "In Western cultures, White racial identity and male gender are treated as cultural expectations. Evidence for this 'White male norm' hypothesis comes from experiments showing that membership in nonnormative groups receives greater attention than membership in normative groups because of its incongruence."

19. The question of whether there is a difference between considering race and considering racial experience surfaced recently in *Coalition to Defend Affirmative Action v. Regents of the University of Michigan,* 539 F. Supp. 2d 924 (E.D. Mich. 2008), where plaintiffs challenged Proposal 2 as unconstitutional. The plaintiffs argued that because race is an important part of how minority students choose to define themselves, state universities cannot delete race and selectively deny applicants the opportunity to have central aspects of their identity considered; this creates in impermissible distinction based on race in violation of the Fourteenth Amendment. *See* Memorandum of Law in support of the Cantrell Plaintiffs' Motion for Summary Judgment, *Coal. to Defend Affirmative Action v. Regents of the Univ. of Mich.,* 539 F. Supp. 2d 924 (E.D. Mich. 2008) (Nos. 06–15024, 06–15637), 2007 WL 4595210. In response, supporters of Proposal 2 countered that while there might be a distinction "between considering race as a per se plus factor in allocating admissions and financial aid," which would be proscribed by Proposal 2, and permitting consideration of "an applicants' unique experiences that might have racial overtones," "any such distinction whether valid or not in principle, [is] highly tenuous in practice, and therefore does not dispute the Cantrell Plaintiffs' implied assumption that Proposal 2's prohibition of 'preferential treatment' on the basis of race prevents the Universities from deliberately providing a forum, in their application process, for applicants . . . to highlight their 'racial identity' to sympathetic reviewers." See Defendant-Intervenor Eric Russell's Memorandum in Opposition to the Cantrell Plaintiffs' Motion for Summary Judgment at *7 n.3, *Coal. to Defend Affirmative Action v. Regents of the Univ. of Mich.,* 539 F. Supp. 2d 924 (E.D. Mich. 2008) (Nos. 06–15024, 06–15637), 2008 WL 2155059. The advocates of Proposal 2 contended that the University of Michigan had in fact improperly provided such a forum in that the University of Michigan's application for undergraduate admission: "def[ies] Proposal 2 and direct[s] all undergraduate applicants to '[c]omment on how your personal experiences and achievements would contribute to the diversity of the University of Michigan.' In light of [the university president's] speech, it is difficult to view this mandatory essay without cynicism, indeed, as a calculated ploy to encourage minority applicants to publish racial information, otherwise forbidden by law, to a sympathetic admissions committee."

The central plaintiff's claims were ultimately rejected and the case was dismissed. *Coalition to Defend Affirmative Action,* 539 F. Supp. 2d at 960.

20. See Seema Mehta, "UCLA Accused of Illegal Admissions Practices," *Los Angeles Times,* August 30, 2008, at B1, http://www.latimes.com/news/local/la-me-ucla30–2008aug30,0,06489043.story (accessed January 15, 2012), quoting Connerly to the effect that any applicant who mentions race in their personal statement should be rejected. In the context of Proposition 209 similar allegations have been made regarding admissions to California's state law schools.

21. Philips could form this conclusion because of stereotypes about blacks as having a poor work ethic. See, e.g., Brezina and Winder 2003. This is not to say

that Philips would be consciously thinking that blacks are lazy. Instead, she could be drawing on implicit biases. See Kang 2005, 1494.

22. Some suggest that blacks are overly focused on race. See, e.g., Fukuyama 1995, 295: "Whites complain that blacks are too race conscious." See also Robinson 2008, 1117–1126, which discusses the differences between attentiveness to race and the disparity of incentives to attend to and perceive racial discrimination between blacks and whites.

23. For an elaboration of these claims, see, generally, Carbado and Harris 2008.

24. See *Grutter v. Bollinger,* 539 U.S. 306, 329 (2003): "Our conclusion that the Law School has a compelling interest in a diverse student body is informed by our view that attaining a diverse student body is at the heart of the Law School's proper institutional mission, and that 'good faith' on the part of a university is 'presumed' absent 'a showing to the contrary.'"

25. See, generally, Carbado and Gulati 2004.

PART THREE

War and the Racial State

The essays in this section center on themes that run across the entire volume: the ways that racial projects always work in concert with other social conditions and identity formations; the critical labor such projects perform in fortifying political hegemony; and the inherent and persistent racialization of the U.S. state. Referring to the race-based struggles of the 1950s and 1960s, Omi and Winant wrote: "The postwar period has indeed been a racial crucible," characterized by "new conceptions of racial identity and its meaning, new modes of political organization and confrontation, and new definitions of the state's role in promoting and achieving 'equality'" (Omi and Winant 1994, 95). The "posts" that define our era—"post–civil rights," "post-9/11," and "post-racial"—are also revealed in this section's essays as being demarcated by new understandings of racial identity constructed in relation to war-making and the recurrence of the U.S. state as an empire. Like Omi and Winant, the contributors in this section reject the notion of a "post-racial America." Instead, they recast Omi and Winant's theoretical net, extending it beyond the United States to examine how global conceptualizations of race are intimately connected to sovereign violence in the age of the "war on terror."

Sherene H. Razack's essay, "We didn't kill 'em, we didn't cut their head off: Abu Ghraib Revisited," takes the Obama administration's "post-torture" official position as the starting point for an analysis of what popular cultural narratives about Abu Ghraib demonstrate about the persistence of empire. Razack focuses on narratives critical of the images of torture inflicted on Iraqi detainees at the notorious penal compound west of Baghdad. Following the anthropologist Michael Taussig, she explores the manner in which the tortured colonial body serves to concretize the empire's superiority. Putting Omi and Winant in dialogue with Taussig, Razack utilizes the concept of colonialism alongside racial formation theory to "understand how the category Muslim/Arab becomes a race and the object of racial terror." For Razack, empire, "in which a superior civilization defends its values against barbarians by annihilating them, is evident in torture talk, whether pro or con, whenever the idea is invoked that an all-powerful America confronts an especially savage, culturally different enemy from which it must defend itself."

The role of "global policing" in maintaining the U.S. empire also figures prominently in Nicholas De Genova's "The 'War on Terror' as Racial Crisis: Homeland Security, Obama, and Racial (Trans)Formations." De Genova argues that America's anti-terrorism politics are characteristic of a historical moment of racial crisis concomitant with Barack Obama's election. Pointing to Obama's speeches leading up to and upon his inauguration, De Genova avers, "Obama alluded obliquely to the racial specificity of his election and to its widely presumed implausibility, only to fold that exceptional distinction into the task of reinvigorating U.S. nationalism." Thus the Obama election does the work of reanimating the war against terror and normalizing the state of emergency—conjoined acts that De Genova theorizes as signifying a commitment to war-making just as they evidence a crisis in race-making. De Genova explicates this dual crisis of race-making and war-making by drawing on Omi and Winant's prescient theorizations, by connecting them to multiple political discourses surrounding Obama's election, and by harkening back to "the sense of global horizon DuBois already understood with astounding perspicuity and forceful urgency in his formulations of 'the color line' as a problem of planetary scope and import."

Nikhil Singh also brings W. E. B. DuBois into conversation with Omi and Winant, in his essay, "Racial Formation in an Age of Permanent War." Here, racial formation theory is deployed alongside DuBois to consider how sovereign violence defines the meanings and effects attached to race. Drawing on examples such as the expansion of U.S. national security after 9/11 and the racial panic over Barack Obama's election, Singh expands racial formation theory to conceptualize race as less "*precipitated out of social relations*" than "remade *as social relation*," in order to expose race as reconstituted in the practices of permanent war and as deeply embedded in "the uniquely violent foundations of Western modernity." Whereas De Genova keenly focuses on political discourse in the form of speeches made about Obama's election, Singh deftly deconstructs racist depictions of the U.S. president as embodying "an enemy within, an inscrutable misleader who possesses unnatural, even superhuman powers, a person backed by foreign moneyed cabals, one who is not even our degraded kin, but whose very birthright is foreign and fraudulent." Like the other essays in this section, Singh highlights the complex and troubling contradictions that Obama's presidency engenders, not only for a white hegemony erected on "post-racial" politics but also for sovereign violence legitimized under the global umbrella of the expanded U.S. national security state.

TEN

"We didn't kill 'em, we didn't cut their head off"

ABU GHRAIB REVISITED

Sherene H. Razack

To overcome extremism, we must also be vigilant in upholding the values our troops defend—because there is no force in the world more powerful than the example of America. That is why I have ordered the closing of the detention center at Guantanamo Bay, and will seek swift and certain justice for captured terrorists—because living our values doesn't make us weaker, it makes us safer and it makes us stronger. And that is why I can stand here tonight and say without exception or equivocation that the United States of America does not torture.

In words and deeds, we are showing the world that a new era of engagement has begun.

PRESIDENT BARACK OBAMA, *in an address to the United States Congress, February 24, 2009*

Most of us know and fear torture and the culture of terror only through the words of others. Hence my concern is with the mediation of terror through narration, and with the problem of writing effectively against terror.

MICHAEL TAUSSIG, *1987*

INTRODUCTION

President Barack Obama has declared that "America does not torture" and that "a new era of engagement has begun." Abu Ghraib has now been rebuilt, ironically in the image of a model American prison. We are officially in a "post-torture" age, though we should not forget that former President George W. Bush also declared that America does not torture. It is significant, too, that President Obama invokes the power of America at the very moment that he announced the end of an era of officially sanctioned torture. More than four years after the Abu Ghraib pictures were first leaked, military trials have come and gone, and most sentences have been served. Significantly, no one above the rank of sergeant has been tried. Rumblings persist, as they did in April of 2009, when memos from the Bush administration authorizing the CIA's use of torture were released. Will the Obama administration charge officials of the Bush administration?[1] Can we be post-torture if there is so little accountability? More important, can we be post torture if we are not post-empire?

How Abu Ghraib is remembered tells us a great deal about the persistence of empire. In this chapter, I examine popular cultural narratives about Abu Ghraib. Although I make passing reference to those narratives that openly endorse what went on at Abu Ghraib, I devote little space to them. Instead, I prefer to examine the responses of those who are critical of what happened at Abu Ghraib. For the most part, critics have focused on the torture policies of the Bush administration, omitting any serious consideration of rank and file torturers. When the latter are considered, it is typically to argue that ordinary people will torture if torture is policy. While it is urgent and necessary to acknowledge the systemic nature of torture at Abu Ghraib, and its basis in official policy, I suggest that the failure to more closely examine the actions of rank and file soldiers, and to insist on a deeper and broader public accountability secures a national innocence for Americans. If Abu Ghraib represents only the problem of a few bad leaders, there need not be any sustained confrontation with the facts of empire, neither then nor now. Most of all, those who were tortured, and the communities to which they belong, have no assurance that the Obama-era denouncement of torture recognizes them as full and valued members of a political and human community. To fully confront what happened at Abu Ghraib, we must consider how political and military leaders, *and* large numbers of American soldiers (not just a few bad apples) came to regard the prisoners at Abu Ghraib as less than human. Further, we need to ask whether public memory of Abu Ghraib suggests condemnation or approval of torture, and whether in fact a new era has begun.

The ghosts of Abu Ghraib return to haunt us in uncanny ways, reminding us that the imprinting of colonial power on their corporeal form was a central way in which the abstract concept of empire was made concrete. Empire, in which a superior civilization defends its values against barbarians by annihilating them, is evident in torture talk, whether pro or con, whenever the idea is invoked that an all-powerful America confronts an especially savage, culturally different enemy from which it must defend itself. Long ago, Michael Taussig pinpointed the racial divide that lies at the heart of this contest, imagined as one of savagery over civility. Writing on colonialism's culture of terror, Taussig ventured that neither the political economy of rubber nor that of labor accounts for the brutalities against the Putumayo Indians of Peru during the rubber boom. Terror—violence that is widespread and systematic—he reminded us, is the mediator of colonial hegemony par excellence, an "inscription of a mythology in the Indian body, an engraving of civilization locked in a struggle with wildness whose model was taken from the colonists' fantasies about Indian cannibalism."[2] Despite a persistent belief that torture is instrumental—designed, that is, to extract life-saving information from an enemy who would not otherwise divulge it—the practice is intrinsically about the staking of identity claims on the bodies of the colonized. Because torture is first and foremost a "memorializing" or imprinting of power on the bodies of the colonized,[3] it has an intimate connection to terror, as Taussig emphasized. Marnia Lazreg explains that for the context of colonial Algeria, torture was "a genuine battle between two embodied realities: in this case, colonial France with its unbounded power and mythologies, and colonized Algeria, with its claim to a full share of humanity. Conversely, the fact of doing torture allows the torturer to voice (albeit freely) *his* identity claims."[4] Torture links the body to the state—individual bodies as well as the military itself. In Algeria, torture "reached deep into the military body which it tied to the political system in a way that supplemented the esprit de corps that normally characterizes the army. Torture was the source of social integration that melded the political and the military, and consumed the structural transformation of the state into a militaristic institution."[5] If the state enjoys its identity through torture, individuals who participate in torture do the same: "Imperial identity is achieved through torture."[6]

In contemporary narratives about torture, the struggle with wildness and the fantasy on which it is based (the imperial identity alluded to by Lazreg) is visible in the idea that a culturally different enemy requires torture. For example, at an academic workshop I attended, a former military interrogator, an anthropologist, a psychologist, and a philosopher each discussed the justification for "new methods of interrogation." We are dealing with a culturally different enemy, several of these academics and military personnel advised. The Arab enemy is more "ideologically driven and more religious."[7] Unlike the cold war, the war on terror and the occupations of Iraq and Afghanistan have produced conditions where military interrogators need cultural help. Without it, "the 18 year old interrogator will fail and will be driven to more violent means to obtain information," warned the interrogator. A well-known anthropologist suggested that with a clandestine enemy, standard ways of operating are no longer useful. (The enemy is usually seen as clandestine, as Joshua Dratel points out, but when Communists were viewed as clandestine there was no argument that torture was the only option for confronting the communist threat.)[8] The anthropologist's suggestion was only a hair's breadth away from the logic of torture itself. As Stephen Holmes explained, the logic behind torture is a simple one: "To respond to the savages who want to kill us, we must cast off our Christian-liberal meekness and embrace a 'healthy savagery' of our own. We must confront ruthlessness with ruthlessness. We must pull out all the stops. After victory we will have plenty of time for civility, guilt feelings, and the rule of law."[9] Savagery or wildness, as Taussig reminds us, is the stuff of colonial fantasy.

It is useful to pause here and consider whether Taussig's colonial paradigm may be applied to the contemporary United States. In *Racial Formation in the United States from the 1960s to the 1990s,* Omi and Winant take the position that to consider how race works in the United States, it is not sufficient to apply what they describe as nation-based theory in which race is understood as a territorial phenomenon. According to this theory, European powers divided up the world between them and reinforced colonial domination through a system of racial distinctions. Race secures territory in this account so that the real issue is not race but land. What happens in the United States with regard to race cannot be so easily linked to land.[10] Presumably, then, we would need to be cautious in applying Taussig's insights about colonial violence and terror to the United States today. In particular, it is not easy, Omi and Winant contend, to see the connection between the United States and global patterns based on the legacy of colonialism. Leaving aside for the moment the fact that the United States continues to have a colonial relationship with the peoples who are indigenous to North America, we might consider whether the struggles in which torture has been an issue have the hallmarks of a quintessential colonialism, involving as they do occupation, control of resources, extreme violence, and persistent marking of Muslims as an inferior race. The racial state that Omi and Winant describe, the state centrally implicated in racial definition and management, is as heavily committed to securing territory and resources as it is to the reproduction of a society organized by white supremacy. Such a state engages in forms of violence and terror in much the same way that Taussig describes, and toward the same end: racial rule.

Omi and Winant prefer the concept of racial formation to colonialism in order to highlight "the process through which social, economic and political forces determine the content and importance of racial categories."[11] Although I consider colonialism to be a more useful concept when thinking about racial violence and terror, racial formation is nonetheless useful for reminding us that racial categories are "formed, transformed, destroyed and re-formed"[12] in racial states, a theory that enables us to understand how the category Muslim/Arab becomes a race and the object of racial terror. Although *Racial Formation* was written at a time when Omi and Winant considered Arab an ambivalent racial category,[13] today it is obvious that Muslim/Arab has acquired the features of a full-blown racial category in the United States, a status it has long held in Europe. Regarded as inherently fanatical and prone to violence, the figure of the Muslim/Arab shows that the strictly biological basis of race is accompanied by the notion that "the truth of race lies in the terrain of innate characteristics of which skin color and other physical attributes provide only the most obvious, and in some respect the lost superficial indicators."[14] As I have written elsewhere, values talk is really race thinking, a division of the world into a hierarchy of modern and premodern peoples, the latter inherently so.[15] Although race thinking varies, for Muslims and Arabs, it is underpinned by the idea that modern enlightened, secular peoples must protect themselves from premodern, religious peoples whose loyalty to tribe and community reigns over their commitment to the rule of law. The marking of a group as belonging to the realm of culture and religion, as opposed to the realm of law and reason, has devastating consequences. There is a disturbing spatializing of morality that occurs in the story of modern versus premodern peoples. We have reason; they do not. We are located in modernity; they are not. Significantly, because *they* have not advanced as we have, it is our moral obligation to correct, discipline, and keep them in line and to defend ourselves against their irrational excesses. In doing all of these things, the West has often denied the benefits of modernity to those it considers to be outside of it. Evicted from the universal, and thus from civilization and progress, the non-West occupies a zone outside the law. Violence may be directed at it with impunity.

The idea of a culturally different enemy first circulated after the release of the photographs of Abu Ghraib. The theory that went furthest in providing an explanation for the practices shown in the photos was the idea that sexualized torture was simply a culturally specific interrogation method. Fitting in nicely with the "clash of civilizations" thesis that had come to dominate Western explanations for conflict between West and non-West,[16] and the Islamic world in particular, pyramids of naked men forced to simulate having sex with each other were to be understood as nothing more than a contemporary form of interrogation. Few in the media questioned the Orientalist underpinnings of this claim. (Unlike us, they are sexually repressed, homophobic, and misogynist and are likely to crack in sexualized situations, particularly those involving women dominating men or those involving sex between men.) No one asked whether such methods would in fact humiliate men of all cultures, both because they are violent and because they target what being a man means within patriarchy.

The "clash of civilizations" approach to torture reinforced the idea of the prisoners' barbarism at the same time that it enabled the West to remain on the moral high ground. First, through the idea of cultural difference, sexualized torture became something more generic—torture for the purpose of obtaining information, something that was not even torture at all. Sexualized torture, then, was simply "to attack the prisoners' identity and values."[17] Believing that the fault had to be traced back to the top, Mark Danner declared the photos "comprehensible" given the cultural characteristics of Arabs *and* the Central Intelligence Agency's (CIA's) manual on interrogations. The photos are "staged operas of fabricated shame intended to 'intensify' the prisoners' guilt feelings, increase his anxiety and his urge to cooperate," Danner wrote, quoting parts of the CIA's interrogation policy.[18] The photos were a "shame multiplier," according to the Red Cross, since they could be distributed to the prisoners' families and used to further humiliate detainees.[19] Second, through the idea of culturally specific interrogation techniques, Americans were marked as modern people who do not subscribe to puritanical notions of sex or to patriarchal notions of women's role in it. The Iraqis, of course, remained forever confined to the premodern.

The idea of a culturally different, more savage enemy persists in several contemporary journalistic accounts. For instance, Heather Macdonald, a journalist and frequent guest on Fox News, writes, "The Islamist enemy is unlike any the military has encountered in the past."[20] The difference, it turns out, is a cultural one. Islamists don't give up information, don't play by the rules of the Geneva Convention, and are mainly interested in homosexual sex. (Macdonald illustrates in this comment the incoherence of racist positions. If the Iraqis were especially humiliated by the idea of men having sex with men, why would they also be characterized as mainly interested in homosexual sex?) Confronted with such an uncivilized enemy, Americans had no other choice but to turn to various "stress techniques," some of which may have gone too far (Macdonald dislikes the use of dogs and is a little concerned about water boarding). The prisoners who were moved from Camp X-ray to Camp Delta at Guantanamo were really upset only because they could no longer have homosexual sex. Although acknowledging some practices of torture, Macdonald concludes: "We don't gas people like the Nazis did."

One sees only a slightly more restrained culturalist argument from lawyers and policy analysts, many of whom use the culture argument to downgrade what happened at Abu Ghraib from torture to interrogation. For example, Andrew C. McCarthy describes the "mortification" of Iraqi prisoners at Abu Ghraib and argues that with a new clandestine and ruthless enemy, America had to legally authorize "a bending of the rules." Dismissing any connection between lawlessness (as in the refusal to grant POW status to detainees) and torture, McCarthy simply agrees with Alan Dershowitz that we should have a system of torture warrants whereby we apply for permission to torture especially high value and presumably especially savage detainees.[21]

In view of the mediation of terror through narration, it is not surprising that news coverage of Abu Ghraib in North America, both then and now, has not typically used the word *torture*. As Timothy M. Jones and Penelope Sheets found, only 19 percent of the American press articles on Abu Ghraib referred to torture, compared to 81.8 percent of European press articles. Canada and Australia reportage referred to torture 41 percent of the time.[22] American civilians and soldiers are massively opposed to torture, but not to abuse or mortification. Polls indicate that many Americans are in favor of sleep deprivation and other techniques.[23] As I show below, narratives about a few bad leaders effectively limit the extent to which Americans can see themselves as implicated in torture, and by extension in empire.

ANTI-TORTURE NARRATIVES

Many scholars now unambiguously condemn torture and show "the mundane banality with which cruelty and torture became official policy of the United States Department of Defense."[24] Analysts share the conclusion that under President George W. Bush, as David Cole put it, "an amoral, blinkered pragmatism ruled the day."[25] In this apparently post-torture age, where so many announce their objections to torture, the opening words of Taussig's classic book *Shamanism, Colonialism, and the Wild Man,* in which he reminds us of the mediation of terror through narration, suggest that we should not assume that the narratives that enable torture have in fact all disappeared. How do contemporary narratives about the *wrongness* of torture at Abu Ghraib mediate terror? How do we write effectively against torture? These questions are as pertinent when writing about torture and the Arab/Muslim enemy today as it was for the Putumayo Indians.

A recent collection of articles on the torture debate in the United States begins with the observation that Americans have been remarkably "apathetic" about the question of torture in the war on terror. The editor speculates that Americans are not uncaring but simply confused about the issue.[26] A spate of films about torture and other excesses in the war on terror, however, suggests otherwise. Americans *have* engaged in a public discussion of the meaning of Abu Ghraib, Guantanamo, and other sites of torture, and they have mostly done so as critics. Documentaries such as *Standard Operating Procedure* (the focus of this chapter) and *The Ghosts of Abu Ghraib,* as well as books such as Jane Mayer's *The Dark Side,*[27] and Hollywood movies such as *Rendition* have become a genre of sorts, works united by a common criticism of the torture policies of the Bush administration. If the majority of critics of American torture policies of the past decade (most do not spare the time to discuss pre-9/11 American torture) focus on the corruption, immorality, and illegality that characterized the Bush administration, very few consider torture itself: what is torture, who is tortured, and what made it so easy for the regime, ordinary soldiers, and ordinary people to torture or to accept torture as official policy. Although we have all become familiar with the list of torture practices (indeed, on the day that I am writing this, my local newspaper in Toronto included a short news item on CIA torture techniques and the torture memos have just been released),[28] it is as though these acts were not in fact committed by people we can name. Instead, the discussion has largely been an abstract one about policies and immoral leadership. On the rare occasion that the questions "Why was it so easy for American soldiers to be amoral?" and "What enabled torture?" are asked, they are answered with the theory that once you create a torture culture, ordinary people find it easy to torture (Stanley Milgram's Stanford experiments are often cited).[29] Importantly, psychological explanations turn our gaze away from history and context, leaving little chance of exploring what kind of Americans the soldiers imagined themselves to be. "Rumsfeld made them do it" (a reference to Donald Rumsfeld, defense secretary under President George W. Bush) seems to suffice as explanation.[30] Such explanations do not explore torture as the historical identity-making practice Taussig, among others, considers it to be. In fact, they studiously avoid *embodying* torture at all; it thus remains a particular policy or law. We seldom hear the voices of the tortured of Abu Ghraib, Guantanamo, or elsewhere, though the recently available information from interviews of detainees compiled by the International Committee of the Red Cross is one exception that may yet change the direction of public consciousness.[31]

It is said that Americans must now live with the story of torture. As Mark Danner wrote recently after reading the Red Cross interviews, the decision to torture "sits before us, a toxic fact, polluting our political and moral life."[32] To confront this toxic fact requires confronting what torture *is:* a systematic dehumanization of the Other. Both in popular culture and officially, the United States has yet to acknowledge and confront the fact that its soldiers were able to torture with abandon. The rank-and-file soldiers involved in torture at Abu Ghraib appear neither to regret it nor to face social censure for it. The remarkable disavowal that prisoners were *persons* who were tortured and the compulsion to exonerate the rank and file ensure that Americans do not confront the toxic fact of empire. This is the argument I make in what follows, an argument about the persistence of racial terror in narratives at a moment when America announces itself to be post-torture. Specifically, I suggest that the soldiers at Abu Ghraib have often aroused compassion and understanding. As a culture, North Americans appear to sympathize with many of them, perhaps believing the Milgram experiment to be a good explanation for their behavior. I note here that less good feeling has been accorded the Winter Soldiers, servicemen and -women who protest the war and the terrible things they were required to do in Iraq and Afghanistan.[33] Through the redemption of the rank-and-file soldiers involved in torture and an almost exclusive focus on the legal and political authorization of torture, Americans have successfully stopped torture from penetrating their consciousness. Along with scholars exploring the productive function of apologies, truth and reconciliation commissions, and other national moments in which state violence is confronted, I suggest that an important question to ask about these ostensibly critical narratives of torture is quite simply, How do the stories make us feel?[34] Put another way, what kind of a moral community is created by contemporary critics of torture?

There is something productive about the argument that *only* the leaders are to blame for torture. American innocence is secured through this focus in much the same way that Canadians were able to affirm their innocence in peacekeeping abuses.[35] Both the nation and rank-and-file soldiers, in this telling, become mere dupes of a corrupt leadership. The work of empire can go on apace when we assume that all the bad guys have gone home. What was done to Iraqis disappears into a story of American innocence, a strange time in American history when "our children" as the filmmaker Errol Morris called the rank-and-file soldiers, were coerced into an "animal house on the night shift" at Abu Ghraib, a phrase Morris borrowed from former defense secretary James Schlesinger.[36] Morris is reluctant to call what went on at Abu Ghraib torture, and the soldiers whose faces appear in the famous pictures are never labeled torturers. At worst, the rank-and-file soldiers charged with abuses at Abu Ghraib are fondly referred to in the media as the "seven bad apples," and their activities described as "unseemly."

I rely on the documentary film made by Morris, titled *Standard Operating Procedure,* and the book of the same title that he coauthored with Philip Gourevitch, based on extensive interviews with the soldiers, to illustrate my argument about the "post-torture" recollections of Abu Ghraib.[37]

Sabrina Harman, Megan Ambuhl, Lynndie England, Jeremy Sivits, Javal Davis—five of the seven soldiers charged for their roles in torture at Abu Ghraib—and others have told their stories in two documentaries and a book; two others, Charles Graner and Ivan Frederick, remain incarcerated and inaccessible to the media.[38] Critics have been remarkably unanimous in their responses to *Standard Operating Procedure,* finding the occasional fault (particularly with Morris's decision to re-enact scenes of torture), but agreeing for the most part with the story line that the real culprits are the leaders. Although I rely on the documentary and the book *Standard Operating Procedure,* and critics' responses to them, it is possible to turn to other documentaries and films. The documentary *The Ghosts of Abu Ghraib* by filmmaker Rory Kennedy, which shows fidelity to the argument that the most important conclusion we can come to about Abu Ghraib is that torture was official policy and that rank-and-file soldiers only did what they were ordered to do. Like Morris, Kennedy feels sympathy for her documentary subjects, believing them to be the likable, hapless victims of a corrupt administration. As Kennedy told Amy Goodman in an interview, "And what I found was that they were, in fact, very likeable, and that I could see their humanity in looking at their eyes, and was able to connect with them. And it was very hard to reconcile that experience with the reality of what I was seeing in the photographs and images."[39] For Kennedy, as for so many, it is possible to reconcile the photos with the apparent niceness of the soldiers by focusing on the responsibility of the chain of command and on the idea (citing Stanley Milgram once again) that ordinary people easily commit acts of torture if someone in authority tells them to do so. What enables this exoneration of ordinary torturers? While there are certainly several reasons, I propose that a crucial part of this response originates in the belief that Arabs/Muslims are culturally different, and less than human.

POST-TORTURE: "I DON'T KNOW WHAT I COULD HAVE DONE DIFFERENT"

By way of moral contrast, let us consider some altogether different narratives about Iraq. In March 2008, hundreds of veterans of the wars in Iraq and Afghanistan gathered in Maryland to give their eyewitness accounts of the occupations of both countries. The veterans modeled their testimony after the Winter Soldier hearings organized by Vietnam Veterans Against the War in 1971. As Amy Goodman reported on *Democracy Now,* "The war veterans spoke of free-fire zones, the shootings and beatings of innocent civilians, racism at the highest levels of the military, and the torturing of prisoners."[40] Most major news outlets did not cover the Winter Soldier event. Goodman, via *Democracy Now,* broadcast the hearings, in which soldiers tearfully described in detail (often illustrating with pictures of themselves) the acts of violence they perpetrated upon Iraqi and Afghan people. In one such account, Jon Michael Turner stripped his medals and ribbons from his chest and ended his testimony as follows: "I just want to say that I am sorry for the hate and destruction I have inflicted on innocent people, and I'm sorry for the hate and destruction that others have inflicted on innocent people. . . . I am sorry for the things I did. I am no longer the monster that I once was."[41] Carl Rippberger, commenting on a slide of himself in Iraq, said: "I am extremely shameful of it. I'm showing it in hopes that none of you people that have never been involved ever let this happen to you. Don't ever let your government do this to you. It's me. I'm holding a dead body, smiling. Everyone in our platoon took two bodies, put them on the back ramp, drove them through a village for show, and dumped them off at the edge the village."[42]

As these excerpts reveal, the Winter Soldiers acknowledge personal responsibility for their actions in Iraq and Afghanistan, even as they believe that they were a part of a systematic campaign of violence orchestrated from the top. Their stories confirm that a pattern of terror begins with individual soldiers who are asked to do, and who do, unspeakable things. Some find the courage to say no on the spot; most do not. But in the case of the Winter Soldiers, all now believe that what they were asked to do, and what they did, was wrong. Their testimony is intended to rectify these wrongs by allowing them to take personal responsibility and speak out against practices of torture and terror and against war and occupation. This response is not one that has occurred to the majority of the soldiers at Abu Ghraib, and it is not one that Morris or Gourevitch ever consider possible. "I'm sorry" has not been uttered by any of the torturers, nor have any of those who condemn torture uttered these words. Of course, the politics of apologies are well-known productive acts. As Richard Weisman discussed (drawing also on others' work), expressions of remorse have to include an unconditional acknowledgement of responsibility, sincere self-condemnation and, most crucially, an awareness that the victim has suffered.[43] Without these components, we are not being invited into a moral community in which torture is wrong. If no one thinks that the acts of torture at Abu Ghraib were really wrong or regrettable, then are Muslims/Arabs full members of the human and political community?

In *Standard Operating Procedure,* Morris intersperses vivid reenactments of torture, the Abu Ghraib photographs, and interviews with the soldiers, the last often shot close up so that their faces fill the entire screen. The viewer has a sense of being face to face with torture and literally present with both torturer and tortured. The tortured, of course, do not speak; their bodies are meant only to contrast with the calm and reasonable voices of the soldiers who give us their accounts of what they did in Abu Ghraib prison. There remains a voyeuristic gaze throughout as we are invited to consume pyramids of naked prisoners. As Lazreg wrote about France, as the former colonial power in Algeria, the "cumulative effect of this speaking and writing about the war [of independence in Algeria] has resulted in a trivialization of the significance of torture as glossy pictures turn war into *an orgiastic intellectual entertainment.*"[44] Similarly, documentaries such as *Standard Operating Procedure* offer vivid descriptions and images of torture that serve to normalize these forms of torture.

The documentary begins by informing us that American soldiers were so depressed and so low when they got to Abu Ghraib that they felt "already dead." In the book, Gourevitch and Morris make sure their readers understand that Abu Ghraib was an intolerable place that was constantly under mortar fire (although in 2003, no American soldier was killed because of this). A combat unit, the 372nd Regiment, made up of reservists, finds out that instead of going home, its members will be posted to guard duty at Abu Ghraib, something for which they are not trained. We are coached to understand that—untrained, alienated, stressed, frustrated, and overcome by the climate—normal, wholesome American soldiers, each with his or her own dreams, soon fall apart in the hell that was Abu Ghraib. The film and the book both begin with this equivalent to the journey into the heart of Africa of Marlow, Joseph Conrad's European character in the novel *Heart of Darkness* who travels by river into the dangerous jungle, encountering savageries along the way that reveal the darkness that lies within man.

As I have shown elsewhere, in the case of the violence of Western peacekeepers toward the populations they supposedly go to help, the savagery of the racial Other, and the savagery of the place of the racial Other, becomes the reason why violence is authorized against them. As Hugh Ridley memorably explained in recalling the themes of colonial novels and the mindset of the masculine subjects who inhabit these fictional colonial worlds, "In Africa, who can be a saint?"[45] The civilized man "loses it" in Africa on account of the dust and heat, as the Canadian government concluded in its inquiry into the violence of Canadian peacekeepers toward Somalis. In Africa, the soldier feels compelled to engage in violence *anticipating* the savagery of the racial Other and the hardships of the land. It is this narrative line, a combination of "Rumsfeld made me do it" and "In Iraq, who could be a saint?" that runs through the accounts of the Abu Ghraib soldiers, an account very much fostered by Morris and carefully installed in the film and book.

What stands out the most about the narratives the Abu Ghraib soldiers offer to the cameras is the almost complete absence of moral conflict. The soldiers do not believe that they *personally* did anything wrong. Instead, we see subjects intent on presenting themselves as victims. Presumably asked by Morris (who does not appear) how they feel now, the soldiers display no shame, little interest in the impact of their actions, and an intense self-absorption. Sabrina Harmon appears puzzled by the question about what she could have done differently. She replies, "I don't know what I could have done different," and as an afterthought adds: "I wouldn't have joined the military. It's just not worth it." In the interview quoted in the book, she expands on what she means: "You always feel guilty thinking you could have changed something—or, I guess, dereliction of duty for not reporting something that went on, even though people did know. I guess you could have went [sic] to somebody else. So I accept the dereliction of duty charge. Personally I accept that one. It would be nice just to put everything behind me. It sucks, but it's a learning experience, I guess. It helps you grow, getting screwed over. I don't know."[46] The spark of remorse that leads Harmon to accept the dereliction of duty charge for not reporting the abuse is quickly put out by the predominant feeling of "getting screwed over."

Similarly, although he felt sorry for a prisoner who died in a bombing just as he was being released, Javal Davis remains most rueful about the loss of his dreams. Davis offers the camera his final thought: "A big chunk of my life is gone. I can never get it back." Jeremy Sivits is sorry that he couldn't make his family proud. Megan Graner simply concludes, "Life's not fair, that's for sure," and if we are in any doubt about whose life is not fair, it is quickly put to rest when, reflecting on her own life, she declares, "I've always known that." Lynndie England announces that she wouldn't change a thing because she got a son out of it. For her, regret centers on Charles Graner. Believing herself to have been victimized by Graner, England has drawn one predominant lesson from Abu Ghraib: "Learn from your mistakes. I learned from mine. It's like I don't need a man to survive. Forget 'em. . . . It's just being young and naïve."[47]

Although self-pity runs like a stream through these narratives, the soldiers are clearly not sorry for what they did to Iraqis. Their recollections reveal that little about the situation troubled them in the first place, other than their own personal discomfort, the discomfort of being in a savage place at a savage time. They work hard to make a moral distinction between humiliation and torture, believing nonetheless in their absolute right to engage in the former.

The journey into the heart of darkness, where torture is transformed into humiliation, is a gendered one. Both the book and the film begin with the story of Sabrina Harman as the epitome of feminine innocence defiled. Harman's soft girlish voice reads from her letters to her wife, Kelly.[48] Faithful to the storyline of someone who descends into hell, Harmon writes of the first time that she saw a prisoner with underwear on his head, stripped naked and handcuffed to the rails with his arms extended over his head in the Palestinian position, used by the Israeli army for the extreme discomfort in which it places the prisoner. Like most soldiers, Harman understood that the prisoner, a taxi driver, was most likely innocent, something that did not stop her from engaging in humiliation and torture. She recalls for Kelly that at first she found the prisoner's situation funny and initially laughed when someone "poked his dick." Editorializing quickly, Harman writes, "Then it hit me that this was molestation." Molestation, but not torture. Claiming that she knew that much that went on was wrong, she says she nonetheless participated and took pictures, apparently believing that the photos would later serve as proof. At no time does it occur to Harman to try to stop the practices or even to complain about them. If she gives a thumbs-up or gleefully smiles for the camera, Harmon suggests that this is simply what she always did in front of a camera.

Gourevitch and Morris sympathetically portray the young girl who dreamed of becoming a forensic photographer. In Harman's letters, the story of taking pictures for the purpose of documenting an abuse is undermined by her recounting of the casual details of life at Abu Ghraib where "we stripped prisoners and laughed at them; we degraded them but we didn't hit them." These casually inserted details of her direct participation in torture, practices that she clearly does not consider to be torture, take second place next to the accounts Harman gives of her kindness. She writes of the young boy who was covered in ants and whom she tried to help, and of the general whose eyebrows were shaved and whom she tried to console for this humiliation. On camera she comments on the famous photograph of the prisoner who was made to believe that the electrodes attached to him were live wires and that he would be electrocuted if he fell off the box: "It would have been meaner if the electrodes were hooked up." Gilligan, as this prisoner was nicknamed, was never physically touched, Harman insists, puzzled by those who saw the photo and thought that it was torture.

The contrived and contradictory nature of Harman's recollections give Gourevitch and Morris pause, and they notice that she is working hard to construct herself as innocent: "By the end of her outpourings she repositioned herself as an outsider at Abu Ghraib, an observer and recorder, shaking her head, and in this way she came clean with her wife. In this way she preserved her sense of innocence."[49] Noting that Harman "imagined herself as producing an exposé, but she did not pretend to be a whistle-blower-in-waiting," they can make no further sense of her performance and instead accept her explanations. When she acknowledges that the grin and the thumbs-up she offered to the camera in most of the photos "look bad" and suggests that this was simply how she always posed for photos, there is little in the book or the film to indicate that this might not be true. Harmon's narrative is indeed full of contradictions. Documenting abuse, yet giving an un-self-conscious account of her own involvement in various torture events, her account nonetheless makes clear that "she was as forgiving of her buddies as of herself."[50]

There is a strange structure to the soldiers' narratives of "the first time I saw abuse." It is the naked detainees wearing women's panties that shock, but not the repeated violence. Although initially sure that what they were seeing was wrong, they soon participate in acts of abuse and describe their participation in various contradictory ways: the leaders made me do it; others did far worse; I just followed orders; the prisoners were ordinary innocent people; the prisoners were people who had happily blown us up; the prisoners had information that would save lives; the prisoners didn't have information; and so on. No soldier takes responsibility for acts of humiliation and torture. If it is ever acknowledged that most of the people in Abu Ghraib were simply ordinary people, this does not give anyone pause to acknowledge that what they did was wrong.

Javal Davis knew from his first encounter with naked prisoners wearing women's pink panties over their heads that "something's not right here." Describing his initial attempt to complain, he notes that the chain of command simply abandoned the rank and file, confirming that however the soldiers felt, they had to do the bidding of Military Intelligence. By his own and others' accounts, he grew numb but participated nevertheless, often with enthusiasm. He acknowledges that in and around Abu Ghraib, soldiers in his unit would simply sweep up every single male "from kids to the local baker" and then set about humiliating them. He soon determined what worked best in destabilizing the prisoners: playing rap music and country music loudly and without cease. In his view what he participated in was not torture but humiliation. "We don't have photos of torture," he states, even though he believes that torture happened all the time. The real torturers, he implies, got off. Megan Ambuhl also insists that the photographs don't show torture and goes further by maintaining that they in fact make things look worse than they were. "We softened them up," Ampuhl casually explains. "We would burn them with a cigarette. We'd just do what they [Military Intelligence] wanted us to do. It didn't seem weird; it was saving lives." Other soldiers calmly describe their own role in water torture.

The soldiers speak casually of the horrors they were involved in, lamenting that the incidents for which they have been condemned were far more innocent than others they knew about. They tell of prisoners whom they were "humiliating" who were already dead; of being asked to help out and doing so in order to be "nice." Sabrina Harmon draws diagrams in her letters home of how dogs are used on prisoners. Others announce their belief that most prisoners were ordinary, innocent people, yet they recall soaking sandbags in hot sauce to be placed over a prisoner's head because "these guys have info." They were able to participate in the brutal beatings of prisoners and maintain at the same time that the most that ever happened was "a really, really bad case of humiliation." As "helpers," Anthony Diaz and Jeffery Frost describe the order to tie a prisoner in a higher-stress position. They find out after some time that the prisoner they were allegedly softening up was already dead. "It kinda felt bad. I know I am not part of this but . . . ," offers Diaz in the film, illustrating the acknowledgement of violence and the disavowal of his participation in it in one breath. Although what felt bad was realizing the prisoner was dead, it apparently did not feel bad to spend days tying prisoners up in intolerable stress positions, stripping them naked, and turning on the showers for water torture. The mundane work of torture elicits little moral conflict. Indeed, it is work that is never named as torture.

The soldiers are not only forgiving of themselves and of each other for engaging in torture, but absorbed in the tragedy of what happened to *them*. Lynndie England, whom Gourevitch and Morris describe as a girl who once looked like a boy and who enlisted at seventeen in order to attend college and lift herself out of a life working at a chicken-processing plant, is dismissive of the public, which saw her holding the leash on a prisoner and called it abuse. "It was no big deal," she observes, explaining that Charles Graner asked her to hold the leash for the photo. Maintaining throughout that all she did was what she was told to do, England presents herself as a woman victimized by a man. "I'm in the brig because of a man," she states flatly to the camera, explaining that women in the army either had to prove their equality to men or be controlled by them. A man's place, the army also turned out to be a place where "people wanted to mess with the prisoners." Offering no comment on this state of affairs, England remains unrepentant as she describes her involvement in the scenes of sexual torture: "We didn't kill 'em, we didn't cut their head off." Unconsciously comparing herself to the barbaric enemy who kills and cuts off heads, England secures for herself a higher place on the scale of civilization.

If the soldiers seem unmoved by their acts of torture, those who bring us their story share this indifference to what was done to Iraqi bodies. Although Gourevitch and Morris write passionately that "the stain is ours," the stain is only torture as policy and the crimes of the upper levels.[51] Of the soldiers they conclude: "Even as they sank into a routine of depravity, they showed by their picture taking that they did not accept it as normal. They never fully got with the program. Is it not to their credit that they were profoundly demoralized by their service in the netherworld?"[52] Inexperienced, untrained, under attack, and under orders to do wrong, the low-ranking reservist military police who implemented the nefarious policy of the war on terror on the MI block of Abu Ghraib knew that what they were doing was immoral, and they knew that if it wasn't illegal, it ought to be. They knew that they had the right, and that it was their duty, to disobey an unlawful order and to report it to their immediate superior; and if that failed—or if that superior was the source of the order—to keep reporting it on up the chain of command until they found satisfaction.[53] If they had the right to refuse to commit acts of torture, and given that this was surely their duty, why didn't they do so, and what do we think about them not having done so? These questions are answered in the film: they didn't do so because it was hard to do so and we should forgive them.

The film and the book are both assembled to minimize the complicity of the lower ranks. Tim Dugan, a civilian interrogator, explains to us at the start of the film that the rank-and-file soldiers were a "bunch of unprofessional schmucks that didn't know their damn jobs, all thrown together, mixed up with a big-ass stick." By the end of the film, he no longer holds this view, and we can guess that he now believes that torture was policy. Brent Pack, lead forensic examiner of the computer crime unit of the U.S. Army, who analyzed the thousands of photographs, lends the full weight of his science to the diagnosis: the pictures depict several events of what was often "standard operating procedure." He classifies the acts of torture and humiliation, clarifying that physical injury amounts to a criminal act and that sexual humiliation is dereliction of duty, but that most other practices are simply standard operating procedure. Agreeing with the other experts interviewed that the soldiers were mostly people in the wrong place at the wrong time, Pack feels sorriest for England. Lynndie was "just in love." If the photos tell us anything, he implies, it is the story of a woman in love. Neither Lynndie England nor Sabrina Harman who writes so lovingly to her wife, are presented as torturers. Although we are given little information on the two men serving the longest sentences (Charles Graner and Ivan Frederick), their stories, too, are ultimately presented as those of victims. Their country betrayed them, we are led to believe.

Perhaps the end point of the equivocation about the rank-and-file soldiers is best revealed in the many interviews Morris has given (some with Gourevitch) in which he explains what most concerned him about Abu Ghraib. Professing himself to be most interested in the role of the photos, Morris wonders about what they reveal and what they conceal. Often turning to Sabrina Harman as an example, he notes that it is tempting to conclude from the thumbs-up and the smiles in the photo of herself with the dead, tortured Iraqi prisoner that she participated in his death or at least approved of it. The smile is an uneasy one, Morris suggests, and Harman's crime is nothing compared to the soldiers who actually murdered the prisoner. In this moment, we are invited to forget that while Harman did not murder prisoners, she did participate directly in moments of torture. Challenging his audience to answer the question, Did Sabrina Harman commit a crime? Morris clearly thinks the answer is no. Admitting that she may not be "lily white" or "uncompromised," we are invited to consider that she is not the culprit.[54] In the end, although he wished to interrogate complicity at the bottom rather than the top, and imagined himself making a film that did more than focus on the chain of command, we arrive in the same place. At no point does it really seize Morris's attention that American soldiers such as Sabrina Harman *tortured* Iraqis. The unchallenged assumption throughout, shared by Morris, Gourevitch, and their subjects, is the idea that there is a valid reason for treating Iraqis as they were treated in Abu Ghraib prison by the rank-and-file soldiers, even if things did go a little wrong.

THE REVIEWERS: "FRIGHTENED, DISORIENTED MEN AND WOMEN"

Despite the obviousness of some of the film's plot devices, it is surprising that reviewers find so little to critique in the work of Morris and Gourevitch. In a review of the book and the film published in the *New York Review of Books,* Ian Buruma begins, as so many reviewers do, by reminding us of Susan Sontag's argument that the torture photographs "were typical expressions of a brutalized popular American culture," but he adds approvingly that Morris's documentary "complicates matters."[55] The complication is that the pictures don't tell the whole story and may "even conceal more than they reveal." What they conceal is torture as policy and the practice of using untrained soldiers, among them those with a "bad boy" reputation such as Charles Graner. Of the other soldiers who participated, Buruma has only kind things to say. Harman, in particular, draws his sympathy, as Morris intended. She is the person about whom her colleagues say that she wouldn't hurt a fly. We are reminded of her dream to become a forensic photographer. For Buruma, Harman is simply telling the truth when she says that she took pictures to document abuses.

She committed no crime, he insists, since the real crime lies in those who tortured a prisoner to death. England was simply in love and did whatever her man told her to do. The photos, Buruma concludes, were "fun and games" compared to the darker secret they hid. The worst condemnation that Buruma musters is that everyone probably got a little "erotic frisson" from his or her participation in these acts. He recalls that Sontag may have been right about the pornographic nature of the encounter. Yet lying at the heart of pornography and the Abu Ghraib encounter is the capacity to objectify and dehumanize, something that contemporary Abu Ghraib commentators such as Buruma seem not to notice. Not surprisingly, any comparison between the soldiers of Abu Ghraib and the Nazis is rejected outright, although it is interesting that reviewers such as Buruma feel compelled to deny the similarity.

Buruma's response is a typical one. The Canadian reviewer Peter Goddard also agrees that Lynndie England was merely goofing around for her boyfriend when she took part in the photo of "Gus," the name given to the prisoner on a leash: "The picture isn't about Gus being dominated by England. It's about England being dominated by Graner."[56] Apparently buying England's gender defense that she wasn't humiliating prisoners but was just trying to please Charles Graner, Goddard is able to sidestep the fact that a prisoner was still in the end being humiliated by jailors who had considerable power over him. Graner's interest in documenting the terrible conditions of his job, Harman's wish to use photos to deflect her own humiliation at being a spectator at a demeaning ritual—both are accepted at face value. Goddard concludes: "The theatricality of the Abu Ghraib photos only adds to the shock of what was really happening there. It's as if Graner and the rest of the picture-takers understood implicitly that they were in that awful place to play a role in this war fantasy. So they did just that, with great big smiles on their faces."[57]

One is struck by the extent to which reviewers are forgiving of the soldiers. They emphasize their "uncertainty and confusion" as well as their "posing and posturing." As Michael S. Roth, president of Wesleyan University, writes, "through the soldiers we are able to grasp the 'slapdash ineptitude' and the incoherence of the war itself."[58] Michael Chaiken, in his review, takes Morris to task for "the heavy-handed reliance on re-creations to shock the audience into recognizing the magnitude of the horrors being recounted."[59] Chaiken's argument is that the re-creations "divert attention from that for which there is no substitute: the faces of those frightened, disoriented men and women tearfully coming to terms with historical forces of which they too are hapless victims." Bemoaning that we suffer a failure of empathy and imagination when we are overly exposed to images of horror (as Susan Sontag argued), these writers leave little doubt about whom our sympathy should be for—the soldiers, not their Iraqi victims.

As many reviewers agree, Morris asks us to think about the relationship between the photos and truth. As Cynthia Fuchs put it, "The movie is more deliberately and (for lack of a better term) more poetically invested in how the crimes were defined by the images."[60] Noticing Lynndie England's "oddly detached" stance, Fuchs explains that the problem was that she was a woman in a man's world, and she reminds us that England's "seeming lack of a perspective becomes a perspective." Again, however, the lack of perspective that is so remarkable is simply evidence of the degree to which these practices were policy. The pictures assembled into a timeline by Pack don't tell us about the "stunning policy-making that determined that sequence." For Fuchs as for all the other reviewers, the real story lies elsewhere. It does not lie with the strange detachment that England and others exhibit to this day, except in so far as the detachment confirms that they, too, were merely hapless victims of a corrupt leadership. A reviewer for the World Socialist Web Site, Joanne Laurier, is the only one to suggest that Morris seems to display "an unwillingness to see how far things have gone," a reluctance, that is, to acknowledge that America "terrorized and intimidated an entire population."[61] But how terror and intimidation is performed by individuals who continue to feel blameless and who are apparently without remorse is not a question any reviewer has pursued. Instead, they have sought redemption for the rank and file, and, by extension, for all Americans.

CONCLUSION: EMBODYING EMPIRE

Torture has what we might regard as an almost built-in connection to race. Quite simply, torture is permissible against those we have evicted from personhood, even as torture itself guarantees this outcome. Nothing committed against *homo sacer* can be regarded as a crime, commented Giorgio Agamben, if the law has determined that the rule of law does not apply.[62] Torture's connection to two levels of humanity can thus be located in law. Whether "enemy combatants" or inhabitants of a refugee camp, the legal distinction that marks who enjoys the rule of law and who does not often thinly disguises the fact that the camp's inmates are *already* regarded as a lower form of humanity. Lazreg commented concerning Algeria that the French classified Algerians as "French Muslims" and as "protected subjects," the latter an especially ironic moniker given that those in this category were marked as outside the law's protection.[63] The Bush administration produced Muslims/Arabs in a state of exception in which the rule of law could be suspended in their case.

Drawing on Elaine Scarry's argument that torture is work mediated by the labor of "civilization," Lazreg notes that "torture finds justification in the alleged barbarity of the enemy."[64] In Algeria the French would often set up torture centers in old wine storehouses. Prisoners would often die from the sulfuric gases from the remnants of fermented alcohol, but there was the added bonus of "simply allowing alcohol, the object of a Muslim taboo, to work its invisible magic on the Muslim body."[65] We should not, therefore, be surprised that torture talk and culture talk merge so often. Cultural difference, the enemy's "innate barbarism," is an important element in the eviction of the tortured from the rule of law, and thus from humanity. The bikini panties wrapped so diligently around the heads of the prisoners tortured at Abu Ghraib present a lesson intended more for the torturer than for the tortured, reaffirming the former's cultural superiority and the latter's lower form of humanity.

Post-torture discussions create community as much as torture itself does, continuing racial terror through narrative. In these narratives, torture is not torture at all but interrogation methods gone awry or soldiers carried away as if at a frat party. Culture talk, or in its absence simply an outright dehumanization of Iraqis, undoubtedly helps Americans become reconciled to having tortured. President Obama's statement that Americans don't torture and President Bush's justification for torture may in the end come to mean the same thing when we consider that not only have officials evaded prosecution for their role in torture, but those of the lower ranks who have been charged remain for the most part unrepentant and socially embraced. Their refusal to take responsibility and the public forgiveness of their acts remind those of us who share color, religion, or region with the tortured that our lives are similarly valued. The femininity of the torturers, so celebrated by filmmakers and reviewers alike, strikes terror in the hearts of anyone who watches and waits for an acknowledgement of the violence done to Iraqis.

POSTSCRIPT: "I WANT YOU TO FEEL THAT IRAQI LIFE
IS PRECIOUS"

Iraqis have certainly understood the meaning of American actions. I began this chapter with a story of cultural difference, and I would like to end with another. On May 4, 2008, an intriguing story appeared in the *Los Angeles Times*: "Blackwater Shooting Highlights a U.S., Iraq Culture Clash."[66] Blackwater workers killed seventeen Iraqis, including the son of an Iraqi man, Abdul Razzaq, in what the Iraqis called a massacre and Blackwater described as a situation that arose because their workers feared for their lives. U.S. officials were investigating the shooting, but in the meantime they attempted to provide monetary compensation to Mr. Razzaq, who refused it. The reporters offered their analysis of this strange impasse:

> Far from bringing justice and closure, the investigations underline the fric-
> tions between Americans and Iraqis that have plagued the five-year U.S.
> presence. The shooting and its aftermath show the deep disconnect between
> the American legal process and the traditional culture of Iraq, between
> the courtroom and the tribal *diwan*. U.S. officials painstakingly examine
> evidence and laws while attempting to satisfy victims' claims through cash
> compensation. But traditional Arab society values honor and decorum
> above all. If a man kills or badly injures someone in an accident, both
> families convene a tribal summit. The perpetrator admits responsibility,
> commiserates with the victim, pays medical expenses and other compen-
> sation, all over glasses of tea in a tribal tent. "Our system is so different
> from theirs," said David Mack, a former U.S. diplomat who has served
> in American embassies in Iraq, Jordan, Lebanon, Libya, Tunisia and the
> United Arab Emirates. "An honor settlement has to be both financial and
> it has to have the right symbolism. We would never accept their way of
> doing things, and they don't accept ours." Framed as a culture clash, the
> article ends with the voice of another victim, Baraa Sadoon Ismail, 29, a
> father of two who was severely injured in the gunfire who is reported as
> "miffed" when asked whether he planned to seek compensation. "I want
> you to feel that Iraqi life is precious," explained Haitham Rubaie, a physi-
> cian who lost his physician wife and medical student son and who rebuffed
> efforts at compensation (offered in the form of a donation to an orphan-
> age). "No amount of money", he added "will sweep this under the rug."

It seems certain that the United States really will never accept this way of doing things, this quaint cultural way of acknowledging that Iraqi life is precious and that fathers whose wives and children have been blown to bits require a meaningful apology. Our system is indeed different from theirs. We are, I suggest, neither post torture nor post empire. Here, cultural explanations reveal the perniciousness of Western refusal to grant that Iraqi life is precious.

Framing the issue as a culture clash, the article ends with the voice of another victim, Baraa Sadoon Ismail, a twenty-nine-year-old father of two who was severely injured in the gunfire and who was reported as having been "miffed" when asked whether he planned to seek compensation. "I want you to feel that Iraqi life is precious," explained Haitham Rubaie, a physician who lost his physician wife and medical student son and who also rebuffed efforts at compensation (offered in the form of a donation to an orphanage). "No amount of money," he added, "will sweep this under the rug." It seems certain that the United States will never really accept this way of doing things, this quaint cultural way of acknowledging that Iraqi life is precious and that fathers whose wives and children have been blown to bits require a meaningful apology. Our system is indeed different from theirs. We are, I suggest, neither post-torture nor post-empire. Here, cultural explanations reveal the perniciousness of Western refusal to grant that Iraqi life is precious.

NOTES

The author thanks Nazira Mawji and Corey Balsam for research assistance, and Leslie Thielen Wilson for her comments.
Epigraphs: President Barack Obama, State of the Union Address, February 24, 2009. My thanks to Carmela Murdocca for the suggestion about the meaning of Obama's declaration and for the idea of a "post-torture" era. Taussig 1987, 3.
    1. Associated Press, "Obama Open to Charging Officials over CIA Interrogations," *Toronto Star,* April 22, 2009.
    2. Taussig, *Shamanism, Colonialism, and the Wild Man,* 27.
    3. Achille Mbembe, "Aesthetics of Superfluity," *Public Culture* 16, no. 3 (2004): 373–405.
    4. Marnia Lazreg, *Torture and the Twilight of Empire: From Algiers to Baghdad* (Princeton: Princeton University Press, 2008) 7.
    5. Ibid., 121.

6. Ibid., 184.

7. I offer this example from my own experience, but prefer that the workshop and its participants remain anonymous.

8. Joshua Dratel, "The Curious Debate," in *The Torture Debate in America*, ed. Karen J. Greenberg (New York: Cambridge University Press, 2006), 113.

9. Stephen Holmes, "Is Defiance of Law a Proof of Success? Magical Thinking in the War on Terror," in *The Torture Debate in America*, ed. Karen J. Greenberg (New York: Cambridge University Press, 2006), 127.

10. Michael Omi and Howard Winant, *Racial Formation in the United States from the 1960s to the 1990s*, 2nd ed. (New York: Routledge, 1994), 53.

11. Ibid., 61.

12. Ibid.

13. Ibid., 145.

14. Ibid., 59.

15. The following two pages are excerpted from my book *Casting Out: The Eviction of Muslims from Western law and Politics* (Toronto: University of Toronto Press, 2008), 65–66.

16. See Samuel P. Huntington, *The Clash of Civilizations and the Remaking of World Order* (New York: Touchstone Press, 1997).

17. John Gray, "Power and Vainglory," in *Abu Ghraib: The Politics of Torture*, ed. Meron Benvenisti and Barbara Ehrenreich (Berkeley, CA: North Atlantic Books, 2004), 50.

18. Mark Danner, "The Logic of Torture," in Benvenisti and Ehrenreich, *Abu Ghraib*, 31.

19. Ibid., 32.

20. Heather Macdonald, "How to Interrogate Terrorists," in Greenberg, *The Torture Debate in America*, 86.

21. Andrew C. McCarthy, "Thinking about the Unthinkable," in Greenberg, *The Torture Debate in America*, 96.

22. Timothy M. Jones and Penelope Sheets, "Torture in the Eye of the Beholder: Social Identity, News Coverage, and Abu Ghraib," *Political Communication* 26, no. 3 (2009): 278–295.

23. Darius Rejali, Paul Gronke, et al., "U.S. Public Opinion on Torture, 2001–2009," http://journals.cambridge.org/action/displayAbstract?fromPage=online&aid=7819652.

24. David Cole, "What to Do about the Torturers?" *New York Review of Books* 57, no. 1 (January 15, 2009): 20.

25. Ibid., 22.

26. Karen J. Greenberg, "Introduction: The Rule of Law Finds Its Golem; Judicial Torture Then and Now," in Greenberg, *The Torture Debate in America*, 1.

27. Jane Mayer, *The Dark Side: The Inside Story of How the War on Terror Turned into a War on American Ideals* (New York: Doubleday, 2008).

28. Michelle Shepherd, "Document Lays Bare CIA Torture Techniques," *Toronto Star*, April 8, 2009.

29. Milgram conducted a series of experiments to study obedience. Subjects were invited to administer electric shocks to a victim. As the experiment progressed, subjects were asked to administer more intense shocks. Milgram examined when subjects refused the orders. More than half of his subjects continued to obey orders until the end even though they exhibited considerable emotional strain while doing so.

30. See, for example, the contributions in Greenberg, *The Torture Debate in America.*

31. Mark Danner, "US Torture: Voices from the Black Sites," *New York Review of Books* 56, no. 6 (April 9, 2009), http://www.nybooks.com/articles/22530 (accessed January 25, 2011).

32. Ibid.

33. Veterans of the conflict in Iraq adopted the term *Winter Soldier* from Vietnam Veterans Against the War, which sponsored a media event called the Winter Soldier Investigation from January 31, 1971, to February 2, 1971, to publicize the war crimes of the United States Armed Forces in Vietnam. See Andrew E. Hunt, *The Turning: A History of Vietnam Veterans Against the War* (New York: New York University Press), 1999; Richard Stacewicz, *Winter Soldiers: An Oral History of the Vietnam Veterans Against the War* (New York: Twayne), 1997.

34. Richard Weisman asked this question in "Showing Remorse at the TRC: Towards a Constitutive Approach to Reparative Discourse," *Windsor Yearbook of Access to Justice* 24 (2006): 221–239.

35. Sherene Razack, *Dark Threats and White Knights: The Somalia Affair, Peacekeeping and the New Imperialism* (Toronto: University of Toronto Press, 2004).

36. "Errol Morris" (video interview), *The New Yorker,* October 5, 2007. www.newyorker.com/online/video/festival/2007/MorrisGourevitch (accessed January 25, 2012).

37. Errol Morris, *Standard Operating Procedure* (Participant Productions and Sony Pictures Classics, 2008), video; Philip Gourevitch and Errol Morris, *Standard Operating Procedure* (New York: Penguin Press, 2008).

38. Joanne Laurier, "Standard Operating Procedure: Images from a Neocolonial War," *World Socialist Website,* June 17, 2008, http://www.wsws.org/articles/2008/jun2008/sop-j17.shtml (accessed January 25, 2012).

39. Amy Goodman, " 'The Ghosts of Abu Ghraib'—Doc Traces Path to Torture of Prisoners at Infamous Iraqi Prison," *Democracy Now,* March 21, 2007, http://www.democracynow.org/2007/3/21/the_ghosts_of_abu_ghraib_doc (accessed January 25, 2012).

40. Amy Goodman, "Winter Soldier: US Vets, Active-Duty Soldiers from Iraq and Afghanistan Testify about the Horrors of War," *Democracy Now,* March 17, 2008, http://www.democracynow.org/2008/3/17winter_soldier_us_vets_active_duty (accessed January 25, 2012).

41. Ibid.

42. Amy Goodman, "Winter Soldier: Hundreds of Veterans of Iraq and Afghanistan Gather to Testify in Echo of 1971 Vietnam Hearings," *Democracy Now*, March 14, 2009, http://www.democracynow.org/2008/3/14/hundreds_of_veterans_of_iraq_and.

43. Weisman, "Showing Remorse at the TRC."

44. Lazreg, *Torture and the Twilight of Empire*, 2 (emphasis added).

45. See Razack, *Dark Threats and White Knights*, 58. "In Africa, who can be a saint?" is my paraphrase of Ridley in *Images of Imperial Rule* (New York: St. Martin's Press, 1983), 71, 104.

46. Gourevitch and Morris, *Standard Operating Procedure*, 273.

47. Ibid., 277.

48. The lesbian relationship is casually inserted and unremarked upon in the story, implying that we are watching a film and reading a book made by progressive people. Unlike the Fox News commentators for whom the label *homosexual* for Arabs marks Arab barbarism, the mark of lesbianism in the soldiers places Americans in modernity.

49. Gourevitch and Morris, *Standard Operating Procedure*, 112.

50. Ibid., 117.

51. Ibid., 160.

52. Ibid., 164.

53. Ibid.

54. Errol Morris, quoted in Omar P. L. Moore, "In American Torture and Terror, Errol Morris Finds Shades of Black, White and Gray," *The Popcorn Reel*, March 1, 2008, http://www.popcornreel.com/htm/errolmorris.htm (accessed January 25, 2012).

55. Ian Buruma, "Ghosts," review of *Standard Operating Procedure*, by Philip Gourevitch and Errol Morris, *New York Review of Books*, June 26, 2008, 6–10.

56. Peter Goddard, "Images of Abu Ghraib," *Toronto Star*, June 1, 2008.

57. Ibid.

58. Michael S. Roth, "Framed," review of *Standard Operating Procedure*, by Philip Gourevitch and Errol Morris, *Los Angeles Times*, May 25, 2008, http://articles.latimes.com/2008/may/25/books/bk-roth25 (accessed January 25, 2012).

59. Michael Chaiken, review of *Standard Operating Procedure*, by Philip Gourevitch and Errol Morris, *Film Society of Lincoln Center*, May 8, 2008, http://www.filmlinc.com/film-comment/article/standard-operating-procedure-review (accessed February 22, 2012).

60. Cynthia Fuchs, "Fraction of a Second," review of *Standard Operating Procedure*, by Philip Gourevitch and Errol Morris, *Pop Matters*, May 2, 2008, http://www.popmatters.com/pm/review/58148/standard-operating-procedure (accessed January 25, 2012).

61. Laurier, "Standard Operating Procedure."

62. Giorgio Agamben, *Homo Sacer: Sovereign Power and Bare Life*, trans. Daniel Heller-Roazen (Stanford: Stanford University Press, 1998), 3.

63. Lasreg, *Torture and the Twilight of Empire,* 4.

64. Ibid., 3.

65. Ibid., 118.

66. Borzou Daragahi and Raheem Salman, "Grieving Iraqis Want Honor First, Not Money," *Los Angeles Times,* May 4, 2008, http://articles.latimes.com/2008/may/04/world/fg-blackwater4 (accessed February 22, 2012).

ELEVEN

The "War on Terror" as Racial Crisis

HOMELAND SECURITY, OBAMA, AND RACIAL (TRANS)FORMATIONS

Nicholas De Genova

The election of Barack Obama to the U.S. presidency in 2008 presents racial formation theory as well as radical racial politics with a crucial historical juncture unsettling some of the very meanings conventionally affiliated with the concept of "race." This is the case for the larger social formation of the U.S. nation-state as well as for a global sociopolitical order in which the United States plays a preponderant role. The stakes for sociopolitical processes of racial formation and transformation have been predictably profound, but not in the facile ways that many observers might have optimistically forecast. In this respect, the mercurial figure of Barack Obama and the equivocal significance of his election must be understood as manifestations of a historical moment of *racial crisis*, situated within the larger, more extended, and distinctly amorphous racial crisis of the so-called War on Terror itself. In a way analogous to the police beating of Rodney King and the Los Angeles rebellion in 1992 following the acquittal of the brutalizers, which Michael Omi and Howard Winant rightly identified as a watershed moment in U.S. racial politics (1994, 145; cf. 1993), we are challenged to discern comparably momentous *racial* significance in the events of September 11, 2001, the devastation of Hurricane Katrina in 2005, and the subsequent Obama presidency. Above all, we must analyze their interrelations and correspondences. In the face of these tumultuous landmark episodes in the recent history of the United States (and despite injunctions to the contrary), we find ourselves, in Omi and Winant's words, "compelled to think racially, to use the racial categories and meaning systems into which we have been socialized"— because "opposing racism requires that we notice race . . . that we afford it the recognition it deserves and the subtlety it embodies" (1994, 159). These flashpoints have plainly not entailed the sorts of crisis instigated or provoked directly by racially self-conscious social movements. Nonetheless, they have represented major disruptions or disjunctures in the "unstable equilibrium" of what Omi and Winant have incisively depicted as "the racial state" and its social order, and have commanded the requisite strategies and tactics of absorption and insulation through which to redomesticate racial unrest and restabilize dominant politics (1994, 86–87). Comparable to the L.A. rebellion, but in ways that are still more variegated, convoluted, and equivocal, these events signal crisis because they intensify and reveal "the ambivalences, fault lines, and polarizations which characterize U.S. racial identities today" (1993, 104–105) and, likewise, summon forth tremendous political energies devoted to the *rearticulation* of their meanings and consequential salience (1994, 89–91).

Notably, the illusions that congealed around the Obama presidency because of the historically unprecedented *racial* singularity of his election were inseparable from the expectation that he would supply a liberal panacea to remedy the anti-terrorist excesses of the administration of George W. Bush. Thus, we must theorize the seeming paradox that Obama was celebrated simultaneously as both a grand *exception* in U.S. history (the first African American president) and also an ostensible "return to *normal.*" Both depictions contributed to the anxious sense that Obama's election signaled a kind of "restoration" of democracy (in contrast with the Bush White House's unabashedly illiberal recourse to often unbridled authoritarianism), while it spectacularly appeared nonetheless to verify democracy's enduring vitality and resilience (supposedly evincing a collective repudiation of the prior administration's securitarianism and unilateral militarism). In short, the seemingly monumental election of this Black man to the U.S. presidency was marshaled to confirm an overarching narrative according to which, finally, all was really well and good in "America." Indeed, Obama was quite evidently eager to be the first one to tell us so.

FROM HOMELAND SECURITY TO A GLOBAL SECURITY STATE?

Anti-terrorism must be recognized as not merely a paranoid and self-serving rhetorical ploy but rather as the intransigent idiom of a new species of security state formation (De Genova 2007a, 2009). As Karl Marx incisively notes, "Security is the supreme social concept of civil society; the concept of the police" (1978, 43). The entrenchment of the Homeland Security State, domestically, has been inextricable from the so-called War on Terror's mission of *global* policing and from the "exceptional" status of the United States regarding the task of subjugating and putting in order the wild new frontiers of an unruly planet. The facile illusion in the wake of the Obama election that the most pernicious aspects of the Bush administration would now be simply ended, or promptly rectified by a new regime in the White House, has had to be tempered by a sober and intrepid assessment of the deeply consequential institutionalization of anti-terrorism. One need only note that in his speech on the evening of the election, Obama found it imperative to proclaim to the world: "And to all those watching tonight from beyond our shores, from parliaments and palaces to those who are huddled around radios in the forgotten corners of our world . . . a new dawn of American leadership is at hand. To those who would tear this world down—we will defeat you."[1] Even as Obama gestured toward a "new" (and by implication, different) style of "leadership," here was the requisite signal and the belligerent affirmation of an imperial will to overpower those who might dare to set themselves up as the enemies of "this world," which is to say, after all, this global regime of capital accumulation and its regnant sociopolitical order.

To adequately assess the meaning of Obama's characteristically "presidential" avowal to assert the role of the United States as caretaker and police enforcer for "this world," however, it is necessary to more fully examine the decidedly *globalist* current in the already well-worn doctrines and dictates established by the Bush administration over the course of its self-anointed Global War on Terror. Of course, this more cosmopolitan dimension of Bush's politics has often been easily overlooked in the face of the bombastic U.S. chauvinism and effusive parochialism of the other alternating current in Bush's discourse—his militaristic and millenarian U.S. nationalism. It is precisely in dialogue with that latter, "American exceptionalist" legacy that Obama also declared: "If there is anyone out there who still doubts that America is a place where all things are possible . . . tonight is your answer. . . . So let us summon a new spirit of patriotism."[2] Thus, Obama alluded obliquely to the *racial* specificity of his election and to its widely presumed implausibility, only to enfold that exceptional distinction into the task of reinvigorating U.S. nationalism. In this regard, more fundamentally, we may detect the work of exalting U.S. "nationhood" and inciting patriotism to be one that has deeply conjoined Obama and Bush, just as much as any dispute between them over the proper conduct of the so-called war against terrorism committed them together to a shared ethos of anti-terrorism and a multifaceted material and practical program of securitization, "domestically" and internationally.[3]

Only two months after his inauguration, upon announcing his new strategy for the war in Afghanistan and Pakistan, Obama spoke in terms luridly reminiscent of his predecessor:

> The situation is increasingly perilous. . . . 2008 was the deadliest year of the war [in Afghanistan] for American forces. . . . So let me be clear: Al Qaeda and its allies—the terrorists who planned and supported the 9/11 attacks—are in Pakistan and Afghanistan. Multiple intelligence estimates have warned that al Qaeda is actively planning attacks on the United States homeland from its safe haven in Pakistan. And if the Afghan government falls to the Taliban—or allows al Qaeda to go unchallenged—that country will again be a base for terrorists who want to kill as many of our people as they possibly can. . . . In the nearly eight years since 9/11, al Qaeda and its extremist allies have moved across the border to the remote areas of the Pakistani frontier. This almost certainly includes al Qaeda's leadership: Osama bin Laden and Ayman al-Zawahiri. . . . For the American people, this border region has become the most dangerous place in the world. But this is not simply an American problem—far from it. It is, instead, an international security challenge of the highest order. . . . The safety of people around the world is at stake.[4]

Here, then, was a prompt reaffirmation and tidy condensation of all the key specters associated with the post–September 11, 2001 historical moment (al-Qaeda, Osama bin Laden, "planning attacks on the home-land," "terrorists who want to kill as many of our people as they possibly can"), reanimating the most vital energies of the so-called war against terrorism. On the other hand, it is simultaneously figured as an "international security challenge," which is to say that it is staged as a matter for global *policing*. Precisely as the official anti-terrorist "state of emergency" appeared to have been downgraded and deliberately understated, its very normalization ensured that its perpetuation would proceed apace.

Following more than seven years of the Bush administration's official and unrelenting "state of emergency," therefore, the ever amorphous, unbounded, and limitless Global War on Terror has continued to fecklessly pursue its ever mobile and always receding target. Thus, social inquiry into the processes of racial formation is challenged to produce a viable critique of the ebullience surrounding the Obama presidency, especially inasmuch as it was celebrated as a presumed "return" to "normal." Indeed, what we have been witness to—and what the Obama presidency has really signified—is precisely the *normalization* of the state of emergency. Apart from his evident and urgent service as caretaker for the U.S. state's supervision of a general resuscitation of neoliberal capitalism in crisis, which will have to be considered beyond the purview of the present essay, Obama's enduring commitment to *war*-making (and global policing) must be theorized in terms of what may otherwise be deemed to be a crisis of *race*-making. This task is especially salient, furthermore, insofar as his presidency has been so excessively celebrated as a watershed for the *un*-making of race. For, the stakes may indeed be precisely a new sort of "price of the ticket," to borrow James Baldwin's memorable phrase (1985), whereby admission into a putatively post-racial "American"-ness for African Americans and other (U.S.-citizen) racial "minorities" is being refashioned in terms of a docile and willing servitude to the securitarian and militarist requirements of U.S. empire. Needless to say, such a revalorizing of "the price of the ticket" likewise recalibrates the qualifications for access to the space of the U.S. state and economy and for eligibility for U.S. citizenship, for the aspiring (migrant or would-be migrant) denizens beyond U.S. borders, on a global scale.

THE AMERICAN EXCEPTIONALIST "STATE OF EXCEPTION"

In his speech on "national security," delivered on the eve of the Memorial Day (militarist) holiday weekend in 2009, Obama implored that "national security . . . must be a cause that unites us as one people and as one nation":

> My single most important responsibility as President is to keep the American people safe. . . . And this responsibility is only magnified in an era when an extremist ideology threatens our people, and technology gives a handful of terrorists the potential to do us great harm. . . . *We know* that al Qaeda is actively planning to attack us again. *We know* that this threat will be with us for a long time, and we must use all the elements of our power to defeat it. (emphases added)

And further: "Now this generation faces a great test in the specter of terrorism. . . . Right now, in distant training camps and in crowded cities, there are people plotting to take American lives."

All of this unnerving menace, Obama declared, using the omniscient "we" of the security state, was to be accepted as a matter of *fact*, something that "we know." Whereas he had previously invoked the ever secretive assurances of "multiple intelligence *estimates*" (emphasis added), now he made indubitable pronouncements. In this context, furthermore, Obama emphatically proclaimed anew: "Now let me be clear: we are indeed at war with al Qaeda and its affiliates," and in the entrenched idiom of the Bush administration's rationalizations for its overseas military adventures, he vowed to "take the fight to the extremists who attacked us on 9/11."[5]

In an astounding confluence of events that coincided (as if fortuitously) with Obama's speech—which gave renewed force to the critical purchase of Guy Debord's concept of the society of the spectacle (1967), and was very much reminiscent of numerous episodes during the Bush years—the universe appeared to conveniently verify the "objective truth" of a persistent terrorist menace, "at home" and abroad.[6] The day before Obama's speech, the Pentagon (in an as yet unreleased report) was reported to have determined that "one in seven" of the suspected terrorists released from their prolonged detentions in the Guantánamo Bay prison camp had "returned" to "terrorist" activity.[7] Furthermore, as reported that same morning, a "home-grown" terror plot involving four Black Muslim ex-convicts (replete with all the trappings of FBI entrapment) was spectacularly foiled in New York City, just the night before, and the alleged participants were indicted on charges of "a conspiracy to use weapons of mass destruction."[8] What Obama called "the specter of terrorism"—indeed, the spectacle of terror—was evidently alive and well (De Genova 2011b, n.d.). And it was not merely a matter of "foreign" malcontents but "home-grown" ones— African Americans and migrants racialized as Black—who would now have to answer to the dominant metaphysics of suspicion within a securitarian economy of culpability (cf. De Genova 2007a).[9]

In defense of an avowed policy of subjecting prospective alleged terrorists to military commissions (albeit a reformed version of them),[10] Obama reiterated one of the decisive metaphysical claims of antiterrorism: "After 9/11, we knew that we had entered *a new era*—that enemies who did not abide by any law of war would present new challenges to our application of the law, that our government would need new tools to protect the American people, and that these tools would have to allow us to *prevent* attacks instead of just prosecuting those who try to carry them out" (emphasis added).[11] In this sense, Obama upheld the logic of the *state of exception* instituted by the Bush administration, even as he openly criticized its "sincere" but "hasty" and ultimately misguided and injudicious excesses. True to the precise extralegality of any such sovereign decision regarding the "exception" for which the juridical order may be suspended (Agamben 2005), Obama maintained that the "new era" of anti-terrorist securitization presents exigencies for policing or military action that simply could not be constrained by existing legal statutes, and that the norms of constitutionality could be preserved, finally, only by means of these exceptional measures. Obama celebrated his strategy in terms of "principles that have been the source of our strength and a beacon to the world." Thus, a reaffirmation of the Rule of Law with regard to what he frankly depicted as the counterterrorist state of exception supplied the predictable signal to again uphold "America" *as exception*—lauding "the unique genius of America . . . what makes the United States of America different as a nation."

"American exceptionalism" has, indeed, always promoted a double-sided notion of the United States as exceptional in human history and worldly affairs. On the one hand, it is trumpeted as a refuge of liberty, a land of opportunity, and the champion of the natural and inalienable "rights of man," and as such, a nation uniquely anointed by divine providence (Tuveson 1968; cf. Horsman 1981). On the other, it is also the "exception" among the world's formerly colonial powers—an "empire of liberty," the bastion of freedom that putatively disavows and repudiates the temptations of colonial subjugation (W. Williams 1980). American exceptionalism paradoxically enables what William Appleman Williams depicts as the odd coupling throughout U.S. history of "an intense consciousness of *uniqueness*" and "a hyperactive sense of *mission*" (1976, 27; emphases in original), by which the grand and supposedly irreducible "exception" in human affairs was to be promoted as the ultimate and exemplary *model*, the worthiness of which was presumed to be self-evident for emulation by all the world (Adas 2001).

The Janus-faced conception of the United States as exception has thus provided an unlimited charter for a kind of explicitly and sanctimoniously "anti-colonial" imperialism (De Genova 2007b; cf. Adas 2001; A. Kaplan 1993, 2002). In the ghastly aftermath of the First World War, reflecting upon the global fact of white supremacy established through European colonialism, W. E. B. DuBois frankly identified this American exceptionalist conceit as blithe ambition. From the standpoint of the experience in the United States of "black and brown and yellow peoples," DuBois proclaimed his terse judgment: "It is curious to see America, the United States, looking on herself, first, as a sort of natural peace-maker, then as a moral protagonist in this terrible time. No nation is less fitted for this role" (1921, 50). At the end of the Second World War, again regarding the global question of colonialism, and with respect to the vexations of race and citizenship at home, so to speak, DuBois once more pronounced upon the inescapable requirement that the United States "abdicate its natural leadership of democracy in the world" (1945, 91). Indeed, the putatively exceptional status of the United States has effectively underwritten a dizzying cascade of exceptions. And yet, as Ann Stoler argues, "imperial states by definition operate as states *of* exception that vigilantly produce exceptions to their principles and exceptions to their laws. From this vantage point, the United States is not an aberrant empire but a quintessential one, a consummate producer of excepted populations, excepted spaces, and its own exception from international and domestic law" (2006a, 139–140). The exception of particular "populations" as intrinsically "suspect" or tendentially "dangerous," furthermore, as DuBois was quick to note, discloses the thoroughly *racial* subtext of this whole exceptionalist narrative of U.S. "national" formation, historically (De Genova 2006; cf. M. Jacobson 2000; Roediger 2008).

AMERICAN RACIAL EXCEPTIONALISM: FROM "COLOR-BLIND" TO "POST-RACIAL" AMERICANISM?

On the night of his victory, Obama himself encouraged the widespread sense of relief and reassurance that his election to the presidency should be presumed to signal a reinstatement of "democratic" *normalcy*. On that occasion, he characterized his campaign and his election as having "proved"—for "anyone out there . . . who still questions the power of our democracy"—"that more than two centuries later, a government of the people, by the people and for the people has not perished from this Earth."[12] The banality of this claim was notably underscored by the fact that Bush himself, in his remarks on the election, likewise celebrated Obama's victory as having "showed a watching world the vitality of

America's democracy."[13] But this chapter is centrally concerned, further-more, with the euphoric celebration of the election of an African Ameri-can to the U.S. presidency as the proverbial crossing of a kind of racial Rubicon—a spectacular and monumental *departure* from the racial status quo—marking the ostensible "end" of a historical norm of exclusive white political domination and inaugurating a new purportedly "post-racial" era. After Obama's election campaign had studiously evaded questions of race in spite of several efforts to cynically mobilize racist suspicion and contempt against his candidacy, therefore, the mass media—finally confronted with Obama's victory—could speak of nothing so much as the election's distinctly racial significance. The eruption that same night of various incidents of overtly racist violence perpetrated against Black people and other people of color, as well as the reports over the ensuing days that (white) "gun owners" were mobilized to secure still larger caches of weapons and munitions, likewise, seemed to verify that the moment of "post-racial" ascendancy was one deeply ensconced in the enduring fact of white supremacy.

On the night of his election, Obama himself dissimulated the racial singularity and salience of his accession to the presidency. Indeed, he compulsively deracialized his election in favor of a precisely American exceptionalist gesture of patriotic *post*-racialism. Obama alluded only ellip-tically to its racial significance when he referred to a 106-year-old woman (understood, strictly by implication only, to be African American) whom he figured as witness to more than a century of "change" and for whom the struggle against racial segregation was, according to Obama, on par with the fall of the Berlin Wall or the national mobilization for war following the bombing of Pearl Harbor. Across these and other examples, Obama contended that the "change" to be lauded was indeed but a feature of U.S. *national* splendor. "For that is the true genius of America," Obama insisted, "that America can change. Our union can be perfected." Obama affirmed repeatedly that the momentousness of the occasion served "to reclaim the American Dream and reaffirm that fundamental truth—that out of many, we are one."[14] Here, indeed, was the consummation of what Omi and Winant so presciently characterized in the early to mid-1990s as *"the new convergence in mainstream racial politics"* (1993, 100; emphasis in original)—"the emerging hegemony of the racial project of *neoliberalism*," which evades any frank acknowledgment of racial themes in order "to close the Pandora's box of race" (1994, 147; emphasis in original).

Many of these themes, now extravagantly deracialized, had in fact been rehearsed already in Obama's famous speech directly and explicitly addressing the question of race. Compelled on that occasion to renounce the presumably "inflammatory" racial opinions of his former minister, the Reverend Jeremiah Wright, Obama spoke in a refreshingly frank way about the legacy of past racial injustices, but rejected Wright's "profound mistake"—his "profoundly distorted view of this country—a view that sees white racism as endemic"—and affirmed that "America can change. That is the true genius of this country." True to the spirit of Omi and Winant's formulation of racial neoliberalism, Obama promoted "a false universalism" that could "only serve to mask underlying racial conflicts" (1994, 152). This false universalism, in Obama's hands, was none other than the parochialism of a reanimated U.S. national chauvinism. Indeed, in that speech, Obama had made a curious but telling assertion that would be widely repeated: "I will never forget that in no other country on Earth is my story even possible."[15] Thus, the stubborn and protracted fact of white supremacy was magically converted into a kind of racial American exceptionalism, whereby U.S. national greatness should now be measured and verified by the supposed "exceptions" to its own most heinous and atrocious rule of racial inequality and violence.

On the night of his election, moreover, in place of any substantive engagement with questions of race, Obama accordingly invoked instead "a new spirit of patriotism" and proclaimed "a new dawn of *American* leadership."[16] Whereas he downplayed the salience of race and sidestepped any and all reference to African American particularity, his defeated opponent, John McCain, in his concession speech on the night of the election, was remarkably forthright: "This is an historic election, and I recognize the special significance it has for African-Americans and for the special pride that must be theirs tonight." He continued:

I've always believed that America offers opportunities to all who have the industry and will to seize it. Senator Obama believes that, too. But we both recognize that though we have come a long way from the old injustices that once stained our nation's reputation and denied some Americans the full blessings of American citizenship, the memory of them still had the power to wound. A century ago, President Theodore Roosevelt's invitation of Booker T. Washington to visit—to dine at the White House—was taken as an outrage in many quarters. America today is a world away from the cruel and prideful bigotry of that time. There is no better evidence of this than the election of an African American to the presidency of the United States. Let there be no reason now for any American to fail to cherish their citizenship in this, the greatest nation on Earth. Senator Obama has achieved a great thing for himself and for his country.[17]

Thus, McCain candidly named the racial specificity of the election's significance, only then to immediately retrieve it for the recuperation of an American exceptionalist narrative of nationalist self-congratulation. Furthermore, he notably insinuated that what in fact distinguished Obama and his singular achievement was precisely his *industriousness* (by implication, in contrast with other Black Americans). McCain did so, moreover, in remarkably overt and utterly revealing reference to none other than Booker T. Washington, who famously advocated the purest of bootstrap-style African American self-help, precisely through "industry," and who likewise, notoriously disavowed the value of political struggles for civil rights and other sorts of entitlements.[18] McCain's oblique endorsement of Washington's homilies for "industry" therefore invoked anew what DuBois criticized at the time as "a gospel of Work and Money," tantamount to promoting a policy of disenfranchisement and submission (1969, 87). Here, then, in McCain's crafty analogy, was an astounding enunciation of the new "post-racialist" and "incorporative" commonsense of what Howard Winant has called "contemporary racial hegemony" (2004, xviii–xix), invoking the racial past in order to more thoroughly efface and erase it in the present. Like Omi and Winant, David Theo Goldberg has depicted this phenomenon in terms of a racial neoliberalism, committed to delegitimizing race in the public sphere and expelling it from the proper purview of the state (2009, 327–376), in effect, desacralizing race (334) and privatizing racism (23, 339).

McCain deployed the Obama election, moreover, to silence any further expression of racial complaint or grievance and to suppress anew any specifically racial objection to the claim that this is indeed "the greatest nation on Earth." Indeed, McCain subtly chastised Michelle Obama, yet again, for her candid remark, in the face of her husband's successes in the Democratic Party primaries, that she felt proud of her country for the first time in her adult life.[19] "Let there be no reason now for any American to fail to cherish their citizenship," he admonished. Indeed, McCain celebrated the momentousness of the Obama election only to still more emphatically relegate the legacy of "the *old* injustices" and "bigotry" to a very distant past, "a century ago" and "a world away." In this manner, the Obama victory was immediately pressed to serve as the index of an American racial exceptionalism with regard to the proverbial "American dilemma" itself, whereby the white supremacy that has shaped the United States from its inception could now be treated merely as an anomaly—a regrettable exception to the rule of U.S. national grandeur. Hence, the momentous surmounting of a monumental racial barrier would suffice to demonstrate that all such legacies of racial oppression were in fact merely a thing of the now remote past.

For his part, Bush celebrated the Obama victory in strikingly similar terms, but evaded any explicit acknowledgment of the particularities of race or any specific reference to African Americans as such. For Bush, overtly taking a cue from Obama himself, the election was evidence, for all the world to behold, of "the strides we have made toward a more perfect union." Furthermore, cannibalizing the American exceptionalism of Obama's depiction of his personal journey, Bush depicted Obama's accession to the presidency ("my story," in Obama's words) as "a triumph of the American story—a testament to . . . faith in the enduring promise of our nation." Nevertheless, Bush did then plainly gesture toward race by way of the only half-coded term "civil rights." Like McCain, he suggested the putative fulfillment and purported closure of a now decidedly *past* era of civil rights struggles over racial injustices: "Many of our citizens thought they would never live to see that day. This moment is especially uplifting for a generation of Americans who witnessed the struggle for civil rights with their own eyes—and four decades later see a dream fulfilled. A long campaign has now ended, and we move forward as one nation."[20] As for McCain, then, so also for Bush: by treating the concerns of the civil rights movement as the fading memories, from decades long past, of a prior and fast-fading generation, the Obama election could be endorsed as the proper "end" of that already *historical* era and as the verification of an American exceptionalist racial narrative of resilient perfectibility, inexorable progress, and dreams "fulfilled." The Obama election was recuperable, therefore, for a renewed and reinvigorated exaltation of U.S. nationalism, as Bush went on to speak of "this amazing country" as "the greatest nation on the face of the earth." Furthermore, with an only half-understated militarism and a precisely imperial worldliness, Bush went on to welcome the accession of "our next Commander-in-Chief" to that "most important responsibility—protecting the American people."

However paradoxically, as we have seen, Obama similarly subordinated any recognition of the racial salience of his election to precisely the same devout post-racialism and authorized its pronouncedly exceptionalist repackaging. In effect, Obama's presidentialism mirrored Bush's, as their respective postures were already prefigured by an obligatory U.S. nationalist script. In his inaugural address, with still more careful understatement than he had exuded on the night of his electoral victory, Obama acknowledged his own status as "a man whose father less than sixty years ago might not have been served in a local restaurant," only then to immediately (and preemptively) underscore "how far we have traveled." Moreover, celebrating the United States as the ultimate simulacrum of global inclusiveness— "shaped by every language and culture, drawn from every end of this Earth"—and referring to the legacies of "civil war and segregation" as but a "dark chapter" from which the nation has "emerged stronger and more united," he reaffirmed to the world that the United States should ever be seen as a beacon of the promise "that the old hatreds shall someday pass; that the lines of tribe shall soon dissolve; that as the world grows smaller, our common humanity shall reveal itself." He concluded that "America must" therefore "play its role in ushering in a new era" of global harmony and integration.[21] Thus, we may discern in this discursive terrain, which so strikingly unites Obama with his ostensible political adversaries, the project of a new regime of avowedly "post-racial" *Americanism*, deeply conjoined with a *global* project of imperial multiculturalism, articulated redundantly and emphatically in the time-worn language of American exceptionalism.

Yet this sort of officially "post-racial" Americanism and its ostentatiously colorful service to the intertwined projects of U.S. nationalism and imperial power may also be understood as, in fact, a culmination of the signature racial project of the Bush White House. Obama may be apprehensible, then, as the veritable culmination of the preceding administration, so prominently ornamented with the likes of Colin Powell, Condoleezza Rice, Alberto Gonzalez, and John Yoo. "Today less than ever," Omi and Winant remarked already in the 1990s, "does minority status correlate with victim status." (1994, 158). Indeed, during the Bush years, it became transparently evident that people of color could dutifully and unreservedly play some of the highest-profile roles in the global administrative work of securitarian and militarized victimization. What was abundantly manifest but devoutly unremarked on in the Bush administration—the fact that it was the most racially diverse presidential cabinet hitherto in U.S. history—may have been carefully enacted as racial neo*conservatism*, a dogmatic "colorblindness" whereby race is implicitly relegated to the status of something incidental that frankly no longer matters and is, in general, simply unspeakable. With the Obama presidency, in accord with the more ecumenical requirements of neo*liberalism*, racism is similarly privatized, and race rendered a matter that the state will now actively disregard (Goldberg 2009; Omi and Winant 1994, 147–157), while it reenlists and reinvigorates the agonistic energies of racial formation for the recuperative hegemonic project of "post-racial" U.S. nationalism (Winant 2004). What deserves further consideration, however, is the manner in which this distinctive American *racial* exceptionalism is finally apprehensible only in relation to what may be designated an *imperial* multiculturalism.

THE MUSLIM QUESTION: ANTI-TERRORISM AS A RACIAL PROJECT

The specter haunting Obama's presidency is indubitably the horrendous spectacle of Black misery that erupted from the vicious abandonment by the U.S. state of the African American citizens of New Orleans in the wake of the Hurricane Katrina disaster in August 2005, rendering them perfectly debased and unprotected (quasi-stateless) "refugees" wholly exposed to the terrifying prospects of mass death, disease, hunger, indefinite displacement, irremediable dispossession, and perpetual poverty. Here, it is instructive to recall DuBois's memorable depiction of the great mass of formerly enslaved African Americans in the aftermath of emancipation—as "a horde of starving vagabonds, homeless, helpless and pitiable, in their dark distress" (1969, 55).[22] Here in the Katrina aftermath, furthermore, was the definitive display, if ever there was one, of the obscene truth of the Homeland Security State and its most elementary conceits about safeguarding and protecting the U.S. population from cataclysmic emergency. The charade of Homeland Security, of course, did not collapse, but rather continued shamelessly grinding along, setting its sights on an ever escalating campaign of terror against deportable migrant labor, especially that of undocumented Latinos—a peculiar "war on terror" indeed, which has fashioned "immigration" as its most precious target (De Genova 2007a, 2009; cf. Fernandes 2007).

If Katrina flagrantly exposed the fatuous logic of securitization domestically, the war in Iraq and the protracted occupation of that country did much the same with respect to the putative "anti-terrorist" rationalizations for reenergized U.S. militarism globally. As Goldberg poignantly suggests, "post-Katrina New Orleans, in short, is simply Iraq come home" (2009, 89). And a vital animating thread linking these apparently disparate processes of U.S. state formation is the force of racism. For it was the enduring and protracted legacy of white supremacy that so predictably and callously set up the Black Americans of New Orleans for extinction domestically, while also so readily fashioning its nefarious and ever elusive transnational Enemy with the figure of the Muslim "terrorist" as a distinctly racialized one (Ahmad 2002, 2004; Bayoumi 2008; Cainkar 2002, 2003, 2004, 2005; Chon and Arzt 2005; Cole 2003, 47–56; Daulatzai 2007; Maira 2004, 2009; Puar 2007; Puar and Rai 2002; Saito 2001; Tehranian 2009; Volpp 2002; cf. Human Rights Watch 2002). Whereas Black hurricane victims were left to fend for themselves against the prospect of death by merciless abandonment, however, any and all Muslims worldwide were now subject to suspicion and surveillance, if not the utter abjection of *indefinite* imprisonment and relentless torture. Thus, the U.S. state's unabashed domestic profiling and selective persecution of Muslims, particularly noncitizen men, as alleged terror "suspects" was a decisive and defining feature of the new racial project of anti-terrorism and the dire need to produce "culprits" in its amorphous and borderless war. Indeed, "detentions"—or, more precisely, indefinite imprisonment without formal charges or any semblance of due process of law—truly became the hallmark of the Homeland Security State, with male Arab and other Muslim noncitizens overwhelmingly figured as its special targets (De Genova 2007a).

Obama's post-racialist racial persona, notably, is a complex condensation of a great heterogeneity of figures of identity and difference, for which the "Muslim Question," in particular, has been a persistent irritant. That his middle name is Hussein is of course only the tip of the proverbial iceberg. For, if Obama could be uniformly, resoundingly, and conclusively figured as "Black" or "African American" on the occasion of his election, his "mixed" racial and "multicultural" heritage has in fact been a remarkably more polyvocal affair, allowing him to be all things for all people, a cipher for the full gamut of post-racialist obsessions—and thus, perhaps also a man of a thousand disguises. Omi and Winant astutely alerted us in the 1990s to the profound complications that have emerged with "the multipolarity of racial identities" (1994, 158). Obama is perhaps the paradigmatic case for this sort of racialized complexity and its multifarious orientations on the shifting terrain of contemporary racial politics.

At various junctures in the course of his campaign, from diverse standpoints, Obama was both too Black (even alleged to be a militant Black nationalist) and also not "Black" enough (not truly African *American*), while also white (indeed, too white for some, and plainly never quite white enough for others), "American" but with a Hawaiian difference, "native" but also "immigrant," and for some, suspiciously "foreign"—perhaps African, perhaps Indonesian, and ultimately, for his most vigilant adversaries, the ultimate embodiment of "the sleeper," the War on Terror's frightful secret agent, alleged to be a madrassa-educated Wahhabi Muslim extremist "passing" as one of "us," merely waiting to be detonated for a mission of mass destruction. There was even a minor legal skirmish surrounding his disputed eligibility for the presidency based on questions regarding the validity of his birth certificate and the credibility of his claim to birthright U.S. citizenship. Beginning in late January 2008, Obama was notoriously pressed to disavow the allegation of his suspected Muslim identity, and to the chagrin of some who sought in his candidacy a kind of racially inclusive redemption, he responded irritably with the requisite quotient of dutifully anti-Muslim aversion. A campaign press statement declared definitively: "To be clear, Senator Obama has never been a Muslim, was not raised a Muslim, and is a committed Christian." The statement went further, though, denouncing the contentions as "malicious, irresponsible charges."[23] His campaign website characterized the allegation that he was a Muslim as a "smear."[24] He never candidly denounced the campaign for its baldly anti-Muslim premises, however. Then, in June 2008 (by which time, Obama had never yet made a campaign appearance in a mosque or before any Muslim or Arab American organization), two Muslim women supporters of Obama's campaign were prohibited from appearing in their head scarves behind their candidate on the podium where he was to address a Detroit rally under the unrelenting and unforgiving gaze of the mass media.[25]

The "Muslim Question" at the center of antiterrorism's racial project, then, commands some further consideration. Rather than a proverbial "specter" haunting the Obama presidency, however, the Muslim Question was inescapably established as its very overt and rather prosaic "problem"—a problem of racial government and domestic policing as much as an enduring and protracted preoccupation of imperial global superintendence and securitization. In his first overseas trip as president, in a speech to the Turkish Parliament, Obama revisited and expounded upon these multiculturalist themes:

> Let me say this as clearly as I can: The United States is not, and will never be, at war with Islam. . . . I also want to be clear that America's relationship with the Muslim community, the Muslim world, cannot, and will not, just be based upon opposition to terrorism. We seek broader engagement based on mutual interest and mutual respect. . . . The United States has been enriched by Muslim Americans. Many other Americans have Muslims in their families or have lived in a Muslim-majority country—I know, because I am one of them.[26]

Thus, the United States is figured as a national formation capacious enough and sufficiently devoted to a universal inclusivity to be able to encompass Islam and to espouse its properly *American* Muslims, while it is yet juxtaposed to a largely homogenized and monolithic "Muslim world." And whether it is explicit or merely implied, this gesture always crucially represents the United States as the epitome of the civilizational formation known under the peculiar heading of "the West."

A "CLASH OF CIVILIZATIONS," OR CIVILIZATION AND ITS MALCONTENTS?

Upon delivering his ultimatum to the Taliban regime as the prelude to war against the people of Afghanistan, it is instructive to recall, George W. Bush explicitly addressed himself to "Muslims throughout the world." He avowed: "We respect your faith. . . . Its teachings are good. . . . The enemy of America is not our many Muslim friends; it is not our many Arab friends."[27] Bush thus made explicit the capricious distinction between "good" Muslims and "evil" ones, enemies who "hate us" (cf. Mamdani 2002, 2004). What was decisive in Bush's magnanimously "multiculturalist" discourse of U.S. power, then, is the more fundamental friend/enemy distinction, which is inevitably premised on submission and conformity to the reign of the global regime of capital accumulation—a world sociopolitical order ultimately upheld and enforced by the United States. Hence, the ultimatum to the Taliban also notoriously provided the occasion for an ultimatum to the world: "Either you are with us, or you are with the terrorists." "Civilization" would be understood to signal submission and conformity; "terrorism" would stand as its all-encompassing alterity, signaling disaffection and defiance.

In this very crucial sense, then, Bush was never fiercely committed to the crudely anti-Muslim sort of discourse implicated in an endorsement of the identitarian "clash of civilizations" thesis propagated by Samuel Huntington (1993, 1996). Instead, Bush's discourse was an assimilationist one preoccupied with the task of hierarchically sorting and ranking Muslim "friends" and "terrorist" malcontents, all the while devoutly affirming a global project of imperial multiculturalism, whereby all merely "cultural" or identitarian differences could ultimately be accommodated and integrated within the planetary rubric of a singular Civilization, more or less coercively safeguarded and regimented under the supervision of U.S. military and political power. What bears repeating here is that Obama's similarly magnanimous gestures of "mutual respect" to "the Muslim world," fundamentally recapitulate this same globalist sensibility.

IMPERIAL MULTICULTURALISM: INDIAN WARS ON THE NEW FRONTIER

The insistence on the futility of imagining the future in any terms that might diverge from those of the anti-terrorist present was forcefully and incessantly sustained throughout the Bush years. That pronounced sense of the permanence of the War on Terror signaled a peculiarly militarized reiteration of Francis Fukuyama's triumphalism in the face of the supposed "end of communism" and the global hegemony of capitalism. In spite of its universalist and teleological rhetoric of inexorable progress, Fukuyama's original vision of the putative "end of history" (1989, 1992) was indeed one replete with the residual historical memory of a long saga of brutal coercion and colonization.

Articulated in the iconic terms of Manifest Destiny and the well-worn heroic mythology in which the West is perpetually reconstituted and reinvigorated through civilization's violent confrontations with, and conquests of, an ever receding frontier, Fukuyama concluded his much-touted essay with a quite revealing allegory:

> Rather than a thousand shoots blossoming into as many different flowering plants, mankind will come to seem like a long wagon train strung out along a road. Some wagons will be pulling into town sharply and crisply, while others will be bivouacked back in the desert, or else stuck in ruts in the final pass over the mountains. Several wagons, attacked by Indians, will have been set aflame and abandoned along the way. . . . But the great majority of wagons will be making the slow journey into town, and most will eventually arrive there. The wagons are all similar to one another: while they are painted different colors and are constructed of varied materials, each has four wheels and is drawn by horses, while inside sits a family hoping and praying that their journey will be a safe one. The apparent differences in the situations of the wagons will not be seen as reflecting permanent and necessary differences between the people riding in the wagons, but simply a product of their different positions along the road. (1992, 338–339)

In short, in Fukuyama's account, the manifest destiny of the entire planet must now be apprehensible as merely the universalization of the United States' colonial subjugation of the North American continent. In this account, accordingly, there are of course incorrigible differences— differences of the sort that can only be dealt with by means of crushingly violent reprisals and the utterly conclusive cultural politics of outright conquest. But the larger multiculuralist script contends nonetheless that "apparent differences" among diverse peoples ought not to count as "permanent and necessary" ones, but should only be the result of their respective positions along a unitary passage toward the eventuality of a global capitalist peace. Fukuyama's universalist claims for post-historical homogenization, then, perfectly express the imperious sort of imperial multiculturalism that seeks to transpose the American exceptionalist narrative of nationhood through inclusion and assimilation into a planetary model for perpetual capitalist peace.

In light of Fukuyama's overt reference to wagon trains "attacked by Indians," the War on Terror's "great divide in our time . . . between civilization and barbarism"[28] may be still more clearly located within the legacies of imperial "civilizing missions" and their multifarious discourses of *savagery*. Here, it bears noting emphatically that the mortal combat between civilization and barbarism is something quite distinct from a purported clash of "civilizations" (in the plural). If anti-terrorism's incorrigible "enemies of the 21st century"[29] are alleged to reject the purportedly *universal* values not of "Western civilization," but of Civilization itself, then the now globalized showdown emerges nevertheless as yet another heroic (and preordained) struggle on a new frontier to conquer the Wild West. And "if the West was at bottom a form of society," as Richard Drinnon has persuasively argued, "then on our round earth, Winning the West amounted to no less than winning the world" (1980, 464–465). Much as "the obverse of Indian-hating" had always been "the metaphysics of empire-building," as Drinnon demonstrates, so also must we discern in the metaphysics of anti-terrorism a renewed imperial project for the superintendence of global capitalism. And its obverse, an ardent loathing for the despicable "terrorist" Enemy, invokes yet another instance of intractable and inassimilable savagery, a residual but recalcitrant barbarism, in stark relief.

The sporadic eruptions of utterly retrograde passions against the illustrious forward march of humanity at the end of history could be principally expected, according to Fukuyama, from the dissensions of "the Islamic world." But as with earlier renditions of the Manifest Destiny theme, Fukuyama's grand finale entails a teleological narrative whose drama is false and empty: the "end of history" spins around a foregone conclusion.

> It is true that Islam constitutes a systematic and coherent ideology . . . with its own code of morality and doctrine of political and social justice. . . . And Islam has indeed defeated liberal democracy in many parts of the Islamic world, posing a grave threat to liberal practices even in countries where it has not achieved political power directly; . . . [however] while nearly a billion people are culturally Islamic . . . they cannot challenge liberal democracy on its own territory on the level of ideas. (1992, 45–46)

This passage was revealingly accompanied by a seemingly prescient footnote: "They can, of course, challenge liberal democracy through terrorist bombs and bullets, a significant but not vital challenge" (347n9). Very much consonant with the prosaic managerial outlook of empire's caretakers during the 1990s, terrorism was apprehensible as a kind of nuisance, not a "vital" threat, and very much an afterthought, literally a footnote to the grandiose dicta of one of global capitalism's most lauded soothsayers. In Fukuyama's account, Muslims could be expected to play the part of wild "Indians," haplessly assaulting some of the less fortunate, "strung out along [the] road," in the wagon train of humanity. Muslims would supply the heroic drama of the end of history with savagery's proverbial last stand.

In the end, what has dominated in the discourse of anti-terrorism is a revised variation of Fukuyama's "end of history" scenario, in which roaming bands of Muslim fanatics (transnational "networks") supply the figure of a reinvigorated savagery, mere "Indians" launching desperate and hopeless attacks. "Terrorists" are depicted not as vital contenders in a monumental "clash of civilizations," however, but rather as precisely *un*-civilized and atavistic naysayers engaged in monstrously irrational and aberrant acts, who pitifully set themselves up as the final Enemy of Civilization itself, and thus relegate themselves to their abject place outside humanity proper. (In Obama's lurid phrase, these anachronistic enemies were merely "those . . . huddled around radios in the forgotten corners of our world . . . who would tear this world down"). The menace of "terrorism" may have come to appear (in the rhetoric of the Bush administration) as posing a truly significant (indeed, epoch-making) challenge beyond Fukuyama's wildest nightmares, and was abundantly staged as a kind of new (unprecedented and unforeseen) world war of monumental proportions—the veritable "clash" of the century, which would continue beyond any reasonable horizon. Nevertheless, this was emphatically not Huntington's war of incommensurable and incompatible "civilizational" identities (at least, not officially). The Global War on Terror promised an indefinite and apparently interminable future of conflict and warfare, but these would be mere Indian wars on a new planetary frontier.

The War on Terror thus adamantly affirmed its post-historical character all the same. Now, indeed, there could be only one global (universal) Civilization—the empire of capital—in which all cultures, religions, and identities could be accommodated and assimilated, as long as they were properly subordinate to the mandates of capital accumulation. The resounding (explicit) ideology of the War on Terror has therefore been a kind of vapid and hypocritical imperial multiculturalism. Its cynical assimilationist universalism appears self-evident, however, only from the standpoint of those whose "differences" have already been effectively subordinated, domesticated, and "civilized." The submerged alternating current—an identitarian "clash of civilizations" devoted to hunting down and persecuting Muslims as always already susceptible to suspicion and, hence, as terrorism "suspects" by presumptive (racialized) definition—remains nonetheless the obscene underside of an unrelenting *disciplinary* mission to discern, sort, and rank, after all, who are the "good" ones and who are ever elusive "enemies."

The most fundamental work accomplished through the War on Terror's global racialization of "Muslim" identity is the production of a racial condensation that is inimical to the white (Christian, "European") identity of "the West," while yet, precisely, *ambiguous* and inherently heterogeneous. The racial ambiguity and instability of the figure of the Muslim is productive, then—subject always to suspicion, commanding surveillance and further investigation in the incessant police work of uncovering the "terrorists," who, it may be supposed, *refuse* to be assimilated.

By now, against this racially ambiguous but unequivocally nonwhite "Muslim" figure of alterity to the Global Security State, it ought not be difficult to discern the complex analogy that may be posited between Fukuyama and Obama.[30] Against the mutually exclusive and intrinsically incompatible identitarian "differences" of "culture" promulgated by Huntington's pluralist "clash of civilizations" thesis, Fukuyama and Obama in their somewhat discrepant but deeply interrelated ways have championed the globalist and assimilationist imperial project of "civilization" that was always the durable ideological centerpiece of Bush's rhetoric. In this respect, of course, they are the not-so-secret agents of U.S. nationalism and the empire of global capital. If Obama's post-racialist discourse of reanimated U.S. nationalism relies thoroughly on American exceptionalism as its proviso for policing the global empire of capital under a resuscitated U.S. military hegemony, Fukuyama's post-historical discourse of the permanence of neoliberal capitalism relies similarly on American exceptionalism as the premise for an imperial multiculturalism, in which virtually all differences of race, "culture," and religion may be subsumed, assimilated, and finally subordinated (De Genova 2010). Both men, of course, literally embody and epitomize white supremacy's post-racial and multiculturalist hegemony. Fukuyama is himself a descendant of migrants who were expressly racialized as not-white and historically rendered ineligible for U.S. citizenship on explicitly racial grounds. Like Obama, Fukuyama can cheerfully claim that his own father might not have been served in Washington, DC's local restaurants. As the iconic spokesmen for a resplendently post-racial Americanism and a devoutly imperial multiculturalism, Fukuyama and Obama dutifully render the service of revivifying American exceptionalism, proffering it as the legitimating narrative of an incipient

Global Security State, securing Civilization itself against the atavistic savagery of its terrorist malcontents.

CODA: THEORIZING RACIAL (TRANS)FORMATIONS

As we have witnessed the dramatic transformation and rearticulation of race *in* the United States since the social upheavals of the 1960s, the racial formations theory originally elaborated by Omi and Winant has proven to be remarkably well suited for analyzing "the *centrality of race*" (1994, 138; emphasis in original) and its constitutive role in U.S. social and political life, as both a premise and an ever malleable refraction of social struggles and political conflicts. In the agonizingly unstable equilibrium that is U.S. global hegemony in the twenty-first century, beleaguered and overextended as it may be, we cannot escape the enduring epistemological and methodological centrality of race, as this essay seeks to demonstrate. However, that centrality must be persistently reconceptualized and still more explicitly formulated in terms sufficiently flexible to apprehend *the imbrication of the United States in the world*, and the inextricable presence of those worldly concerns within the ostensibly "national" space of the U.S. racial state.

Omi and Winant's insistence that "race" is always entangled in dynamic social relations of struggle and political conflicts, and therefore retains a pervasive and persistent (seemingly intractable) significance—precisely because its forms and substantive meanings are always eminently historical and mutable—has proven enduringly versatile. The analytic framework of racialization and racial projects, furthermore, attends to the unforeseen extension and rearticulation of racial meanings to social relations, practices, or groups that may have previously been racially unclassified, or differently classified, in the unresolved historically specific contexts of struggle (1994, 55–56; cf. Winant 1994, 58–68). Nevertheless, today more than ever, it is evident that the United States cannot be adequately conceptualized as simply an insular and self-contained "society," a parochial "national" social formation unto itself. Rather, the United States is a historically specific spatial and political conjuncture that particularizes the global relation of *the political* in terms of a necessary *mediation* between the global regime of capital accumulation and the territorial definition of coercive state power on a "national" scale (Holloway 1994). In fact, it was never sufficient to comprehend the United States—and its racial order in particular—in any terms except those that could problematize the restless and relentless (veritably colonial) production of the ever unstable "inside" and "outside" of its nation-state space (De Genova 2006).

If the study of race does indeed ensnare us within "a world of paradox, irony, and danger" (Omi and Winant 1994, xi), the contemporary economic and political weight and military dominance of the United States on a planetary scale necessarily also insinuate the politics of race and the processes of racial formation into the world at large, with all manner of incumbent paradoxes, ensuing ironies, and explosive perils (De Genova 2007b). One need only note that it is a standard and long-established convention of U.S. militarism to refer to the theater of warfare or colonial occupation, always and everywhere, as "Indian country" (see, e.g., R. Kaplan 2004, 2005; cf. Drinnon 1980; Silliman 2008). Or one need only recall the facility with which the term nigger could be deployed to disparage such disparate overseas racial targets as Filipinos during the U.S. invasion in 1898 or Iraqi "sand niggers," particularly during the first Gulf War in 1991. Simultaneously, the processes of racial formation "in" the United States cannot be adequately comprehended as long as they are treated as somehow autochthonous. The imperial project of the United States and its compulsive war-making, globally, have been a constant source of reanimated and reenergized struggles over race-making "domestically." Thus, the subtle meanings and putative substance of "race," however treacherously misleading in its apparently "national" involution, have become ever more transnationally convoluted.

This, indeed, is the sense of *global* horizon that DuBois already understood with astounding perspicuity and forceful urgency in his formulation of "the color line" as a problem of planetary scope and import.[31] DuBois was perhaps singularly eloquent in his damning interrogation of white supremacy in the early part of the twentieth century as "the ownership of the earth forever and ever, Amen" (1921, 30) with its "new religion of whiteness" (31) and its unanimous global "doctrine of the divine right of white people to steal" (48). By the middle of the twentieth century, while still confronting a world thoroughly throttled by European and Euro-American colonialism and white racial dominance, DuBois already noted the steady demise of the bankrupt ideology of racial inferiority and the putative "natural" incompetence of people of color for "civilization" and self-government. "We are not nearly so sure today as we used to be," he wrote at the end of World War II, "of the inherent inferiority of the majority of the people of the earth who happen to be colored." However, because "government and economic organization [had] already built a tremendous financial structure upon the nineteenth-century conception of race inferiority," DuBois contended, such altered perspectives on race (and the accumulation of historical, anthropological, and biological facts to bolster them) continued to change little or nothing about actual human behavior in the modern world. In this context, DuBois could recognize the persistence of the colonial system as "a method of investment yielding unusual returns" (1945, 55), "a method of carrying on industry and commerce and of distributing wealth" (56), which was therefore a crucial part of a global "battle between capital and labor" (55) and which had ensured that the colonies were "the slums of the world" (17). "This," he concluded, "is what the imperialism of our day means" (54).

If Du Bois had famously forecast in 1903 that "the problem of the Twentieth Century is the problem of the color line" (1969, 3), by mid-century he had come to rearticulate this key insight as "the problem of the future of colonies" (1945, 57). "The color line," therefore, always already implied an open-ended sense of futurity that would be grounded, nevertheless, in the racialized historicity of a precisely colonial universality. And, much as DuBois had earlier forecast that "a belief in humanity is a belief in colored men" and women, that "the destinies of this world will rest ultimately in the hands of darker nations" (1921, 49), he remained resolute in his sense that this problem of the future of colonized humanity would be "fundamental for the future of the world" (1945, 9). Certainly, the tumultuous drama of decolonization that ensued irreversibly discredited the most intransigent dogmas and most tawdry rationalizations of the colonial racisms. However, the enduring material and practical consequences of a world rigorously organized and regimented according to the pallid doctrines of white racial supremacy predictably ensured that the ostensibly decolonized future of the colonies has not ceased to be a world of slums inhabited by "the majority of the people of the earth who happen to be colored" (54). DuBois supplied a memorable descriptive outline of the quintessential features of life in the colonies of his time: "black boys diving for pennies; human horses hitched to rickshaws; menial service in plethora for a wage near nothing; absolute rule over slaves, even to life and death;

fawning, crawling obeisance; high salaries, palaces, and luxury coupled with abject, nauseating, diseased poverty" (19–20). Much of this admittedly "imperfect" sketch of the bygone colonial world has changed only inasmuch as it is now crowned with the semblance of national sovereignty and "independence" and superintended locally—by elites of color. By the grace of neoliberalism's most stalwart and sacrosanct conceits about the bright prospects for "developing countries" and their "emerging markets," furthermore, postcolonial elites are now unencumbered as never before by any residual sense of responsibility for the "uplift" of "the people," much less any lingering sense on the part of the impoverished multitudes that they should expect from their putative leaders anything other than self-aggrandizement (see, e.g., Mbembe 1992).

This postcolonial travesty and its inevitable and unapologetic "post-racialism," as this chapter seeks to elucidate, has furthermore been extended and intensified in unforeseen ways. For even some of the highest-profile (and publicly visible) work of global superintendence over the avowedly "anti-colonial" empire of capital has now fallen into the capable hands of men and women of color. It ought not surprise us that such unprecedented racial (trans)formations should have finally ensued within the United States. Indeed, to understand these developments otherwise would be tantamount to reinscribing yet again the racial American exceptionalism that has been the hallmark of the Obama presidency. It was exactly the profundity of decolonization (and the most telling evidence of its truly planetary scope and scale) that conditioned and incubated the radicality of the insurgency against the racial state and the severities of white supremacy, "domestically," within the United States, during that same historical period (see, e.g., Singh 2004). The inescapable enlistment and capacitation of "native" ruling elites in the formerly colonized zones of the earth—mirrored by the political incorporation of people of color into the administration of U.S. cities in the immediate aftermath of what Omi and Winant rightly designated "the Great Transformation" (1994, 95–112)—have now been matched by an analogous racial recruitment of seasoned and exceedingly competent personnel in the topmost echelons of the state within the world's greatest military power. "This," if we may recall DuBois's haunting phrase, "is what the imperialism of our day means." This, indeed, is one of the most remarkable distinctions of the contemporary global empire of capital, and perhaps its signature innovation.

Acknowledgments: An earlier version of this essay was written as a keynote lecture and delivered to the conference "The New Frontiers of Race: Criminalities, Cultures, and Policing in the Global Era," sponsored by the Center for the Study of Race, Politics, and Culture, at the University of Chicago (May 29, 2009). I owe a note of warm appreciation and thanks to the organizers, Gilberto Rosas and Ramón Gutiérrez, for their gracious invitation; to all who participated in the workshop and enriched this paper with their own fine work; and to Jasbir Puar, Elana Zilberg, and Ralph Cintrón, in particular, for their thoughtful comments. Portions of this text were previously published as an essay in the journal *Identities* (2010). I am deeply grateful for the critical engagement and thoughtful reflections of several other colleagues, who responded in various ways to the text: Amanda Gilliam, Nisha Kapoor, Maria Kromidas, Nathalie Peutz, Josh Price, Dave Roediger, Sunonda Samaddar, Justin Stearns, and Howie Winant. My thinking in this revised essay has also enjoyed the benefit of insights from Nahum Chandler, Noel Ignatiev, and Daniel HoSang.

1. Barack Obama, "Remarks of President-Elect Barack Obama: Election Night," Chicago, www.barackobama.com.

2. Ibid.

3. Obama's long-standing commitment to escalate and expand the war in Afghanistan—and then, within the first months of his presidency, also Pakistan—only further corroborated these extravagant, seemingly gratuitous gestures of distinctly imperial "presidentialism" (cf. D. Nelson 2006). In fact, it was *Pakistan* that quickly came to be identified as the centerpiece of this revised War on Terror. A 2009 White Paper outlined the administration's new policy: "*In Pakistan,* al Qaeda and other groups of jihadist terrorists are planning new terror attacks . . . the core goal of the U.S. must be to disrupt, dismantle, and defeat al Qaeda and its safe havens *in Pakistan.*" White House, "White Paper of the Interagency Policy Group's Report on U.S. Policy toward Afghanistan and Pakistan," Washington, DC, http://www.whitehouse.gov/assets/documents/afghanistan_pakistan_white_paper_final.pdf (accessed January 16, 2012), p. 1; emphases added.

4. Barack Obama, "Remarks by the President on a New Strategy for Afghanistan and Pakistan," White House Office of the Press Secretary, March 27, 2009, http://www.whitehouse.gov/the_press_office/Remarks-by-the-President-on-a-New-Strategy-for-Afghanistan-and-Pakistan/.

5. Barack Obama, "Text: Obama's Speech on National Security," *New York Times,* May 21, 2009.

6. For more extended elaborations of Debord's conception of the society of the spectacle, see De Genova 2011a, n.d.

7. Upon closer inspection, of the seventy-four former prisoners alleged by the Pentagon report to have been engaged in terrorism, only twenty-nine were identified by name, and only five could be independently verified to have either

engaged in or even simply threatened to engage in "terrorist" activity. See Elisabeth Bumiller, "Later Terror Link Cited for 1 in 7 Freed Detainees," *New York Times,* May 20, 2009.

8. Among the so-called "home-grown" terrorists, denigrated as "jailhouse converts," the alleged plot was strictly "aspirational" in that the FBI "fully controlled" the whole affair, which "played out on a veritable soundstage of hidden cameras and secret microphones." An FBI informant previously arrested and sentenced to five years' probation for "identity theft" cultivated and effectively recruited a motley crew comprising an alleged "crack addict," a drug dealer, an unemployed purse snatcher medicated for schizophrenia or a bi-polar disorder and "living in squalor" amidst "bottles of urine," and a "particularly violent" steak-house employee who "lately had grown a beard and taken to reading the Koran." Mosque members reported that the suspected government informant, "the stranger with all the money," conspicuously "seemed to focus most of his attention on younger black members and visitors." See Al Baker and Javier Hernandez, "4 Accused of Bombing Plot at Bronx Synagogues," *New York Times,* May 20, 2009; Michael Wilson, "In Bronx Bomb Case, Steps and Missteps, on Tape," *New York Times,* May 22, 2009; and William K. Rashbaum and Kareem Fahim, "Informer's Role in Bombing Plot," *New York Times,* May 22, 2009.

9. For an important discussion of the particular salience of the figure of migrants who come to be racialized as "Black," see Nopper 2008.

10. Obama gestured on this occasion toward the statutory institutionalization of "preventative detention"—something that even the Bush administration had never broached. See Sheryl Gay Stolberg, "Obama Is Said to Consider Preventive Detention Plan," *New York Times,* May 21, 2009. For an extended legal elaboration of the reasoning in favor of a statutory delimitation of permissible "preventative" detention, see Cole 2009.

11. Obama, "Text: Obama's Speech on National Security."

12. Obama, "Remarks of President-Elect Barack Obama: Election Night."

13. George W. Bush, "President Bush on Obama's Victory," Real Clear Politics, press statement, November 5, 2008, http://www.realclearpolitics.com/articles/2008/11/president_bush_on_obamas_victo.html (accessed January 16, 2012).

14. Obama, "Remarks of President-Elect Barack Obama: Election Night."

15. Barack Obama, "Barack Obama's Speech on Race" (Philadelphia), transcript, *New York Times* March 18, 2008.

16. Obama, "Remarks of President-Elect Barack Obama: Election Night."

17. John McCain, "McCain's Concession Speech," transcript, *New York Times* November 5, 2008.

18. One need only recall Washington's lament, with regard to Black Americans: "Among a large class there seemed to be a dependence upon the Government for every conceivable thing. The members of this class had little ambition to create a position for themselves, but wanted the federal officials to create a position for them" (1995, 43). And further: "I had a strong feeling that what our people most

needed was to get a foundation in education, industry, and property, and for this I felt that they could better afford to strive than for political preferment" (44).

19. Fox News, "Michelle Obama Takes Heat for Saying She's 'Proud of My Country' for the First Time," February 19, 2008, http://www.foxnews.com/story/0,2933,331288,00.html (accessed April 24, 2012).

20. Bush, "President Bush on Obama's Victory."

21. Barack Obama, "President Barack Obama's Inaugural Address," White House Office of the Press Secretary, January 21, 2009. Available at: http://www.whitehouse.gov/the_press_office/president_barack_obamas_inaugural_address/ (accessed January 16, 2012).

22. Indeed, following what DuBois called the Reconstruction era's "full-fledged government" (1968, 66) of "the emancipated Negro as the ward of the nation" (62), post-emancipation African American mobility came to routinely signal for the propertied classes precisely a failure of government—a dangerously inadequate reconstruction of Black servitude, such that Black people's freedom of movement had likewise to be reconstructed as willful "vagrancy," shadowing literal bondage with the ostensible "crime" of vagabondage (Hopper and Milburn 1996, 124). I am grateful to Lynn Lewis, whose research as an activist and scholar concerned with race and homelessness in the United States, brought this particular reference and the convergence of these themes into clarity for me.

23. See Lynn Sweet, "Obama 'Has Never Been a Muslim': Obama's Gibbs' Memo on Madrassa Smear," *Chicago Sun-Times,* http://blogs.suntimes.com/sweet/2007/01/obama_has_never_been_a_muslim.html (accessed February 4, 2012).

24. See "The Truth about Barak Obama's Faith," Fight the Smears, n.d., http://my.barackobama.com/page/invite/christian.

25. Andrea Elliot, "Muslim Voters Detect a Snub From Obama," *New York Times,* June 24, 2008, http://www.nytimes.com/2008/06/24/us/politics/24muslim.html?fta=y (accessed January 16, 2012). In all of this, furthermore, it is instructive to recall that the ideological antecedent to racial whiteness in British colonial North America was, precisely, the concise protonational and deeply racialized figure of "Christian," in permanent and hostile opposition to Native American "savagery" (Roediger 2008, 9, 28).

26. Barack Obama, "Remarks by President Obama to the Turkish Parliament," Ankara, Turkey, April 6, 2009, http://www.whitehouse.gov/the_press_office/Remarks-By-President-Obama-To-The-Turkish-Parliament/ (accessed January 16, 2012).

27. George W. Bush, "Address to a Joint Session of Congress and the American People," White House, September 20, 2001, http://georgewbushwhitehouse.archives.gov/news/releases/2001/09/20010920-8.html (accessed February 4, 2012).

28. George W. Bush, "We're Fighting to Win—And Win We Will," Remarks by the President at USS *Enterprise* Naval Station, Norfolk, Virginia, on Pearl Harbor Day,

White House, December 7, 2001, http://georgewbush-whitehouse.archives.gov/news/releases/2001/12/20011207.html (accessed February 4, 2012).

29. George W. Bush, "President Speaks on War Effort to Citadel Cadets," White House, December 11, 2001, http://georgewbush-whitehouse.archives.gov/news/releases/2001/12/20011211–6.html (accessed February 4, 2012).

30. In the aftermath of the reckless occupation of Iraq in 2003, Fukuyama eventually distanced himself from the so-called neoconservative movement associated with the Project for a New American Century and became a vocal critic of Bush's policies of apparently failed "nation-building"; see Fukuyama 2004, 2006. Notably, Fukuyama endorsed the candidacy of Barack Obama for president in 2008.

31. For a crucial theoretical exegesis of DuBois's deployment of the idea of the color line, with particular attention to its original formulation as a concept operating within a *global* horizon, see Chandler 2006, 2010.

TWELVE

Racial Formation in an Age of Permanent War

Nikhil Singh

> The road which leads from the Indian massacres of the last
> century to the Pentagon and another from the oppressive slave
> plantation to the ghetto are the major conjunctive highways
> running through the very center of US life and history.
>
> JACK O'DELL, *"The July Rebellions and the Military State,"* 1967

> We are a nation of war; I mean a nation of law.
>
> CHRIS WALLACE, *Fox News Anchor, interviewing former New York
> mayor Rudy Giuliani, November 16, 2009*

> A Sovereign People are an Armed People.
>
> *Tea Party slogan, 2010*

In their important book, *Racial Formation in the United States from the
1960s to the 1980s,* Michael Omi and Howard Winant offered what might
be described as a first draft of the racial politics of the post–civil rights era.
Omi and Winant define "race" as "an unstable and decentered complex of
social meanings" that is at once foundational to, and made and remade in
the course of, political struggles (Omi and Winant 1986, 68). This way of
describing race marked a salutary theoretical development that expressly
worked against an incipient, neoconservative discourse of "colorblindness" that sought to undermine (with increasing success) normative, legal,
and political claims about the racial inequality in the United States in
the wake of advances toward civil rights and formal equality by erasing
positivist racial classification from law and social policy. Omi and Winant
acknowledge naturalistic reference to differentiated human embodiment
as the ideological kernel of race (a notion preserved by colorblind ortho-
doxy). They suggest, however, that when viewed in formation, conceptions of racial difference at once exceed references to phenotype and gross
morphology and come already embedded within broader struggles over

political power, social reproduction, and questions of governance. Understood this way, race is a historically given and politically reconstituted field of projected meaning and investment integral to the aggregation of socially significant identities—a form of collective imagination, and a way of imagining collectivity, that is secondarily codified in legal and biological (among other) terms. Such a perspective has presented a strategic and theoretical challenge to all static, particularistic, and essentialist framings of racial identity and conflict, insisting both on the universal effects of racial division across the social field and on the increasingly flexible and recombinant dynamics of U.S. racial orders.

More specifically, Omi and Winant's was a comprehensive attempt to capture within a new set of analytical rubrics the dimensions of change and relative permanence in the ordering of racial hierarchy and domination in the context of the tremendous victories, declines, and political reversals of the black freedom movement in the United States. It was also an effort—perhaps more implicit than explicit—to provide intellectual resources for reconstructing an *integrated* and *majoritarian,* yet also expressly *transformational,* anti-racist politics in one country, against a host of contending visions from the left that either heralded a return to the putative fundamentals of class division from the armchairs of defeated social democracy, or abandoned the field of social politics altogether, regrouping within the niche markets of multiculturalism or within the shrinking silos of "identity politics." Written against these currents, and at the height of "Reagan's America," *Racial Formation* was in this sense a brave and ambitious book. It sought to teach us how to talk about race in a period when "it was all about race," that is, one marked by a redeployment of the most vicious and invidious forms of pseudo-positivist racial description (and prescription), from Charles Murray's *Bell Curve* to Laurence Mead's "welfare queen"— and yet a period that asserted the normative value of colorblindness in which "nothing is about race" (Hancock 2004, 58). Indeed, the steady bifurcation of reality and reference in which an invidious racialism could successfully masquerade as neutral empiricism while racial justice claims could be dismissed as without basis or foundation represented a novel condition, one that still characterizes the present.

Like a number of other texts and approaches with which it might be grouped, *Racial Formation* was also situated within and sought to theorize broad transitions in the use and importance of racial ordering in the United States in the context of what has subsequently proved to be a fairly decisive unwinding of institutional supports and policy orientations of welfare-state liberalism. In one sense, this meant looking backward to what Omi and Winant described as the "great transformation" of the early post–World War II years through the end of the 1960s, during which white supremacy was normatively discredited and an inclusive, modestly ameliorative form of racial liberalism gained intellectual ascendancy. As numerous scholars have argued, this transition coincided with and was analogue to the U.S. emergence as the world's leading capitalist nation-state in the wake of world war and economic depression, a role defined by an unprecedented commitment to "secure," by force if necessary, multilateral commodity production and exchange across the planet (Dudziak 2004). In this context, the overcoming of historic racial exclusion was widely described as a legitimating frame for assessing U.S. claims to global leadership. As fungible as slavery was as a way of indexing white freedoms across the nineteenth century, to claim to be fighting "Communist slavery" was not easily reconciled with severe, ongoing, state-sanctioned discrimination against the descendants of U.S. slaves. From the 1950s, when the U.S. State Department intervened in support of school integration (on precisely these grounds), to the contemporary period, in which policymakers and pundits claimed that the 2003 invasion of Iraq was acceptable to the world because it was based on demonstrated U.S. achievement of democracy for all, rather than on the "white man's burden," public assertions of normative commitment to racial equality have become a banal truth, a staple of U.S. consensus ideology and official public discourse.

Within the generic, normalizing frame of racial liberalism, however, a much sharper conflict raged across the broad front of civil society within the United States concerning the speed and scope of racial reform at the end of the 1960s. At one end of the political spectrum, a heterogeneous black freedom movement broadly coalesced around a critique of the limits of racial liberalism—despite debilitating tactical and strategic differences about how those limits should be confronted. In this view, the formal achievements of civil and political rights for black people was viewed as merely an initial stage in a longer, ongoing social and political struggle aimed at dislodging possessive investments in white privilege that structured (and distorted) both libidinal and political economies of U.S. society writ large. At the other end of the political spectrum, a similarly heterogeneous politics of white self-interest regrouped across a range of discourses and strategies from states' rights, victims' rights, meritocratic individualism, and legal formalism, to selective withdrawal from or privatization of public domains and (for the least advantaged) a vigorous, at times violent defense of occupational sinecures and local neighborhood boundaries. The great irony, of course, is that looking forward, blacks would be blamed for upsetting the consensual applecart of racial liberalism, even as racial liberalism increasingly provided cover for restocking rotten defenses of racial privilege and articulating new ones.

It is fair to say that we have not yet taken a full or comprehensive inventory of the broad reconstitution of racialized disparity in the ensuing "post–civil rights" period, during which racial matters have increasingly become an unspoken referent and code for right-wing politics and social policy in the United States. Ronald Reagan's election was an inflection point, as the self-proclaimed states' righter confidently launched his presidential campaign in Philadelphia, Mississippi, site of the notorious murders of civil rights activists Chaney, Schwerner, and Goodman. At the same time, it would also be wrong to assume that the field of battle had been vacated: racial liberalism remained a normative baseline against which campaigns for the equalization of distribution and recognition along racial lines continued to be waged, and with notable successes, particularly in the media-sports-entertainment complex and educational sectors. Jesse Jackson's Rainbow Coalition and Harold Washington's Chicago mayoralty campaign, moreover, demonstrated new scalable potentialities for black-led, multiracial coalition politics within the electoral arena. On college campuses, the movement for South African divestment again signaled that racial exclusion and domination remained a universal concern with the capacity to galvanize social justice activism. Growing attention to the "intersectional" and intraracial politics of gender and sexuality, particularly within the arenas of law and social policy, augured new and expansive articulations of queer, feminist, and anti-racist perspectives. Meanwhile, across the color line, productive diversification of frames of reference occurred as hidden histories of Asian and Latino presence in the United States complemented and at times contended with monopolization of racial concerns by black/white paradigms.

It is arguable, however, that an understandable sense of a more or less even contest filled with both gains and reversals constituted the backdrop against which *Racial Formation* was written, and that this backdrop concealed a deeper process of bifurcation and fragmentation that had begun to reshape the possible trajectories of progressive racial politics on local, national, and global scales. The neoliberal restructuring project that arose in response to the global economic downturn of the 1970s and that became associated with the triumph of the Reagan-Thatcher administrations in the 1980s marked the consolidation of an increasingly repressive, upwardly redistributionist governmental regime within the developed zones of the world economy that sought to secure rising rates of corporate profitability through a more ruthless imposition of market discipline on those at the bottom of the social order. This was of course most discursively marked in Anglo-America, where the purified liberalism of the "Washington Consensus" resonated with long-standing cultural predilections and corporate constituencies. These were, not coincidentally, also places where "moral panics" over race, crime, and national security became the means for "shifting the very character of hegemony": rather than seeking a new, expanded consensus, elite and governmental preference became one of "managed dissensus" in which coercive projects—policing, punishment, and confinement—were both key social policy instruments and legitimating frameworks for securing ever narrowing bases of popular consent (Hall et al. 1978).

Put differently, a racialized law-and-order project was introduced during this period as the opening wedge in a broader reorientation of the very forms and dispositions of governance—what Stuart Hall and his collaborators in their landmark text *Policing the Crisis* (1978) described as the emergence of an "exceptional state." It is generally forgotten that alongside Lyndon Johnson's vaunted "war on poverty," which ostensibly aimed at maximizing welfare-state inclusion for the black poor (and the Vietnam War escalation that gradually starved it of resources), came the most dramatic expansion of federal crime control funding in U.S. history, with passage of the 1968 Omnibus Crime Control and Safe Streets Act (Mirpuri 2010). This was followed by a more or less continuous period in which policing infrastructures and practices in the United States were augmented, militarized, and gradually released from legal stricture in the face of a host of implicit and explicit fabrications of irredeemable black pathology, from wild youth to gangbangers, drug lords, and "street terrorists." Indeed, this period represented another sort of inflection point as the legal regime protecting the rights and bodily integrity of the accused and incarcerated, which had achieved its maximum extension in a series of landmark Supreme Court decisions in the 1960s and early 1970s, was inexorably rolled back (Singh 2006; Dayan 2008). In many ways Britain was in the vanguard of these developments, as its new emergency powers for preventive detention of potential domestic terrorists established an administrative regime of "anticipatory policing" increasingly freed from political oversight and judicial review (Hall et al. 1978, ch. 10). Developing both incrementally and substantively from the "war on drugs" to today's "global war on terror," what may be most characteristic of the new dispensation within Anglo-American liberalism has been a gradual blurring of and reciprocity between the discourses of crime and war, with criminalization of threats to the social order met with a consistent militarization of policing strategies and tactics, even as military action was increasingly justified in the name of policing the appetites of criminal regimes.

Emerging in such proximity to the 1960s racial upheaval and its fundamental expansion of welfare-state provision, the social engineering of the Reagan-Thatcher era retained the premise that the silent (national) majority would be spared the unforgiving cut of austerity, criminalization, and disposability. Thatcher's famous statement that "there is no such thing as society, only individuals and families," rested on the fantasy of "Little Britain" as a self-regulating moral and political domain—that is, it imagined a prior racial-sexual caesura within a population whose presumptive political membership was naturalistically ascribed, rather than being the disorderly product of distended migration. Similarly, Reagan's statement that he was performing a ritualistic and violent carving of the public domain drew on racial and gendered distinctions between a virtuous, hardworking citizenry whose unquestioned possession of a sovereign right to have rights contrasted with those whose rights were the artificial product of elite condescension, minoritarian maneuvering, special interests, and activist jurists, and therefore (at least potentially) politically revocable. The conceptual and legal challenge that those who sought the regeneration of white identity politics faced was to find new ways to exclude or limit inclusion of those for whom legal barriers and exclusionary stigma had been substantively reduced. Added to the growth of the carceral regime, and the enduring infrastructural barriers to mobility and employment, particularly for the black poor, the legal arena became a domain of especially fierce, racially inflected contestation. The gradual triumph of colorblind jurisprudence over the ensuing decades ensured that claims for redress under the terms of anti-discrimination law would be subject to the strictest scrutiny, even as assessment of the wide-ranging disparate impact of collective forms of racial inequality were rendered invisible or inaccessible under the minimalist, individualist, and reversible criteria of juridical formalism.[1]

At the same time, as much as the hard-edged racial themes of the Reagan restoration may have been a necessary condition for the rightward political realignment and electoral successes of the Republican Party during the 1980s and early 1990s, they proved insufficient for serving the more ambitious goal of permanently shifting the modalities of governance. Moderate racial inclusiveness in the form "diversity" and "tolerance" retained their ideological appeal, even in a public discourse that largely disavowed and disowned the historical depth and scope of the white supremacist distortion of social relations. While opposition to affirmative action and anti-poverty programs became central to advancing a politics of white self-interest, particularly at state and local levels, popular Great Society expansions of welfare-state provision like Medicare and Head Start early-childhood education remained in force. In retrospect, Lee Atwater's infamous, politically devastating "Willie Horton" ad, suggesting that George H. W. Bush's Democratic opponent Michael Dukakis's "softness on crime" would unleash black rapists and murderers upon an unsuspecting public, seems crude and caricatured in its overt appeals to racial fear. Indeed, it may now be difficult to recall how figures like Rudolph Giuliani rose to prominence leading a police riot on the steps of City Hall while promising to put "white guys back in charge" of New York City. Significant national opposition to the establishment of a holiday to commemorate the life of Martin Luther King Jr. now seems the project of a shrinking rearguard. Indeed, it is telling that the leader of the first congressional Republican majority in four decades, Newt Gingrich, publicly conceded that the one great success of modern liberalism had been its support for racial equality. However disingenuous we might judge such pronouncements (including Atwater's deathbed mea culpa), particularly in light of the increasingly well established tendency to code racial appeals in "colorblind" discourse and nonracial language, it seems clear that anti-black racism had diminishing political returns, even if the pacification and subjugation of the disproportionately black urban poor proceeded apace.

The point here is not to endorse a thesis of a "declining significance of race" or to suggest that anti-black racism does not retain an everyday significance and latent force that can be activated instantaneously; rather it is once again to point to the growing complexity of and sharp bifurcations within the field of racial meanings (W. Wilson 1980). It is hardly incidental that elite recognition of the need to rejigger the balance between consensus and coercion began precisely when formal democracy and legal inclusion for blacks had been stretched to its maximum within the welfare-state framework. Indeed, it is to be expected that as that framework was unwound, blacks—the perennial "canaries in the coal mine"—would be the first to suffer the consequences (Guinier and Torres 2003). Less obvious or foreseeable was the extent to which this process would far exceed prophecies of "benign neglect" and turn instead toward such ambitiously coercive institutionalizations, including the largest spate of prison construction in human history in the last two decades of the twentieth century. It is arguable, moreover, that social analysis and political organization have substantially lagged these developments (even though advances have been made in recent years). Indeed, it may be, as Adolph Reed argues, that the very normalization of racial liberalism had the effect of fundamentally narrowing, if not distorting entirely, the frame of social justice politics, as if demonstration of racial inclusion and "diversity" could be an exclusive means for marking a just settlement of social affairs, even as the most (racially) marked casualties of market society in a moment of neoliberal restructuring were increasingly abandoned, rendered disposable, or subjected to quarantine (Reed and Warren 2010). In other words, not only have racial exclusion and racial inclusion paradoxically risen in tandem, but also colorblindness and multiculturalism arguably stabilized as nonantagonistic (if contradictory) poles of contemporary (racial) common sense. Both sides tend to contend with each other from the baseline of a shrunken conception of polity, public, and personhood, underneath which the real axes of differentiation within orders of humanity at both local and global scales have grown increasingly obscure.

Indeed, the neo-Gramscian notion of a "racial war of position" advanced in *Racial Formation,* a conflict that unfolds across the terrain of civil society and constitutes the domain of "normal" politics, ideology, and group identity, may proceed alongside and partially obscure social and institutional processes that have gradually and surreptitiously reattached racial meanings to state capacities for violently excluding categories of persons as "exceptional" security threats; that is to say, the reanimation of a racialized relation as a zone of violence and insecurity that calls forth active state augmentation and intervention as its corollary. "Conventional wisdom holds that the United States faced an actual crime problem in the 1960s that was infused with racial politics," writes scholar Naomi Muru-kawa. The fact is that the "US did not confront a crime problem that was then racialized[;] it confronted a race problem that was then criminalized" (Murukawa 2008, 236). Put another way, what began to develop at the end of the 1960s was a process of reracialization that cut horizontally across the social field—that is, reactivation of an old reciprocity between acts of "legitimate" state violence and the "inhuman" worlds that become their object and rationale. In this mode of thought and social policy, violent state action and biopolitical security are paramount concerns and take precedence over any understanding of politics rooted in consensual demo-cratic action—even if democratic consent is sought to ratify these agendas. Moreover, in this view, any visible manifestation of what is deemed to be illegitimate violence—regardless of its reality, source, or etiology—becomes prima facie evidence for the necessity of preemptive violence on the part of state powers, or powers that act in the name of the state. In this way, violence becomes the figure and ground, the consequence and cause, of a categorically "new" social relation. That is to say, even though such violence may be mapped along the lines of existing social cleavages and (racial) differentiations, it also produces differentiating effects at the point of its application.

This approach might help us approach the vexing question of how the invidious racial differentiation of social relations persists and reconstitutes itself across profound changes in and challenges to sociolegal, spatial, and racial orders (e.g., plantation slavery, segregation, civil rights) (Wacquant 2002). More specifically, it can begin to unravel the apparent contradiction between the ongoing normalization of racial liberalism and the intensifica-tion of racially inscribed domination over the past several decades. If racism is defined, following Ruth Wilson Gilmore, as state-sanctioned production of group-differentiated vulnerability to premature death, then acts of state violence take precedence over ideological discourses as differentiating prac-tices (Gilmore 2007; see also Balibar 1991). In other words, to answer the vexing question, What is racism? one needs to begin not by identifying a set of preexisting, already categorized groups that are done to, but rather by delineating the formation and institutionalization of structures and situations of protection and vulnerability for which post hoc, descriptive accounts of dishonored group characteristics serve as a form of rationalization or justification. Retrospective rationalizations have consequences, of course, and become central to reinforcing and reproducing disparate vulnerability, which is why ideological forms of racism are important and need to be combated on their own terms. These also often become part of the formation of (counter)cultures of resistance, group identification, and linked fates among oppressed, stigmatized peoples that become a stake in reversing the valences of their own negation. In ideological terms, racism is knowable as a narrative structure of positions and habits of perception that corresponds with and responds to a *preceding, preexisting* regime of racial categorization and differentiation.[2] What remains to be explained, however, is how new racial orders are constituted. In other words, forms of past racial ordering are only partially predictive of racial (or nonracial) futures, particularly when we recognize the extent to which racial meaning crystallizes in the course of ongoing political struggles and across periods of vast social and economic change. The important point is that social differentiations that come to be known as racial have been and continue to be produced *in advance* of stable orders of racial reference and in contexts in which fields of racial reference are actively destabilized.

This understanding seems particularly important today, when historic forms of racist attribution and common sense have been widely challenged if not wholly discredited, and when the continuing reproduction of racial disparity proceeds through a powerful discourse of disavowal. If racial liberalism has tended to reduce racial meaning to problems of individual perception and prejudice, perhaps an unintended consequence of the intellectual challenges to ontological views of race that now underpin social constructionist and historicist accounts of the production of racial meaning is a tendency to hypostatize race as "merely" ideological—that is, as the more or less coherent expression of contending collective mentalities or group identities. As already suggested, the notion of race as a "decentered complex of social meaning" put forth in *Racial Formation* marks an important advance on this view. *Racial Formation* not only expressly resists efforts to cast race as "epiphenomenal" but also attempts to think through "racialization" as an active social process—"the extension of racial meaning to a previously unclassified relationship, social practice or group" (Omi and Winant 1986, 64). At the same time, the identification of race as primarily

a question of social meaning—even when that meaning has been understood to be productive of "structures" of inequality in wealth, employment,
housing, law enforcement, and the like—continues to operate within a
methodological discourse that imagines the category of race as something
that can ultimately be *precipitated out of social relations,* rather than as
something that is constantly made and remade *as a social relation.* In other
words, the problem continues to revolve around how to specify what makes
a certain social relation "racial'—which generally means identifying the
resurfacing of established, already recognized forms of racial discourse or
ideology to describe, interpret, or justify that social relation. This is why
so much intellectual and political debate continues to turn on the positivist validity of racial classification, the question of discriminatory intent,
or degrees of inclusion and exclusion, and yet fails to even recognize, let
alone explain, the extraordinary resiliency of institutionalized racial disparity and domination—in the absence of either extensive legal support or
strong ideological justification for such disparity.

Ironically, critical discourse about race today is most likely to task itself
with identifying a situation as "racial" in the face of public absence of such
recognition. In addition to its obvious intellectual and political weaknesses,
the claim that race (still) matters or that such-and-such is racist, however,
rarely captures the paradoxical durability and novelty of contemporary
racial conditions, which now include the delegitimization of formal racial
categories and ideologies by anti-racist struggles. The reality is that the
political decomposition of white supremacy has turned anti-racists into
detectives in search of the traces of racialized power, even as it has imposed
unprecedented ideological burdens upon putatively racist social movements and racially invidious policy prescriptions, which are now forced
to defend their nonracist bona fides even as they attempt to reconstitute
an exclusive sense of political constituency along racial lines. We are likely
to misconstrue this situation entirely, however, if we imagine that ideological racism has ever been fully disarticulated from the complex forms
of identification and modalities of political action in which it is always
already embedded. Racist adherence neither would be effective nor would
infuse collectivities were it not also a theory of political action and a persuasive account of the bases of social reproduction—including questions
of labor, gender, sexuality, and above all, nationality. At the same time,
the specifically racial component within contemporary political struggles
is increasingly difficult, perhaps even impossible, to definitively isolate.

Indeed, the political complexity and contradictions of the racial past/present in the United States have arguably never been so clearly on display as they are today. A highly visible coterie of black people, for example, have become enriched, powerful players in the U.S. media, sports, entertainment, and military complexes, even as a massive prison complex locks up one in nine black men between the ages of twenty and thirty-four and strips one in seven of the right to vote on the grounds of felon disfranchisement statutes (Alexander 2010). Three decades of more or less continuous immigration and household formation by peoples from Latin America and Asia now augurs a remarkable minority-majority demographic shift in the United States, even as police and military powers to confine, detain, deport, and kill predominantly Latino "illegal" immigrants and predominantly South Asian and Muslim "enemy combatants" have been expanded on unprecedented scales. The United States has its first popularly elected black president, and yet one who is assailed with unprecedented challenges to the very legitimacy of his birthright by groups who attempt to claim the mantle of the civil rights movement, even as they seek to reinterpret the Fourteenth Amendment by establishing new prerequisites for "birthright" citizenship (*jus soli*) for the children of "illegal" immigrants.

One would be hard-pressed to support the colorblind claim that the field of contemporary U.S. politics is not thoroughly racialized. As suggested by *Racial Formation,* moreover, racial meanings continue to inform and to be transformed by political struggle. What remains more difficult to explain in the contemporary period, however, is how extremely violent and unequal social relations—including those that may map onto preexisting racial cleavages—can now be immediately produced and publicly sanctioned without explicit reference to preexisting racial categories. Disfranchised felon, enemy combatant, and illegal immigrant, each enact a violent and exclusive social relation through a discursive and institutional process of criminalization without the requirement of a racial prerequisite. This raises the question whether all social relationships constituted through forms of extreme state violence should be considered "racial" or "racist"—which is to say, it broaches the central and unresolved question of how we can know something is "racial" or "racist" and why we might want to retain "race" as a category of analysis even when its epistemological grounds are shaky and its ontological basis largely refuted. The partial answer to this question is that race talk (and especially critical discourse about race) provides the vocabulary that allows us to record and index the recurrent institutionalization of and the ongoing, unfinished contest over the uniquely violent foundations of Western modernity in slavery and freedom, subjugation, and self-determination during a period when those foundations are increasingly obscured by platitudes about global markets, even as they are actively reconstituted by practices of permanent war (Goldberg 2009; Dirlik 2008).

To attain a political relevancy adequate to contemporary conditions, however, it is necessary to challenge the implicit or explicit nationalist horizons that still tend to define the posing of racial questions and challenges—that is, still tend to frame race as a question *for* the nation, rather than *of* the nation. From the standpoint of racial liberalism, for example, race and nation (and this goes back as far as Renan's famous disquisition) are antagonistic constructs of social and political identity (Renan 1996). Racial liberalism often retains traces of a primordialist or naturalist conception of racial difference, but it invariably consigns it to the temporal past and argues for the relativization, if not the wholesale disappearance of, racial particularity with respect to universal citizenship and socially consequential forms of political identity and equalization instituted by the nation form. Whereas racial liberalism imagines race and nation as antithetical ways of categorizing people and posits nationalism as a species of universalism that progressively triumphs over forms of racial particularity, the agonistic notion of the nation as a racial formation, and the state as a racial state, tends to see racism as an ever active, more or less permanent ideological constellation internal to the nation-state. At the same time, even in this conception the nation-state continues to be imagined as the political horizon of ultimate *deracialization.* That is, projects of racial egalitarianism remain linked to the nation form both as a pragmatic political reality and as an order of social mediation that is at least in some incipient sense nonracial, or racially neutral.

But what if we think of race less as a meaning complex that is pre-given and anchored in a set of antecedent biological or ethnic classifications of specific population groups within a particular nation-state, and more as an epistemic field that has been extended and filled with content according to specific historical imperatives of national sovereignty itself—Western modernity's preeminent governing rubric? Such a perspective, I would suggest, can enable a fuller appreciation of both the empty foundationalism and ceaseless reinventedness that seems to characterize the operation of race in modernity, what poet Leroi Jones once famously described as "the changing same." First and foremost is the distinction between sovereign and nonsovereign space, and the concomitant development of legal and ethical doctrines of sovereignty as a right to legitimate violence (up to and including the right to kill) within the colonial confrontation (Anghie 2007). Racial classification emerged within this context as a flexible rubric for both collectively marking and individualizing a kind of "anti-civilizational chaos" or excess, categorically opposed to sovereignty as a civil domain and life-protecting agency.[3] Phenotype was merely one element among many within heterogeneous assemblages of racial classification, which encompassed a wide range of markers for naturalizing colonial schematics of social, spatial, embodied difference, including language, geography, behavior, culture, technology, religion, sound, sexuality, and so forth (T. McCarthy 2009).

For the last half-century, one of the central ideological tasks of U.S. global power has been to cleanse sovereignty of its colonial-racial taint. Thus, as Nazi Germany and to a lesser extent imperial Japan came to be seen as the apotheosis of murderous racist states, and as violent decolonization proceeded fitfully, the colonial contexts for the production of modern sovereignty were gradually erased. Ironically, the global visibility of U.S. racial dramas played an important role throughout this process. For even as transnational contexts shaped the U.S. federal government's disavowals of white supremacy after World War II in the course of formally dismantling de jure racial segregation, black struggles were portrayed as a domestic, national concern without any particular relationship to the global context of decolonization. Over time, in other words, a U.S. "exceptionalist" account of race carefully excised the colonial context of its genesis. This was implicitly recognized by astute commentators like Gunnar Myrdal and diplomats like Ralph Bunche who understood that intranational racial reform within the United States was essential to modeling a form of global power capable of winning the affections of the emerging and soon-to-be (sovereign) darker nations. Of course, the toxic brew of white supremacist intransigence and anti-communist paranoia consistently poisoned the reservoirs of respect and good feeling that anti-colonial nationalists from West Africa to Southeast Asia may have held toward the United States. Meanwhile, radical black freedom movement activists within the United States repeatedly challenged the discourse of domestication as well as the accession to imperial foreign policy and colonial war that it supported, with accounts that emphasized the "special type" or "internal" form of colonization they suffered.[4]

With respect to political strategy and collective organization, comparative colonial global accounts of black suffering have fallen on hard times since the late 1960s and early 1970s, even as transnational and diasporic accounts of black cultural and intellectual production have achieved scholarly respectability and recognition. The consensus view defines racial reform, democratic expansion, and national inclusion as the main current of the U.S.-led phase of global history. From the mid-twentieth century to the present day, and particularly in the context of the partial successes of the civil rights movement (up to and including the election of Barack Obama), this conception has mostly gained force. The severing of the link between race and coloniality was part and parcel of the reification of race as a more or less exclusive figure for domestic law and positive science, which once again produced a situation in which a narrow (nationalist) politics of racial classification and identification submerged more expansive arguments about the relationship between race, ethics, political economy, and foreign policy. As Barnor Hesse writes, this not only represented a profound reduction of the scope and significance of race but also began to obscure its "prolonged historical invention and enactment" as a complex marker of inferior social status, civil incapacity, and civil threat that has continued to constellate contemporary social relations (Hesse forthcoming; see also Quijano 2000).

With the dominant narrative of civil rights success at the center, processes of citizen deliberation, legal reform, and inclusive nation-state building have thus been placed in the forefront of public understanding of U.S. racial politics. In recent years, a host of bizarre and troubling formulations have been built upon this ideological edifice, from Michael Ignatieff's aforementioned assertion that the 2003 U.S. invasion of Iraq was acceptable to the world because it was not based on "the white man's burden," to U.S. secretary of state Condoleeza Rice's claim that the African American civil rights movement helped the United States to "find its voice" as an armed champion of democracy overseas. A recent *New York Times* article by Adam Liptak purporting to explain the exceptionally high incarceration rates for blacks in the United States today is especially revealing on this score, "Many specialists dismissed race as an important distinguishing factor in the American prison rate," Liptak wrote. "It is true that blacks are much more likely to be imprisoned than other groups in the United States, but that is not a particularly distinctive phenomenon. Minorities in Canada, Britain and Australia are also disproportionately represented in those nation's prisons, and the ratios are similar to or larger than [those in] the United States."[5] Where Ignatieff and Rice link civil rights successes to an exceptional overcoming of the ordering mechanism of race within the post–World War II United States, Liptak effectively short-circuits a potentially lingering negative racial exceptionalism that might still define the nation; he does so through a comparative gesture that renaturalizes racial disparities at the global scale. What is remarkable here is how a demonstrated statistical consistency of invidious racial disparity across the leading national formations of white settler colonialism supposedly illustrates the putative normalcy and race neutrality of *all of them*. While this may represent a particularly glaring instance of sophistry, it again illuminates how race can persist as empirical description and effect that informs the texture of observations about everyday life, even as it is now disqualified a priori as a source of social action and power that might require adjudication. In a deeper sense, however, the quoted passage suggests quite precisely what may be the necessary parameters of our inquiry today—that is, not only how racial formation is irreducible to any specific national social formation, but also how it has been comparatively elaborated, assembled, and operationalized in relation to institutionalized, yet ideologically flexible zones of state-sanctioned violence and exclusion across the modern world system.

Indeed, when we consider the long durée of modern social formations, including the United States, we might consider how sovereign violence, rather than political struggle, or legal and scientific codification "overdetermines" the field of racial meanings and effects. This is what W. E. B. DuBois may have had in mind when he described the globally dominant racist formation of white supremacy of his day as "a kind of public and psychological wage" (DuBois 1998). Commentators on this phrase have tended to focus on the association between whiteness and wages with respect to the racial monopolization of fields of employment and the production of differentials within laboring populations that cut across the field of class struggle. As important, however, are the words *public* and *psychological,* for they highlight the transfer of whiteness to the threshold of nationality as an imagined community or public, or the constitution of race as a relation that links "democratic participation with the management of public authority and its specific mechanisms of violence" (Quijano 2000, 566). In his classic argument about the origins of race in colonial Virginia, for example, Edmund Morgan showed how carefully elaborated gradations in modes of punishment were one of the keys to the elaboration of racial status distinctions between African slaves and European indentured servants—black bodies could be whipped naked, whites would remain clothed (Morgan 1975). Although Morgan was interested in illuminating the power of law to codify or ratify a racial project, this example contains a deeper meaning. The long eighteenth-century expansion of white rights to political participation in the United States was articulated as an increasingly privileged relationship to the modalities of official violence and its legal narration: what defined the race relation was the fact that blacks and Indians could be killed with impunity.

The prospect of state violence, even war, has never been far from either the figuration or the conceptualization of race as a form of social relation. Beyond the obvious pecuniary and erotic interests that weighed against his tortured conscience, for example, Thomas Jefferson believed that racial slavery had implanted an impossible security threat at the heart of the U.S. republic. Blacks needed either to be quarantined or to be removed beyond the reach of admixture. If they were not, the "deep-rooted prejudices entertained by the whites: ten thousand recollections, by the blacks, of the injuries they have sustained," he wrote, would eventually lead to a war of "extermination of one of the other race" (Jefferson 1999, 149). Race war in Jefferson's account is explicitly imagined as civil war—the result of a traumatic and recurring state of injury that produces a divided collective experience that can be neither forgiven nor forgotten, and that thus remains outside the domain of the political understood as a regulated space of collective organization, rational action, and conflicts of interest. Blackness in this context is knowable only as threat—what Jefferson elsewhere described as that "immovable veil" that obscures what can only be a murderous wish or intention. The affinities of blackness with a discourse of crime are already emergent here. The great irony, as Jefferson implicitly recognized, is that it was the crimes committed by whites that constituted the real historical basis for the threat that was in turn displaced onto and into black bodies.

It is worth noting here that it is the potential for black equality—one might say black sovereignty or self-possession—that activates the fantasy of race war. Race war, moreover, needs to be distinguished from "normal" war—that is, war fought under terms of mutual recognition between equal sovereigns. Race war and colonial war are forms of war in which there can only be one sovereign and wars in which the enemy is not recognized as a political enemy, but rather viewed as an unjust enemy—or a criminal. In *Settler Sovereignty* (2010), Lisa Ford elaborates with great specificity how this process began with indigenous people across the settler colonial world in the mid-nineteenth century. It may be surprising to learn, given the weight of expansionist teleology, that the early U.S. republic largely tolerated plural forms of sovereignty under rubrics of warfare and treaty agreements that regulated conduct among different indigenous "tribes" and the U.S. federal state, all of which were considered to be distinct sovereigns. By the 1830s, settler sovereignty, however, decisively expanded its purview, precisely by describing indigenous violence (and countervio-lence) as a type of crime, and by in turn creating new legal narratives for settler violence. According to Ford (2010), the shift from a discourse of war to a discourse of crime is central to the substantive erasure of native sovereignty—a process that she tracks with remarkable consistency in the two decades before the 1850s.

Interestingly, this period gives rise to a fairly wide-ranging conversation that concerns how to mark the boundaries of war in which we can observe how violence against colonial and racial subjects—subjects deemed to be constitutively lacking sovereignty—is quite precisely unbracketed or sus-pended. War in racial and colonial situations, then, rather than marking a breach of normal politics—and "the continuation of politics by other means," as Clausewitz famously defined it—becomes instead the primary means of mediating and structuring social relations with those who are deemed in advance to be potentially criminal or unjust enemies. In an early iteration of this logic, Kant's *Metaphysics* (1797), after having laid out principle interdictions to war (including a ban on wars of extermi-nation and subjugation), quite stunningly asserts that contrary to what he has just been arguing, "the rights of a state against an unjust enemy are unlimited in quantity or degree." Who is the "unjust enemy" in the Kantian formulation? "Someone, whose publicly expressed will, whether expressed in word or in deed, displays a maxim which would make peace among nations impossible and would lead to a perpetual state of nature if it were made into a general rule" (see Baucom 2009). John Stuart Mill provided another turn on the same argument in "A Few Words on Non-intervention," written just after the Sepoy Revolt of 1857. Here, Mill suggests that principles of "non-intervention" scrupulously followed in relations among sovereign powers needed to be categorically suspended in the case of "barbarians," who "could not be depended upon to observe any rules" or "to place their wills under the influence of distant motives" (see Singh 2006).

If U.S. settler sovereignty begins and ends with Indians, as Ford suggests, it comes to linger in complex ways on blacks and blackness. In contrast to the frontier, where the eliminationist project was deemed successful from the standpoint of settlers, blackness cultivated and reproduced under the auspices of the slave regime remained suspended as a permanent threat, one that required investing every white person with the sovereign right to kill. Here, once again, we see a blurring of a military and police relation: citizen militias and slave patrols were functional equivalents, the routes they charted along the plantation hinterlands aptly called "the beat" (McCurry 1997). The incipient race war, moreover, did in fact manifest as a civil war—the greatest industrialized, mass slaughter in modern history up to that time. After the war, blackness would be legally suspended in freedom, much as it had been suspended in slavery, posing a consistent crisis for democratic sovereignty—even as it gradually also became a means to meditate upon the possibilities of fundamentally expanding the domain of democratic politics. The Reconstruction- and post-Reconstruction–era south was marked by an ongoing articulation of legal and extralegal police and white vigilante violence focused on disrupting, if not destroying, black social relations at the point of social reproduction (free labor, household formation), and by the constitution of the field of politics across the color line along paramilitary lines (Rosen 2008; Hahn 2005).

It is arguable that the "civil war" never really ended for blacks in the South: both legal and extralegal violence became a norm of black life. As one U.S. senator put it, "The black man does not incite antagonism because he is black, but because he is a citizen" (quoted in Logan 1954; see also Singh 2004, ch. 2). It is telling, moreover, that the signal innovation in racial science following Reconstruction was the development of racial crime statistics. As Khalil Gibran Muhammad shows, criminality rapidly became the key measure to adjudicate the fitness of black people for modern life, and black criminality became the most durable and "widely accepted basis for justifying prejudicial thinking, discriminatory treatment and the acceptance of racial violence as an instrument of public safety" (Muhammad 2010, 4). The Thirteenth Amendment had already shown the way forward by abolishing slavery, except as punishment for crime. The period that black historian Rayford Logan called the nadir was marked by a legal and quasi-legal regime of white terror in which thousands of black people were lynched and in which tens of thousands were murdered in prison and on convict-lease plantations (Perkinson 2010). The resolution of formal black freedom—civil and political rights—was, in this sense, explicitly calibrated to the augmentation of police power in relation to the ongoing social reproduction of blacks and blackness. As *Plessy v. Ferguson* put it in nationalizing miscegenation statutes, "Laws forbidding intermarriage of the two races may be said in a technical sense to interfere with the freedom of contract"; such regulation, however, "has been universally recognized as within the police power of the state" (quoted in Pascoe 2009, 74).

Police powers here mark the emergence of biopowers in the Foucauldian sense, but biopowers that are quite distinctly articulated to juridical right as the exception that underpins the rule by investing the police with a formless authority precisely correlated to zones of rightlessness and statelessness elaborated through colonial and racial violence. In other words, this is neither a strictly formal nor a functionalist aspect of modern sovereignty; rather it is the repetition of the founding logic of sovereignty along an increasingly widening axis of police power. Redeemer historian and founder of U.S. political science John Burgess put it in the following revealing formulation in 1893: "The police power is the Dark Continent of our jurisprudence" (quoted in Wagner 2010, 12). As Brian Wagner writes, from the standpoint of power, what constitutes blackness is its ongoing rearticulation to the conditions of statelessness. Statelessness, or nonsovereign existence, might further be characterized as a condition of social dissolution understood as *anathema* to social reproduction. The modern police power is precisely correlated to the "Dark Continent" as the domain in which social and political life is always already suspended. This condition constitutes a permanent state of emergency. From the standpoint of power, it has no knowable properties beyond its criminal propensity and open-ended threat potential. In other words, these threats are such that they require rigorous and ongoing applications of "legitimate" violence along a potentially limitless vector.

While the modern police power was articulated to a politics of white supremacy, it is important to note that its prerogatives were defined not as a defense of racial particularity, but as a defense of the constituent power of democratic (national) sovereignty. Put another way, we might say that racial distinctions have been made and remade as differentiations of zones of protection and vulnerability with respect to sovereign violence. Sovereignty, in turn, is simultaneously the object of popular-democratic claims and also a form of institutionalized (or state) authority. Racial politics has unfolded quite precisely within this space; yet it has hardly been an even contest. Drawing upon a liberal-democratic tradition, anti-racist movements across the twentieth century tended to appeal to institutionalized (state) authority for recognition and protection of individual rights within a civil domain understood as a negotiated plurality. By contrast, racist and exclusionary movements have consistently based themselves on a pre-constituted understanding of the homogenous fundament of sovereignty ("the rights of those who have rights") and in turn sought an identity or reciprocity with institutionalized (or constituted) power. For most of U.S. history, such reciprocity was easily achieved as ongoing and ever expanding institutionalizations of the military-police function have been articulated and operationalized in relation to figures of nemesis drawn from both readily at hand and available and newly fashioned and exotic regimes and repertoires of difference.

What may be exceptional, or at least notable, about the United States is the depth, duration, and significance of its intranational struggle and debate about racial exclusion. At the same time, when we recognize the extent to which sovereign violence constitutes law, we can also recognize the relative ease with which questions of racial difference and their attendant conflicts have been more or less immediately constituted as a threat to the very survival of the state. Speaking at the height of the civil rights movement and in opposition to impending civil rights legislation, Barry Goldwater declared, "Security from domestic violence, no less than from foreign aggression, is the most elementary and fundamental purpose of any government" (quoted in D. Rodriguez 2006, 20). Goldwater was drawing on a nascent discourse that pitted the "rights" of citizens against the chaos, disorder, and incipient criminality of racial protest politics. Modern conservatives who followed in his wake increasingly understood that one did not need to uphold statutory racial discrimination, but merely to draw compelling distinctions between law-abiding citizens and those who threatened their security. A neoconservative, as Irving Kristol famously put it, was merely "a liberal who had been mugged by reality." It was often the case of course, that race made all the difference when it came to producing a compelling distinction. But it is also the case that the very category of "illegality" or "criminal," particularly as it became part of the logic of an administrative apparatus, could increasingly do the work of racial sorting without explicitly maintaining the forms of racial codification that had been central to its origination.

In 1995 the passage of another large omnibus crime bill under President Bill Clinton established the preliminary legal and institutional architecture of what subsequently emerged in the wake of the terrorist attacks of 9/11/2001 as the massively expanded U.S. national security state, something that grew paradoxically and in spite of the end of the cold war, which had supplied the entire rationale for its initial growth.[6] Statutory provisions for the "rendition" of foreign drug traffickers and for the suspension of ancient strictures around the use of military resources and personnel within U.S. territorial borders accelerated the dissolution of moral and conceptual boundaries between inwardly concentrated practices of policing and public safety and outwardly tested military aggression, with effects on both sides of the equation. Self-styled global strategist and futurologist Robert Kaplan (reputedly Clinton's favorite public intellectual) captured the zeitgeist in his widely read essay "The Coming Anarchy." Writing in the wake of the Los Angeles riot of 1992, Kaplan tellingly diagnosed a fundamental mutation with the organization of the U.S. nation-state as an engine of homogenization and conflict stabilization, ascribing both (yet again) to the pathologies of black urban dwellers, who unlike the Jews and Irish before them, preferred the hostilities and illusory gratifications of "negritude" for the virtuous trials of assimilation. Kaplan went further still, suggesting that the dangers of inner (racial) fragmentation of the nation-space were magnified by a global situation in which a contagion of state failure, particularly in "Africa" (where else?), had the potential to inflame conflicts along racial and civilizational lines. In this context, he suggested (following the urban military theorist Martin van Creveld), fighting crime and waging war were gradually becoming indistinguishable, and "national defense" was no longer defined by unitary territorial logic but rather by multiscalar tactics and strategies of pacification and control.[7]

Kaplan's fixation on the disruptive and dangerous presence of black ontology at the internal borders of U.S. nationhood is once again highly telling, as is his sense that the disruption of national homogeneity constitutes a threat to sovereignty that is the functional equivalent of an undeclared (race) war. It is important, however, to recognize what Fred Moten has termed "the paraontological distinction between blackness and black people" if we are to grasp the ever fungible articulation and rearticulations of race and sovereignty in the contemporary moment (Moten 2008). If blackness has been the principle figure and ground for defining and enacting a racialized *inhumanity*, particularly in U.S. history, it has also proven to be at once analogically flexible and only one part of a heterogenous repertoire of racializing motifs that have in turn informed the creation of a heterogenous military-policing apparatus at home and abroad. It was the trigger event of 9/11, moreover, that gave such neo-Spenglerian racial-civilizationist declensionism a new impetus, providing both retrospective and prospective logic for what now appears as a definitive substitution of warfare for welfare models as the guarantor of social security within shrinking kingdoms of privileged prosperity across the Western world. Where pioneering Islamaphobe Bernard Lewis explicitly linked "terror and migration" as the twin specters haunting European civilization, John Lewis Gaddis reached deep into the American past, justifying new Bush administration doctrines of preemptive war on the grounds of a still-more-ancient sovereign right—that is, when the new nation needed to protect an open frontier against the depredations of "native Americans, pirates, and other marauders" (Gaddis 2003).

If *Racial Formation* correctly diagnosed the ways in which racial investments and referents were increasingly embedded within (if not constitutive of) broadly "hegemonic" political struggles and policy debates on a national scale, it did not (perhaps could not) foresee the extent to which race would continue to be operationalized in novel ways as a technology of wholesale, violent political and civil exclusion for large segments of the population, not only in the United States but anywhere people could be exposed to (a lack of protection from) sovereign violence (much of which, incidentally, can be traced back to the globalization of U.S. models and practices of police, security, and war). In this context, the laudable goal of reanimating race as a vehicle of collective, egalitarian political aspiration faced a number of challenges and obstacles, ones for which extant languages and frames of civil-inclusionist, let alone nation-based, politics have proven increasingly inadequate. Indeed, the recent turn in intellectual discourse to a largely *anti-political* rubric comprising terms like "state of exception," "bare life," "social death," and even "race war" might be said to index this state of affairs; that is, such approaches attempt to formally diagnose the limit conditions of the (exceptional) state form that has emerged as the norm in recent decades, even as they also express a certain pessimism, if not impotency, when it comes to thinking about conjunctural possibilities and ameliorative, let alone broadly transformative, political strategies. Thinking at the limit, it would seem, tends to limit thinking (especially critical thinking) to the most austere conceptualizations of enduring, if not entirely unchanging, modalities of racial dominance and state violence (without hegemony) across time.

This is a challenging, paradoxical situation. On the one hand, contemporary historical understanding, comparative elaboration, and theoretical conceptualization of U.S. racial formation has achieved a level of complexity and comprehensiveness unimaginable two decades ago. Building at least in part on the innovations of *Racial Formation,* hundreds of monographs and research projects have outlined the ways racial dispositions and powers have been shaped in the interstices of ideological struggle and institutional change, within a dialectic of social movement actors and governmental agencies, and at the nexus of foreign and domestic policies across the colonial and settler-colonial world. At the same time, a shift has occurred in which the expansion of the domains of application of state violence in the production of forms of group-differentiated spatial confinement, bodily dispossession, denial of civic honor and recognition, and vulnerability to violence, injury, and ill health (up to and including premature death) now proceeds largely without the requirement of an explicit codification of, or reference to, preexisting forms of group differentiation. This situation is ironically mirrored in certain critical tendencies toward formalist, ahistorical theorization. Whether this is termed a "new racism," "color-blind racism," or "racism without race," it is a form of power that produces disparate consequences in the absence of prior ideological rationalization or explicit group targeting: indeed, the express absence of particularistic, or "racial," intent (often in the form of disavowal) in part constitutes the "legitimacy" of such violence.

With specific attention to the U.S. context, we might say that concrete institutionalizations of militarized-carceral regimes over the past three decades, rather than the heroic struggle against "Jim Crow" and white supremacy, now form the principal background condition to the contemporary theorization of race. Of course, it might be objected that the popular election of Barack Obama, a black man, to the U.S. presidency fundamentally alters this picture, as Obama's rise was scripted from a carefully selected combination of African American civil rights narrative elements and post-racial prescriptive postures, colorblind adherence, and multicultural pabulum. The racial panic his election engendered among elements of the far right, moreover—from the "birther" movement to the Tea Party's "Obama as Hitler" rhetoric—attests to the destabilization and consequent scrambling of right-wing racial codes. Rather than a figure of black subhumanity and dishonored kinship that needs to be fixed in place through one of many peculiar institutions, racist depictions of Obama often tend toward those of Orientalism and anti-Semitism, in which the racial other is an enemy within, an inscrutable misleader who possesses unnatural, even superhuman powers, a person backed by foreign moneyed cabals, one who is not even our degraded kin, but whose very birthright is foreign and fraudulent.[8] In another sense, however, Obama merely entrenches the ideological baseline of multicultural post-racialism against which a resurgent white supremacy will contend only with great difficulty, particularly in the face of unfavorable, secular demographic trends.

Indeed, an underlying aspect of contemporary crisis, as Kaplan's writing demonstrates, is an increasingly audible panic about "the quotient of homogeneity" required for the continued existence of the nation-state form.[9] In the United States this question has long been mediated by the application of the equally fungible and strategically indeterminate term *white*, which reflexively precedes the constitution of political identity that "founds" democratic sovereignty. Yet the power of whiteness to do this work has been substantively, perhaps even fatally, diminished. The fundamental promise of Obama is his symbolic representation of an alternative national sovereignty no longer grounded in the history of white supremacy. Instead, it would seem, Obama represents the completion of the post-1960s passive revolution in which the exceptional state born of the accumulation crisis of the West in its incipient moment of globalization is given (a perhaps brief) new legitimacy. With his election, the historic impasse of black liberation against which colorblind discourse protested too much and multicultural discourse softened or acceded too readily can now be officially disavowed as completed, leaving so many to reinvent the wheel in empty forms of critique that would again fundamentalize race against its apparent erasure and therefore grasp neither what has changed nor what remains fundamentally the same in the current conjuncture. The danger, of course, is that the center will not hold and that the apparent truce or at least stalemate in the ongoing civil war will give way to something far more atrocious in its next incarnation, and the formidable machineries of surveillance, violence, and control assembled by the exceptional state these past decades will again be captured by those whose solution to the crisis of stasis is the project of race war—not only in distant theaters but across the broad front of civil society.

NOTES

1. For detailed analyses see Crenshaw et al. 1995.

2. This phrasing is indebted to Dyer 1997.

3. I am indebted to Gopal Balakrishnan for this formulation. See Balakrishnan 2009, 70.

4. While acknowledging the strengths of internal colonialism perspectives in connecting the intranational and global dimensions of racial oppression, Omi and Winant suggest that "nation-based approaches" to racial questions have been politically rather than analytically grounded, and more specifically that they are unable to specify what is "national about racial oppression." The remainder of the essay might be considered a kind of extended answer to this question.

5. Michael Ignatieff, "The Burden," *New York Times*, January 5, 2003; "Rice, in Alabama, Draws Parallels for Democracy Everywhere," *New York Times*, October 22, 2005, A4; Adam Liptak, "Inmate Count in US Dwarfs Other Nations," *New York Times*, April 23, 2008.

6. Dana Priest and William Arkin, "A Hidden World Growing beyond Control," http://projects.washingtonpost.com/top-secret-america/articles/a-hidden-world-growing-beyond-control/ (posted 7/19/2010; accessed 9/12/2010).

7. Robert Kaplan, "The Coming Anarchy," *The Atlantic*, February 1994.

8. This is not to say that historic anti-black themes are not present. Glenn Beck, for example, has described Obama as someone who hates white people and who wants to "settle old racial scores," presumably from the baseline of historically black racial grievances. More recently, Dinesh D'Souza and Newt Gingrich have sought to mau-mau Obama, as a figure of (African) violence and deranged anti-colonial and anti-Western grievance. Although the latter cases deploy historically anti-black themes, they also draw from a largely non-U.S. repertoire that in turn reassociates blackness with a sense of threats of the foreign and unfamiliar.

9. This phrase is from Balakrishnan 2009, xiv.

Racial Formation Rules

CONTINUITY, INSTABILITY, AND CHANGE

Michael Omi and Howard Winant

A LONG, STRANGE TRIP

When we initially advanced our concept of racial formation in the mid-1980s, we did not have the slightest inkling that it would prove both durable and flexible as a framework for understanding the changing meaning of race. The credit for its vitality goes not to us alone but also to scholars and activists from a wide range of fields who have creatively engaged racial formation theory and given it much of its ongoing significance, coherence, and utility. The contributors to this collection are among those leading the way in deepening our understanding of ongoing processes of racialization and interpreting the broader political meaning of "racial projects" both historically and in the present.

With this essay we seek both to situate racial formation theory in the historical period from which it first emerged and to apply it to racial politics today in the age of Obama. In the first subsection, "The Origins of Racial Formation Theory," we consider the problems that the theory was initially designed to address, and the thinkers and movements who influenced us. In a short transition, "Breaking with the Past: Trajectories of Racial Politics," we move to the present, drawing attention to the breadth and depth of the shifts in the meaning and social structure of race that the United States and the world as a whole have experienced over just the past few decades. In the following subsection, "Post-racial Scenarios?" we survey some contemporary analyses of changing U.S. racial dynamics and their implications.

After that, we present our own take on new patterns of race and racism. In "Racial Classification and Its Discontents," we examine the ongoing instability and changing meaning of the race concept and discuss such matters as census politics, the "new racial science," and concepts of race in popular culture. In "The Racial Regime and Its Discontents," we consider such issues as "colorblind" racial ideology, the U.S. demographic shift toward a "majority-minority" population, the role of race in electoral politics, race and empire, immigrant rights and resurgent nativism, and the racial dimensions of neoliberalism.

As this long list of topics indicates, we continue to see race and racism as fundamental dimensions of U.S. politics and society—deeply structuring social life at both macro and micro levels and profoundly shaping political discourse and ideology. Our concluding subsection, "Reconstructing Race," looks at U.S. racial prospects: a combination of chronic racial crisis and glimmers of hope for an expanding and deeper democracy.

THE ORIGINS OF RACIAL FORMATION THEORY

Our concept of racial formation emerged in the 1980s as a reaction to the then-dominant modes of theorizing about race in mainstream social science. We were trained in the social sciences; we were experienced anti-racist activists. We had come to reject the way race was conceptualized and operationalized, both in social science research and in left anti-racist thought and political practice. In mainstream social science, scholars failed to address the changing meaning of race over historical time and in distinct social settings. Race was ubiquitous, but the changing meaning of race and the "content" of racial identity went largely unnoticed. Conceiving race in a fixed and static way meant that researchers did not have to engage the very category of race itself and its social determinants. Treating race in a binary manner, for example as present/absent, 0/1, allowed researchers to correlate it simply and nonreflexively with the other variables in assessing patterns of residential segregation, income inequalities, health disparities, and so on. Of course, understanding racial inequality is important. But what is the meaning of race itself? How did race assume a given reality, a given significance, at a specific historical moment and in a specific social site? Such questions were rarely, if ever, asked.

Trying to address these problems ourselves led us to think of race as a social concept, something that needed to be critically engaged in its own right. One could not effectively analyze patterns of residential segregation, for example, without considering the racial categories that were utilized and encoded in research, in public documents, and in legal decisions at a given place and time. One had to ask not only how race shaped segregation but also how segregation reciprocally shaped race, how it invested racial categories with content and meaning. To assert that race is a social concept marks the beginning, not the conclusion, of "doing" racial theory.

Our initial take was to emphasize the "political determination" of race. This emphasis came from our simultaneous engagement and disenchantment with theories of race and racism on the political left. While firmly committed to the democratic, egalitarian, and social justice goals espoused by the left, we were critical of several assumptions that guided Marxist analyses of race. Race was seen as epiphenomenal to class, while racism was regarded as a specific form of "false consciousness" that muted class-based opposition to capitalist exploitation. From this perspective, race was strategically utilized by the capitalist class to sow discontent and create divisions within the working class, thus preventing the emergence of unified class consciousness and organization.[1] The task for the left was to challenge false racial consciousness and promote the primacy of class-based politics.

Skeptical of this position, we began to consider race as a legitimate and salient social category in its own right, on par with class. Adopting this approach allowed us to think about race as a fundamental principle of social organization in the United States. From there, we could discover how race could shape class categories as well as be shaped by them, and also how race was inextricably bound up with other axes of stratification and difference such as gender and sexuality.

Of course the concept of racial formation did not emerge out of thin air. We were inspired by some of the magnificent scholars who had gone before us, and we pillaged and borrowed from a variety of sources. The pioneering work of W. E. B. DuBois, E. Franklin Frazier, and Oliver C. Cox, among others, helped us understand the multiple ways in which race was a foundational and organizing principle of U.S. society, and how profoundly it had shaped social stratification historically. In particular, DuBois's notion of "double consciousness" (1969) was fundamental to how we thought about individual identity and collective consciousness. Bob Blauner's concept of "internal colonialism" (1972) was also instrumental in our rethinking of race. Although we criticized that paradigm in *Racial*

Formation, Blauner's treatment of the distinctions between "colonized and immigrant minorities" and the attention he directed toward the problem of cultural domination influenced us greatly. His efforts to link the "Third World abroad" to the "Third World within" continue to hold relevance for contemporary racial theory. Herbert Blumer (1958) and Troy Duster's symbolic interactionist account of race and racism (Blumer and Duster 1980) allowed us to think about "group position" and the consolidation of racial hierarchy. They showed how racial stratification profoundly shapes relations between racially defined groups. A crucial insight we took from symbolic interactionism was its emphasis on individual and collective agency and the ways identities and relationships were continually forged in social interaction.

The writings of Antonio Gramsci (1971) spurred us to rethink Marxism and supplied the key conceptual frames for understanding the transition from racial dictatorship to racial democracy. Gramsci's notion of *hegemony,* constituted by a combination of coercion and consent, allowed us to explore the consolidation, depth, and persistence of racial power. Through Gramsci we were able to conceptualize historical changes in the U.S. racial system and the ways in which a "war of maneuver"—a pitched battle between clearly located antagonists, between dominant and subordinate racialized groups—had given way to a "war of position," a pervasive conflict being fought out everywhere at once. Adam Przeworski's concept of "class formation" (1977) not only helped us rethink class but also provided a reference point for theorizing about race. Przeworski critiqued the notion that class was a distinct location within a mode of production and instead emphasized the highly relational and contingent political dimensions of class conflict. Ernesto Laclau's work (1977) demonstrated that ideological positions did not necessarily reflect discrete class positions but that themes such as populism and nationalism could be taken up and refashioned to express the interests and aspirations of different and antagonistic political blocs. Populism or nationalism could have authoritarian or emancipatory political framings. From such work we grasped the importance of political struggles over racial meaning and adopted the concept of *rearticulation* to illustrate how racial ideology could be refashioned to suit a variety of different and sometimes competing political positions.[2] To us, these were "better" Marxian analyses.

The theoretical insights of feminist scholars such as Sheila Rowbotham, Shulamith Firestone, and bell hooks, among others, also shaped our ideas in several important ways. Second-wave feminism was flowering as we wrote, and questions of race-gender "intersectionality" were first being raised. Thinking about gender as a distinct axis of stratification and differ- ence prodded us to conceptualize the category of race in a parallel fashion. The feminist movement advanced an understanding of gender, both ana- lytically and politically, as a social category—arguing convincingly that gender was not reducible to class. Feminism facilitated and deepened our critique of Marxist and left analyses of race and racism. Feminist theory also insisted on comprehensively linking both the micro and macro levels of social analysis. It dramatically revealed how concepts of gender were deeply embedded at all levels of human interaction and organization— from intimate relations within the family to the overall structure of pre- and postindustrial societies. Such an analysis was succinctly expressed by radical feminist Carol Hanisch's notion that "the personal is political."[3] We took such formulations to heart in our analysis of race. We paid atten- tion to the ways race was conceived, constructed, and practiced at both the micro level of everyday social relationships and at the macro level of institutional arrangements and social structure.

Our concept of racial formation was forged in struggle. We were inspired by and engaged in the new social movements of the 1960s and 1970s: the black power movement, the feminist movement, the antiwar movement, the student movement, the insurgent labor movement, and the struggles for ethnic studies on university campuses. The insights, issues, and contra- dictions generated by these social justice struggles became foundational to our work. Racial formation also reflected debates between the two of us. We worked out our positions through intense discussion, endless rewriting, and compromise. Our collaboration, now more than thirty years old, is a model for collective political and intellectual labor. It sometimes seems like a miracle, a marvelous gift that we have been able to give each other. Our work has truly been sustained by a great friendship.

The concept of racial formation was first advanced in a two-part article, "By the Rivers of Babylon: Race in the United States," published in the journal *Socialist Review,* with which we were associated (Omi and Winant 1983). The first edition of the book *Racial Formation in the United States* appeared in 1986.

Then came disappointment. We were dismayed that our work was ignored for several years by the very social scientists we sought to influ- ence. Anti-racist activists took no notice. Much to our surprise, our initial fans were from other academic disciplines, notably history, literary studies, and law. Historians used our ideas to examine and periodize shifts in the racial order, literary theorists and critics analyzed racial representations and discourse in their canonical texts, and legal scholars interrogated the fluidity and ambiguity of race in doctrinal law, jurisprudence, and legal practice. The fact that contemporary introductory sociology textbooks on race and ethnicity now have a section on "racial formation" is quite gratifying for us. We can at last find validation in our own discipline—one that had initially ignored our call to critically examine the social construction of race.

Over the years, numerous criticisms have been made of the concept of racial formation. The political determinism we embraced early in our collaboration has often been challenged, but we continue to uphold our commitment to *the primacy of the political.* Such an emphasis, we think, allows us to discern the contours of the current racial order, to understand what racial hegemony looks like, to specify its contradictions, and to envision alternative scenarios.

We continue to emphasize the *instability* of the race concept. This condition derives from the multiply determined "social space"—both very broad and very deep—that race occupies. Race operates at the crossroads between social structure and experience.[4] It is both historically determined and continuingly being made and remade in everyday life.[5] In this sense, race is simultaneously synchronic and diachronic, as Lévi-Strauss (1966) might say.

The instability of race accounts for both the ongoing volatility and the continuity of the concept. Why, for example, are racial attributions so prone to violence, so "hot," so fiercely upheld and contested, so necessary in the modern world as components of both self and social structure? Why is race so available as a "scavenger concept": a default variable on the basis of which so many disparate phenomena are supposedly explained (Fredrickson 2002; Gilroy 1999)? How can a social distinction be both so determining—of life chances and status, of freedom, of social structure, of identity itself—and at the same time so undetermined, inchoate, and indeed unreal on so many levels? These are but a few of the many questions we were asking about race and racism more than three decades ago.

We are asking them still. And while racial conditions have changed dramatically since our book was first published, the legacy of the past, the vast *waste* of structural racism,[6] accumulated over the centuries, continues to weigh us down as well. We do indeed live in history.

BREAKING WITH THE PAST: THE TRAJECTORIES OF RACIAL POLITICS

There have been "cycles" or "trajectories" of racial reform and reaction since the rise of the race concept in tandem with the development of the "modern world-system." But the post–World War II racial "break" was the most profound transformation in world racial history. Never before had there been a racial upsurge so *wide*: so comprehensively driven by extensive global conflicts—such as World War II and the Cold War—and so propelled by mass action, by vast demographic transformations, massive migrations, urbanization, and above all, by popular mobilization. Never has any racial upheaval cut so *deep*: indeed, under intense pressure that was often radical and sometimes revolutionary, many racial states officially "switched sides" in the postwar years, shifting from upholding apartheid, racial exclusion, and colonial rule to opposing—at least officially—these policies and practices (Winant 2001).

Enormous changes have occurred over the past few decades as parts of a shift, a rupture, a break that we called (*pace* Polanyi) the "great trans-formation" (Polyani 2011 [1944]). De jure segregation and state-enforced Jim Crow were effectively challenged in the 1960s, and the South African apartheid system finally fell in 1994. Some explicitly "racist regimes" (Fred-rickson 2002) have been overthrown, and the ideologies that undergirded them have been largely discredited.[7]

The U.S. encounter with race and racism in the second half of the twentieth century and beyond constitutes a case study of a global racial transition. The great transformation, the worldwide racial "break," was the cumulative result of states, empires, and elites on a world scale being challenged by their own people—by "natives," and by the descendants of former slaves and colonial subjects—to "pay up" for the practices of superexploitation, exclusion, domination, and nonrecognition to which they had been so long subjected. The former "wretched of the earth" demanded greater social equality, a fundamental expansion of democracy, and a dramatic extension of *popular sovereignty*. The great wave of postwar political movements—anti-imperialist movements, civil rights movements, and the "identity politics" of the 1960s—all contributed to the radical transformation of the global racial order.

Not only was the vast upsurge of demands for racial justice more than merely a U.S.-based phenomenon, but the resistance to those demands, what we called the "racial reaction," was correspondingly global in scope. Neoconservatism, nonracialism, neoliberalism, backlash, multiculturalism, rollback, colorblindness,[8] and racial differentialism—to pick some of the key terms of that reaction—were responses, sometimes right-wing and sometimes centrist or even liberal,[9] to the hugely disruptive, redistributive, democratic, and egalitarian demands of the worldwide racial upsurge. Here too the United States was but a "case," however important, of a global process in which displaced elites, empires, and ideologies struggled to reconstruct and indeed reimagine their racial regimes after the war.

POST-RACIAL SCENARIOS?

This brings us to the present moment. Have racist regimes been dismantled as a result of the "great transformation," or has racism simply mutated into new and perhaps more flexible and less discernible forms? Some political observers have interpreted the election of Barack Obama as the dawning of a new, "post-racial" era. Obama's ascent to the highest post in the land is popularly regarded as stunning testimony of how far the nation has come in moving beyond the racial barriers and exclusions of the past. This post-racial optimism reflects contemporary "colorblind" racial ideology: the belief that the goals of the civil rights movement have been substantially achieved, that overt forms of racial discrimination are a thing of the past, and that the United States has successfully transitioned to a "post-" or even "nonracist" society. As an ideological frame, colorblindness denies that race should inform perceptions, shape attitudes, or influence individual or collective action. Indeed from a colorblind standpoint any hints of race consciousness are tainted by racism; hence, the most effective anti-racist gesture, policy, or practice is simply to ignore race. The hope is that by ignoring race, we can transcend racism and embrace a post-racial future.[10]

Such an optimistic scenario, of course, misses the enduring persistence and significance of race, and the ways that structural racism continues to shape present conditions.[11] The "colorblind" framework has been the target of scathing criticism across the social sciences, humanities, and professions that has demonstrated the persistence of racial inequalities and argued for "race conscious" policies and practices to address them (Carbado and Harris 2008; Brown et al. 2003; Feagin 2006; Bonilla-Silva 2006).

But while race still matters, changes are always afoot. The color line itself has been rendered more complex in the twenty-first century transition to a majority-minority society. How will racial transformations reshape issues of racial hierarchy and broader patterns of racial domination and subordination?

Many have speculated about these questions, peering through a glass darkly in their attempts to predict the racial future. Jennifer L. Hochschild (2005) assesses future racial trends and poses several possible scenarios contingent on different racial constructions and practices. In her "black exceptionalism" scenario, a black/nonblack racial divide is the crucial axis of racial division: Asians and Latinos are slowly drawn to the white side of the color line. An alternative is the "white exceptionalism" scenario, which posits a white/nonwhite racial divide in which groups of color would share a common subordinate status. Her third possibility is the "South African" scenario, in which the nation is re-sorted into three groups: whites and "honorary whites" (most Asians, some Latinos, and some biracials), coloreds (some Asians, most Latinos, some biracials and a few blacks), and blacks and almost-blacks. This last "triracial" system is similar to Eduardo Bonilla-Silva's notion (2004) of the "Latin Americanization" of race relations. A fourth scenario Hochschild considers is the dramatic growth of a "mixed-race" or multiracial population with the requisite blurring of distinct racial and ethnic groups. "A crucial divide in this scenario," writes Hochschild, "would be between those who identify as monoracials and seek to protect cultural purity and those who identify as multiracials and celebrate cultural mixing" (2005, 81).

Certainly persistent white supremacy has historically required that groups of color be politically and economically marginalized and subject to cultural forms of domination. Such a position of subordination found expression, for example, in the internal colonialism account: there, groups of color shared a common situation of oppression that offered a potential basis for political unity. But just as previous "outsiders" such as the Irish and Jews have been incorporated into prevailing notions of who is white,[12] some scholars speculate that groups such as Asian Americans and Latinos are increasingly being included in an expanded definition of whiteness. For example, George Yancey (2003) argues that Latinos and Asian Americans are undergoing significant structural, marital, and identity-based assimilation and that a black/nonblack divide is emerging as these groups become "white," while blacks continue to experience what Yancey calls "racial alienation." The emergence of a triracial order in which some groups are positioned as intermediate buffers between black and white might at first glance appear more pluralistic and fluid than a biracial order shaped by the rule of hypodescent, the so-called one-drop rule. But, as Bonilla-Silva warns, a triracial system of stratification would also be an effective means of maintaining white supremacy. The "Latin Americanization of race" thesis anticipates a U.S. transition to a society with "more rather than less racial inequality but with a reduced forum for racial contestation" (Bonilla-Silva 2006, 198).

We question aspects of the "Latin Americanization of race" thesis. Because the United States now relates to the global South and global East through a master policy of "accumulation by dispossession,"[13] it fosters immigration. Displaced and impoverished workers and peasants from Latin America and the Caribbean, as well as from the Pacific Rim, continue to immigrate, their human flow modulated but hardly contained by boom and bust, "bubble," and recession.[14] And because the United States has also become more predatory domestically, practicing a similar policy of "accumulation by dispossession" in post-Katrina New Orleans or the subprime housing crisis—to pick just two prominent examples—it is less able to integrate immigrants than it was in previous historical periods. Where will the United States find an "engine of mobility" to parallel that of the late nineteenth and early twentieth centuries, the epochs of mass labor recruitment to the industrial economy? In short, the country's economic capacity to absorb enormous numbers of immigrants, low-wage workers and their families, and a new, globally based (and largely female) servant class (see Glenn 2002), without generating the sort of established subaltern groups we associate with the terms *race* and *racism,* seems to us more limited than was the "whitening" of Europeans a century earlier, this argument's key precedent.[15]

And then there is the question of "mixed-race" or multiracial individuals, another key aspect of the "Latin Americanization" thesis. The issue of multiraciality problematizes deeply held notions of race, racial classification, and racial identity itself. Indeed, the very concept of being of "mixed race" presupposes the existence of clearly defined, discernible, and discrete races.[16] Our view is that any discussion of multiraciality must resist "racial lumping": the tendency to locate multiracial individuals in a collective category that fails to consider not only the enormous diversity within multiracial populations but also the varied political and cultural meanings of multiraciality itself. For example, the *mestizaje* framework conflicts with the white/nonwhite North American system. And in many social or institutional settings the experience and consciousness of being mixed-race white-Asian is significantly different from that of being black-Asian. Whether multiracial identity, consciousness, and organization will seriously subvert or merely reinforce racial hierarchy in the United States remains very much an open question.

An opposite and equally pernicious tendency is to reject group identity *tout court* by elevating social constructionist approaches to ethnicity, race, and nationality to an all-encompassing framework, a sort of universal solvent of all identity, all particularity. Perhaps driven by frustration that not only racial but also ethnic and national identities remain flexible and unstable and resist social scientific specification, Rogers Brubaker, Mara Loveman, and Peter Stamatov (1994; see also Brubaker 2004) repudiate "groupism" across the board. They argue that ethnic, racial, and national social categories can be more effectively conceived as matters of social psychology. Ethnic, racial, or national identities are thereby reduced to quite subjective processes: how one (or many) interpret their social location, their differences or similarities with others, and so forth. This has the consequence of diminishing the political dimensions of these themes, as well as relegating lived experience, not to mention world-historical events and widely distributed beliefs, to little more than commonly held illusions.

All these issues—the possibility or desirability of a post-racial society, the realities of demographic transformation and racial stratification, the varieties of multiracial consciousness, and the parameters of collectivity as well—continually and inexorably point to the continuing instability of the concept of race itself. This instability is a fundamental preoccupation of the racial formation approach. It is reflected, for example, in the endemic mismatches between state-based racial classifications and individual/collective social identities. Such inconsistencies are political in nature and embody profound differences over racial meaning—differences that reveal who wields power in establishing definitions and categories and how such boundaries are contested and negotiated.

Consider the U.S. census. As this is written the 2010 census is under way. We cannot yet evaluate its findings. But according to the Census Bureau, 40 percent of Latinos in the 1980, 1990, and 2000 censuses filled out the race and ethnicity questions "wrong." The bureau's preference was to have Latinos respond both to the question "Is this person Spanish/Hispanic/ Latino?" *and* the question "What is this person's race?" A dark-skinned Puerto Rican, for example, might check off that she or he was "Hispanic/ Puerto Rican" *and* "Black," while a light-skinned Mexican might describe himself or herself as "Hispanic/Mexican" *and* "White." But many Latino respondents did not understand, or perhaps did not accept, the racial and ethnic categories presented. They did not know how—or perhaps refused—to situate themselves within the choices the census offered. It is estimated that about 95 percent of respondents who simply checked "some other race" were in fact Latino (Omi 1997; Rodríguez 2000).

The shifting context of race has a profound impact on claims for recognition that are validated (or ignored) in state-sanctioned racial categories. In the mid-1990s, during the planning for Census 2000, key Arab American civil rights organizations unsuccessfully lobbied the Office of Management and Budget for a "Middle Eastern" category on the census. They were critical of the classification of Arab Americans as "white" and argued that with respect to hate crime reporting (among other social indicators and issues), Arab Americans should be a distinct racial category. We are not surprised that in the wake of 9/11 *no* Arab American organization is now lobbying for such a separate "Middle Eastern" category. The line between group recognition and racial profiling is a thin one.[17]

The issue of racial profiling reveals an intriguing contradiction in the meaning of race and its relationship to the racial ideology of colorblindness. Profiling raises questions of when and under what circumstances we want to "notice" race. When do we want to be race-conscious, and when do we want to be "colorblind"? After decades of touting colorblindness as the only appropriate guide to policymaking regarding race, some conservative political figures and commentators are now finding it expedient to make exceptions. In the context of the continuing "war on terror," it is argued that our national security may rest on the state's adoption of explicitly *race-conscious* policies. Since the 9/11 attacks, the 2004 Atocha railroad bombings in Spain, the July 2005 attacks in London, and various other similar events, renewed calls have gone out for authorities to use racial and ethnic profiling to identify potential terrorists at airports and elsewhere. The "scavenger concept" of race resurfaces.

After the attempt to blow up a passenger jet in December 2009, New York assemblyman Dov Hikind (D-Brooklyn) introduced legislation to "authorize law enforcement personnel to consider race and ethnicity as one of many factors that could be used in identifying persons who can be initially stopped, questioned, frisked and/or searched." In 2005 Hikind had sponsored a bill to allow New York state police to zero in on "Middle Easterners" when conducting terrorism prevention searches. "They all look a certain way," he said. "It's all very nice to be politically correct here, but we're talking about terrorism."[18] This is a call for policies and practices that *notice* race and attempt to rationalize and justify such moves as serving a broader public interest. Law professor John Banzhaf states, "A very compelling argument can be made that the government's interest in protecting the lives, safety and health of thousands of its citizens from another major terrorist attack similar to those carried out in New York, London and other cities . . . is at least as 'compelling' as a racially diverse student body."[19]

The pervasive instability of the concept of race is revealed not only in ongoing policy debates but also in the biological sciences. The dominant mantra in the social sciences and humanities is that "race is a social construction, not a biological one." This view reflects scientific critiques of race as a biological concept that emerged at the close of World War II as a direct response to the eugenic ideologies and practices of Nazi Germany. An editorial in the *New England Journal of Medicine* in 2001 sought to provide the definitive word on the subject by flatly stating that "race is biologically meaningless." But in the wake of the Human Genome Project, geneticists are once again debating whether race is a meaningful and useful genetic concept.

Geneticist Neil Risch contends that genetic differences have arisen among people from different continents and employs the term "race" to aggregate the human population into five major groups. This recognition of race, he contends, is important for understanding genetic susceptibility to certain diseases and receptivity to medical interventions such as drug treatments.[20] This biological turn has repercussions in fields such as pharmacogenomics. The ultimate goal of pharmacogenomics is to deliver the precise type of medication—and the precise dose—to a patient based on her or his individual genome. Drugs would be specifically tailored for the treatment of an individual's specific condition. Given that an individual's genome has yet to be sequenced in a quick and cost-effective manner, the question has been raised as to whether one's race can serve as a suitable proxy for determining how one might fare with a specific drug.

The question is not an abstract one. Consider the introduction of BiDil as the first "ethnic designer drug." Produced by the biotech firm NitroMed, BiDil is marketed to African Americans who suffer from congestive heart failure. Some medical researchers fear that BiDil sets a dangerous precedent by linking race and genetics in ways that could distract from alternative ways of understanding the causes of a disease and the means to treat it (Kahn 2004). Legal scholar and bioethicist Jonathan Kahn suggests that by approving BiDil, the federal government was "giving its imprimatur, its stamp of approval, to using race as a biological category. To my mind, it's the road to hell being paved with good intentions."[21]

The issue of race and genetics finds expression in popular culture as well. In 2010, PBS aired *Faces of America, with Henry Louis Gates, Jr.,* a four-episode documentary series that traced the ancestral roots of prominent celebrities through "genealogy and genetics." Gates's series inspired a growing popular quest by individuals to find their "roots" through purportedly scientific means. There are currently at least two dozen companies that market "genetic ancestry tests"; more than 460,000 people have purchased these tests over the past six years (Bonick et al. 2007). In 2007 Gates stated: "We are living through an era of the ascendance of biology, and we have to be very careful. We will all be walking a fine line between using biology and allowing it to be abused."[22] There is indeed a fine line. The rebiologization of race will significantly contribute to and trouble debates about the very concept of race.

Somewhat ironically, new patterns and developments in racialization, such as the rebiologization question, destabilize the prevailing racial ideology of colorblindness. It is hard to maintain a colorblind posture if there is indeed a "scientific" basis to race and racial categories. Given the inherent instability of the race concept, it becomes increasingly important to make clear distinctions between colorblind and race-conscious policies and practices, and to discern their larger purpose and intent.

In August 2006 Mark Burnett, the creator of CBS's *Survivor,* caused a furor when he revealed that in the upcoming fall season, the twenty *Survivor* contestants would be divided into four "tribes"—Asian American, black, Hispanic, and white. Local and national protests ensued. Several

New York City Council members demanded that CBS cancel the show. Their demand prompted *New York Times* columnist Clyde Haberman to observe sarcastically that the very city officials incensed by the show were members of the black, Latino, and Asian caucuses that operate in New York City's political system. "In other words," wrote Haberman, "leading the condemnation of CBS for creating teams defined by race and ethnicity was a team that created itself using race and ethnicity as the definition."[23]

Haberman's comment is indicative of the dilemmas of racial classification. Those engaged in challenging racial inequality need to specify with greater clarity (and consistency) when, where, and under what circumstances we want to be "colorblind" and when we want to be race-conscious in the broader pursuit of social justice.

THE RACIAL REGIME AND ITS DISCONTENTS

The instability of the race concept and the controversies it generates are emblematic of the *racially contradictory* society in which we live. In the United States a system of racial rule has always been in place, operating not merely through macro-level, large-scale activities but also through micro-level, small-scale practices. The racial regime is enforced and challenged in the schoolyard, on the dance floor, on talk radio, and in the classroom as much as it is in the Supreme Court, electoral politics, or the battlefield of Helmand province. Because racial formation processes are dynamic, the racial regime remains unstable and contested. We live in racial history.

While the "great transformation" contributed to the demise of explicitly racist state policies, discredited essentialist racial ideologies, and ushered in a set of (ostensibly) egalitarian reforms, it obviously did not complete those tasks. Given the persistence of structural racism and racial inequality in the "post–civil rights era," is the racial regime's supposed "switching of sides," the supposed transition "from domination to hegemony" we described in *Racial Formation,* anything more than a thinly veiled cosmetic makeover? In the United States, after all, segregation proceeds quite effectively without explicit state sponsorship, and indeed still receives quite a bit of tacit state support. Anti-discrimination laws are barely enforced, and when an occasional plaintiff of color wins a rare victory in court, the costs to discriminators don't even begin to offset the benefits derived from discrimination in the first place. The old forms of systematic voter disenfranchisement—by terror—have largely ended, but new forms of election rigging (for example, "vote caging" and the permanent denial of voting rights to ex-felons) achieve many of the same effects. Since the enactment of civil rights laws, incarceration rates in the United States have increased so dramatically (nearly a tenfold increase since 1980; see Mauer 2006; Alexander 2010; Gilmore 2007), and with such extreme racial disproportionality, that carceral policy has now to be viewed as a prime example of "backlash" racial politics.

And come to think of it, how relegated to the past is the question of empire? In the modern world, empires are always distinctively racist; race and empire walk hand in hand. Occupying and subduing other nations is justified today by reference to the putative backwardness of the "natives" (Afghanistan) as well as by claims that they are suffering under horrific regimes that fail to provide elementary democratic or human rights (Iraq). How different is this from the French *"mission civilisatrice"* or the British "white man's burden"—or for that matter, the U.S. "manifest destiny"—of past epochs?[24] One notes that the effort to tutor these "backward" peoples in the "higher values" of advanced civilization also involves dispossessing them of resources and/or labor, not to mention mass slaughter (Mbembe 2001). As for popular sovereignty, forget it. In 2008 the United States maintained military bases in 132 countries. While publically fighting wars of occupation in Iraq and Afghanistan, it was covertly involved in military operations in at least a dozen other supposedly sovereign nations. The meaning and structure of race, both in the United States and worldwide, remain fundamentally unstable and troubled and are the source of unresolved contradictions and dilemmas.

The "great transformation" after World War II overturned the old racial logics, enabled anti-racist movements to enter mainstream politics and initiate racial "wars of position," and resulted in the rearticulation and reorganization of racial regimes in more incorporative and less coercive forms. This shift transformed but hardly precluded the recurrence of "old school" racial repression and violence. In many respects it allowed the perpetuation of discrimination, profiling, nativism, empire, and other forms of racial injustice as it "regrooved" these practices, making use of the very racial reforms for which earlier civil rights and anti-imperialist activists had successfully struggled.[25] Condoleeza Rice compared the U.S. occupation of Iraq to the 1963 movement led by Dr. Martin Luther King Jr. in her native Birmingham, Alabama.

The crisis of race is now a chronic condition. "Crisis," Gramsci wrote, "consists precisely in the fact that the old is dying and the new cannot be born: in this interregnum, morbid phenomena of the most varied kind come to pass" (1971, 276). On the one hand, the old verities of established racism and white supremacy have been officially discredited, not only in the United States but fairly comprehensively around the world; on the other hand, racially informed action and social organization, racial identity and race consciousness, continue unchecked in nearly every aspect of social life.

Given this, why doesn't the manifest contradiction between the *repudiation* of race—both official and personal—and the continuing, constant, and near-ubiquitous *recognition* of race in virtually every aspect of social and political life provoke enormous uncertainty and confusion in public life, political activity, and personal identity? Why don't our heads *explode* under the pressures of such cognitive dissonance?

The answer once again lies in the instability of the race concept, the processual characteristics of racial formation. Because racial categories remain unstable and subject to contention, and because the trajectory of racial reform and racial reaction remains volatile, the U.S. racial regime is permanently unstable as well. Here we note, necessarily very briefly, some of the major contradictions of the present U.S. racial system.

Electoral Politics

The election of Barack Obama transformed the U.S. presidency in ways we cannot yet fully appreciate. Obama is not simply the first nonwhite (that we know of) to occupy the office. He is the first to have lived in the global South, the first to be a direct descendent of colonized people, the first to have a genuine movement background. Without question Obama is by far the most progressive, the most "left" person ever to have occupied the White House. But he is no more powerful than any of his predecessors; he is constrained, as they were, by the U.S. system of rule, by the U.S. racial regime, by structural racism.

Not just the Obama victory but also a host of recent developments have demonstrated the isolation and marginalization of the Republican Party. It has become the white people's party, driven in large measure by racial, religious, and gender/sexuality-based *ressentiment*. In U.S. history, there has generally been one political party that took charge of racial rule. This has been especially true vis-à-vis black-white demarcations; for example, the organization by the Democratic Party of white supremacist rule in the Jim Crow era. But rapid swings are possible. After the critical election of 1932 U.S. blacks (those who could vote) shifted their loyalties away from the "party of Lincoln" en masse (Weiss 1983; Katznelson 2005). This occurred even though Roosevelt's New Deal coalition effectively delegated control of the South to the plantocratic/agrarian/racist/Dixiecrat wing of his party. After the civil rights reforms of the mid-1960s, large numbers of white voters, particularly those based in the South, similarly embraced the Republicans.

The appearance of the "Tea Party" movement since the 2008 election signals a clearly reactionary racial agenda. This "movement"—white, predominantly male, and very much in the Republican Party orbit—is both an "Astroturf" phenomenon, a loose network of fake grass-roots organizations cobbled together by corporate lobbyists, and a genuine right-wing populist phenomenon rooted in resentment of Obama and the resurgence—still quite feeble—of the welfare state. Its whining politics— "I want my country back!"—incarnates a certain incredulity directed at present political conditions, both class-based and race-based. The "movement" has greater disruptive potential than it has adherents: just whose country is the United States, anyway?[26]

Resurgent Nativism and Immigrants' Rights

Reforms in 1965 and 1986 removed many of the overtly racist components of the immigration laws that had shaped U.S. policy since the 1920s, and thereby set off enormous shifts in U.S. racial demography. These changes in turn have dramatically heightened nativist ideologies and mobilizations, reiterating racially framed political conflicts that stretch back to the founding of the U.S. nation-state (Ngai 2005; Chavez 2008).

The ineluctable demographic transition to a majority-minority population may impose some limits on the intensity and depth of contemporary nativist mobilization, however. Although nativism continues to flourish, it confronts other obstacles that did not exist in past cycles of alternating clampdowns and relaxations of immigration laws. In contrast to the sweeping anti-immigrant upsurges of the past (Higham 2002), a significant immigrants' rights movement exists today in the United States; nothing like it has ever developed before. The civil rights connection to immigrants' rights remains strong—most notably embodied in the legacy of the Immigration Reform Act of 1965, a civil rights bill in its own right and a priority of the Kennedys. And immigration reform has huge consequences for voting patterns, especially over the medium and long term; this has been clear with respect to Latino voting patterns since 1994, when what had been seen as a swing constituency was pushed over to the Democrats as a result of California governor Pete Wilson's promotion of Proposition 187 (R. Jacobson 2008; Ono and Sloop 2002; Wroe 2008).

In contrast, before the "great transformation" and the rise of the modern civil rights movement, exhortations on behalf of "Anglo-conformity" (M. Gordon 1964) were taken quite seriously. Virulent nativist assaults such as the anti-Irish movements of the 1840s (the American Native party or "Know-Nothings"), the 1870s and 1890s assaults on West Coast Asian communities (Saxton 1971; Pfaelzer 2007), and the 1930s mass deportations of Mexicans from Southern California (Balderrama and Rodríguez 1995) would prove considerably harder to stage today. The outcome of present-day immigration struggles depends on much political contention at the local, national, and global levels. Catastrophic events on the order of the 9/11 tragedy are always possible—and such tragedies remain susceptible to racialization. In the past the United States often recurred to "domestic foreign policy" in response to political threats. The country has tended to address major social conflicts (and sometimes international ones) by recourse to racist domestic practices. This is exemplified by the internment of Japanese Americans during World War II, the Palmer raids on Eastern and Southern Europeans in the 1920s, and the enormous waves of Islamophobia that followed the 9/11 attack.

In April 2010 the state of Arizona enacted SB 1070, an act "relating to unlawfully present aliens" that authorized police to stop suspected "illegal immigrants" and to demand proof of citizenship. National polls conducted in the wake of the law's passage revealed significant popular support for the law[27]—an ominous sign that immigration reform and the racialization of undocumented workers continue to be vexing issues. Does Arizona SB 1070 represent a new instance of "domestic foreign policy" in addition to being an obvious reiteration of U.S. nativism? Or is it a "gift to the Democrats," as some political commentators have suggested, cementing the loyalties of Latino voters to the Democratic Party, much as Proposition 187 did in California in 1994?[28]

As the Republican Party locks in its identity as the U.S. white people's party, and as the rise in the U.S. Latino population continues, it is hard to avoid the impression that Arizona's institutionalization of racial profiling via SB 1070 represents a last-ditch and probably doomed effort to deny brown people access to the ballot. But that's in the medium to long term, when demographic trends favor another cycle of legalization, as happened in 1965 and 1986. The sheer impracticality of deporting large numbers of undocumented denizens from the United States, and the ferocious state repression that would be required to carry out such a policy, seem to rule out the strategy of *la mano dura* that SB 1070 implies. Numerous other negative consequences would also derive from such measures, notably massive disruptions in the labor market and untold amounts of personal suffering. In the short term, though, there are undoubtedly some political gains to be made through immigrant-bashing.

The Crisis of Neoliberalism and the Assault on the Welfare State

The shifting demographics of race also affect other key political and policy arenas, such as education, labor policy, and social security. The rise of neoliberalism, which began under Reagan, meant the vitiation of an already beleaguered welfare state: notably in the 1996 Clinton welfare "reforms" that abandoned AFDC in favor of the more draconian policies of TANF.[29] By shredding the "safety net" that had been established in the 1930s and was only belatedly and grudgingly extended to racial minorities in the 1960s, the U.S. racial regime greatly widened the gap between the formal ("visible"), largely white economy and the informal ("invisible"), largely nonwhite economy. This trend also increased the distance between city and suburb, hardened policing and criminal "justice" patterns (often relying on a "national security" rationale),[30] and reinforced segregation in schooling and residential patterns—vis-à-vis both blacks and Latinos (Boger and Orfield 2005).

Education is a key battleground in the racial restructuring of U.S. society. The student body in the U.S. public education system is moving toward majority-minority status, though it is still some decades away from that. Census Bureau estimates of that transition locate it around the year 2025.[31] Who will teach these students? What career prospects will they have? As the U.S. economy becomes increasingly centered in the "knowledge industries," it will require major investments in public education and far more effective integration between curricular content and shifting patterns of employment. Neoliberal educational policy ("No Child Left Behind," "Race to the Top," the privatization of higher education) is headed in precisely the opposite direction: disinvesting; relying on mechanistic and formulaic testing of basic skills rather than teaching adaptive and creative thought processes ("intelligence" in the Deweyan use of the term); and abandoning large numbers of low-income children (disproportionately black and brown) to permanent subemployment.

A closely related question is the *racial composition of the U.S. workforce.* As informal labor markets grow (Vogel 2006) in size and importance, it becomes more difficult to assess employment patterns with specificity (Toossi 2002). Consider the Social Security system, perhaps the most durable element of the New Deal–based welfare state. Already there are fewer and fewer white workers paying the FICA taxes to support social security payments to largely white baby boomers. The Social Security system—forced savings through regressive payroll taxation, pay-as-you-go financing—has long been seen both as a powerful guarantor of political legitimacy and as a "third rail" of the welfare state: a New Deal achievement that worked to curtail and regulate excessive and highly ideological "free market" pressures from the political right. George W. Bush's blundering campaign for Social Security "privatization" was but the most recent assault on that system from the HQ of reaction.[32] But by the mid-twenty-first century a majority of U.S. workers will be nonwhite. To the extent that they are employed in the formal economy, they will be paying their FICA/payroll taxes (as of now still organized regressively, exempting annual incomes above $106,800 in 2009) to support those largely white retirees born in the mid-twentieth century and later. Well before 2050, in short, the calculus of cost and benefit in the Social Security system will shift: it will no longer afford political legitimacy or constitute an unshakeable pillar of support to many working people. We may very well see revolts against this remaining bastion of the welfare state (or against its inadequacy) on the part of people of color. Might we see future opposition to Social Security from the "left"? Now that would be something new![33]

Racial rule is increasingly difficult to maintain. The *costs of racial repression*—imprisonment and arming the U.S.-Mexican border, for example—directly compete with the costs of social investment. *Postcolonial warfare*—a distinctly racial policy—is perhaps the most egregious example of this: the cost of U.S. wars since 2001 is now in the trillions.[34] *Cultural transformations* generally tend to delegitimize racial rule, especially in the context of demographic transition toward a majority-minority society: in the arts, popular media, language use, "styles," the dynamics of personal life and intimate relationships, and indeed in working concepts of identity, racial rearticulation is commonplace.

Racial rule *requires* repression, not because of some functionalist law, but because it inspires resistance. Exclusion, superexploitation, violence, and despotism inevitably generate opposition. In the past the opposition of those who were not white, who lacked citizenship rights and therefore could not access the political system, necessarily took subversive and largely spontaneous forms: sabotage, slacking, subaltern forms of action (Scott 1990). After "the great transformation," after the movement "from protest to politics" (Kelley 1992; Tate 1993; see also Waskow 1966), however, the racially subordinate could both act within mainstream political parameters and continue to subvert those boundaries in search of greater democratic and human rights. Yet racial repression remains very much a part of everyday life and social structure in the United States.

RECONSTRUCTING RACE

The prevailing ideology of colorblindness is a failed attempt to construct a new racial hegemony, based on the limited reforms of the civil rights era. Center-right in political orientation, informed by an uneasy admixture of new right and neoconservative racial ideology,[35] colorblind racial ideology cannot overcome the gap between the promises of reform and the realities of ongoing inequality and racial despotism.

While advocates of "colorblind" racial ideology vehemently argue against state policy "taking race into account," the state also *needs* race to rule. This is true in virtually every area of state activity. Structural racism persists; democratic reforms have not undone the legacy of systematic exclusion, violence, exploitation, and marginalization that race embodies. Thus social control via race continues: in criminal "justice," in corporate welfare as well as the evisceration of the welfare state, in the organization of labor, credit, and housing markets, and of course in the U.S. militarization of the world. Racial repression continues to furnish brutal reminders of the incompleteness of democracy and the shallowness of post-racial celebrations. Consider the victims: who are the prisoners, the families dropped from the welfare rolls, the permanent residents deported, and those disproportionately dispossessed by the home mortgage crisis (Rivera 2008)?

But while the state needs race to rule, it is also confronted by anti-racist opposition and constrained by its own commitment to the achievement of racial hegemony through the colorblindness construct. In general, it is forced to exercise racial rule covertly. The effects of the "great transformation" still resonate. The contradictions of this situation, in which the racial regime must simultaneously disavow its raciality and deploy it as broadly and deeply as ever, is arguably the greatest single factor in the continuing instability of race in the state's unavoidable ratification of neoliberal policies of superexploitation and "accumulation by dispossession." Here we see the limits of President Obama's post-racial appeals, the enormous difficulties involved in stemming, much less cleaning up, the ongoing accumulation of racial "waste."

So what does the crisis of colorblindness suggest for the racial future? What does it mean for the United States that a new racial hegemony cannot be consolidated, that achieving some new post–civil rights era racial commonsense seems very unlikely, at least for now? Does it mean persistent structural racism, unremitting racial despotism, the impossibility of democratization? Or does our present racial condition contain hints and suggestions about *alternative routes*—not toward racial "progress" (a much too incrementalist, too meliorist term), but at least toward a greater and deeper democracy? Can we see new ways of situating the racial self, of inhabiting our racial identities—both individually and collectively—in greater freedom?

The desire remains strong—not only in our hearts but in those of millions—for a more emancipatory concept of race and a more fulfilling, less conflicted race consciousness. What would that look like? To be very specific, what do you want *your* race consciousness to be?

If the "colorblind" perspective has failed to achieve hegemony, failed to consolidate a new racial "common sense," what comes next? From a "colorblind" perspective, one is exhorted not to "notice" race, not to see it, for if one did, one wouldn't be "blind" to it, right? But what happens to *race consciousness* under conditions of "colorblind" hegemony? Quite clearly, awareness of raciality does not dry up like a raisin in the sun. Just as "colorblind" racial ideology serves as a means to occlude recognition of race beneath the veneer of a supposedly already accomplished universality, race consciousness works to highlight racial differences and particularities. It can be linked to despotic or democratic ends, articulated in defense of coercion, privilege, and undeserved advantage; alternatively it can be deployed in support of inclusion, human rights, and social justice.

Yet despite our strong criticism of racism and of the "colorblind" racial project, race consciousness exhibits certain contradictions as well. We can make errors in conceptualizing race or in attributing racial identity. Just when does race matter, anyway? Always? Sometimes? If the answer is "sometimes," what about those situations when race "doesn't matter"? Are there situations in which we should *not* notice race? Isn't racial identity often ambiguous and contradictory? What is its significance for transracial solidarity and alliance? What is its significance for transracial friendship, or indeed love? These old themes no doubt retain something of their transgressive and unsettling character, but they are also increasingly normal, regular, and unremarkable. Can trust and solidarity exist across racial lines? Is it possible either in individual or collective social practice to "get beyond" race, and what exactly would that mean? How definitive is racial identity, and what are the implications for democracy, humanism, and antiracism (Gilroy 2002)?

Parallel to the question, What do you want *your* race consciousness to be? is another: What would a racial justice–oriented *social policy* look like *to you*? What types of policies and practices—at the level of the state, civil society, and major institutions—would help us achieve a more comprehensive, deeper, and longer-lasting racial democracy in the United States?

Some General Answers to These Questions

Since racism is so large, combating it must also be a large-scale practice. The historically recurrent theme of racial reparations provides a valuable guidepost here (Henry 2007). *Reparation* means repairing, making whole, making good what was evil. As a sociopolitical project, reparations can be seen to extend from the large to the small, from the institutional to the personal (Yamamoto 1999). Clearly, abolishing the debt (not "forgiving," for who is to forgive and who is to be forgiven?) fits within the reparations logic, as does affirmative action.

Redistribution fits as well, but here we must be careful: the politics of income and wealth distribution are "double-entry" bookkeeping items. Not only the allocation of resources but also the derivation of revenues are involved. If reparations were to be paid for the crime against humanity that was African slavery, it would be important to look at both the inflow and the outflow sides of the process. On the outflow side, reparations should take the form of social investment (think of a "Marshall Plan for the Cities" or something similar). On the inflow side, there is a danger that reparations would be paid out of general revenues, unduly assessing present-day working people for the crimes of past colonialists and elites, perpetuating rather than attenuating racial conflicts, and allowing new variants of the "colorblind" argument to loom up in the future. An alternative revenue-oriented strategy would raise the money by means of a wealth tax, thus recognizing how many present-day capital hoards had their origins in slavery.[36]

Beyond reparations, anti-racist practice can be understood macropolitically in terms of *social citizenship* and micropolitically in terms of *acculturation and socialization*. The concept of social citizenship was proposed by T. H. Marshall (1950) as an obligation of the postwar welfare state, the proximate stage in the achievement of popular sovereignty. Rights, Marshall argued, had been acquired by the populace in stages: first economic, then political. The time had now come for the achievement of social rights. Of course, this formulation was offered when the British flag still flew over Lagos and Singapore and Jim Crow still flourished in the United States; it was proposed when postmodern criticism of the limits of "rights talk" (in critical race theory, for example) had not yet been made; and it certainly did not encompass the diasporic and globalized issues anti-racists face today. Yet we can make use of it to think anew about political inclusion, social provision, even world citizenship.

By *acculturation and socialization* we mean the reawakening of the 1960s concept that "the personal is political" as a key principle of anti-racist personal practice. No one—no matter what their racial identity is—can be free of racism in their heads or hearts; it is too deeply ingrained a social structure. Yet a great deal of thought and action has been devoted to the problem of fostering anti-racist practice at the individual and experiential level. Developing these skills, fostering the interruption and interrogation of racism, and extending the reach of anti-racism in family, school, and cultural life constitute an important dimension of the practice we want to support.

While we have offered here some tentative and sketchy answers to these questions, on a deeper level such serious issues can be adequately addressed only through the creative thought and political action of many people—the masses, the multitudes, whose "freedom dreams" (Kelley 2003) can transfigure and rearticulate the unstable and conflicted racial system yet again. We began this essay by noting that racial formation theory emerged from an earlier set of challenges to the system of racial oppression. Surely those movement-based challenges were not the last we shall ever know. If our approach has any value, it lies in the suggestion that racial politics is an ongoing creative practice, both individual and collective. Our actions and ideas—both individual and collective—should be seen as political projects that have the potential to undo racial injustice and generate broader racial equality, and indeed greater freedom in every way. Racial formation theory should help us think about race and racism as *continuing encounters between despotic and democratic practices*, in which individuals and groups, confronted by state power and entrenched privilege but not entirely limited by those obstacles, make choices and locate themselves over and over in the constant racial "reconstruction" of everyday life.

NOTES

1. A neo-Marxist critique of this approach that influenced us in important ways was Bonacich 1972.

2. In retrospect we can see that we were developing arguments that paralleled emerging perspectives in post-structural and in radical pragmatist theoretical approaches. This was not our primary purpose, though; we sought better explanations for race/racism dynamics, and reinvented the wheel only in pursuit of that specific aim.

3. There is some debate as to the origins of the phrase. "The Personal Is Political" was the title of an essay by Carol Hanisch, an early second-wave feminist activist and veteran of the civil rights movement. The essay was published in 1969 by the Redstockings organization. See Carol Hanisch, "The Personal Is Political," http://www.carolhanisch.org/CHwritings/PIP.html (accessed January 19, 2012).

4. The crossroad is deeply significant in the black vernacular. Cf. Robert Johnson, "Cross Roads Blues," originally Vocalion Records, catalog no. 3519 (1937); reissued on idem, *King of the Delta Blues Singers*, Columbia catalog, no. CL 1654 (1966); see also Litwack 1998, 410–411.

5. In a well-known article (1997), Eduardo Bonilla-Silva argued for a "structural interpretation" of racism. Focusing on rac*ism*, he did not deeply explore the race concept, instead invoking the notion of "racialized social systems" to link race to racism. Lévi-Strauss's approach effectively grasps the interplay between the everyday (synchronic) and historically imbedded (diachronic)

dimensions of "social structure"; that's why we cite him here. Although we have some disagreements with the Bonilla-Silva piece, we still consider it a major contribution.

6. On racism as "waste," see Feagin, Vera, and Batur 2000. The concept is drawn from Georges Bataille.

7. Of course, others remain: Israel-Palestine, Kurdistan, the conditions of many indigenous peoples . . . It's a long list.

8. This term requires some clarification. *Colorblindness* is a problematic term, a neologism twice over. First and most obviously, it is rooted in an ophthalmic condition that has no relevance to race, unless we understand race as being "about" skin color, which involves a deep reductionism in the race concept's meaning. Second, the term's application to the race concept derives from its appearance in the dissent of Justice John Marshall Harlan in the 1896 *Plessy v. Ferguson* case, where the justice's insistence that "our Constitution is colorblind," coexists blissfully with a range of support claims for eternal white superiority and supremacy (see Gotanda 1995).

9. We use the term *liberal* here in the U.S. sense, signifying "center-left."

10. We discuss colorblindness more extensively later in this essay.

11. The structural racism perspective allows us to see racism in terms of its consequences, not as a matter of intentions or beliefs. In *Racial Formation* we describe it this way as well: "a structural feature of US society, the product of centuries of systematic exclusion, exploitation, and disregard of racially defined minorities" (Omi and Winant 1994, 69). Grant-Thomas and powell offer a similar interpretation: "We can describe a social system as structurally racist to the degree that it is configured to promote racially unequal outcomes. For example, a society marked by highly interdependent opportunity structures and large interinstitutional resource disparities will likely be very unequal with respect to the outcomes governed by those institutions and opportunity structures" (Grant-Thomas and powell 2006, 5).

12. Of the vast literature on this topic, see Jacobson 1998; Roediger 2005; and Guglielmo 2003.

13. "Accumulation by dispossession" is an idea taken from David Harvey (2004). Among its many theoretical and analytical applications, the concept effectively describes such exploitative and predatory practices as "payday lending" (spatially concentrated in ghetto and barrio locations) and "steering" of subprime mortgages to working-class black and brown borrowers.

14. Elsewhere in the global system, parallel patterns prevail, overlapping to a large extent with U.S. processes: Maghrebines and Caribbeans migrate to France, Spain, and Italy; sub-Saharan Africans and South Asians are on the move; in the Philippines the state exports labor (particularly female labor) systematically; the global economy of remittances constitutes the most reliable and "progressive" (so to speak) foreign aid. For a good overview, see Massey et al. (2005).

15. See also Perlmann and Waters 2005; Perlmann 2005; Foner and Fredrickson 2004.

16. "Mixed-race" identity is also a race-gender/sexuality issue of "intersectionality" par excellence. See Stoler 2006b.

17. In 2003 the Census Bureau shared data on Middle Eastern, Arab, and South Asian Americans with the Department of Justice and the newly created Department of Homeland Security. The details of this cooperation—which seems to have violated pledges on the confidentiality of census data and on the bureau's abstention from politics—remain themselves confidential.

18. Quoted in Edward Epstein, "Calls for Racial, Ethnic Profiling Renewed after Transit Attacks" *San Francisco Chronicle,* August 10, 2005.

19. Ibid.

20. Nicholas Wade, "Race Is Seen as Real Guide to Track Roots of Disease," *New York Times,* July 30, 2002.

21. Quoted in Carolyn Johnson, "Should Medicine Be Colorblind?" *Boston Globe,* August 24, 2004.

22. Quoted in Amy Harmon, "In DNA Era, New Worries about Prejudice," *New York Times,* November 11, 2007.

23. Clyde Haberman, "NYC: Separating Common Sense from Reality," *New York Times,* September 1, 2006.

24. Indeed contemporary U.S. imperial misadventures generally take place on the very same terrains on which Americans' European predecessors sought in vain to impose their will in the past. "Globalization" is hardly a new phenomenon.

25. Contemporary civil rights jurisprudence exemplifies these trends. The Supreme Court has proved unwilling, in case after case, to tackle the ongoing dynamics of racial discrimination, unless that discrimination is construed to harm the interests of white people (Kairys 1996). The Court now thinks that whites are the main victims of racial discrimination in the United States. In a 2007 decision on two school desegregation cases, the Court outlawed school desegregation plans that were voluntary and had substantial community support, on the grounds that they invoked racial categories. See *Parents Involved in Community Schools Inc. v. Seattle School District No. 1,* and *Meredith v. Jefferson County (Ky.) Board of Education,* 551 U.S. 701 (2007).

26. For recent survey research on the Tea Party and its members' racial attitudes, conducted by a team of University of Washington political scientists, see Christopher S. Parker, "2010 Multi-State Survey of Race & Politics," WISER (University of Washington Institute for the Study of Ethnicity, Race, and Sexuality), http://depts.washington.edu/uwiser/racepolitics.html (accessed January 23, 2012).

27. According to a Pew Research Center poll conducted May 6–9, 2010, 73 percent approved of requiring people to produce documents verifying legal status, while 67 percent approved of allowing police to detain anyone unable to verify legal status. See "Broad Approval for New Arizona Immigration Law," Pew Research Center for the People & the Press, http://people-press.org/report/613/arizona-immigration-law (accessed January 23, 2012).

28. Conservative columnist Michael Gerson, writing in the *Washington Post*, noted opposition to the law from many Republican elected officials, and argued: "Unlike, say, a conservative magazine or blog, it is the purpose of a political party to win majorities within the broad bounds of its convictions. And each time a portion of the conservative movement demonstrates this particular form of ideological purity—in California's Proposition 187, the 2006 House immigration debate and now Arizona—they create resentments toward the Republican Party among Latinos that will last for generations. In all these cases, Republicans have gained little, sacrificed much, and apparently learned nothing." See Michael Gerson, "The Authors of Arizona's Immigration Law Retreat," *Washington Post*, May 3, 2010.

29. Clinton's welfare program (Temporary Assistance to Needy Families, or TANF), which replaced the previous, Aid to Families with Dependent Children (AFDC) program in 1996, forced welfare recipients (particularly women of color) into "workfare" jobs and substantially eroded the well-being of low-income children across a wide range of health, housing, education, and indeed survival issues. See Edelman 2004.

30. For a good overview of these connections, see Hayden 2004.

31. Calculated from Table M, U.S. Census Bureau, Current Population Reports, *Population Projections of the United States by Age, Sex, Race, and Hispanic Origin: 1995 to 2050* (issued February 1996; updated April 13, 1999), 16–17.

32. Social Security privatization was also presented as benefiting blacks, a claim doubtful at best. See Peter Wallsten and Tom Hamburger, "Blacks Courted on Social Security," *Los Angeles Times*, February 28, 2005; Paul Krugman, "Little Black Lies," *New York Times*, January 28, 2005.

33. We are indebted to Joe Feagin for first drawing our attention to this point.

34. See National Priorities Project, http://costofwar.com/ (accessed January 23, 2012); see also Stiglitz and Bilmes 2008.

35. New right and neoconservative racial ideologies are quite distinct; their political alliance remains shaky. The new right diverges from neoconservatism in its willingness to practice racial politics subtextually, through coding, manipulation of racial fears, and so on. De facto, it recognizes the persistence of racial difference in United States society. The new right understands perfectly well that its mass base is white and that its political success depends on its ability to interpret white identity in positive political terms. The resurgent nativism discussed above, the hostility and indeed blatant attacks on President Obama (and threats of violence against him), the return to talk of "states' rights" and even secession in the "Tea Party" and Republican far right, all show that the strategy of authoritarian populism addressed to the mass base of the white people's party (the Republicans) is far from exhausted. Neoconservatism at least professes post-raciality and "colorblindness." It has not, and could not, deliver such tangible political benefits, and in fact lacks an equivalent mass political base. Thus the uneasy alliance between the two tendencies.

36. Insurance companies indemnified slave owners if their slaves escaped or ship-bound Africans revolted, for example. British slaveowners were compensated for their "losses" in 1833 when Parliament abolished slavery, and North American slavocrats regained their autarchic local autonomy in the "Compromise" of 1877, which DuBois (1998) called a counterrevolution.

BIBLIOGRAPHY

Adas, Michael. 2001. From Settler Colony to Global Hegemon: Integrating the Exceptionalist Narrative of American Experience into World History. *American Historical Review* 106 (5): 1692–1720.

Agamben, Giorgio. 1998. *Homo Sacer: Sovereign Power and Bare Life*, trans. Daniel Heller-Roazen. Stanford: Stanford University Press.

Agamben, Giorgio. 2005. *State of Exception*, trans. Kevin Attell. Chicago: University of Chicago Press. Original edition published in Italian, 2003.

Ahmad, Muneer I. 2002. Homeland Insecurities: Racial Violence the Day after September 11. *Social Text* 20 (3): 101–115.

————. 2004. A Rage Shared by Law: Post–September 11 Racial Violence as Crimes of Passion. *California Law Review* 92 (5): 1259–1330.

Alarcón, Norma. 1990. The Theoretical Subject(s) of *This Bridge Called My Back* and Anglo-American Feminism. In *Making Face, Making Soul: Haciendo Caras; Creative and Critical Perspectives by Feminists of Color*, ed. Gloria Anzaldua. San Francisco: Aunt Lute Books.

————. 1991. The Theoretical Subjects of *This Bridge Called My Back* and Anglo-American Feminism. In *Criticism in the Borderlands: Studies in Chicano Literature, Culture, and Ideology*, ed. Hector Calderón and Jose Davíd Saldívar. Durham, NC: Duke University Press.

Albrecht, Stan L., Melvin L. DeFleur, and Lyle G. Warner. 1972. Attitude-Behavior Relationships: A Reexamination of the Postulate of Contingent Consistency. *Pacific Sociological Review* 15: 149–168.

Alexander, Michelle. 2010. *The New Jim Crow: Mass Incarceration in an Age of Colorblindness*. New York: The New Press.

Alfred, Taiaiake. 1999. *Peace, Power, Righteousness: An Indigenous Manifesto*. Oxford: Oxford University Press.

Almaguer, Tomás. 1994. *Racial Fault Lines: The Historical Origins of White Supremacy in California*. Berkeley: University of California Press.

American Freedmen's Inquiry Commission. 1863. *Preliminary Report Touching on the Condition and Management of Emancipated Refugees: Made to the Secretary of War*. New York: John F. Trow Printer.

Anderson, Benedict. 1983. *Imagined Communities: Reflections on the Origin and Spread of Nationalism.* London: Verso.

Andrien, Kenneth. 1985. *Crisis and Decline: The Viceroyalty of Peru in the Seventeenth Century.* Albuquerque: University of New Mexico Press.

Amnesty International. 2007. *Maze of Injustice.* New York: Amnesty International.

Anghie, Anthony. 2007. *Imperialism, Sovereignty and the Making of International Law.* Cambridge: Cambridge University Press.

Appadurai, Arjun. 1991. Global Ethnoscapes: Notes and Queries for a Transnational Anthropology. In *Recapturing Anthropology: Working in the Present,* ed. Richard Fox. Santa Fe: School of American Research Press.

Austin, Andrew. 2004. Review Essay. Explanation and Responsibility: Agency and Motive in Lynching and Genocide. *Journal of Black Studies* 34 (5): 719–733.

Axel, Brian, ed. 2002. *From the Margins: Historical Anthropology and Its Futures.* Durham, NC: Duke University Press.

Baade, Hans. 1996. The Gens de Coleur of Louisiana: Comparative Slave Law in Microcosm. *Cardozo Law Review* 18 (2): 535–586.

Balakrishnan, Gopal. 2009. *Antagonistics: Capitalism and Power in an Age of War.* New York: Verso.

Balderrama, Francisco, and Raymond Rodríguez. 1995. *Decade of Betrayal: Mexican Repatriation in the 1930s.* Albuquerque: University of New Mexico Press.

Baldwin, James. 1985. *The Price of the Ticket: Collected Nonfiction, 1948–1985.* New York: St. Martin's/Marek.

Balibar, Etienne. 1991. Racism and Nationalism. In *Race, Nation, Class: Ambiguous Identities.* London: Verso.

Bambara, Toni Cade. 1977. The Sea Birds Are Still Alive. In *The Sea Birds Are Still Alive.* New York: Random House.

Bardacke, Frank. 2011. *Trampling Out the Vintage: Cesar Chavez and the Two Souls of the United Farm Workers.* New York: Verso, 2011.

Basch, Linda. 2001. Transnational Social Relations and the Politics of National Identity: An Eastern Caribbean Case Study. In *Islands in the City: West Indian Migration to New York,* ed. Nancy Foner. Berkeley: University of California Press.

Baucom, Ian. 2009. Cicero's Ghost: The Atlantic, the Enemy, and the Laws of War. In *States of Emergency: The Object of American Studies,* ed. Russ Castronovo and Susan Gillman. Chapel Hill: University of North Carolina Press.

Bayoumi, Moustafa. 2008. *How Does It Feel to Be a Problem? Being Young and Arab in America.* New York: Penguin.

Beam, Joseph, ed. 1986. *In the Life: A Black Gay Anthology.* Boston: Alyson.

Beatty, Paul. 1996. *The White Boy Shuffle.* Boston: Houghton Mifflin.

Bedolla, Lisa Garcia. 2007. Intersections of Inequality: Understanding Marginalization and Privilege in the Post–Civil Rights Era. *Politics and Gender* 3 (2): 232–249.

Bell, Derrick A. 1973. *Race, Racism, and American Law.* Boston: Little, Brown.

———. 1995. Racial Realism. In *Critical Race Theory,* ed. Kimberlé Crenshaw et al. New York: The New Press.

Bennett, Herman L. 2003. *Africans in Colonial Mexico: Absolutism, Christianity, and Afro-Creole Consciousness, 1570–1640.* Bloomington: Indiana University Press.

Bentley, George. 1974. *A History of the Freedmen's Bureau.* New York: Octagon Books.

Benton, Lauren. 2002. *Law and Colonial Cultures: Legal Regimes in World History, 1400–1900.* Cambridge: Cambridge University Press.

Bhattacharyya, Gargi, John Gabriel, and Stephen Small. 2002. *Race and Power: Global Racism in the Twenty-First Century.* London: Routledge.

Blauner, Robert. 1972. *Racial Oppression in America.* New York: Harper & Row.

Blumer, Herbert. 1958. Race Prejudice as a Sense of Group Position. *Pacific Sociological Review* 1 (1): 3–7.

Blumer, Herbert, and Troy Duster. 1980. Theories of Race and Social Action. In *Sociological Theories: Race and Colonialism,* ed. Marion O'Callaghan. Paris: UNESCO.

Bobo, Lawrence, James Kluegel, and Ryan A. Smith. 1997. Laissez-faire Racism: The Crystallization of a Kinder, Gentler, Antiblack Ideology. In *Racial Attitudes in the 1990's: Continuity and Change,* ed. Steven A. Tuch and Jack K. Martin. Westport, CT: Praeger.

Boger, John Charles, and Gary Orfield, eds. 2005. *School Resegregation: Must the South Turn Back?* Chapel Hill: University of North Carolina Press.

Bonacich, Edna. 1972. A Theory of Ethnic Antagonism: The Split Labor Market. *American Sociological Review* 37 (5): 547–559.

Bonick, Deborah A., et al. 2007. The Science and Business of Genetic Ancestry Testing. *Science* 318 (5849): 399–400.

Bonilla-Silva, Eduardo. 1997. Rethinking Racism: Toward a Structural Interpretation. *American Sociological Review* 62 (3): 465–480.

———. 2003a. "New Racism," Color-Blind Racism, and the Future of Whiteness in America. In *White Out: The Continuing Significance of Race,* ed. Eduardo Bonilla-Silva and Ashley "Woody" Doane. New York: Routledge.

———. 2003b. *Racism without Racists: Color-Blind Racism and the Persistence of Racial Inequality in the United States.* New York: Rowman & Littlefield.

———. 2004. From Bi-racial to Tri-racial: Towards a New System of Racial Stratification in the USA. *Ethnic and Racial Studies* 27 (6): 931–950.

———. 2006. *Racism without Racists: Color-Blind Racism and the Persistence of Racial Inequality in the United States.* 2nd edition. Lanham, MD: Rowman & Littlefield.

Brezina, Timothy, and Kenisha Winder. 2003. Economic Disadvantage, Status Generalization, and Negative Racial Stereotyping by White Americans. *Social Psychology Quarterly* 66 (4): 402–418.

Briggs-Cloud, Marcus. 2010. The United States as Imperial Peace: Decolonization and Indigenous Peoples. *Journal of Race, Ethnicity, and Religion* 1 (5) (December). Available at http://raceandreligion.com/JRER/Volume_1_%282010%29.html. Accessed March 2, 2012.

Bronfman, Alejandra. 2004. *Measures of Equality: Social Science, Citizenship, and Race in Cuba, 1902–1940*. Chapel Hill: University of North Carolina Press.

Brown, Elsa Barkley. 1992. "What Has Happened Here": The Politics of Difference in Women's History and Feminist Politics. *Feminist Studies* 18 (2): 295–312.

Brown, Michael K., Martin Carnoy, Elliot Currie, Troy Duster, David B. Oppenheimer, Marjorie M. Shultz, and David Wellman. 2003. *Whitewashing Race: The Myth of a Color-Blind Society*. Berkeley: University of California Press.

Brubaker, Rogers. 2004. *Ethnicity without Groups*. Cambridge, MA: Harvard University Press.

Brubaker, Rogers, Mara Loveman, and Peter Stamatov. 2004. Ethnicity as Cognition. *Theory and Society* 33 (1): 31–64.

Butler, Judith. 1993. *Bodies That Matter: On the Discursive Limits of "Sex."* New York: Routledge.

———. 1997. *The Psychic Life of Power*. Stanford: Stanford University Press.

Cahill, David. 1994. Colour by Numbers: Racial and Ethnic Categories in the Viceroyalty of Peru, 1532–1824. *Journal of Latin American Studies* 26 (2): 325–346.

Cainkar, Louise. 2002. No Longer Invisible: Arab and Muslim Exclusion after September 11. *Middle East Report* 224. Available at www.merip.org/mer/mer224/no-longer-visible (accessed May 7, 2012).

———. 2003. Special Registration: A Fervor for Muslims. *Journal of Islamic Law and Culture* 7 (2): 73–101.

———. 2004. The Impact of the September 11 Attacks and Their Aftermath on Arab and Muslim Communities in the United States. *GSC Quarterly* 13 (Summer–Fall).

———. 2005. Space and Place in the Metropolis: Arabs and Muslims Seeking Safety. *City & Society* 17 (2): 181–209.

Camiscioli, Elisa. 2009. *Reproducing the French Race: Immigration, Intimacy, and Embodiment in Early 20th Century France*. Durham, NC: Duke University Press.

Candelario, Ginetta E. B. 2007a. Color Matters: Latina/o Racial Identities and Life Chances. In *A Companion to Latino Studies*, ed. Juan Flores and Renato Rosaldo. Malden, MA: Blackwell.

———. 2007b. *Black behind the Ears: Dominican Racial Identity from Museums to Beauty Shops*. Durham, NC: Duke University Press.

Carbado, Devon. 2009. Yellow by Law. *California Law Review* 97 (3): 633–692.

Carbado, Devon, and Mitu Gulati. 2004. Race to the Top of the Corporate Ladder: What Minorities Do When They Get There. *Washington and Lee Law Review* 61 (4): 1645–1693.

Carbado, Devon, and Cheryl Harris. 2008. Taking Initiative on Initiatives: Examining Proposition 209 and Beyond; The New Racial Preferences. *California Law Review* 96: 1139–1214.

Carby, Hazel. 1999. *Cultures in Babylon: Black Britain and African America*. New York: Verso.

Castro-Klarén, Sara, and John Charles Chasteen, eds. 2003. *Beyond Imagined Communities: Reading and Writing the Nation in Nineteenth-Century Latin America.* Baltimore: Johns Hopkins University Press.

Chandler, Nahum D. 2006. The Figure of W. E. B. Du Bois as a Problem for Thought. *CR: The New Centennial Review* 6 (3): 29–56.

————. 2010. Of Horizon: An Introduction to "The Afro-American" by W. E. B. Du Bois—circa 1894. *Journal of Transnational American Studies* 2 (1). Available at http://escholarship.org/uc/acgcc_jtas. Accessed January 23, 2012.

Chang, Grace. 2000. *Disposable Domestics: Immigrant Women Workers in the Global Economy.* Boston: South End Press.

Chavez, Leo R. 2008. *The Latino Threat: Constructing Immigrants, Citizens, and the Nation.* Stanford: Stanford University Press.

Chon, Margaret, and Donna E. Arzt. 2005. Walking While Muslim. *Law and Contemporary Problems* 68: 215–254.

Churchill, Ward. 1983. *Marxism and Native Americans.* Cambridge, MA: South End Press.

————. 1993. *Struggle for the Land.* Monroe, ME: Common Courage Press.

Coalicion de Derechos Humanos. 2011. On the Wrong Side of History Again: Supreme Court Upholds Law Aimed at Immigrant Workers. *National Network for Immigrant and Refugee Rights,* June 3. Available at http://nnirr.blogspot.com/2011/06/on-wrong-side-of-history-again-supreme.html. Accessed March 3, 2012.

Cohen, Cathy. 1999. *The Boundaries of Blackness: Aids and the Breakdown of Black Politics.* Chicago: University of Chicago Press.

Cole, David. 2003. *Enemy Aliens: Double Standards and Constitutional Freedoms in the War on Terrorism.* New York: The New Press.

————. 2009. Out of the Shadows: Preventive Detention, Suspected Terrorists, and War. *California Law Review* 97 (3): 693–750.

Collins, Patricia Hill. 1990. *Black Feminist Thought: Knowledge, Consciousness, and the Politics of Empowerment.* New York: Routledge.

Combahee River Collective. 1983. The Combahee River Collective Statement. In *Home Girls: A Black Feminist Anthology,* ed. Barbara Smith, 264–274. New York: Kitchen Table Press.

Cook, David N., ed. 1968. *Padrón de los Indios de Lima en 1613.* Lima: Universidad Nacional Mayor de San Marcos.

Cook-Lynn, Elizabeth. 1997. Who Stole Native American Studies? *Wicazo Sa Review* 12 (1): 9–28.

Cooper, Frederick, Thomas Holt, and Rebecca Scott. 2000. *Beyond Slavery: Explorations of Race, Labor, and Citizenship in Postemancipation Societies.* Chapel Hill: University of North Carolina Press.

Coronado, Jorge. 2009. *The Andes Imagined: Indigenismo, Society and Modernity.* Pittsburgh: University of Pittsburgh Press.

Coulthard, Glen. 2007. *Subjects of Empire: Indigenous Peoples and the "Politics of Recognition" in Canada.* Contemporary Political History 6 (4): 437–460.

Crenshaw, Kimberlé. 1991a. Demarginalizing the Intersection of Race and Sex: A Black Feminist Critique of Antidiscrimination Doctrine, Feminist Theory, and Antiracist Politics. In *Feminist Legal Theory*, ed. Katherine Bartlett and Rosanne Kennedy, 57–80. Boulder, CO: Westview Press.

———. 1991b. Mapping the Margins: Identity Politics, Intersectionality, and Violence against Women. *Stanford Law Review* 43: 1241–1299.

———. 2002. The First Decade: Critical Reflections, or "A Foot in the Closing Door." In *Crossroads, Directions, and a New Critical Race Theory*, ed. Francisco Valdes, Jerome McCristal Culp, and Angela P. Harris. Philadelphia: Temple University Press.

Crenshaw, Kimberlé, Neil Gotanda, Garry Peller, and Kendall Thomas, eds. 1995. *Critical Race Theory: The Key Writings That Formed the Movement*. New York: The New Press.

Danner, Mark. 2004. The Logic of Torture. In *Abu Ghraib: The Politics of Torture*, ed. Meron Benvenisti and Barbara Ehrenreich. Berkeley, CA: North Atlantic Books.

Daulatzai, Sohail. 2007. Protect Ya Neck: Muslims and the Carceral Imagination in the Age of Guantánamo. *Souls* 9 (2): 132–147.

Davila, Arlene. 2004. *Barrio Dreams: Puerto Ricans, Latinos, and the Neoliberal City*. Berkeley: University of California Press.

Davis, Angela. 2003. *Are Prisons Obsolete?* New York: Seven Stories Press.

Davis, Dána-Ain. 2006. *Battered Black Women and Welfare Reform: Between a Rock and a Hard Place*. Albany: State University of New York Press.

Dawson, Ashley, and Malini Johar Schueller. 2007. Introduction: Rethinking Imperialism Today. In *Exceptional State: Contemporary U.S. Culture and the New Imperialism*, ed. Ashley Dawson and Malini Johar Schueller. Durham, NC: Duke University Press.

Dayan, Colin. 2008. *The Story of Cruel and Unusual*. Cambridge, MA: MIT Press.

De Certeau, Michel. 1988. *The Writing of History*, trans. Tom Conley. New York: Columbia University Press.

de Contreras, Miguel, Noble David Cook, and Mauro Escobar Gamboa. 1968. *Padrón de los Indios de Lima en 1613*. Lima: Universidad Nacional Mayor de San Marcos, Seminario Rural Indio.

De Genova, Nicholas. 2005. *Working the Boundaries: Race, Space, and "Illegality" in Mexican Chicago*. Durham, NC: Duke University Press.

———. 2006. Introduction: Latino and Asian Racial Formations at the Frontiers of U.S. Nationalism. In *Racial Transformations: Latinos and Asians Remaking the United States*, ed. Nicholas De Genova. Durham, NC: Duke University Press.

———. 2007a. The Production of Culprits: From Deportability to Detainability in the Aftermath of "Homeland Security." *Citizenship Studies* 11 (5): 421–448.

———. 2007b. The Stakes of an Anthropology of the United States. *CR: The New Centennial Review* 7 (2): 231–277.

———. 2009. Conflicts of Mobility, and the Mobility of Conflict: Rightslessness, Presence, Subjectivity, Freedom. *Subjectivity* 29: 445–466.

————. 2010. Migration and Race in Europe: The Trans-Atlantic Metastases of a Post-Colonial Cancer. *European Journal of Social Theory* 13 (3): 405–419.

————. 2011a. Alien Powers: Deportable Labor and the Spectacle of Security. In *The Contested Politics of Mobility: Borderzones and Irregularity,* ed. Vicki Squire. London: Routledge.

————. 2011b. Spectacle of Security, Spectacle of Terror. In *Accumulating Insecurity: Violence and Dispossession in the Making of Everyday Life,* ed. Shelley Feldman, Charles Geisler, and Gayatri Menon. Athens: University of Georgia Press.

————. n.d. "The Spectacle of Terror: Immigration, Race, and the Homeland Security State." Unpublished book manuscript.

De Genova, Nicholas, and Ana Y. Ramos-Zayas. 2003. *Latino Crossings: Mexicans, Puerto Ricans, and the Politics of Race and Citizenship.* New York: Routledge.

De la Cadena, Marisol. 1999. Myths of Racial Democracy: Cuba, 1900–1912. *Latin American Research Review* 34 (3): 39–73.

————. 2000. *Indigenous Mestizos: The Politics of Race and Culture in Cuzco, Peru, 1919–1991.* Durham: Duke University Press.

De la Fuente, Alejandro. 1999. Myths of Racial Democracy: Cuba, 1900–1912. *Latin American Research Review* 34 (3): 39–73.

————. 2004. Slave Law and Claims-Making in Cuba: The Tannenbaum Debate Revisited. *Law and History Review* 22 (2): 340–369.

Debord, Guy. 1995. *The Society of the Spectacle,* trans. Donald Nicholson-Smith. New York: Zone Books.

Delgado, Richard, and Jean Stefancic. 2000. *Critical Race Theory: The Cutting Edge.* Second Edition. Philadelphia: Temple University Press.

Deloria, Vine. 1969. *Custer Died for Your Sins: An Indian Manifesto.* New York: Macmillan.

————. 1970. *We Talk, You Listen: New Tribes, New Turf.* New York: Dell.

Denetdale, Jennifer. 2008. Carving Navajo National Boundaries: Patriotism, Tradition, and the Dine Marriage Act of 2005. *American Quarterly* 60 (2): 289–294.

Devos, Thierry, and Mahzarin Banaji. 2005. American = White? *Journal of Personality and Social Psychology* 88 (3): 447–466.

Dirlik, Arif. 2008. Race Talk, Race, and Contemporary Racism. *PMLA* 123 (5): 1363–1379.

Dominguez Ortiz, Alejandro. 1952. La Esclavitud en Castilla durante la Edad Moderna. *Estudios de Historia Social* 2: 369–428.

Douglass, John Aubrey. 2007. *The Conditions for Admission: Access, Equality, and the Social Contract of Public Universities.* Stanford: Stanford University Press.

Dratel, Joshua. 2006. The Curious Debate. In *The Torture Debate in America,* ed. Karen J. Greenberg. New York: Cambridge University Press.

Drinnon, Richard. 1980. *Facing West: The Metaphysics of Indian-Hating and Empire-Building.* Minneapolis: University of Minnesota Press.

Duany, Jorge. 2002a. Neither Black nor White: The Representation of Racial Identity among Puerto Ricans on the Island and in the U.S. Mainland. In

The Puerto Rican Nation on the Move: Identities on the Island and in the United States. Chapel Hill: University of North Carolina Press.

———. 2002b. *The Puerto Rican Nation on the Move: Identities on the Island and in the United States.* Chapel Hill: University of North Carolina Press.

———. 2003. Nation, Migration, Identity: The Case of Puerto Ricans. *Latino Studies Journal* 1 (3): 424–444.

———. 2007. Nation and Migration: Rethinking Puerto Rican Identity in a Transnational Context. In *None of the Above: Puerto Ricans in the Global Era,* ed. Frances Negron-Muntaner. New York: Palgrave MacMillan.

DuBois, W. E. B. 1921. The Souls of White Folk. In *Darkwater: Voices from Within the Veil.* New York: Harcourt, Brace & Co.

———. 1945. *Color and Democracy: Colonies and Peace.* New York: Harcourt, Brace & Co.

———. 1969. *The Souls of Black Folk.* New York: Penguin/Signet.

———. 1998. *Black Reconstruction in America, 1860–1880.* New York: Free Press.

Dudziak, Mary. 2004. *Cold War Civil Rights.* Princeton: Princeton University Press.

Dudziak, Mary, and Leti Volpp, eds. 2006. *Legal Borderlands: Law and the Construction of American Borders.* Baltimore: Johns Hopkins University Press.

Dyer, Richard. 1997. *White: Essays on Race and Culture.* New York: Routledge.

Edelman, Peter. 2004. Welfare and the Politics of Race: Same Tune, New Lyrics. *Georgetown Journal on Poverty Law & Policy* 11 (3): 389–404.

Edin, Kathryn, and Laura Lein. 1997. *Making Ends Meet: How Single Mothers Survive Welfare and Low-Wage Work.* New York: Russell Sage Foundation.

Edsall, Thomas Byrne, and Mary D. Edsall. 1992. *Chain Reaction: The Impact of Race, Rights, and Taxes on American Politics.* New York: W. W. Norton.

Edwards, Laura F. 1997. *Gendered Strife and Confusion: The Political Culture of Reconstruction.* Urbana: University of Illinois.

Elinson, Elaine, and Stan Yogi. 2009 *Wherever There's a Fight: How Runaway Slaves, Suffragists, Immigrants, Strikers, and Poets Shaped Civil Liberties in California.* Berkeley, CA: Heyday Books.

Escobar, Arturo. 2008. *Territories of Difference: Place, Movements, Life, Redes.* Durham, NC: Duke University Press.

Estenssoro Fuchs, Juan Carlos. 2000. Los colores de la plebe: Razón y mestizaje en el Perú colonial. In *Los Cuadros del Mestizaje del Virrey Amat,* ed. Natalia Mahluf, 66–107. Lima: Museo de Arte de Lima.

Etzioni, Amitai. 1959. The Ghetto: A Re-evaluation. *Social Forces* 37: 255–262.

Evans, E. Raymond. 1977. Fort Marr Blockhouse: The Last Evidence of America's First Concentration Camps. *Journal of Cherokee Studies* 2 (Spring): 256–263.

Farmer, Mary. 1999. "Because They Are Women": Gender and the Virginia Freedmen's Bureau's "War on Dependency." In *The Freedmen's Bureau and Reconstruction: Reconsiderations,* ed. Paul A. Cimbala and Randall M. Miller. New York: Fordham University Press.

Fausto-Sterling, Anne. 2000. *Sexing the Body: Gender Politics and the Construction of Sexuality.* New York: Basic Books.

Feagin, Joe R. 2001. *Racist America.* New York: Routledge.

———. 2006. *Systemic Racism: A Theory of Oppression.* New York: Routledge.

———. 2009. *The White Racial Frame.* New York: Routledge.

Feagin, Joe R., Hernán Vera, and Pinar Batur. 2000. *White Racism: The Basics.* Second Edition. New York: Routledge.

Feldman, Heidi. 2006. *Black Rhythms of Peru: Reviving African Musical Heritage in the Black Pacific.* Middletown, CT: Wesleyan University Press.

Fêo Rodrigues, Isabel. 2003. Islands of Sexuality: Theories and Histories of Creolization in Cape Verde. *International Journal of African Historical Studies* 36 (1): 83–104.

Fernandes, Deepa. 2007. *Targeted: Homeland Security and the Business of Immigration.* New York: Seven Stories Press.

Ferreira da Silva, Denise. 1998. Facts of Blackness: Brazil Is Not (Quite) the United States . . . and Racial Politics in Brazil? *Social Identities* 4 (2): 201–235.

———. 2007. *Toward a Global Idea of Race.* Minneapolis: University of Minnesota Press.

Fields, Barbara J. 1990. Slavery, Race, and Ideology in the United States of America. *New Left Review* 181: 95–118.

Flores Galindo, Alberto. 1986. *Buscando un inca: Identidad y Utopia en los Andes.* Lima: Instituto de Apoyo Agrario.

Foley, Neil. 1997. *The White Scourge: Mexicans, Blacks, and Poor Whites in Texas Cotton Culture.* Berkeley: University of California Press.

———. 2007. "God Bless the Law, He Is White": Legal, Local, and International Politics of Latina/o and Black Desegregation Cases in Post–World War II California and Texas. In *A Companion to Latino Studies,* ed. Juan Flores and Renato Rosaldo. Malden, MA: Blackwell Publishing.

Foner, Nancy, and George M. Fredrickson, eds. 2004. *Not Just Black and White: Historical and Contemporary Perspectives on Immigration, Race, and Ethnicity in the United States.* New York: Russell Sage.

Ford, Lisa. 2010. *Settler Sovereignty: Jurisdiction and Indigenous People in American and Australia, 1788–1836.* Cambridge, MA: Harvard University Press.

Forman, Tyrone A., Carla Goar, and Amanda E. Lewis. 2002. Neither Black nor White? An Empirical Test of the Latin Americanization Thesis. *Race and Society* 5: 65–84.

Foucault, Michel. 1998. On the Ways of Writing History. In *Michel Foucault: Aesthetics, Method, and Epistemology,* ed. James D. Faubion. New York: The New Press.

Franke, Katherine. 1999. Becoming a Citizen: Reconstruction Era Regulation of African American Marriages. *Yale Journal of Law and the Humanities* 11: 251–309.

Frankel, Noralee. 1999. *Freedom's Women: Black Women and Families in Civil War Era Mississippi.* Bloomington: Indiana University Press.

Franklin, Cynthia G. 1997. *Writing Women's Communities: The Politics and Poetics of Contemporary Multi-genre Anthologies*. Madison: University of Wisconsin Press.

Fredrickson, George M. 1988. *The Arrogance of Race: Historical Perspectives on Slavery, Racism and Inequality*. Middletown, CT: Wesleyan University Press.

———. 2002. *Racism: A Short History*. Princeton: Princeton University Press.

Freyre, Gilberto. 1961. *Luso e o Trópico*. Lisbon: Executive Committee for the Commemoration of the Fifth Centenary of the Death of Prince Henry the Navigator.

———. 1986. *The Masters and the Slaves: A Study in the Development of Brazilian Civilization*. Berkeley: University of California Press.

Friedman, Ray, and Martin Davidson. 1999. The Black-White Gap in Perceptions of Discrimination: Its Causes and Consequences. In *Research on Negotiation in Organizations*, ed. Robert Bies, Roy Lewicki, and Blair Sheppard. Greenwich, CT: JAI Press.

Fujikane, Candace, and Jonathan Okamura, eds. 2008. *Asian Settler Colonialism*. Honolulu: University of Hawaii Press.

Fukuyama, Francis. 1989. The End of History? *The National Interest* (Summer 1989). Available at http://www.wesjones.com/eoh.htm. Accessed February 22, 2012.

———. 1992. *The End of History and the Last Man*. New York: Free Press.

———. 1995. *Trust: The Social Virtues and the Creation of Prosperity*. New York: Free Press.

———. 2004. Nation-Building 101. *Atlantic Monthly* (January–February). Available at http://www.theatlantic.com/doc/200401/fukuyama. Accessed January 16, 2012.

———. 2006. Introduction: Nation-Building and the Failure of Institutional Memory. In *Nation-Building: Beyond Afghanistan and Iraq*, ed. Francis Fukuyama. Baltimore: Johns Hopkins University Press.

Fuss, Diana. 1989. *Essentially Speaking: Feminism, Nature, and Difference*. New York: Routledge.

Gaddis, John Lewis. 2003. *Surprise, Security, and the American Experience*. Cambridge, MA: Harvard University Press.

Ganz, Marshall. 2009. *Why David Sometimes Wins: Leadership, Organization, and Strategy in the California Farm Workers Movement*. New York: Oxford University Press.

Garcia, Matthew. Forthcoming. *A Moveable Feast: César Chávez and the United Farmworkers' Boycott*. Berkeley: University of California Press.

García Canclini, Néstor. 1995. *Hybrid Cultures: Strategies for Entering and Leaving Modernity*. Minneapolis: University of Minnesota Press.

Gilmore, Ruth Wilson. 2007. *Golden Gulag: Prisons, Surplus, Crisis, and Opposition in Globalizing California*. Berkeley: University of California Press.

Gilroy, Paul. 1987. *"There Ain't No Black in the Union Jack": The Cultural Politics of Race and Nation*. London: Hutchinson.

———. 1993. *The Black Atlantic*. London: Verso.

———. 1999. The End of Anti-Racism. In *Racism*, ed. Martin Bulmer and John Solomos. New York: Oxford University Press.

————. 2002. *Against Race: Imagining Political Culture beyond the Color Line.* Cambridge, MA: Harvard University Press.

Glenn, Evelyn Nakano. 1999. The Social Construction and Institutionalization of Race and Gender: An Integrative Framework. In *Revisioning Gender,* ed. Myra Marx Ferree, Judith Lorber, and Beth Hess. Thousand Oaks, CA: Sage.

————. 2002. *Unequal Freedom: How Race and Gender Shaped American Citizenship and Labor.* Cambridge, MA: Harvard University Press.

Glick Schiller, Nina, Linda Basch, and Cristina Szanton-Blanc. 1992. Towards a Transnationalization of Migration: Race, Class, Ethnicity, and Nationalism Reconsidered. In *Towards a Transnational Perspective on Migration: Race, Class, Ethnicity, and Nationalism Reconsidered,* ed. Nina Glick Schiller, Linda Basch, and Cristina Szanton-Blanc. New York: New York Academy of Sciences.

Goldberg, David Theo. 2008. *The Threat of Race: Reflections on Racial Neoliberalism.* New York: Wiley-Blackwell.

————. 2009. *The Threat of Race: Reflections on Racial Neoliberalism.* Malden, MA: Wiley-Blackwell.

Gómez, Laura E. 2007. *Manifest Destinies: The Making of the Mexican American Race.* New York: New York University Press.

————. 2009. Opposite One-Drop Rules: Mexican Americans, African Americans, and the Need to Reconceive Turn-of-the-Century Race Relations. In *How the United States Racializes Latinos: White Hegemony and Its Consequences,* ed. Jose A. Cobas, Jorge Duany, and Joe R. Feagin. Boulder: Paradigm.

————. 2010. Understanding Race and Law as Mutually Constitutive: An Invitation to Explore an Emerging Field. *Annual Review of Law and Social Science* 6: 487–505.

Gordon, Avery. 1997. *Ghostly Matters: Haunting and the Sociological Imagination.* Minneapolis: University of Minnesota Press.

Gordon, Leonard. 1989. Racial Theorizing: Is Sociology Ready to Replace Polemic Causation Theory with a New Polemic Model? *Sociological Perspectives* 32 (1) (Spring): 129–136.

Gordon, Linda. 1994. *Pitied but Not Entitled: Single Mothers and the History of Welfare 1890–1935.* New York: Free Press.

Gordon, Milton. 1964. *Assimilation in American Life: The Role of Race, Religion, and National Origins.* New York: Oxford University Press.

Gotanda, Neil. 1995. A Critique of "Our Constitution Is Colorblind.'" In *Critical Race Theory: The Key Writings That Formed the Movement,* ed. Kimberlé Crenshaw, Neil Gotanda, Garry Peller, and Kendall Thomas. New York: The New Press.

Gourevitch, Philip, and Errol Morris. 2008. *Standard Operating Procedure.* New York: Penguin Press.

Gramsci, Antonio. 1971. *Selections from the Prison Notebooks,* ed. Quinton Hoare and Geoffrey Nowell-Smith. New York: International.

Grant-Thomas, Andrew, and john a. powell. 2006. Toward a Structural Racism Framework. *Poverty & Race* 15 (6): 3–6.

Gray, John. 2004. Power and Vainglory. In *Abu Ghraib: The Politics of Torture*, ed. Meron Benvenisti and Barbara Ehrenreich. Berkeley, CA: North Atlantic Books.

Greenberg, Karen J. 2008. Introduction: The Rule of Law Finds Its Golem: Judicial Torture Then and Now. In *The Torture Debate in America*, ed. Karen J. Greenberg. New York: Cambridge University Press.

Greene, Shane. 2006. Getting over the Andes: The Geo-Eco Politics of Indigenous Movements in Peru's Twenty-First Century Inca Empire. *Journal of Latin American Studies* 38 (2): 327–354.

Gross, Ariela. 2008. *What Blood Won't Tell: A History of Race on Trial in America*. Cambridge, MA: Harvard University Press.

Guglielmo, Thomas A. 2003. *White on Arrival: Italians, Race, Color, and Power in Chicago, 1890–1945*. New York: Oxford University Press.

———. 2006. Fighting for Caucasian Rights: Mexicans, Mexican Americans, and the Transnational Struggle for Civil Rights in World War II Texas. *Journal of American History* 92 (4): 1212–1237.

Guinier, Lani, and Gerald Torres. 2003. *The Miner's Canary: Enlisting Race, Resisting Power, Transforming Democracy*. Cambridge, MA: Harvard University Press.

Gutiérrez, Ramón A. 1991. *When Jesus Came, the Corn Mothers Went Away: Marriage, Sexuality, and Power in New Mexico, 1500–1846*. Stanford: Stanford University Press.

———. 2009. Hispanic Identities in the Southwestern United States. In *Race and Classification: The Case of Mexican Americans*, ed. Ilona Katzew and Susan Deans-Smith. Stanford: Stanford University Press.

Guzman, Manolo. 2005. *Gay Hegemony/Latino Homosexualities*. New York: Routledge.

Haas, Lisbeth. 1995. *Conquests and Historical Identities in California, 1769–1936*. Berkeley: University of California Press.

Hahn, Steven. 2005. *A Nation under Our Feet: Black Political Struggles from Slavery to the Great Migration*. Cambridge, MA: Harvard University Press.

Hale, Charles. 2002. Does Multiculturalism Menace? Governance, Cultural Rights, and the Politics of Identity in Guatemala. *Journal of Latin American Studies* 34 (3): 485–524.

Hall, Stuart. 1990. Cultural Identity and Diaspora. In *Identity: Community, Culture, Difference*, ed. Jonathan Rutherford. London: Lawrence & Wishart.

———. 1993. What Is This "Black" in Black Popular Culture? In *Black Popular Culture*, ed. Gina Dent. New York: Dia Center for the Arts.

———. 1996. New Ethnicities. In *Black British Cultural Studies: A Reader*, ed. Houston A. Baker, Manthia Diawara, and Ruth H. Lindeborg. Chicago: University of Chicago Press.

Hall, Stuart, Chas Critcher, Tony Jefferson, John Clarke, and Brian Roberts. 1978. *Policing the Crisis: Mugging, the State, and Law and Order*. London: Palgrave MacMillan.

Han, Sora. 2002. Veiled Threats. Paper presented to the American Studies Association, Houston, November 2002.

———. 2006. Bonds of Representation: Vision, Race and Law in Post–Civil Rights America. PhD dissertation, University of California, Santa Cruz.

Hancock, Ange Marie. 2004. *The Politics of Disgust and the Public Identity of the Welfare Queen.* New York: New York University Press.

Haney-López, Ian. 1996. *White by Law: The Legal Construction of Race.* New York: New York University Press.

———. 2004. *Racism on Trial: The Chicano Fight for Justice.* Cambridge, MA: Harvard University Press.

Hardisty, Jean. 1999. *Mobilizing Resentment: Conservative Resurgence from the John Birch Society to the Promise Keepers.* Boston: Beacon Press.

Hardisty, Jean, and Deepak Bhargava. 2005. Wrong about the Right. *The Nation,* November 7, 2005. Available at http://www.thenation.com/article/wrong-about-right. Accessed February 10, 2012.

Harris, Angela P. 2000. Embracing the Tar-Baby: Latcrit Theory and the Sticky Mess of Race. In *Critical Race Theory,* Second Edition, ed. Richard Delgado and Jean Stefancic. Philadelphia: Temple University Press.

Harris, Cheryl. 1995. Whiteness as Property. In *Critical Race Theory: The Key Writings That Formed the Movement,* ed. Kimberlé Crenshaw, Neil Gotanda, Garry Peller, and Kendall Thomas. New York: The New Press.

———. 2002. Critical Race Studies: An Introduction. *UCLA Law Review* 49: 1215–1239.

Harrison, Faye V. 1995. The Persistent Power of "Race" in the Cultural and Political Economy of Racism. *Annual Review of Anthropology* 24: 47–74.

Hartman, Saidiya. 1997. *Scenes of Subjection: Terror, Slavery, and Self-Making in Nineteenth-Century America.* Oxford: Oxford University Press.

Harvey, David. 2004. The New Imperialism: Accumulation by Dispossession. *Socialist Register* 40: 63–87.

Hattam, Victoria. 2005. Ethnicity and the Boundaries of Race: Rereading Directive 15. *Daedalus* 134 (1): 61–69.

Hayden, Tom. 2004. *Street Wars: Gangs and the Future of Violence.* New York: The New Press.

Hearn, Marcellene. 2000. *Dangerous Indifference: New York City's Failure to Implement the Family Violence Option.* New York: NOW Legal Defense and Education Fund.

Hemphill, Essex, ed. 1991a. *Brother to Brother: New Writings by Black Gay Men.* Boston: Alyson.

Hemphill, Essex. 1991b. Introduction. In *Brother to Brother: New Writings by Black Gay Men,* ed. Essex Hemphill. Boston: Alyson.

Henry, Charles P. 2007. *Long Overdue: The Politics of Racial Reparations.* New York: New York University Press.

Hesse, H. Barnor. Forthcoming. *Creolizing the Political: A Genealogy of the African Diaspora.* Durham, NC: Duke University Press.

Higham, John. 2002. *Strangers in the Land: Patterns of American Nativism, 1860–1925.* Second Edition. New Brunswick, NJ: Rutgers University Press, 2002.

Hirsch, Marianne. 2005. Editor's Column: In Medias Res. *PMLA* 120 (2): 321–326.

Hochschild, Jennifer L. 2005. Looking Ahead: Racial Trends in the United States. *Daedalus* 134: 70–81.

Holloway, John. 1994. Global Capital and the National State. *Capital and Class* 52: 23–49.

Holmes, Stephen. 2006. Is Defiance of Law a Proof of Success?: Magical Thinking in the War on Terror. In *The Torture Debate in America,* ed. Karen J. Greenberg. New York: Cambridge University Press.

Hong, Grace Kyungwon. 2006. *The Ruptures of American Capital.* Minneapolis: University of Minnesota Press.

———. 2007. The Ghosts of Transnational American Studies: A Response to the Presidential Address. *American Quarterly* 59 (1): 33–39.

Hooker, Juliet. 2005. Indigenous Inclusion/Black Exclusion: Race, Ethnicity, and Multicultural Citizenship in Latin America. *Journal of Latin American Studies* 37: 285–310.

Hopper, Kim, and Norweeta G. Milburn. 1996. Homelessness among African Americans: A Historical and Contemporary Perspective." In *Homelessness in America,* ed. Jim Baumohl, 123–131. Phoenix: Onyx Press.

Horsman, Reginald. 1981. *Race and Manifest Destiny: The Origins of American Racial Anglo-Saxonism.* Cambridge, MA: Harvard University Press.

HoSang, Daniel Martinez. 2010. *Racial Propositions: Ballot Initiatives and the Making of Postwar California.* Berkeley: University of California Press.

Hull, Gloria, and Barbara Smith. 1982. Introduction. In *All the Women Are White, All the Blacks Are Men, But Some of Us Are Brave,* ed. Gloria Hull, Patricia Scott, and Barbara Smith. New York: Feminist Press.

Hull, Gloria, Patricia Bell Scott, and Barbara Smith, eds. 1993. *All the Women Are White, All the Blacks Are Men, but Some of Us Are Brave.* New York: Feminist Press.

Human Rights Watch. 2002. Presumption of Guilt: Human Rights Abuses of Post–September 11 Detainees. Available at www.hrw.org/reports/2002/us911. Accessed January 23, 2012.

Hunt, Andrew E. 1999. *The Turning: A History of Vietnam Veterans Against the War.* New York: New York University Press.

Huntington, Samuel P. 1993. The Clash of Civilizations? *Foreign Affairs* 72 (3): 22–49.

———. 1996. *The Clash of Civilizations and the Remaking of World Order.* New York: Free Press.

———. 1997. *The Clash of Civilizations and the Remaking of World Order.* New York: Touchstone Press.

———. 2005. *Who Are We? The Challenges to America's National Identity.* New York: Simon & Schuster.

Ignatieff, Michael. 1978. *A Just Measure of Pain.* New York: Pantheon Books.

Incite!: Women of Color Against Violence. 2006. *The Color of Violence: The Incite! Anthology.* Boston: South End Press.

Jackson, Robert. 1999. *Race, Caste and Status: Indians in Colonial South America.* Albuquerque: University of New Mexico Press.

Jacobson, Matthew F. 1998. *Whiteness of a Different Color: European Immigrants and the Alchemy of Race.* Cambridge, MA: Harvard University Press.

———. 2000. *Barbarian Virtues: The United States Encounters Foreign Peoples at Home and Abroad, 1876–1917.* New York: Hill & Wang.

———. 2002. History, Historicity, and the Census Count by Race. In *The New Race Question: How the Census Counts Multiracial Individuals,* ed. Joel Perlmann and Mary C. Waters. New York: Russell Sage.

Jacobson, Robin Dale. 2008. *The New Nativism: Proposition 187 and the Debate over Immigration.* Minneapolis: University of Minnesota Press.

Jefferson, Thomas. 1999. *Notes on the State of Virginia.* New York: Penguin.

Jendian, Matthew Ari. 2001. Assimilation and Ethnicity: Adaptation Patterns and Ethnic Identity of Armenian-Americans in Central California. PhD dissertation, Department of Sociology, University of Southern California.

Johnson, Lyman, and Sonya Lipsett-Rivera, eds. 1998. *The Faces of Honor: Sex, Shame, and Violence in Colonial Latin America.* Albuquerque: University of New Mexico Press.

Jones, Jacqueline. 1992. *The Dispossessed: America's Underclasses from the Civil War to the Present.* New York: Basic Books.

Jones, Timothy M., and Penelope Sheets. 2009. Torture in the Eye of the Beholder: Social Identity, News Coverage, and Abu Ghraib. *Political Communication* 26 (3): 278–295.

Jung, Moon-Kie, and Tomás Almaguer. 2004. The State and the Production of Racial Categories. In *Race and Ethnicity: Across Time, Space, and Discipline,* ed. Rodney D. Coates. Leiden, The Netherlands: Brill.

Kairys, David. 1996. Unexplainable on Grounds Other Than Race. *American Law Review* 45 (3): 729–749.

Kamen, Henry. 2003. *Empire: How Spain Became a World Power, 1492–1762.* New York: Harper Collins.

Kandaswamy, Priya. 2010. "You trade in *a* man for *the* man": Domestic Violence and the U.S. Welfare State. *American Quarterly* 62 (2): 253–277.

Kang, Jerry. 2005. Trojan Horses of Race. *Harvard Law Review* 118 (5): 1489–1593.

Kaplan, Amy. 1993. "Left Alone with America": The Absence of Empire in the Study of American Culture. In *Cultures of United States Imperialism,* ed. Amy Kaplan and Donald E. Pease. Durham, NC: Duke University Press.

———. 2002. *The Anarchy of Empire in the Making of U.S. Culture.* Cambridge, MA: Harvard University Press.

Kaplan, Robert D. 2004. Indian Country. *Wall Street Journal* (September 21, 2004), A22.

———. 2005. *Imperial Grunts: The American Military on the Ground.* New York: Random House.

Katznelson, Ira. 2005. *When Affirmative Action Was White: An Untold History of Racial Inequality in Twentieth-Century America.* New York: W. W. Norton.

Keleher, Terry. 2005. Contested Questions about Race. *Applied Research Center,* 2005. Hard copy in author Gary Delgado's possession.

Kelley, Robin D. G. 1992. The Black Poor and the Politics of Opposition in a New South City, 1929–1970. In *The "Underclass" Debate: Views from History,* ed. Michael B. Katz. Princeton: Princeton University Press.

———. 2003. *Freedom Dreams: The Black Radical Imagination.* Boston: Beacon Press, 2003.

Kellstedt, Paul. 2003. *Mass Media and the Dynamics of American Racial Attitudes.* New York: Cambridge University Press.

Kennedy, Bill, Emily Fisher, and Colin Bailey. 2010. Framing in Race-Conscious Antipoverty Advocacy: A Science-Based Guide to Delivering Your Most Persuasive Message. *Clearinghouse Review: Journal of Poverty Law and Policy* 43 (9–10): 408–421.

Kerber, Linda K. 1998. *No Constitutional Right to Be Ladies: Women and the Obligations of Citizenship.* New York: Hill & Wang.

Konetzke, Richard. 1958. *Colección de documentos para la formación social de Hispanoamérica, 1493–1810.* Madrid: Consejo Superior de Investigaciones Científicas.

Koshy, Susan. 2008. Why the Humanities Matter for Race Studies Today. *Publications of the Modern Languages Association of America* 123 (5): 1542–1549.

Kuznesof, Elizabeth. 1995. Ethnic and Gender Differences in Spanish Creole Society in Colonial Spanish America. *Colonial Latin American Review* 4 (1): 153–176.

Laclau, Ernesto. 1977. *Politics and Ideology in Marxist Theory.* London: New Left Books.

Lakoff, George. 2004. *Don't Think of an Elephant! Know Your Values and Frame the Debate—The Essential Guide for Progressives.* White River Junction, VT: Chelsea River.

———. 2009. Why Environmental Understanding, or "Framing," Matters: An Evaluation of the EcoAmerica Summary Report. *Huffington Post.* May 19. Available at http://www.huffingtonpost.com/george-lakoff/why-environmental-underst_b_205477.html. Accessed January 10, 2012.

Landale, Nancy S., and Ralph Salvatore Oropesa. 2002. White, Black, or Puerto Rican?: Racial Self-Identification among Mainland and Island Puerto Ricans. *Social Forces* 81 (1): 231–254.

LaPiere, Richard Tracy. 1930. The Armenian Colony in Fresno County, California: A Study in Social Psychology. PhD dissertation, Department of Sociology, Stanford University.

Larson, Brooke. 2004. *Trials of Nation Making: Liberalism, Race, and Ethnicity in the Andes, 1810–1910.* Cambridge: Cambridge University Press.

Lazreg, Marnia. 2008. *Torture and the Twilight of Empire: From Algiers to Baghdad.* Princeton: Princeton University Press.

Lau, Estelle. 1997. Can Money Whiten? Exploring Race Practice in Colonial Venezuela and Its Implications for Contemporary Race Discourse. *Michigan Journal of Race & Law* 3: 417–474.

Lavallé, Bernard. 2001. *Amor y Opresión en los Andes Coloniales.* Lima: Institut Français d'études Andines.

Lee, Chang-Rae. 1995. *Native Speaker.* New York: Riverhead.

Lemert, Charles. 1995. *Sociology after the Crisis.* Boulder, CO: Westview Press.

Lévi-Strauss, Claude. 1966. *The Savage Mind,* trans. John Weightman and Doreen Weightman. Chicago: University of Chicago Press.

Lewis, Laura. 2000. Blacks, Black Indians, Afromexicans: The Dynamics of Race, Nation, and Identity in a Mexican *Moreno* Community (Guerrero). *American Ethnologist* 27 (4): 898–926.

Lipsitz, George. 1990. *Time Passages: Collective Memory and American Popular Culture.* Minneapolis: University of Minnesota Press.

———. 1998. *The Possessive Investment in Whiteness: How White People Profit from Identity Politics.* Philadelphia: Temple University Press

———. 2006. *The Possessive Investment in Whiteness: How White People Profit from Identity Politics.* Revised and expanded edition. Philadelphia: Temple University Press.

Litwack, Leon F. 1998. *Trouble in Mind: Black Southerners in the Age of Jim Crow.* New York: Vintage.

Logan, Rayford. 1954. *The Negro in American Life and Thought: The Nadir, 1877–1901.* New York: Dial Press.

López, Ian. 1996. *White by Law: The Legal Construction of Race.* New York: New York University Press.

Lorde, Audre. 1983. The Master's Tools Will Never Dismantle the Master's House. In *This Bridge Called My Back: Writings by Radical Women of Color,* ed. Cherríe Moraga and Gloria Anzaldúa, Second Edition. New York: Kitchen Table, Women of Color Press.

Loveman, Mara. 1999. Is "Race" Essential? *American Sociological Review* 64 (6): 891–898.

Loveman, Mara, and Jeronimo O. Muniz. 2007. How Puerto Ricans Became White: Boundary Dynamics and Inter-census Racial Reclassification. *American Sociological Review* 72 (6): 915–939.

Lowe, Lisa. 1996. *Immigrant Acts: On Asian American Cultural Studies.* Durham, NC: Duke University Press.

Lugones, María. 2007. Heterosexualism and the Colonial/Modern Gender System. *Hypatia* 22 (1): 186–209.

Luker, Kristen. 1996. *Dubious Conceptions: The Politics of Teenage Pregnancy.* Cambridge, MA: Harvard University Press.

Lyons, Scott. 2010. *X-Marks.* Minneapolis: University of Minneapolis Press.

Macdonald, Heather. 2006. How to Interrogate Terrorists. In *The Torture Debate in America*, ed. Karen J. Greenberg. New York: Cambridge University Press.

Maira, Sunaina. 2002. *Desis in the House: Indian American Youth Culture in New York City.* Philadelphia: Temple University Press.

————. 2004. Youth Culture, Citizenship, and Globalization: South Asian Youth in the United States after September 11th. *Comparative Studies of South Asia, Africa, and the Middle East* 24 (1): 219–31.

————. 2009. *Missing: Youth, Citizenship, and Empire after 9/11.* Durham, NC: Duke University Press.

Mallon, Florencia. 1995. *Peasant and Nation: The Making of Postcolonial Mexico and Peru.* Berkeley: University of California Press.

Mamdani, Mahmood. 2002. Good Muslim, Bad Muslim: A Political Perspective on Culture and Terrorism. *American Anthropologist* 104 (3): 766–775.

————. 2004. *Good Muslim, Bad Muslim: America, the Cold War, and the Roots of Terror.* New York: Pantheon Books/Random House.

Mannarelli, Maria Emma. 1993. *Pecados Públicos: La Ilegitimidad en Lima, Siglo XVII.* Lima: Centro de la mujer peruana Flora Tristán.

Marable, Manning. 2004. Globalization and Racialization. ZNet. Available at http://www.zcommunications.org/globalization-and-racialization-by-manning-marable. Accessed January 24, 2012.

Maracle, Lee. 1988. *I Am Woman.* Vancouver: Write On Publishers.

Marshall, T. H. 1950. Class, Citizenship, and Social Development. In *Citizenship and Social Class and Other Essays.* Cambridge: Cambridge University Press.

Martínez, María Elena. 2008. *Genealogical Fictions: Limpieza de Sangre, Religion, and Gender in Colonial Mexico.* Stanford: Stanford University Press.

Marx, Anthony. 1998. *Making Race and Nation: A Comparison of the United States, South Africa, and Brazil.* Cambridge: Cambridge University Press.

Massey, Douglas, et al. 2005. *Worlds in Motion: Understanding International Migration at the End of the Millennium.* New York: Oxford University Press.

Matory, James Lorand. 2005. *Black Atlantic Religion: Tradition, Transnationalism, and Matriarchy in the Afro-Brazilian Candomble.* Princeton: Princeton University Press.

Matsumoto, Valerie. 1993. *Farming the Home Place: A Japanese American Community in California, 1919–1982.* Ithaca, NY: Cornell University Press.

Mauer, Marc. 2006. *Race to Incarcerate.* 2nd ed. New York: The New Press.

Mbembe, Achille. 1992. The Banality of Power and the Aesthetics of Vulgarity in the Postcolony. *Public Culture* 4 (2): 1–30.

————. 2001. *On the Postcolony.* Berkeley: University of California Press.

————. 2004. Aesthetics of Superfluity. *Public Culture* 16 (3): 373–405.

McCall, Leslie. 2005. The Complexity of Intersectionality. *Signs: Journal of Women in Culture and Society* 30 (31): 1771–1800.

McCarthy, Andrew C. 2006. Thinking about the Unthinkable. In *The Torture Debate in America*, ed. Karen J. Greenberg. New York: Cambridge University Press.

McCarthy, Thomas. 2009. *Race, Empire, and the Idea of Human Development*. Cambridge: Cambridge University Press.

McCurry, Stephanie. 1997. *Masters of Small Worlds: Yeoman Households, Gender Relations, and the Political Culture of the Antebellum South Carolina Low Country*. New York: Oxford University Press.

McKinley, Michelle. 2010. "Such Unsightly Unions Could Never Result in Holy Matrimony": Mixed-Status Marriages in Seventeenth-Century Colonial Lima. *Yale Journal of Law and Humanities* 22 (2): 217–255.

Means, Russell. 1995. *Where White Mean Fear to Tread*. New York: St. Martin's Griffin.

Menchaca, Martha. 2001. *Recovering History, Constructing Race: The Indian, Black, and White Roots of Mexican Americans*. Austin: University of Texas Press.

———. 2007. Latinos/as and the *Mestizo* Racial Heritage of Mexican Americans. In *A Companion to Latino Studies*, ed. Juan Flores and Renato Rosaldo. Malden, MA: Blackwell.

Merton, Robert K. 1949. Discrimination and the American Creed. In *Discrimination and the National Welfare*, ed. R. MacIver. New York: Harper & Row.

Messer-Davidow, Ellen. 1993. Manufacturing the Attack on Liberalized Higher Education. *Social Text* 36: 40–80.

Mignolo, Walter. 1995. Afterword: Human Understanding and (Latin) American Interests—The Politics and Sensibilities of Geocultural Locations. *Poetics Today* 16 (1): 171–214.

Miles, Robert, and Rudy Torres. 2007. Does 'Race' Matter? Transatlantic Perspectives on Race after "Race Relations." In *Race and Racialization: Essential Readings*, ed. Tania Das Gupta, Carl E. James, Roger C. A. Maaka, Grace-Edward Galabuzi, and Chris Andersen. Toronto: Canadian Scholar's Press.

Minasian, Edward. 1983. *The Armenian Community of California: The First One Hundred Years*. Los Angeles: Armenian Assembly Resource Center.

Mink, Gwendolyn. 1995. *The Wages of Motherhood*. Ithaca, NY: Cornell University Press.

Mirpuri, Anoop. 2010. "Slated for Destruction: Race, Black Radicalism, and the Meaning of Captivity in the Postwar Exceptional State." PhD dissertation, Department of English, University of Washington, Seattle.

Mohanty, Chandra Talpade. 1988. Under Western Eyes: Feminist Scholarship and Colonial Discourses. *Feminist Review* 30: 61–88.

Montejano, David. 1987. *Anglos and Mexicans in the Making of Texas, 1836–1986*. Austin: University of Texas Press.

Monture-Angus, Patricia. 1999. *Journeying Forward*. Halifax, Nova Scotia: Fernwood.

Moraga, Cherríe, and Gloria Anzaldúa, eds. 1981. *This Bridge Called My Back*. Watertown, MA: Persephone Press.

Morgan, Edmund S. 1975. *American Slavery, American Freedom: The Ordeal of Colonial Virginia*. New York: W. W. Norton.

Mörner, Magnus. 1967. *Race Mixture in the History of Latin America*. Boston: Little, Brown.

Morning, Ann. 2011. *The Nature of Race: How Scientists Think and Teach about Human Difference.* Berkeley: University of California Press.

Morris, Errol. 2008. *Standard Operating Procedure.* United States: Participant Productions and Sony Pictures Classics. Video.

Moten, Fred. 2003. *In the Break: The Aesthetics of the Black Radical Tradition.* Minneapolis: University of Minnesota Press.

———. 2008. Black Op. *PMLA* 123 (5): 1743–1748.

Muhammad, Kahil Gibran. 2010. *The Condemnation of Blackness: Race, Crime, and the Making of Modern Urban America.* Cambridge, MA: Harvard University Press.

Murukawa, Naomi. 2008. The Origins of the Carceral Crisis: Racial Order as "Law and Order" in Postwar American Politics. In *Race and American Political Development,* ed. Joseph Lowndes, Julie Novkov, and Dorian Warren. New York: Routledge.

Murguia, Edward, and Tyrone Forman. 2003. Shades of Whiteness: The Mexican American Experience in Relation to Anglos and Blacks. In *White Out: The Continuing Significance of Race,* ed. Eduardo Bonilla-Silva and Ashley "Woody" Doane. New York: Routledge.

Myrdal, Gunnar. 1944. *An American Dilemma: The Negro Problem and Modern Democracy.* New York: Harper & Bros.

Nazzari, Muriel. 1996. Concubinage in Colonial Brazil: The Inequalities of Race, Class, and Gender. *Journal of Family History* 21 (2): 107–124.

Nelson, Dana D. 2006. The President and Presidentialism. *South Atlantic Quarterly* 105 (1): 1–17.

Ngai, Mae M. 2005. *Impossible Subjects: Illegal Aliens and the Making of Modern America.* Princeton: Princeton University Press.

Nguyen, Viet Thanh. 2008. At Home with Race. *Publications of the Modern Languages Association of America* 123 (5) (October): 1557–1564.

Nobles, Melissa. 2000. *Shades of Citizenship: Race and the Census in Modern Politics.* Stanford: Stanford University Press.

Nopper, Tamara K. 2008. Why Black Immigrants Matter: Refocusing the Discussion on Racism and Immigration Enforcement. In *Keeping Out the Other: A Critical Introduction to Immigration Enforcement Today,* ed. David Brotherton and Philip Kretsedemas. New York: Columbia University Press.

O'Brien, Eileen. 2008. *The Racial Middle: Latinos and Asian Americans Living beyond the Racial Divide.* New York: New York University Press.

Okada, John. 1976. *No-No Boy.* Seattle: University of Washington Press.

Omi, Michael. 1997. Racial Identity and the State: The Dilemmas of Classification. *Law and Inequality* 15 (1): 7–23.

Omi, Michael, and Howard Winant. 1983. By the Rivers of Babylon: Race in the United States, Parts I and II. *Socialist Review.* 71–72.

———. 1986. *Racial Formation in the United States: From the 1960s to the 1980s.* New York: Routledge.

————. 1993. The Los Angeles "Race Riot" and Contemporary U.S. Politics. In *Reading Rodney King, Reading Urban Uprising*, ed. Robert Gooding-Williams. New York: Routledge.

————. 1994. *Racial Formation in the United States: From the 1960s to the 1990s.* Second Edition. New York: Routledge.

Ong, Aiwa. 1999. *Flexible Citizenship: The Cultural Logics of Transnationality.* Durham, NC: Duke University Press.

Ongiri, Amy Abugo. 2009. Prisoner of Love: Affiliation, Sexuality, and the Black Panther Party. *Journal of African American History* 94 (1): 69–86.

Ono, Kent A., and John M. Sloop. 2002. *Shifting Borders: Rhetoric, Immigration, and California's Proposition 187.* Philadelphia: Temple University Press.

O'odham Solidarity Across Borders Collective. 2010. Attack the Root! May 2, 2010. Available at http://oodhamsolidarity.blogspot.com/. Accessed May 16, 2010.

Ortíz, Fernando. 1942. Cuba, Martí and the Race Problem. *Phylon* 3 (3): 250–276.

————. 1995. *Cuban Counterpoint: Tobacco and Sugar.* Durham, NC: Duke University Press.

Padilla, Mark. 2007. *Caribbean Pleasure Industry: Tourism, Sexuality, and AIDS in the Dominican Republic.* Chicago: University of Chicago Press.

Pagden, Anthony. 1982. *The Fall of Natural Man: The American Indian and the Origins of Comparative Ethnology.* Cambridge: Cambridge University Press.

Pascoe, Peggy. 1996. Miscegenation Law, Court Cases, and Ideologies of "Race" in Twentieth-Century America. *Journal of American History* 83 (1): 44–69.

————. 2009. *What Comes Naturally: Miscegenation Law and the Making of Race in America.* Oxford: Oxford University Press.

Pawel, Miriam. 2009. *The Union of Their Dreams: Power, Hope, and Struggle in César Chávez's Farm Worker Movement.* New York: Bloomsbury Press.

Perez, Gina M. 2004. *The Near Northwest Side Story: Migration, Displacement, and Puerto Rican Families.* Berkeley: University of California Press.

Perkinson, Robert. 2010. *Texas Tough: The Rise of America's Prison Empire.* New York: Metropolitan Books.

Perlmann, Joel. 2005. *Italians Then, Mexicans Now: Immigrant Origins and Second-Generation Progress, 1890 to 2000.* New York: Russell Sage.

Perlmann, Joel, and Mary C. Waters, eds. 2005. *The New Race Question: How the Census Counts Multiracial Individuals.* New York: Russell Sage.

Pfaelzer, Jean. 2007. *Driven Out: The Forgotten War against Chinese Americans.* New York: Random House.

Piedra, José. 1993. The Black Stud's Spanish Birth. *Callaloo* 16 (4): 820–846.

Pike, Ruth. 1967. Sevillan Society in the Sixteenth Century: Slaves and Freedmen. *Hispanic American Historical Review* 47 (3): 344–359.

Piven, Frances Fox, and Richard Cloward. 1971. *Regulating the Poor: The Functions of Public Welfare.* New York: Random House.

Polyani, Karl. 2011 (1944). *The Great Transformation: The Political and Economic Origins of Our Time.* Boston: Beacon Press.

Polkinhorn, Harry, Alfredo Velasco, and Malcom Lambert. 2005. *El Libro de Calo: The Dictionary of Chicano Slang.* Revised Edition. San Francisco: Floricanto Press.

Portes, Alejandro. 2007. The New Latin Nation: Immigration and Hispanic Population in the United States. In *A Companion to Latino Studies,* ed. Juan Flores and Renato Rosaldo. Malden, MA: Blackwell.

Povinelli, Elizabeth. 2006. *Empire of Love.* Durham, NC: Duke University Press.

powell, john a., Stephen Menendian, and Jason Reece. 2009. The Importance of Targeted Universalism. *Poverty & Race* 18 (2): ID 11577.

Prashad, Vijay. 2006. Ethnic Studies Inside Out. *Journal of Asian American Studies* 9 (2): 157–176.

Pratto, Felicia, Josephine Korchmaros, and Peter Hegarty. 2007. When Race and Gender Go without Saying. *Social Cognition* 25 (2): 221–247.

Premo, Bianca. 2005. *Children of the Father King: Youth, Authority, and Legal Minority in Colonial Lima.* Chapel Hill: University of North Carolina Press.

Price, Patricia L. 2009. At the Crossroads: Critical Race Theory and Critical Geographies of Race. *Progress in Human Geography* 34 (2): 147–174.

Przeworski, Adam. 1977. Proletariat into a Class: The Process of Class Formation from Karl Kautsky's *The Class Struggle* to Recent Controversies. *Politics and Society* 7 (4): 343–401.

Puar, Jasbir K. 2007. *Terrorist Assemblages: Homonationalism in Queer Times.* Durham, NC: Duke University Press.

Puar, Jasbir K., and Amit S. Rai. 2002. Monster, Terrorist, Fag: The War on Terrorism and the Production of Docile Patriots. *Social Text* 20 (3): 117–148.

Quadagno, Jill. 1994. *The Color of Welfare: How Racism Undermined the War on Poverty.* New York: Oxford University Press.

Quijano, Anibel. 2000. Coloniality of Power, Eurocentrism, and Latin America. *Nepantla: Views from South* 1 (3): 533–580.

Ramos-Zayas, Ana Y. 2003. *National Performances: The Politics of Class, Race, and Space in Puerto Rican Chicago.* Chicago: University of Chicago Press.

Raphael, Jody. 1996. *Prisoners of Abuse: Domestic Violence and Welfare Receipt.* Chicago: Taylor Institute.

Razack, Sherene. 2002. When Place Becomes Race. In *Race, Space and the Law: Unmapping a White Settler Society.* Toronto: Between the Lines.

———. 2004. *Dark Threats and White Knights: The Somalia Affair, Peacekeeping and the New Imperialism.* Toronto: University of Toronto Press.

———. 2008. *Casting Out: The Eviction of Muslims from Western Law and Politics.* Toronto: University of Toronto Press.

Reed, Adolph, Jr., and Kenneth Warren. 2010. *Renewing Black Intellectual History: The Ideological and Material Foundations of African American Thought.* New York: Paradigm.

Reid Andrews, George. 2009. Afro-Latin America: Five Questions. *Latin American and Caribbean Ethnic Studies* 4 (2): 191–210.

Renan, Ernest. 1996. What Is a Nation? [lecture at the Sorbonne, March 11, 1882]. In *Becoming National: A Reader*, ed. Geoff Eley and Ronald Grigor Suny. New York: Oxford University Press.

Restall, Matthew. 2000. Black Conquistadors: Armed Africans in Early Spanish America. *The Americas* 57 (2): 171–205.

Richie, Beth. 2005. A Black Feminist Reflection on the Antiviolence Movement. In *Domestic Violence at the Margins: Readings on Race, Class, and Culture*, ed. Natalie J. Sokoloff and Christina Pratt. New Brunswick, NJ: Rutgers University Press.

Ridley, Hugh. 1983. *Images of Imperial Rule*. New York: St. Martin's Press.

Rivera, Amaad, et al. 2008. *Foreclosed: State of the Dream 2008*. Boston: United for a Fair Economy. Available at http://www.faireconomy.org/dream. Accessed January 24, 2012.

Roberts, Dorothy. 1997. *Killing the Black Body: Race, Reproduction, and the Meaning of Liberty*. New York: Pantheon.

Robinson, Russel. 2008. Perceptual Segregation. *Columbia Law Review* 108: 1093–1180.

Rodríguez, Clara E. 2000. *Changing Race: Latinos, the Census, and the History of Ethnicity in the United States*. New York: New York University Press.

———. 2009. Counting Latinos in the U.S. Census. In *Race and Classification: The Case of Mexican Americans*, ed. Ilona Katzew and Susan Deans-Smith. Stanford: Stanford University Press.

Rodriguez, Dylan. 2006. *Forced Passages: Imprisoned Radical Intellectuals and the U.S. Prison Regime*. Minneapolis: University of Minnesota Press.

———. 2010. *Suspended Apocalypse: White Supremacy, Genocide, and the Filipino Condition*. Minneapolis: University of Minnesota Press.

Rodriguez, Juana Maria. 2003. *Queer Latinidad: Identity Practices, Discursive Spaces*. New York: New York University Press.

Roediger, David R. 1991. *The Wages of Whiteness: Race and the Making of the American Working Class*. New York: Verso.

———. 2005. *Working toward Whiteness: How America's Immigrants Became White; The Strange Journey from Ellis Island to the Suburbs*. New York: Basic Books.

———. 2008. *How Race Survived US History: From Settlement and Slavery to the Obama Phenomenon*. New York: Verso.

Rolph-Trouillot, Michel. 1995. *Silencing the Past: Power and the Production of History*. Boston: Beacon Press.

Rosen, Hannah. 2008. *Terror in the Heart of Freedom: Citizenship, Sexual Violence, and the Meaning of Race in the Post-Emancipation South*. Chapel Hill: University of North Carolina Press.

Ruiz, Vicki L. 2004. *Morena/o, blanca/o y café con leche:* Racial Constructions in Chicana/o Historiography. *Mexican Studies / Estudios Mexicanos* 20 (2): 343–359.

Rumbaut, Ruben G. 2009. Pigments of Our Imagination: On the Racialization and Racial Identity of "Hispanics" and "Latinos." In *How the United States*

Racializes Latinos: White Hegemony and Its Consequences, ed. Jose A. Cobas, Jorge Duany, and Joe R. Feagin. Boulder, CO: Paradigm.

Russell, Thaddeus. 2008. The Color of Discipline: Civil Rights and Black Sexuality. *American Quarterly* 60 (1): 101–128.

Russell-Wood, A. J. R. 1978. Iberian Expansion and the Issue of Black Slavery: Changing Portuguese Attitudes, 1440–1770. *American Historical Review* 83 (1): 16–42.

Said, Edward. 1994. *Orientalism.* New York: Vintage.

Saito, Natsu Taylor. 2001. Symbolism under Siege: Japanese American Redress and the "Racing" of Arab Americans as "Terrorists." *Asian Law Journal* 8: 1–29.

San Juan, E., Jr. 2009. Re-visiting Race and Class in Post 9/11 USA. *Counter Currents* April 24. Available at http://www.countercurrents.org/sanjuan240409.htm. Accessed January 24, 2012.

Saranillio, Dean Itsuje. 2009. *Seeing Conquest: Colliding Histories and Cultural Politics of Hawai'i Statehood.* Ann Arbor: University of Michigan. Available at http://hdl.handle.net/2027.42/64824. Accessed January 26, 2012.

Sassen, Saskia. 1998. *Globalization and Its Discontents: Essays on the New Mobility of People and Money.* New York: The New Press.

Saxton, Alexander. 1971. *The Indispensable Enemy: Labor and the Anti-Chinese Movement in California.* Berkeley: University of California Press.

Scarry, Elaine. 1985. *The Body in Pain: The Making and Unmaking of the World.* New York: Oxford University Press.

Schlesinger, Arthur M. 1998. *The Disuniting of America: Reflections on a Multicultural Society.* New York: W. W. Norton.

Scott, James C. 1990. *Domination and the Arts of Resistance: Hidden Transcripts.* New Haven: Yale University Press.

Seed, Patricia. 1982. Social Dimensions of Race in Mexico City, 1753. *Hispanic American Historical Review* 62 (4): 569–606.

Sen, Kasturi, and A. Yunas Samad. 2007. *Islam in the European Union: Transnationalism, Youth, and the War on Terror.* Oxford: Oxford University Press.

Sexton, Jared. 2008. *Amalgamation Schemes.* Minneapolis: University of Minnesota Press.

Sharma, Nandita, and Cynthia Wright. 2009. Decolonizing Resistance: Challenging Colonial States. *Social Justice* 35 (3): 120–138.

Shaw, Randy. 2008. *Beyond the Fields: Cesar Chavez, the UFW, and the Struggle for Justice in the 21st Century.* Berkeley: University of California Press.

Shryock, Andrew. 2008. The Moral Ambiguities of Race. In *Race and Arab Americans before and after 9/11,* ed. Amaney Jamal and Nadine Naber. Syracuse, NY: Syracuse University Press.

Silliman, Stephen W. 2008. The "Old West" in the Middle East: U.S. Military Metaphors in Real and Imagined Indian Country. *American Anthropologist* 110 (2): 237–247.

Silverblatt, Irene. 2004. *Modern Inquisitions: Peru and the Origins of the Civilized World.* Durham, NC: Duke University Press.

Singh, Nikhil Pal. 2004. *Black Is a Country: Race and the Unfinished Struggle for Democracy.* Cambridge, MA: Harvard University Press.

———. 2006. The Afterlife of Fascism. *South Atlantic Quarterly* 105 (1): 71–93.

Skerry, Peter. 2002. Multiracialism and the Administrative State. In *The New Race Question: How the Census Counts Multiracial Individuals,* ed. Joel Perlmann and Mary C. Waters. New York: Russell Sage.

Skrentny, John D. 2002. *The Minority Rights Revolution.* Cambridge, MA: Belknap Press of Harvard University Press.

Slack, Jennifer Daryl. 1996. The Theory and Method of Articulation in Cultural Studies. In *Stuart Hall: Critical Dialogues in Cultural Studies,* ed. David Morely and Kuan-Hsing Chen. London: Routledge.

Smith, Andrea. 2004. Beyond the Politics of Inclusion: Violence against Women of Color and Human Rights. *Meridians* 4 (2): 121–124.

———. 2005. *Conquest: Sexual Violence and American Indian Genocide.* Cambridge, MA: South End Press.

———. 2006. Heteropatriarchy and the Three Pillars of White Supremacy. In *The Color of Violence,* ed. Incite! Cambridge, MA: South End Press.

———. 2008. *Native Americans and the Christian Right: The Gendered Politics of Unlikely Alliances.* Durham, NC: Duke University Press.

Smith, A. Wade. 1981. Racial Tolerance as a Function of Group Position. *American Sociological Review* 46: 525–541.

Smith, Barbara. 1983. *Home Girls: A Black Feminist Anthology.* New York: Kitchen Table Press.

Smith, Robert Courtney. 2006. *Mexican New York: Transnational Lives of New Immigrants.* Berkeley: University of California Press.

Song, Min Hyoung. 2005. *Strange Future: Pessimism and the 1992 Los Angeles Riots.* Durham, NC: Duke University Press.

Spatz, Diana, and Sheila Katz. 2005. *Family Violence Is Not an Option: The Failure of CalWORKS to Serve Battered Women with Children.* Oakland: LIFETIME.

Springer, Kimberly. 2005. *Living for the Revolution: Black Feminist Organizations, 1960–1990.* Durham, NC: Duke University Press.

Stacewicz, Richard. 1997. *Winter Soldiers: An Oral History of the Vietnam Veterans Against the War.* New York: Twayne.

Steele, Claude. 1997. A Threat in the Air: How Stereotypes Shape Intellectual Identity and Performance. *American Psychologist* 52 (6): 613–629.

Stepan, Nancy L. 1991. *The Hour of Eugenics: Race, Gender and Nation in Latin America.* Ithaca, NY: Cornell University Press.

Stephen, Lynn. 2007. *Transborder Lives: Indigenous Oaxacans in Mexico, California, and Oregon.* Durham, NC: Duke University Press.

Stevenson, Winona. 1998. "Ethnic" Assimilates "Indigenous": A Study in Intellectual Neocolonialism. *Wicazo Sa Review* 13 (1): 33–51.

Stiglitz, Joseph E., and Linda J. Bilmes. 2008. *The Three Trillion Dollar War: The True Cost of the Iraq Conflict.* New York: W. W. Norton.

Stroessner, Steven. 1996. Social Categorization by Race or Sex: Effects of Perceived Non-normalcy on Response Times. *Social Cognition* 14 (3): 247–276.

Stocking, George. 1994. The Turn of the Century Concept of Race. *Modernism/Modernity* 1 (1): 4–16.

Stoler, Ann Laura. 2006a. On Degrees of Imperial Sovereignty. *Public Culture* 18 (1): 125–146.

———. 2006b. *Haunted by Empire: Geographies of Intimacy in North American History.* Durham, NC: Duke University Press.

Sue, Christina A. 2009. The Dynamics of Color: *Mestizaje*, Racism, and Blackness in Vera Cruz, Mexico. In *Shades of Difference: Why Skin Color Matters*, ed. Evelyn Nakano Glenn. Stanford: Stanford University Press.

Sweet, James. 1997. The Iberian Roots of American Racist Thought. *William & Mary Quarterly* 54 (1): 143–166.

Tannenbaum, Frank. 1946. *Slave and Citizen: The Negro in the Americas.* New York: Vintage.

Tate, Katherine. 1993. *From Protest to Politics: The New Black Voters in American Elections.* Cambridge, MA: Harvard University Press.

Taussig, Michael. 1987. *Shamanism, Colonialism, and the Wild Man: A Study in Terror and Healing.* Chicago: University of Chicago Press.

Tehranian, John. 2000. Performing Whiteness: Naturalization Litigation and the Construction of Racial Identity in America. *Yale Law Journal* 109 (4): 817–848.

———. 2009. *Whitewashed: America's Invisible Middle Eastern Minority.* New York: New York University Press.

Teles, Steven Michael. 2008. *The Rise of the Conservative Legal Movement: The Battle for Control of the Law.* Princeton: Princeton University Press.

Thomas, Deborah A., and Kamari Clarke. 2006. Introduction. In *Globalization and Race: Transformations in the Cultural Production of Blackness*, ed. Deborah A. Thomas and Kamari M. Clarke. Durham, NC: Duke University Press.

Thornton, James. 1992. *Africa and Africans in the Making of the Atlantic World, 1400–1680.* Cambridge: Cambridge University Press.

Tienda, Marta, and Vilma Ortiz. 1986. "Hispanicity" and the 1980 Census. *Social Science Quarterly* 67 (1): 3–20.

Toossi, Mitra. 2002. A Century of Change: The U.S. Labor Force, 1950–2050. *Monthly Labor Review* 125 (5): 15–28.

Torres-Saillant, Silvio. 1998. The Tribulations of Blackness: Stages in Dominican Racial Identity. *Latin American Perspectives* 25 (3): 126–146.

———. 2007. Afro-Latinas/os and the Racial Wall. In *A Companion to Latino Studies*, ed. Juan Flores and Renato Rosaldo. Malden, MA: Blackwell.

Tuveson, Ernest Lee. 1968. *Redeemer Nation: The Idea of America's Millennial Role.* Chicago: University of Chicago Press.

U.S. Bureau of the Census. 2010. *Overview of Race and Hispanic Origin: 2010.* Issued March 2011 http://www.census.gov/prod/cen2010/briefs/c2010br-02.pdf. Accessed January 8, 2012.

Valdes, Francisco, Jerome McCristal Culp, and Angela P. Harris, eds. 2002. *Crossroads, Directions, and a New Critical Race Theory.* Philadelphia: Temple University Press.

Vasconcelos, José. 1967. *La raza cósmica: Mission de la raza ibero-americana.* Mexico DF: Aguilar.

Vaughn, Bobby. 2005. Afro-Mexico: Blacks, *Indigenas,* Politics, and the Greater Diaspora. In *Neither Enemies nor Friends: Latinos, Blacks, and Afro-Latinos,* ed. Anani Dzidzienyo and Suzanne Oboler. New York: Palgrave MacMillan.

Vidal-Ortiz, Salvador. 2004. On Being a White Person of Color: Using Autoethnography in Understanding Puerto Rican's Racialization. *Qualitative Sociology* 27 (2): 179–203.

Vidal-Ortiz, Salvador, Carlos Decena, Hector Carrillo, and Tomás Almaguer. 2010. Revisiting Activos and Pasivos: Toward New Cartographies of Latino/Latin American Male Same-Sex Desire. In *Latina/o Sexualities: Probing, Powers, Passions, Practices, and Policies,* ed. Marysol Asencio. New Brunswick, NJ: Rutgers University Press.

Viotti da Costa, Emilia. 1985. The Portuguese African Slave Trade: A Lesson in Colonialism. *Latin American Perspectives* 12 (1): 41–61.

Vogel, Richard D. 2006. Harder Times: Undocumented Workers and the U.S. Informal Economy. *Monthly Review* 58 (3): 29–39.

Volpp, Leti. 1996. Talking Culture: Gender, Race, Nation and the Politics of Multiculturalism. *Columbia Law Review* 96 (6): 1573–1617.

———. 2002. The Citizen and the Terrorist. *UCLA Law Review* 49: 1575–1598.

Wacquant, Loic. 2002. From Slavery to Mass Incarceration: Rethinking the "Race" Question in the United States. *New Left Review* 13: 41–60.

Wade, Peter. 1993. *Blackness and Race Mixture: The Dynamics of Racial Identity in Colombia.* Baltimore: Johns Hopkins University Press.

———. 1997. *Race and Ethnicity in Latin America.* London: Pluto Press.

Wagner, Brian. 2010. *Disturbing the Peace.* Cambridge, MA: Harvard University Press.

Warren, Jonathon, and Frances Windance Twine. 2002. Critical Race Studies in Latin America: Recent Advances, Recurrent Weaknesses. In *A Companion to Racial and Ethnic Studies,* ed. David Theo Goldberg and John Solomos. Oxford: Blackwell.

Washington, Booker T. 1995. *Up from Slavery.* New York: Dover Thrift Editions.

Waskow, Arthur. 1966. *From Race Riot to Sit-in: 1919 and the 1960s.* New York: Doubleday.

Watson, Alan. 1989. *Slave Law in the Americas.* Athens: University of Georgia Press.

Waziyatawin. 2008. *What Does Justice Look Like?* St. Paul: Living Waters Press.

Wegner, Daniel, David Schneider, Samuel Carter III, and Teri White. 1987. Paradoxical Effects of Thought Suppression. *Journal of Personality and Social Psychology* 53 (1): 5–13.

Weiss, Nancy J. 1983. *Farewell to the Party of Lincoln: Black Politics in the Age of FDR.* Princeton: Princeton University Press.

Weisman, Richard. 2006. Showing Remorse at the TRC: Towards a Constitutive Approach to Reparative Discourse. *Windsor Yearbook of Access to Justice* 24: 221–239.

Westie, Frank. 1965. The American Dilemma: An Empirical Test. *American Sociological Review* 30: 527–538.

Williams, Patricia. 1991. *The Alchemy of Race and Rights*. Cambridge, MA: Harvard University Press.

Williams, Robert. 2005. *Like a Loaded Weapon*. Minneapolis: University of Minnesota Press.

Williams, William Appleman. 1976. *America Confronts a Revolutionary World, 1776–1976*. New York: Morrow.

———. 1980. *Empire as a Way of Life*. New York: Oxford University Press.

Wilson, William Julius. 1980. *The Declining Significance of Race: Blacks and Changing America's Institutions*. Chicago: University of Chicago Press.

Winant, Howard. 1992. Rethinking Race in Brazil. *Journal of Latin American Studies* 24 (1): 173–192.

———. 1994. *Racial Conditions: Politics, Theory, Comparisons*. Minneapolis: University of Minnesota Press.

———. 2001. *The World Is a Ghetto: Race and Democracy since World War II*. New York: Basic Books.

———. 2002. Durban, Globalization, and the World after 9/11: Toward a New Politics. *Poverty and Race* 11 (1): 19–22.

———. 2004. *The New Politics of Race: Globalism, Difference, Justice*. Minneapolis: University of Minnesota Press.

Winchell, Lilbourne Alsip. 1933. *History of Fresno County and the San Joaquin Valley*. Fresno, CA: A. H. Cawston.

Wing, Bob. 2007. Harry Chang: A Seminal Theorist of Racial Justice. *Monthly Review* 58 (7): 23–31.

Wise, Tim. 2007. Majoring in Minstrelsy: White Students, Blackface, and the Failure of Mainstream Multiculturalism. *Lip Magazine*. June 22.

Wroe, Andrew. 2008. *The Republican Party and Immigration Politics: From Proposition 187 to George W. Bush*. New York: Palgrave MacMillan.

Womack, Craig. 1999. *Red on Red*. Minneapolis: University of Minnesota Press.

Yamada, Mitsuye. 1983. Asian Pacific American Women and Feminism. In *This Bridge Called My Back: Writings by Radical Women of Color*, ed. Cherríe Moraga and Gloria Anzaldúa. New York: Kitchen Table Press.

Yamamoto, Eric. 1999. *Interracial Justice: Conflict and Reconciliation in Post–Civil Rights America*. New York: New York University Press.

Yancey, George. 2003. *Who Is White? Latinos, Asians, and the New Black/Nonblack Divide*. Boulder, CO: Lynne Rienner.

Yellow Bird, Michael. 2006. Why Are Indigenous Soldiers Serving in Iraq? *New Socialist*, no. 58 (September–October): 38. Available at <newsocialist.org/attachments/128_NewSocialist-Issue58.pdf>. Accessed February 20, 2012.

Yu, Henry. 2007. Ethnicity. In *Keywords for American Cultural Studies*, ed. Bruce Burgett and Glenn Hendler. New York: New York University Press.

CONTRIBUTORS

TOMÁS ALMAGUER is Professor of Ethnic Studies at San Francisco State University and a scholar of Latino studies, gender, and sexuality. His book, *Racial Fault Lines: The Historical Origins of White Supremacy in California,* was published by the University of California Press (1994; 2009).

DEVON W. CARBADO is Professor of Law at the University of California, Los Angeles, and writes in the areas of critical race theory, employment discrimination, criminal procedure, constitutional law, and identity. A former vice dean of the faculty, he has coedited four volumes and published more than twenty-five scholarly articles and chapters. His book *Acting White?* (with Mitu Gulati) is forthcoming from Oxford University Press.

GARY DELGADO is founding director of the Center for Third World Organizing and the Applied Research Center. A Visiting Scholar at the Center for Research on Social Change at the University of California, he has published more than thirty articles on social change practice and produced a documentary film on race and public policy titled *Racing California* (2008).

NICHOLAS DE GENOVA is a Senior Lecturer in the Department of Anthropology at Goldsmiths, University of London. An anthropologist, theorist, and social critic, his book *Working the Boundaries: Race, Space, and "Illegality" in Mexican Chicago* was published by Duke University Press in 2005.

RODERICK A. FERGUSON is Professor of Race and Critical Theory and Chair of the Department of American Studies at the University of Minnesota, Twin Cities. In 2000, he received the Modern Language Association's Crompton-Noll Award for "best essay in lesbian, gay, and queer studies in the modern languages" for his article "The Parvenu Baldwin and the Other Side of Redemption." From 2007 to 2010, he was associate editor of *American Quarterly: The Journal of the American Studies Association.* He is author of *Aberrations in Black: Toward a Queer of Color Critique* (2004) and *The Reorder of Things: The University and Its Pedagogies of Minority Difference* (2012) and coeditor (with Grace Hong) of *Strange Affinities: The Gender and Sexual Politics of Comparative Racialization* (2011).

MATTHEW GARCIA is Professor of History and Transborder Studies and Director of the Comparative Border Studies Program at Arizona State University. He is the author of *A World of Its Own: Race, Labor and Citrus in the Making of Greater Los Angeles, 1900–1970*, published by the University of North Carolina Press in 2001.

CHERYL I. HARRIS is the Rosalinde and Arthur Gilbert Professor of Civil Liberties and Civil Rights at the University of California, Los Angeles. She is the author of leading works in critical race theory including "Whiteness as Property," published in the *Harvard Law Review* (1993).

DANIEL MARTINEZ HOSANG is Associate Professor of Ethnic Studies and Political Science at the University of Oregon and specializes in U.S. racial politics, political history, and political identity. His book, *Racial Propositions: Ballot Initiatives and the Making of Postwar California*, was published in 2010 by the University of California Press.

ONEKA LABENNETT is Associate Professor of African and African American Studies, and Women's Studies and Research Director of the Bronx African American History Project, Fordham University. Her research and teaching interests include popular youth culture, race, gender, West Indian migration, and transnationalism. Her book, *She's Mad Real: Popular Culture and West Indian Girls in Brooklyn*, was published in 2011 by New York University Press.

JAMES KYUNG-JIN LEE is Associate Professor in and Chair of the Department of Asian American Studies and Director of the Ph.D. Program in Culture and Theory at the University of California, Irvine. His book, *Urban Triage: Race and the Fictions of Multiculturalism*, was published by the University of Minnesota Press in 2004.

PRIYA KANDASWAMY is Assistant Professor of Women's, Gender, and Sexuality Studies at Mills College in Oakland, California. Her research focuses on the regulation of women of color's labor and sexuality through U.S. social welfare policy. Her articles have appeared in *American Quarterly, Sexualities,* and *Radical Teacher.*

MICHELLE MCKINLEY is Associate Professor of Law at the University of Oregon and specializes in law, culture, and society; immigration law; public international law; and refugee and asylum law. Her articles have appeared in the *Yale Journal of Law and Humanities, Berkeley Journal of Gender, Law and Justice,* and *Unbound: Harvard Law Journal of the Legal Left.*

MICHAEL OMI is Associate Professor of Ethnic Studies at the University of California, Berkeley, and the coauthor of *Racial Formation in the United States.* His research specialties include racial theory and politics, racial/ethnic classification and the census, Asians Americans and racial stratification, and racist and antiracist social movements.

LAURA PULIDO is Professor of American Studies and Ethnicity at the University of Southern California. Her most recent book, co-written with Laura Barraclough and Wendy Cheng, is *A People's Guide to Los Angeles,* published by the University of California Press in 2012.

SHERENE H. RAZACK is Professor of Sociology and Equity Studies in Education at the Ontario Institute for Studies in Education of the University of Toronto. Her research specialties include critical race studies, feminism and human rights, law, aboriginal issues, and violence. Her most recent book, *Casting Out: Race and the Eviction of Muslims from Western Law and Politics,* was published in 2008 by the University of Toronto Press.

NIKHIL SINGH is Associate Professor of Social and Cultural Analysis at New York University. He is the author of the award-winning *Black Is a Country: Race and the Unfinished Struggle for Democracy,* published by Harvard University Press in 2004, and *Climbin' Jacob's Ladder: The Black Freedom Movement Writings of Jack O'Dell,* published by the University of California Press in 2009.

ANDREA SMITH is Associate Professor in the Department of Media and Cultural Studies at the University of California, Riverside. Her most recent book, *Native Americans and the Christian Right: The Gendered Politics of Unlikely Alliances,* was published by Duke University Press in 2008.

HOWARD WINANT is Professor of Sociology at the University of California, Santa Barbara, and Director of the University of California Center for New Racial Studies, a Multi-campus Research Program. He is coauthor of *Racial Formation in the United States* and author of *The New Politics of Race: Globalism, Difference, Justice* (University of Minnesota Press, 2004) and *The World Is a Ghetto: Race and Democracy since World War II* (Basic Books, 2001).

ACKNOWLEDGEMENTS

Collaborations—when they are as congenial, dynamic, and productive as this one has been—can be one of the most rewarding experiences in academic life. We are grateful to all of the contributors for the intellectual labor and engagement that made the superb essays in this volume possible.

Michael Omi and Howard Winant deserve our appreciation not only for the trenchant and far-reaching analysis they first developed in *Racial Formation in the United States* twenty-five years ago, but also for their generous support of this project over several years. At every turn, they welcomed critical engagement with their work and were eager to see scholarship on racial formation pushed in new directions.

Many of the essays included here were presented at the Racial Formation in the 21st Century conference at the University of Oregon, Eugene, in 2009. We thank all of the presenters who made that conference a tremendous success: Tomás Almaguer, Eduardo Bonilla-Silva, Devon Carbado, Gary Delgado, Denise Ferreira da Silva, Matt Garcia, Neil Gotanda, John L. Jackson Jr., Catherine Lee, Michelle McKinley, Michael Omi, Sherene Razack, Ellen Scott, Nikhil Singh, Andrea Smith, Martin Summers, Deborah A. Thomas, and Howard Winant.

At the University of Oregon, the conference was generously funded by the College of Arts and Sciences, the Office of Institutional Equity and Diversity, the Wayne Morse Center for Law and Politics, the Oregon Humanities Center, and the School of Law, with additional support from the Departments of Anthropology, Sociology, History, Geography, Women and Gender Studies, Political Science, Ethnic Studies, and International Studies. Margaret Hallock and the unparalleled staff at the Morse Center expertly managed the coordination and logistics of the conference, with support from Donella Elizabeth Alston in the Department of Ethnic Studies as well as Jeannine Anderson, Brian Guy, Kristina Mollman, Tish Ramey, and Mark Turner in the Department of Political Science.

This project began with a panel at the American Studies Association conference in Philadelphia in 2007, organized to commemorate the twentieth anniversary of the original publication of *Racial Formation in the United States*, featuring Gary Delgado, Daniel HoSang, Evelyn Hu-DeHart, Oneka LaBennett, Michael Omi, and Howard Winant.

Niels Hooper has been a thoughtful and engaged editor at the University of California Press. The astute and insightful feedback of two anonymous reviewers brought greater narrative clarity to the volume as a whole. At the University of Oregon, Robin Barklis, Kathryn Miller, and Brian Guy provided invaluable research and production assistance. Celeste Newbrough produced a superb index on a short timeline. Orlando Serrano expertly proofread the entire volume during production.

Finally, this volume is dedicated to the memories of two extraordinary colleagues and friends, Peggy Pascoe (1954–2010) and Clyde Woods (1957–2011), whose respective work on race and racial formation has influenced and enriched a generation of scholars.

INDEX

Abiko, Kyutaro, 102
Abu Ghraib, 1, 14–15, 213–14, 217; analysis
of documentary (*see* Morris, Errol,
Standard Operating Procedure video);
book on (*see under* Gourevitch, Philip
and Morris); colonial culture of
terror and, 219, 223; gender used in
exonerating female soldiers, 231–32,
237, 239–40; racial stereotyping of
prisoners, 218; soldiers' narratives, 227,
229, 230–34. *See also* torture; war
Adams, Elbert G., 102
affirmative action, 3, 11, 14, 92, 119, 170,
172, 174; issue of essentialism and,
188–89; jurisprudence on, 201–02,
211n19; non-affirmative action
institutions, 200–201; pro-affirmative
action discourse, 171, 179; racial
preferences and race-neutrality issue
(*see also* race-neutral approaches), 189,
191, 199–200; whether a racial project,
183–86, 282. *See also* anti-affirmative
action policies and initiatives
Afghanistan war, 11, 220, 226, 227–28,
249, 262, 272n3, 317. *See also* War on
Terror
African Americans. *See* black Americans
Afro-Latinos, 119, 135–39, 142n16; African
lineage underestimated, 157; racialized
sexualization of, 156
Agamben, Giorgio, 238
agricultural history, 95–96

Agricultural Labor Relations Board,
California, 105
Alarcón, Norma, 54
Alcala, María de, annulment petition,
124–25, 131–32
Alexander, Michelle, 80
Alfred, Taiaiake, 80
Almaguer, Tomás, "Race, Racialization,
and Latino Populations in the United
States," 13, 92
al Qaeda, 249, 250, 251, 272n3. *See also*
War on Terror
Ambuhlz, Megan, 233
American exceptionalism, 169, 250–53;
racial exceptionalism, 253–59, 271
American Indian Movement (AIM), 77
American myths, 169t., 169, 172. *See also*
frame systems
American Native Party ("Know-
Nothings"), 320
Anderson, Benedict, 118
Angola, Antonia Jiménez, 134, 140
anti-affirmative action policies and
initiatives, 163, 168–69, 171, 175,
178, 183, 184, 193; discrediting or
dismantling racial gains, 2–3, 34, 47,
58, 281–82; as racial projects, 92, 164,
201, 209, 281–82. *See also* California
ballot measures; Michigan Proposal 2
anti-imperialist activism, 84, 317
anti-racism, 15–16, 20, 48, 53; anti-racist
movements, 44–46

367

anti-terrorism, as a racial project, 259–62. *See also* War on Terror

anti-welfare discourse, 34, 39. *See also* welfare

Anzaldúa, Gloria, 5

apartheid, 10, 50, 84, 308

Arab Americans, 74, 313. *See also* Muslims and Arab peoples

Arakelian, Krikor, 100–101

Arizona SB 1070, 320

Armenian grape growers, 13, 96, 97–98, 110–11, 113; debate over racial identity, 98–101. *See also* California grape growers

articulation processes, 45, 48, 64, 279; rearticulation of race, 3, 47, 49, 51, 81, 247, 295, 305, 320

Asian Americans, 65; destabilizing the category of, 70; grape growers (*see also* California grape growers), 13, 92, 95; as a "model minority," 62–63, 111–12

Asian American feminism, 49

Asian American studies, 62

Asian (world population), 67f.

assimilationism, 140n1, 263, 266–67

Azalea magazine, 51

backlash opposing racial gains, 2–3, 7, 12, 45–46, 111, 317, 320

Baldwin, James, 250

ballot initiatives, and racial discourse, 165–66, 173–74. *See also by* state, e.g., California ballot measures

Bambara, Toni Cade, 64

Banzhaf, John, 314

Beatty, Paul *The White Boy Shuffle*, 64

Beck, Glenn, 301n4

Bedolla, Lisa Garcia, 8

belief archetypes, 166, 168–69. *See also* frame systems

Bell, Derrick, 71–72, 79

Berkeley School of Law, UC, 196

Bhattacharyya, 10

BiDil drug, 315

bilingual education, 11, 174; anti-bilingual education initiatives, 178

biology and race, 5–6, 7. *See also* genetics; social construction of race

"black exceptionalism," 73, 310

black Americans, 8, 13, 260, 287; diasporic identity, 9; equality of, 292–93; radical activists, 289–90. *See also by topic*, e.g., civil rights movement

black feminism, 49–50; black lesbian feminists, 50, 51, 52; critique of the women's movement, 26–27. *See also* feminist movement; women of color

black gay men's movement, 51, 52

"blackness," 64, 67f., 68, 73, 74, 128, 151–56, 292, 294, 295, 298, 301n8. *See also* "whiteness"

black/non-black binary, 310

Black Panther Party, 50

Blackwater Shooting, 240

black/white binary, 74–75, 77, 88–89n2, 143, 185

black women: bodies of, 33, 36–37; circular logic regarding, 39. *See also* black feminism; women of color

Black Women's Liberation Committee, SNCC, 50

Blauner, Bob, 304–5

BLK magazine, 52

blood mixing, hierarchies of, 13, 123, 128–31

blood purity, Iberian (*pureza de sangre*), 121, 128

Blumer, Herbert and Troy Duster, 305

Boas, Franz, 7, 99. *See also* ethnicity paradigm

Bonilla-Silva, Eduardo, 310–11, 327–28n5

Briggs-Cloud, Marcus, 84

Brother to Brother anthology, 52

Brown, Elsa Barkley, 28

Brown, Gerald (Jerry), 108

Brown, Orlando, 37

Brown v. Board of Education, 89n6

Brubaker, Rogers and colleagues, 312

Burgess, John, 295

Buruma, Ian, 236–37

Bush, George H. W., 282

Bush, George W., 14, 217, 239, 247, 257; his discourse on terrorism, 26, 248–50, 262–63; effort to privatize Social Security, 322; preemptive war policy,

284, 298; War on Terror and, 250–52,
253, 257, 258–59, 266, 267, 275n30
Butler, Judith, 62

Cadena, Marisol de la, 140n6
calidad (social class), 127, 131
California Agricultural Labor Relations
Act, 105
California Associated Raisin Company,
100
California ballot measures, 183, 209;
Proposition 14 (farm workers
initiative), 105, 106, 107; Proposition
54 ("Racial Privacy Initiative"), 174,
177–78; Proposition 209 ("Civil Rights
Initiative"), 166, 192, 196, 209
California grape growers: conservative
society of, 102, 110; Japanese and
Armenian growers, 13, 97–102;
opposing Proposition 14, 105
capitalism: capitalist state, 7, 31, 40, 278;
capitalist system, 68f., 68–69, 278;
land as property, 83; private property,
107–8, 112
Carbado, Devon and Cheryl Harris, "The
New Racial Preferences," 14, 92–93
Carter, Jimmy, 163–64
Cartozian, Tatos O., 99
CBS, *Survivor*, 315–16
Census, U.S., 119, 313, 321; 1850 decennial
census, 146; 1970 Census, 146–47;
Census 2000, 144, 147, 149, 157
Certeau, Michel de, 55–56
Chaiken, Michael, 237–38
Chávez, César, 92, 104, 106–8
Cherokee Nation, 74, 78, 80; Trail of
Tears, 89n3
Chicano movement, 152. See also Mexicans
in the U.S.
Churchill, Ward, 76–77
Citizens for a Fair Farm Labor Law, 105–6
citizenship, conceptions of, 39, 48
"civilizing" race, 47
Civil Liberties Act, 109
"Civil Rights Initiative" (Proposition 209),
166, 192, 196, 209
civil rights: anti-discrimination laws,
148, 316, 319; anti-miscegenation laws

overturned, 148; backlash against,
2–3, 7, 12, 45–46, 111, 317, 320;
contemporary jurisprudence, 329n25;
post-civil rights era, 30–31, 44
civil rights movement, 3, 11, 148, 177,
290; heteronormative values, 48;
problematic results, 8. See also "great
transformation;" racial justice
civil rights remediation efforts: majority-
minority districts, 186–87; "racial
lumping" issue, 186, 187, 188, 312;
Thomas' opposition to, 201
Civil War, U.S., 294
"clash of civilizations" thesis, 222–23, 241,
262–63; Huntington on, 263, 266, 267.
See also Muslims and Arab peoples;
Orientalism
class formation, 305; as key analytic
category, 6–7, 304
classification and determination of
race, 13–14, 31, 313–16; elasticity of
categories, 131–32, 159–60; genetics
and, 315; Latin American colonial
enumerations, 120–21, 133, 135; legal
(*see* legal determination of race);
perceptions of difference, 135;
scientific discourses on, 121, 141n10,
314–15. See also Census, U.S.; racial
hybridity
Clausewitz, Carl von, 293
Clinton (William, "Bill") administration,
5, 297, 321. See also welfare reform
Coalition for Economic Survival (CES),
107
Cohen, Cathy, 31–32
college admissions process, 189–92,
211n19; "colorblind" approach,
207–9; discursive self-representation
analyzed, 193–207, 211n19; Obama's
self representation analyzed, 195–200;
Thomas's self representation analyzed,
202–7
colonial culture of terror, 219, 220–21, 223.
See also Abu Ghraib
colonialism, 1, 13, 213; accumulation by
dispossession, 311, 324, 328n13
colonial discourse on race, 30, 122, 126,
128–29; imperialism and, 89n9, 90n10;

colonial discourse on race *(continued)*
  Spanish colonial racializations, 14. *See
  also* settler colonialism
Colorado ballot initiative, 177
colorblindness, 5, 6, 13, 15–16, 58, 93,
  170, 279, 287; as a guise for racism,
  163, 169–70, 299, 309–10, 328n8;
  emergence of, 95; legal cases and,
  112, 119; meritocracy and, 14, 112;
  neoconservatism and, 113, 114; and
  post-racial optimism, 309; race
  consciousness vs., 324–25. *See also* race-
  neutral approaches
Combahee River Collective, 27, 50, 54
Communists, 220
compulsory labor. *See* forced labor
Connerly, Ward, 169, 177–78
Conrad, Joseph, *Heart of Darkness,* 229
Contreras, Juan, census of Peruvian
  Indians, 133–35
"cosmic race," the *(la raza cósmica),* 123.
  See also mestizaje system
Coulthard, Glen, 76, 80
court rulings on race, 98–99. *See also*
  Supreme Court, U.S.; *and by* case
Crenshaw, Kimberlé, 19, 27, 32. *See also*
  intersectionality
criminality, 284
critical race theory, 5, 117, 304; race as
  foundational to social structure, 1,
  4, 6, 19, 30, 71, 267; U.S. as central
  to analysis, 7, 8, 71. *See also* Omi,
  Michael and Howard Winant
Cuba, racial hybridity in, 117
Culp, Jerome McCristal, 8
cultural politics, 52, 61–62, 264. *See also*
  identity politics
cultural transformations, 322

da Silva, Denise, 10, 73
Davey, Lynn and Susan Bales, *Framing
  Race,* 171–72
Davis, Javal, 227, 230–31, 233
Debord, Guy, 251
declension hypothesis (Omi and Winant),
  12, 46–48, 51–52
decolonization, 76–77, 79–80, 88–89n10;
  movements for, 84–88. *See also*

Indian law; settler
  colonialism
De Forest, John William, 38
De Genova, Nicholas, 155, 158; with
  Ana Y. Ramos-Zayas, *Latino
  Crossings,* 150–51, 158; " 'The
  War on Terror' as Racial Crisis,"
  15, 214–15
Delgado, Gary, 8; "Can We Achieve
  Racial Justice without Mentioning
  Race?," 14, 92
Deloria Jr., Vine, 89n5
Democratic Party, centrist New
  Democrats, 11
democracy, racial, 136–38; and
  multiculturalism, 135; vs. racial
  tyranny, 120
Democracy Now program, 228
Democratic Party, U.S., 256, 319, 320;
  centrist New Democrats, 11
Denetdalez, Jennifer, 87
desegregation of schools, 2–3, 201
Diaz, Anthony, 233–34
domesticity, and forced labor, 36, 39, 40
domestic violence, 41–42, 50, 296
Dratel, Joshua, 220
Dred Scot decision, 78
Drinnon, Richard, 265
Duany, Jorge, 156–58
DuBois, W. E. B., 62, 201, 214, 252–53,
  256, 259, 269, 270–71, 274n72, 291; on
  "double consciousness," 304–5
Dugan, Tim, 235
Dukakis, Michael, 282

ecclesiastical courts (Lima), 1, 13, 92
Edin, Kathryn and Laura Lein, 34
egalitarian values, 177
El Libro de Calo, 155
embodiment, 1, 219; bodies of black
  women, 33, 36–37
enemy as Other, 220, 234, 239; the racial
  or dehumanized Other, 223, 229–30,
  239, 300
England, Lynndie, 227, 231, 234, 235, 237,
  238
English-only instruction in public schools,
  165

Escobar, Inés de, annulment petition, 124
essentialism (racial), 9, 58, 164, 185, 187,
  297–98; affirmative action and, 188–89;
  anti-essentialism, 10
ethnicity: ethnic studies, 66, 67f.; genetic
  design of, 315; racial categories and,
  13–14; ethnicity paradigm, 7, 9, 97
eugenics, racial, 314
Executive Order 9066, 103

"family values," 33
Family Violence Option (FVO), 41–42
farm workers, California, 13; farm workers
  initiative (Proposition 14), 105, 106, 107
Farrakhan, Louis, 185
Feagin, Joe, 72, 88–89n2; *The White Racial
  Frame*, 167–68
feminist movement: Anglo-American
  influence, 11, 55; criticized as
  marginalizing racial structures, 26–27,
  42, 55; black nationalists and, 48–49;
  second wave theory, 305–6. *See also*
  black feminism; women of color
  movement
Ferguson, Roderick A., "On the
  Specificities of Gender and Sexuality
  in the Historiographies of Race," 12
Fields, Barbara Jeanne, 6
Filipinos, 70
Firestone, Shulamith, 305–6
First Amendment, 191–92
Fjikane, Candace, 75
forced labor: domestic labor and, 37–39,
  40; racialized thinking and, 36, 40. *See
  also* Reconstruction
Ford, Lisa, *Settler Sovereignty*, 293
Foucault, Michel, 48, 49, 295
frame systems, 166–68; American myths,
  169, 172; belief archetypes, 166,
  168–69; framing race and public
  policy, 176–77; *Framing Race* (Lynn
  and Bales), 171–72. *See also* political
  discourse on race
Freedmenliub, Virginia, 37
Freedmen's Bureau, 12, 32, 36–38;
  compared to welfare reform of
  the 1990s, 38–43; domestic labor
  contracts, 38; promoting labor for

freedwomen, 38; promoting marriage,
  37–38, 40
Freyre, Gilberto, 123–24, 137, 140n3; *The
  Masters and the Slaves*, 122
Frost, Jeffery, 233–34
Fuchs, Cynthia, 238
Fukuyama, Francis, 263–65, 267–68,
  275n30
Fuss, Diana, *Essentially Speaking*, 184–85

Gaddis, John Lewis, 298
Ganz, Marshall, 105
Garcia, Matthew, "The Importance of
  Being Asian," 13, 91–92, 95
gays and lesbians, "secondary
  marginalization" of, 31–32. *See also*
  queer movement
gender defense: of female soldiers involved
  in Abu Ghraib, 231–32, 237, 239–40;
  imperialist interventions and, 26
gender formation, 1, 231–32, 306;
  articulations of race in, 12, 30–31,
  32–33, 44, 51–53; citizenship concepts
  and, 39, 48; gender as a marker of race,
  39; hierarchies of, 37. *See also* feminist
  movement; queer movement
genetics, 1, 140, 314, 315
Geneva Convention rules, 223
genocide, 13, 59, 68f., 68, 69, 75, 77; logic
  of, 71; Native genocide, 71, 72–73; and
  settler colonialism, 73
Gerson, Michael, 330n28
Gilroy, Paul, 8, 9
Gingrich, Newt, 282
"global apartheid" (DuBois), 10
globalist nationalism. *See also* imperial
  state
globalization, 139; global political vision,
  84, 85, 87, 117; global racial transition,
  308–9
global security state (de Genova), 247–50,
  258, 268; global policing, U.S., 214,
  248, 249, 250, 253, 267. *See also*
  imperial state; War on Terror
Goddard, Peter, 237
Goldberg, Theo, 256, 260
Goldwater, Barry, 296
Good Fox, Julia, 84

Goodman, Amy, 227, 228
Gordon, Leonard, 6, 16–17n7, 16–17, 61
Gourevitch, Philip and Morris, *Standard Operating Procedure*, 228, 229, 231, 232, 234, 236
Gramsci, Antonio, 4, 59, 305; on hegemony, 60–61, 305; neo-Gramscian notions, 283
Graner, Charles, 227, 231, 234, 236, 237
Granerz, Megan, 227, 231–32
grape growers. *See* California grape growers
Great Society, 282
"great transformation," 48, 57–58, 316, 317–18, 323; forging of racial identities, 53; paradigm shifts in racial landscape, 3, 45. *See also* civil rights movement; racial justice
Gutiérrez, Ramón, 160n

Haberman, Clyde, 316
Hall, Stuart, 5, 8, 9
Han, Sora, 68, 69, 75
Hancock, Ange Marie, 8
Hanisch, Carol, 306, 327n3
Hardisty, Jean and Deepak Bhargava, 179–80
Harlan, John Marshall, 78, 79, 328n8
Harmon, Sabrina, 227, 230, 231–32, 233, 235–37
Harris, Angela P., 8, 68, 73, 75
Harris, Cheryl, 74
Harrison, Faye, 7
Hartman, Saidiya, 68
Harvey, David, 328n13
hegemony and racial rule, 60–61, 305, 316–17, 322–23; global hegemony (*see also* imperial state), 268, 298–99; Gramsci on, 60–61, 305. *See also* state power
Hemphill, Essex, 51, 52
Hesse, Barnor, 290
heteronormativity, 33–34, 37–38, 40
heteropatriarchy, 84, 87, 89
Hikindz, Dov, 314
Hirsch, Marianne, 59
Hispanic population, U.S., 145, 147–48
historical-materialist approach, 7

histories of racialization, 91–93, 138
historiographies of race, 11, 44–45, 55–56, 91
Hochschild, Jennifer, 176–77, 310
Holmes, Stephen, 220
Home Girls anthology, 48, 51
Homeland Security, U.S. Dept. of, 247, 329n17
homeland security state (de Genova), 15, 248, 259, 260
homophobia, 87
Hong, Grace Kyungwon, 29
Hooker, Juliet, 138
hooks, bell, 305–6
HoSang, Daniel Martinez, *Racial Propositions: Ballot Initiatives and the Making of Postwar California*, 165
Hull, Gloria, Patricia Bell Scott and Barbara Smith, *All the Women Are White, All the Blacks Are Men, but Some of Us Are Brave*, 27, 49
Human Genome Project, 314
Huntington, Samuel, 263, 266, 267. *See also* "clash of civilizations" thesis
Hurricane Katrina disaster, 246, 259, 260; post-Katrina New Orleans, 311

Iberia/Iberian language, 116, 118, 141n8. *See also* Moors
identity politics, 19, 53–54, 57, 167, 277; disruptions in narratives of identity, 55–56; group identity, 312; identification process, 7, 54–55, 130, 285–86; importance and limitations of anti-racist movements, 53–54; persistence of racial identities, 53
ideologies about race, 13, 46, 55, 78, 170, 208–9. *See also* blood purity; white supremacy
Ignatieff, Michael, 290
immigrants, 11, 14; of color, 34, 35; rights of, 319–20; undocumented, 2, 21, 85, 173, 178, 200, 259, 320–21
immigration policy, 147–48; anti-immigration discourse and measures, 85–87, 173–74, 320; immigration reform, 172, 320; paradigm of exclusion, 75

Immigration Reform Act of 1965, 320
imperial multiculturalism, 258–59, 263–66;
colonialism and, 89n9, 90n10; globalist
nationalism and, 253–59, 288, 317,
323; imperial identity, 6, 219–20,
248, 252–53, 257, 262, 267, 269–71,
289; imperial "presidentialism,"
272n3; Manifest Destiny doctrine
and, 263–65, 317; and torture (*see also*
torture), 1, 14–15, 213–14, 217–20, 222.
See also state power
inclusion, 28
Indian rights, 78–79. *See also*
decolonization; indigeneity
Indian wars, 263, 266
indigeneity, 1, 12, 66, 84, 139; indigenous
rights and critical race theory, 78–80;
liberal vs. genealogical perspectives, 82;
Peruvian Indian population, 133–35,
142n19. *See also* Native nationhood
individualism, 177
institutional racism, 9, 72. *See also* racial
state
intermarriage or miscegenation, 116,
118, 140n3; anti-miscegenation
laws overturned, 148; cross-ethnic,
101; cross-racial, 13, 73, 134, 148;
overturning of anti-miscegenation
laws, 148. *See also* racial hybridity
internal colonialism thesis (Blauner),
71, 165, 301n4, 310, 3304–5. *See also*
colonialism
intersectionality: concept of (Crenshaw),
6, 8, 19, 27; critique of, 27–28; racial
formation theory and, 28–31, 31, 39,
42–43, 80, 88, 306. *See also* gender
formation
intersectional organizing, 49
Iraq War, 11; Blackwater Shooting, 227,
240–41. *See also* Abu Ghraib; war
Irish and Italian immigrants, 6, 320
Ismail, Baraa Sadoon, 241

Jackson, Andrew, 74
Jackson, Jesse, 279
Japanese grape growers, 13, 97, 110–11;
anti-Japanese sentiments, 102–3;
local resistance to, 102; Nisei (second

generation) farmers, 96, 101, 104,
113–14. *See also* California grape
growers
"Japanese Problem," 102
Jefferson, Thomas, 292
Jendian, Matthew, 114n7
Jews, Latin American, 141n7
Johnson, Lyndon, 178, 280
Johnson v. McIntosh, 80
Jones, Timothy M. Penelope Sheets,
223–24
Julien, Isaac, *Looking for Langston*, 52

Kahn, Jonathan, 315
Kandaswamy, Priya, "Gendering Racial
Formation," 12, 19
Kant, Immanuel, *Metaphysics*, 293
Kaplan, Robert, "The Coming Anarchy,"
297–98, 300
Katrina. *See* Hurricane Katrina disaster
Katz, Irwin and R. Glen Hass, 177
Kellstedt, Paul, *Mass Media and the
Dynamics of American Racial Attitudes*,
176–77
Kennedy, Rory, 227
Kennedy (John F.) administration, 320
King, Martin Luther, 112, 169, 282, 317
King, Rodney, 64, 246
Kirby v. Kirby, 112
Koshy, Susan, 9
Kristol, Irving, 296
Kubo, Harry: life of and upward mobility,
92, 96, 103–4, 109–12; a model for
colorblind ideology, 113–14; opposing
workers' rights measure, 105–8
Kyung-Jin Lee, James, 5

labor movements, 1
Laclau, Ernesto, 305
Lakoff, George, 166–67
land ownership, 1
LaPiere, Richard Tracy, 99–100
Lasreg, Marnia, 219, 220, 229, 239
"Latin Americanization" of race relations
(Bonilla-Silva), 310–11, 327–28n5
Latin American hybridity, 67f., 70, 92,
116, 128; *casta* charts, 129–30; colonial
enumerations, 120–21, 133, 135;

Latin American hybridity *(continued)*
criollo (ethnic elite), 125, 127;
hierarchies of blood mixing, 13, 123,
128–31; *mestizaje* system, 118, 122, 136,
137, 312; *moriscos* (Muslim/Catholic)
heritage, 124, 125–26, 141n7; *mulatos*,
124–25, 131
Latinos/Latinas in the U.S., 13–14, 34,
143–44; bureaucratic racialization of,
144–48, 160; internal racializations,
148–59; voting patterns, 320. *See also*
Afro-Latinos
Laurier, Joanne, 238
Lee, Chang-Rae, *Native Speaker*, 62
Lee, James, "The Transitivity of Race and
the Challenge of the Imagination," 12
Lee, Rex E., 2–3
left politics, U.S., 4
legal determination of race: the "common
knowledge" test, 99; court rulings,
98–99, 112, 117; Roman law and
the *Siete Partidas*, 122; U.S. Census
categories (*see also* Census, U.S.), 119
Lemert, Charles, 57
Lévi-Strauss, Claude, 307, 328–29n5
Lewis, Bernard, 298
liberalism: liberal family archetype., 167;
political campaigns and strategic
framing, 14, 168, 169t.
Lima, Peru, blood purity, 13, 92
Lipsitz, George, 74, 110
Livingston Chronicle, 102
Llanos, Agustin de, 124–25
López, Ian Haney, 99
Lorde, Audre, "The Master's Tools Will
Never Dismantle the Master's House,"
61, 62
Los Angeles Times, 240
Los Angeles uprisings, 62–63
Loveman, Mara, 6
Loving v. Commonwealth of Virginia, 112,
148
Lowe, Lisa, 57, 63
Luker, Kristin, 34–35
Lyons, Scott, *X-Marks*, 84, 87

Macdonald, Heather, 223
majority-minority districts, 186–87

Manifest Destiny, 263–65, 317
Marable, Manning, "New Racial
Domain," 10
Maracle, Lee, 77
marriage, 35, 37–38, 39–40, 42;
annulments on claims of racial
inequality, 124–25, 126; Freedman
bureau's promotion of, 37–38;
interracial marriages, 73, 112, 124–25,
134, 148, 198, 295; inter ethnic
marriages, 100
Marshall, T. H., 326
Martí, José, 117, 137
Marx, Karl, Marxism, 248, 304, 305, 306
mass median, 176–77
mayate, 155–56
McCain, John, 256
McCall, Leslie, 8
McCarthy, Andrew C., 223
McKinley, Michelle, "The Unbearable
Lightness of Being (Black)," 13, 92
Merced County, anti-Japanese sentiments,
102–3
mestizaje system, 118, 122, 136, 137, 312. *See
also* Latin American hybridity; post-
emancipation systems; racial hybridity
Mexicans in the U.S., 13–14, 92, 106,
154–55; deportations, 320; shifting
definitions of ethnicity, 145–46, 152–56;
terms designating blackness, 155–56
Michigan Proposal 2, 183, 192, 202, 206, 209
migration, 84
Miles, Robert, 6
Milgram, Stanley, 225–26, 227, 243n29
Mill, John Stuart, "A Few Words on
Nonintervention," 293–94
minorities: claims to whiteness, 146,
152–53, 157, 161n9; complicity with
hegemonic practices and ideas, 13,
85, 110, 111–12; emergent groups, 58;
internal racializing, 150–52; model
minorities, 61–62. *See also by* group
e.g., Asian-Americans
miscegenation. *See* intermarriage or
miscegenation
Missouri v. Jenkins, 201–2
"model minority," Asian Americans as a,
62–63, 111–12

Montesclaros, colonial census under, 132, 133–34
Moors: Iberian Muslims, 124–25, 141n7; *moriscos* (Muslim/Catholic) heritage, 124, 125–26, 141n7
Moraga, Cherrie, 5; and Gloria Anzaldúa, *This Bridge Called My Back,* 27, 51, 54
Morales, Evo, 139
morenos, 155
Morgan, Edmund, 292
Morgono, Pamela, 173
Morris, Errol: reviews of the video, 236–38; *Standard Operating Procedure* (video), 226–27, 229–31, 235–36, 238; with Gourevitch (book) (*see* under Gourevitch, Philip)
Morrison, Toni, *The Bluest Eye,* 61
Moten, Fred, 64, 297–98
multiculturalism, 62, 66, 74, 138, 139–40, 266; and early ideas of universal humanism, 13; imperial multiculturalism, 258–59, 263–66; imperial or global multiculturalism, 258–59, 263–66; and racial democracy, 135, 310. *See also* ethnicity
multiracial populations, 135, 149–50, 310. *See also* racial hybridity
Murukawa, Naomi, 284
Muslims and Arab peoples, 67f., 259–62, 263; Arab Americans, 74, 313; Iberian Muslims, 124–25, 141n7; *moriscos,* 124, 125–26, 141n7; racialized marking of, 214, 220, 221–22, 223, 267
Myrdal, Gunnar, 289; *An American Dilemma,* 122

National Council of Negro Women, 51
nationalism, 81, 118, 214, 248–49, 257–58, 259, 305
National Network for Immigrant and Refugee Rights, 173
National Third World Lesbian and Gay Conference, 51
Native nationhood, 81–84; identity as relation to land, 83, 84; U.S. Indian law and, 79–80. *See also* decolonization; indigeneity; sovereignty

Native studies, 76, 77–81, 88
neoconservatism, 179–80, 185, 296–97, 330n28; backlash opposing anti-racist gains, 2–3, 7, 12, 45–46, 111, 317; belief archetypes, 166–67; contrasted with the New Right, 330n35
neoliberalism: as a racial project, 15, 254, 255–56, 259, 280, 283, 303, 321–23; crisis of, 321–23; racial liberalism and, 278, 279, 283, 285, 288, 296
New Deal (Roosevelt), 322
"new ethnicities" concept, 9. *See also* ethnicity paradigm
"new racism" (Omi and Winant), 3–4, 276, 299; colorblindness and, 163, 169–70, 299, 309–10
New Right: civil rights movement and, 2–3, 7, 12, 317; contrasted with neoconservatism, 330n35; rise of, 12, 47, 111, 279
Newton, Huey, 50
New York Review of Books, 236
New York Times, 290–91, 316
9/11 attacks, 214, 249, 297, 298, 313–14, 320; post 9/11 era, 14, 163, 213, 251. *See also* War on Terror
Nisei Farmers League, 104, 105–6, 109
Nuestra América, 117

Obama, Barack, 11, 14, 93, 162, 179, 192; discourse on terrorism, 248, 250–52, 267; as a "post-racial" subject, 15, 162, 247, 253–61, 267, 299–300, 309, 318–19; as a target of racism, 163–64, 300, 301n8, 330n35; discursive self representation analyzed, 195–200, 209; *Dreams from My Father* excerpts, 194–95; and "imperial presidentialism," 272n3; Muslim identity accusations, 261; and the War on Terror, 214, 217–18, 246, 258. *See also* post-racial era
O'Connor, Sandra Day, 187
O'Dell, Jack, 276
Office of Management and Budget, U.S.: Directive 15, 144, 145; "Hispanic or Latino" category, 145, 147; racial/ethnic cartography, 144, 149, 160. *See also* Census, U.S.

Office on Violence Against Women, 32
Okada, John, *No-No Boy*, 64
Omi, Michael and Howard Winant,
  1, 45, 184; on the centrality of race
  (*see* critical race theory); declension
  hypothesis, 12, 46–48, 51–52; on
  the future of race, 57–58; on model
  minorities, 61–62; on the new
  convergence in racial politics, 254, 308;
  on the "new racism," 3–4, 276, 299; on
  race as unstable and decentered, 1, 4,
  60, 164, 276, 285; on racial crisis, 246;
  on the racial project, 12, 13, 35, 45–46,
  91–93, 116; on the racial state (*see also*
  state power), 7, 21, 30–31, 180, 220–21;
  on transformations of race, 15, 268–71,
  277–78. *See also* critical race theory;
  racial formation theory
Omi, Michael and Howard Winant
  works: "By the Rivers of Babylon,"
  3–4, 306; *Racial Formation in the
  United States* (*see also* racial formation
  theory), 4–5, 7, 10–11, 15, 16–17n7,
  44–45, 55–56, 58–60, 116, 164, 183–85;
  "Racial Formation Rules," 302
Omnibus Crime Control and Safe Streets
  Act, U.S., 289, 297
Ongiri, Amy Abugu, 50
O'odham Solidarity Across Borders
  Collective, 85–86
Orientalism, 68f., 69, 222
Other, the, 223, 229–30, 239, 300. *See also*
  enemy as Other
Ozawa, Takao, 98–99

Pack, Brent, 235
padrón, 120. *See also* Latin America
Pascoe, Peggy, 112
paternity identification, 33, 41, 130
patriarchy, 28, 30, 31, 42, 54–55, 126,
  222, 748; family ideal, 166–67;
  heteropatriarchy, 84, 87, 89; state
  interests and, 33–34
PBS, *Faces of America* documentary, 315
people of color, classification model, 67f.
  See also ethnicity; minorities
Pérez, Juan, 130–31, 140
periodization, 48–49, 53, 56

Perlman, Selig, 5
Personal Responsibility and Work
  Opportunity Reconciliation Act
  (PRWORA), 33, 41
Peru, colonial, 13, 92, 132–33
Piedra, José, 141n8
Plessy v. Ferguson, 295
political analysis of race, 1, 4–5, 7–10,
  283–91, 302; as anachronistic, 4, 5;
  black/ non-black paradigm (Sexton),
  73; nation-based approaches, 119–20,
  301n4; the political dimension as
  dominant, 307; race as a marker of
  other social factors, 6; racial war of
  position, 283–84, 305. *See also* racial
  formation theory
political discourse on race, 14, 15, 52,
  61–62, 170t., 264; do's and don'ts of,
  172; not mentioning race, 175–76;
  the "politics of resentment," 3;
  strategic framing, 168, 169, 172. *See
  also* frame systems; identity politics;
  neoconservatism; race-neutral
  approaches
political leadership, 179–80
popular sovereignty, 308–9, 317
pornography and torture, 237. *See also*
  torture
postcolonial welfare, 322–23
post-emancipation systems, 122–23; chattel
  slavery, 122; manumission, 122. *See also
  mestizaje* system; Reconstruction
post-racial era, 4, 213, 267, 282; globalist
  nationalism and, 253–59, 288;
  multiracial populations and, 135,
  149–50, 310; Obama and, 15, 162, 247,
  253–61, 267, 299–300, 309, 318–19;
  the restructuring of race and, 321–25;
  scenarios of, 15–16, 309–11
postwar movements, 213, 308–9. *See
  also* civil rights movement; feminist
  movement; "great transformation"
Povinelli, Elizabeth, 81
power. *See* state power
precolonial people. *See* indigeneity
Price, Patricia, 8, 19
prison complex and population, 11, 68,
  291

privatizing inequality, 40

Przeworski, Adam, 305

public messaging, 166–67; recommended frames, 169t. *See also* frame systems

Puerto Rican racial identity, differing valuation of lineages, 156–58

Puerto Ricans, 13–14

queer movement, 48–49, 51–53; queers of color, 45, 50

race: colonialism and (*see also* colonialism), 77–78, 80; ethnicity and, 13–14; global racial transition, 308–9; the racial Other, 229–30, 300; the racial regime, 316–18; racial subjectivity, 3, 6, 62; reductionist vs. nonreductionist concepts of, 5, 164; social construction of, 8, 61, 119, 141n10, 285; theory of (*see* racial formation theory); transitivity of, 13–14, 57, 60, 64–65, 184

race-based ideologies. *See* ideologies about race

race-based movements. *See under* social movements

race-neutral approaches, 14, 174–75, 189, 189–92, 200, 207, 291; achievement evaluations and, 189; race-positive applicants, 199–200, 210n9. *See also* colorblindness; post-racial subject

racial crisis, 246–47, 318. *See also* War on Terror

racial formation theory, 1–7, 10–16, 116, 140n6, 327; as a political category (*see* political analysis of race); and class (*see also* class formation), 305; and the concept of intersectionality (*see* intersectionality); essentialist (*see* essentialism (racial); feminist theory and (*see also* gender formation), 12, 30–31, 32–33, 44, 51–53, 305–6; historiographies of race and racialization, 11, 44–45, 55–56, 91–93, 96–97, 138–39; instability of race concepts, 1, 4, 60, 164, 276, 285, 307–8, 316, 318; intersections with gender (*see also* intersectionality),

28–31, 31, 39, 42–43, 80, 88, 306; origins of, 303–7; reracialization process, 150–52, 155, 284, 321; transformations of race, 15, 164, 268–71, 277–78; transnational theories, 9–10, 15. *See also* critical race theory; political analysis of race

racial hybridity, 14, 117, 118, 119, 137; elasticity of categories, 131–32, 159–60; internal racializing and, 150–52; Latinos/Latinas in the U.S., 148–50, 159; "some other race" census category, 149–50. *See also* intermarriage or miscegenation; Latin American racial hybridity; multiracial populations; transformations of race

racial justice, 14, 92, 162, 176, 177, 179, 180, 277, 309; racial restructuring, 321–25; social policy of, 16, 325–27. *See also* civil rights movement

"Racial Privacy Initiative"(Proposition 54), 174, 177–78

racial profiling, 86, 176, 313–14, 321

racial project: defined, 29, 183; Omi and Winant on, 12, 13, 35, 45–46, 91–93, 116; and racism, 184–85

racial silence, 14, 175–76

racial state, 14, 40, 71, 213, 221, 247, 288, 308; Omi and Winant on, 7, 21, 30–31, 180. *See also* imperial state; war

racism: anti-black racism, 68–69, 89n9, 162–64, 283, 301n8; beliefs about anti-white racism, 181n7, 185; defining, 284–85; evaluating racial projects regarding, 184–85; permanency of, 79, 165; structural racism, 6, 308, 309–10, 316, 318, 323, 324, 328n11. *See also* capitalism; slavery

Razack, Sherene H., "Abu Ghraib Revisited," 14–15, 213–14

Razzaq, Abdul, 240–41

Reagan (Ronald) administration, 5, 47, 109, 279, 281; discrediting or dismantling racial gains, 2–3, 34, 47, 58, 281–82, 321; and the notion of whites as victims, 47. *See also* Republican Party

Reagan-Thatcher era, 281

Reconstruction, Southern, 12, 274n72; state promotion of marriage, 37–39, 40. *See also* Freedmen's Bureau
redistribution, 325–26
Red Power movement, 77
reducciones, 132, 142n12
Reed, Adolph, 283
reform and new convergence in racial politics, 80, 254, 308. *See also* civil rights movement; transformations of race
reparation, 325
repression hypotheses, 55
reproductive justice, 11
Republican Party, U.S., 109, 282, 318, 319, 321, 330n28. *See also* Tea Party activists
restructuring of race, 321–25
Rice, Condoleeza, 290, 317
Ridley, Hugh, 230
Riggs, Marlon, *Tongues Untied,* 52
right-wing movements. *See* neoconservatism; New Right
Risch, Neil, 314–15
Roberts, Dorothy, 35
Rodriguez, Dylan, 70
Rodriguez, Juana Maria, *Queer Latinidad,* 53–54
Roth, Michael S., 237
Rowbotham, Sheila, 305–6
Rubaie, Haitham, 241
Rumbaut, Ruben, 144, 145
Rumford Act, California, 108
Russell, Thaddeus, "Civil Rights and Black Sexuality," 48
Ruth Pike, 141n7

Said, Edward, 69
San Joaquin Abstract Company, 98
San Joaquin Valley, 91, 102
San Juan Jr., E., 6–7
Saranillio, Dean, 75
Saxton, Alexander, 5
Scarry, Elaine, 239
scientific discourses on race, 121, 141n10, 314–15
Scott, James, 141n10
Seed, Patricia, 141n10
Senate Bill 1070, Arizona, 85, 87

settler colonialism, 12–13, 66, 72–73, 88, 293, 294; exclusion of immigrants, 75; the logic of, 71, 73, 76; removal of Native peoples, 73, 74, 78, 83, 84. *See also* colonialism; decolonization; war
"settlers of color," 80, 81
Sexton, Jared, 68, 75; *Amalgamation Schemes,* 72–73
sexuality, 1, 2. *See also* gender formation
Sharma, Nandita and Cynthia Wright, 81–84
*Shaw v. Reno*m, 187
Shryock, Andrew, 74
Singh, Nikhil, "Racial Formation in the Age of Permanent War," 15, 214–15
Sivits, Jeremy, 227, 230
Skocpol, Theda, 174–75
Slack, Jennifer, 45
slavery, 1, 8–9, 13, 30, 68f., 68, 140–41n7, 292, 331n36; comparative studies of, 119, 122, 123; racism and, 124; the slaveability of black people (belief), 68; status of slaves, 125. *See also* post-emancipation systems
Smith, Andrea, "Indigeneity, Settler Colonialism, and White Supremacy," 12–13
Smith, Barbara, *Home Girls,* 48, 51
social citizenship, 326
social class. *See* class formation
social construction of race, 8, 61, 119, 141n10; structures of inequality, 285
Socialist Review, 3, 5
social movements, 1, 32; of the postwar era, 308–9; race-based, 46, 46–49, 53, 60, 77, 78, 80, 97, 119, 170; and state power, 12, 30, 40–41. *See also* civil rights movement; feminist movement; queer movement
Social Security system, 322
Sojourner: A Third World Women's Research Newsletter, 51
Song, Min, 63
Sontag, Susan, 236, 237, 238
"South African" scenario, 310. *See also* post-racial era
sovereignty, 76, 78–79, 81, 89n6

sovereign violence, 15, 213, 214–15, 291, 292, 296, 298, 299
state power, 7, 31, 40, 278, 295–96; hegemony and racial rule, 60–61, 305, 316–17, 322–23; patriarchal interests, 33–34; as the site of racial structure, 14, 40, 71, 213, 221, 247, 288, 308, 316; and social movements, 12, 30, 40–41. *See also* imperial state; racial state; sovereignty
state security, 15, 247–50, 248, 259, 260, 329n17
Steele, Claude, 196
Stocking, George, 135, 140n2
structural racism, 6, 308, 309–10, 316, 318, 323, 324, 328n11
subjectivity, racial, 3, 6, 62. *See also* identity
Supreme Court, U.S., 27, 112, 148, 281, 316, 329n25

Taala Hooghan Infoshop, Arizona, 87
Taino Indians of Puerto Rico, 157–58
Taliban regime, 249, 262, 263
Tannenbaum, Frank, 122
Taussig, Michael, 213–14, 217, 220–21
Tea Party activists, 179, 276; reactionary racial agenda, 300, 319, 329n26, 330n35. *See also* Republican Party, U.S.
teenage pregnancy, 34–35
terror. *See* War on Terror; colonial culture of terror; al Qaeda
Thatcher, Margaret, 282
Thind, Bhagat Singh, 98–99
Thind decision, 99
Third World Lesbian Writers Conference, 51
Third World Women's Alliance, 50
Third World Women's International, 50
This Bridge Called My Back anthology, 27, 51
Thomas, Clarence, 14, 93, 192; discursive self representation analyzed, 203–7; opposing race-conscious remediation, 201; *Pieces of My Life as My Grandfather's Son*, 202–3
Thomas, Deborah and Kamari Clarke, 9, 10

Torres, Rudy, 6
torture, 222–23, 225–26, 227, 230, 237, 243n29; anti-torture narratives, 224–27; and the "clash of civilizations" thesis, 222–23; exoneration of, 227, 231–38; imperialism and, 1, 14–15, 213–14, 217–20, 222; as policy, 236, 238; and the racial state (*see also* racial state), 238–40; torture warrants, 223
transformations of race, 15, 268–71, 277–78, 310, 312, 313; global racial transition, 308–9. *See also* classification and determination of race; racial hybridity; racial formation theory
transnational theories of race, 9–10, 15
Treaty of Guadalupe Hidalgo, 146, 149
Tridentine rule (marriage as a sacrament), 126, 130, 141–42n11
triracial systems, 310

United Farm Workers (UFW), 13, 92, 97, 105, 107. *See also* Chávez, César
United States (U.S.): as a racially contradictory society, 316–18; Arizona law against immigrants, 85–87; as a settler state (*see also* settler colonialism; white supremacy), 77, 80; Civil War, 294; critical race theory and (*see also* critical race theory), 7, 8, 70; demographic shifts in (*see also* Census, U.S.), 147–48, 319–20, 321; global power (*see also* hegemony and racial rule; imperial state), 11, 268, 298–99; legitimacy issues, 76, 77; racial composition of workforce, 322. *See also* by state, e.g., California
United States (U.S.) laws and institutions: Civil Liberties Act, 109; Executive Order 9066, 103; Indian law, 78–80; OMB racial categories (*see* Office of Management and Budget); Omnibus Crime Control and Safe Streets Act, 289, 297; Supreme Court rulings, 27, 112, 148, 281, 316, 329n25; Thirteenth Amendment, 294–95
United States v. Cartozian, 99
United States v. Fordice, 201

universal humanism, 13. *See also* multiculturalism

University of Michigan Law School, 203

U.S.-Mexico War, 145–46

Valcárcel, Luis, 140n1
Valdes, Francisco, 8
Vasconcelos, José, 123
veterans' narratives, 227–29
Vietnam Veterans Against the War, 228
violence: criminality, 284; domestic, 41–42; state or sovereign, 15, 213, 214–15, 291, 292, 296, 298, 299. *See also* torture; war

Wagner, Brian, 295
Wallace, Chris, 276
Wallace, George, 3
war, 68f., 69, 85, 145; as an activity of the racial state, 1, 12, 180, 213, 221, 247, 288, 308; the enemy as Other, 220, 234, 239; military intelligence, 23. *See also* Iraq War; state power; World War II
War on Terror, 15, 220, 246, 266, 273n8, 313–14; as a racial crisis, 246–47; racial profiling and, 313–14; and U.S. global policing, 214, 248, 249, 250. *See also* 9/11 attacks; *and under* Bush, George W.; and Obama, Barack
Washington Times, 172–73
Waziyatawin, 87, 88–89n10
Weisman, Richard, 228–29
welfare, 11; anti-welfare discourse, 34, 39; racially stratified meanings, 39–40
"welfare queen," 34; historical context, 35–36; as mythical, 34–35
welfare reform of the mid-1990s, 12, 32–36; compared to the Freedmen's Bureau of Reconstruction, 38–43; and dismantling of the welfare state, 321–23; Family Violence Option

(FVO), 41–42; Personal Responsibility and Work Opportunity Reconciliation Act (PRWORA), 33, 41
welfare state, U.S., 12
"whiteness," 13, 73, 74, 98–100, 111, 128, 210n18, 269, 311; minority and ethnicity claims to, 146, 152–53, 157, 161n9; trajectory toward (*see also mestizajo* system), 128–29. *See also* "blackness"
white political identity politics, 3, 47, 281. *See also* settler colonialism
white racial frame, 167–68
white supremacy, 12–13, 21, 66, 68, 73–74, 88, 269–71; delegitimation of, 286; normalization or persistence of, 78, 310–11; structure and logic of (*see also* Orientalism; genocide; slavery), 68f., 68–70, 75, 76, 82. *See also* ideologies about race
Williams, Robert, 77–80
Willie Horton ad, 282
Winant, Howard, 6, 10
Winter Soldiers, 228, 243n33
women of color, 19, 45, 50; black "welfare queens," 34–36; civilizing projects for black freedwomen, 36. *See also* black women; Latinos/Latinas in the U.S.
women of color movement, 48–51, 52, 53; splits in, 54, 55. *See also* feminist movement
women's studies, 24, 43n1
World Social Forum, 83
World Socialist Web Site, 238
World War II, 317
Wright, Jeremiah, 255

Yamada, Mitsuye, 49
Yamato colonists. *See* Japanese grape growers
Yancey, George, 311
Yellow Bird, Michael, 84–85